Monty Python's Flying Circus
Just the Words

Other publications by Monty Python available from Methuen

The Brand New Monty Python Papperbok

The Fairly Incomplete and Rather Badly Illustrated Monty Python Songbook

Monty Python's Big Red Book

Monty Python's Flying Circus Just the Words (Volume One)

Monty Python and The Holy Grail (Screenplay)

Monty Python's Life of Brian (Screenplay)

Monty Python and the Meaning of Life

The Very Best of Monty Python

Monty Python's Flying Circus

Just the Words

Volume Two
(except for the animation bits)

Written and conceived by
GRAHAM CHAPMAN
JOHN CLEESE
TERRY GILLIAM
ERIC IDLE
TERRY JONES
MICHAEL PALIN

Methuen

Acknowledgements

Enormous, Mr Equator-like thanks to those who put so much effort into assembling this book:
Roger Wilmut, Geoffrey Strachan, Alison Davies, Suzanne Lindop, Roger Saunders.

First published in Great Britain by Methuen London in 1989
First published in paperback as an omnibus edition (containing *Just the Words: One* and
Just the Words: Two) by Mandarin Paperbacks in 1990
This paperback edition published in 2019 by Methuen & Co Ltd, Orchard House,
Railway Street, Slingsby, York, YO62 4AN
www.methuen.co.uk
Copyright © Python Productions 1989, 2019
Edited from the original scripts by Roger Wilmut
Editor's Introduction Copyright © Rogert Wilmut 1989, 2019
Moral Rights have been asserted. All Rights Reserved

Methuen & Co Ltd Reg No. 05278590

A CIP catalogue record for this book is available from the British Library

ISBN: 978 0 413 77820 8

Typeset by SX Composing DTP, Rayleigh, Essex

Printed and bound in Great Britain by Clays Ltd., Elcograf S.p.A.

This paperback edition is sold subject to the condition that it shall not, by way of trade or
otherwise be lent, resold, hired out or otherwise circulated in any form of binding or cover
other than that in which it is published and without a similar condition, including
this condition, being imposed on the subsequent purchaser.

To Ian MacNaughton,
who somehow understood it all,
and everyone else who joined the Circus,
especially Carol Cleveland

Editor's note

The complete scripts from the four Monty Python series, first shown on BBC television between 1969 and 1974, have been collected in two companion volumes, the first twenty-three episodes in volume one and the second twenty-two in volume two. Transmission details are given in the appendix on p. 342.

Characters' names – often not spoken – are given as in the original camera scripts, with the name of the actual performer added on their first appearance (usually on their first line of dialogue). Small parts taken by walk-ons have not always been identified.

A deliberate decision was made not to include most of the cartoon animations, and in most cases the presence of the cartoon has been simply noted, with occasional reference to the subject matter.

Roger Wilmut

Contents

1 **Twenty-four** — *Conquistador coffee campaign; Repeating groove; Ramsay MacDonald striptease; Job hunter; Agatha Christie sketch (railway timetables); Mr Neville Shunt; Film director (teeth); City gents vox pops; 'Crackpot Religions Ltd'; 'How not to be seen'; Crossing the Atlantic on a tricycle; Interview in filing cabinet; 'Yummy yummy'; Monty Python's Flying Circus again in thirty seconds.*

15 **Twenty-five** — *'The Black Eagle'; Dirty Hungarian phrasebook; Court (phrasebook); Communist quiz; 'Ypres 1914' – abandoned; Art gallery strike; 'Ypres 1914'; Hospital for over-actors; Gumby flower arranging; Spam.*

30 **Twenty-six** — *The Queen will be watching; Coal mine (historical argument); The man who says things in a very roundabout way; The man who speaks only the ends of words; The man who speaks only the beginnings of words; The man who speaks only the middles of words; Commercials; How to feed a goldfish; The man who collects birdwatcher's eggs; Insurance sketch; Hospital run by RSM; Mountaineer; Exploding version of 'The Blue Danube'; Girls' boarding school; Submarine; Lifeboat (cannibalism); Undertaker's sketch.*

45 **Twenty-seven** — Whicker's World: *Court scene - multiple murderer; Icelandic saga; Court scene (Viking); Stock Exchange report; Mrs Premise and Mrs Conclusion visit Jean-Paul Sartre; Whicker Island.*

60 **Twenty-eight** — *Emigration from Surbiton to Hounslow; Schoolboys' Life Assurance Company; How to rid the world of all known diseases; Mrs Niggerbaiter explodes; Vicar/salesman; Farming Club; 'Life of Tschaikowsky'; Trim Jeans Theatre; Fish-slapping dance; World War One; The BBC is short of money; Puss in Boots.*

75	Twenty-nine	'The Money Programme'; 'There is nothing quite so wonderful as money' (song); Erizabeth L; Fraud film squad; Sabation fuzz; Jungle restaurant; Apology for violence and nudity; Ken Russell's 'Gardening Club'; The Lost World of Roiurama; Six more minutes of Monty Python's Flying Circus; Argument clinic; Hitting on the head lessons; Inspector Flying Fox of the Yard; One more minute of Monty Python 's Flying Circus.
91	Thirty	'Blood, Devastation, Death, War and Horror'; The man who speaks in anagrams; Anagram quiz; Merchant banker; Pantomime horses; Life and death struggles; Mary recruitment office; Bus conductor sketch; The man who makes people laugh uncontrollably; Army captain as clown; Gestures to indicate pauses in a televised talk; Neurotic announcers; The news with Richard Baker (vision only); 'The Pantomime Horse is a Secret Agent film'.
105	Thirty-one	The All-England Summarize Proust Competition: 'Summarize Proust Competition'; Everest climbed by hairdressers; Fire brigade; Our Eamonn; 'Party Hints' with Veronica Smalls; Language laboratory; Travel agent; Watney's Red Barrel; Theory on Brontosauruses by Anne Elk (Miss).
121	Thirty-two	Tory Housewives' Clean-up Campaign; Gumby brain specialist; Molluscs – 'live' TV documentary; The Minister for not listening to people; Tuesday documentary/children's story/party political broadcast; Apology (politicians); Expedition to Lake Pahoe; The silliest interview we've ever had; The silliest sketch we've ever done.
134	Thirty-three	Biggles dictates a letter; Climbing the north face of the Uxbridge Road; Lifeboat; Old lady snoopers; 'Storage jars'; The show so far; Cheese shop; Philip Jenkinson on Cheese Westerns; Sam Peckinpah's 'Salad Days'; Apology; The news with Richard Baker; Seashore interlude film.
148	Thirty-four	The cycling tour: *Mr Pither; Clodagh Rogers; Trotsky; Smolensk; Bingo-crazed Chinese; 'Jack in a Box'.*
165	Thirty-five	Bomb on plane; A naked man; Ten seconds of sex; Housing project built by characters from nineteenth-century English literature; M1 interchange built by characters

		from 'Paradise Lost'; Mystico and Janet – flats built by hypnosis; 'Mortuary Hour'; The Olympic hide-and-seek final; The Cheap-Laughs; Bull-fighting; The British Well-Basically Club; Prices on the planet Algon.
180	Thirty-six	Tudor jobs agency; Pornographic bookshop; Elizabethan pornography smugglers; Silly disturbances (the Rev. Arthur Belling); The free repetition of doubtful words sketch, by an underrated author; 'Is there?'... life after death?; The man who says words in the wrong order; Thripshaw's disease; Silly noises; Sherry-drinking vicar.
194	Thirty-seven	'Boxing Tonight' – Jack Bodell v. Sir Kenneth Clark; Dennis Moore; Lupins; What the stars foretell; Doctor; 'TV4 or not TV4' discussion; Ideal Loon Exhibition; Off-Licence; 'Prejudice'.
210	Thirty-eight	Party Political Broadcast (choreographed); 'A Book at Bedtime'; 'Redgauntlet'; Kamikaze Scotsmen; No time to lose; Penguins; BBC programme planners; Unexploded Scotsman; 'Spot the Loony '; Rival documentaries; 'Dad's Doctors' (trail); 'Dad's Pooves' (trail).
227	Thirty-nine	Grandstand: Thames TV introduction; 'Light Entertainment Awards'; Dickie Attenborough; The Oscar Wilde sketch; David Niven's fridge; Pasolini's film 'The Third Test Match'; New brain from Curry's; Blood donor; International Wife-Swapping; Credits of the Year; The dirty vicar sketch.
240	Forty	The golden age of ballooning: Montgolfier Brothers; Louis XIV; George III; Zeppelin.
257	Forty-one	Michael Ellis: Department store; Buying an ant; At home with the ant and other pets; Documentary on ants; Ant communication; Poetry reading (ants); Toupee; Different endings.
276	Forty-two	Light entertainment war: 'Up Your Pavement'; RAF banter; Trivializing the war; Court Martial; Basingstoke in Westphalia; Anything Goes In' (song); Film trailer; The public are idiots; Programme titles conference; The last five miles of the M2; Woody and tinny words; Show-jumping (musical); Newsflash (Germans); 'When Does A Dream Begin?' (song).

x   Monty Python's Flying Circus Volume Two

293 Forty-three   Hamlet: *Bogus psychiatrists; 'Nationwide'; Police helmets; Father-in-law; Hamlet and Ophelia; Boxing match aftermath; Boxing commentary; Piston engine (a bargain); A room in Polonius's house; Dentists; Live from Epsom; Queen Victoria Handicap.*

310 Forty-four   Mr Neutron: *Post box ceremony; Teddy Salad (CIA agent); 'Conjuring Today.*

326 Forty-five   Party Political Broadcast: *'Most Awful Family in Britain'; Icelandic Honey Week; A doctor whose patients are stabbed by his nurse; Brigadier and Bishop; Appeal on behalf of extremely rich people; The man who finishes other people's sentences; David Attenborough; The walking tree of Dahomey; The batsmen of the Kalahari; Cricket match (assegais); BBC News (handovers).*

342   Appendix: transmission details

344   Index

Twenty-four

An office. Boss is reading a book, 'Chinese for Business Men'. He tries out a few Chinese words. There is a knock at the door.

Boss (JOHN) Come in. *(Mr Frog comes in)* Ah, Frog.
Frog (ERIC) S. Frog, sir.
Boss Shut up, I want to have a word with you, Frog.
Frog S. Frog, sir.
Boss Shut up. It's about your advertising campaign for Conquistador Coffee. Now, I've had the managing director of Conquistador to see me this morning and he's very unhappy with your campaign. *Very* unhappy. In fact, he's shot himself.
Frog Badly, sir?
Boss No, extremely well. *(lifts up a leg belonging to a body behind desk, and holds up a card saying joke)* Well, before he went he left a note with the company secretary *(opens a nearby door; a dead company secretary falls out),* the effect of which was how disappointed he was with your work and, in particular, why you had changed the name from Conquistador Instant Coffee to Conquistador Instant Leprosy. Why, Frog?
Frog S. Frog, sir.
Boss Shut up. Why did you do it?
Frog It was a joke.
Boss A joke? *(holds up card saying joke)*
Frog No, no not a joke, a sales campaign. *(holds up a card saying 'No, a Sales Campaign')*
Boss I see, Frog.
Frog S. Frog, sir.
Boss Shut up. Now, let's have a look at the sales chart. *(indicates a plummeting sales graph)* When you took over this account, Frog, Conquistador were a brand leader. Here you introduced your first campaign, 'Conquistador coffee brings a new meaning to the word vomit'. Here you made your special introductory offer of a free dead dog with every jar, and this followed your second campaign 'the tingling fresh coffee which brings you exciting new cholera, mange, dropsy, the clap, hard pad and athlete's head. From the House of Conquistador'.
Frog It was a soft-sell, sir.
Boss Why, Frog?
Frog S. Frog, sir.
Boss Shut up! Well?
Frog Well, people know the name, sir.

Boss They certainly do know the name – they burnt the factory down. The owner is hiding in the bathroom *(shot heard)* – the owner *was* hiding in my bathroom. *(holds up 'joke' card again)*

Frog You're not going to fire me, sir?

Boss Fire you? Three men dead, the factory burnt down, the account lost and our firm completely bankrupt, what ... what ... what ... can you possibly say? What excuse can you possibly make?

Frog Sorry, father. *(holds up the 'joke' card)*

Boss Oh, yes. Oh, incidentally your film's won a prize.

He opens a Venetian blind on the window to reveal the film: a coastline. Panning shot of hills rolling down into the sea, waves breaking on the shore. Travelogue music (Malcolm Arnold type) over this. Suddenly the music sticks, and keeps repeating one phrase. The pan continues. We come across an old-fashioned gramophone on which the record is sticking. A hand comes in and lifts the needle off; the pan continues – it's the hand of the announcer who is sitting at his desk.

Announcer (JOHN) Sorry about that. And now for something completely diff ... *(the film sticks and repeats the end of the sentence several times)* something completely diff ... completely diff ... completely diff ... completely diff ... completely different.

It's Man (MICHAEL) It's ...

After about fifteen seconds of the credits the music and animation sticks, and keeps repeating. We finally get on to the right track, and complete the titles.

Stock film of Ramsay MacDonald arriving at Number 10 Downing Street and any others of that period.

Voice Over (JOHN) 1929. Stanley Baldwin's Conservative Government is defeated and Ramsay MacDonald becomes, for the second time, Prime Minister of England.

MacDonald walks into an empty room (black and white film).

Ramsay MacDonald (MICHAEL) My, it's hot in here.

He proceeds to take off his clothes, strips down to black garter belt and suspenders and stockings.

Cut to Mr Glans who is sitting next to a fully practical old 8mm home projector. There is a knock at the door. He switches the projector off and hides it furtively. He is sitting in an office, with a placard saying 'Exchange and Mart, Editor' on his desk. He points to it rather obviously.

Glans (JOHN) Hello, come in. *(enter Bee, a young aspirant job hunter)* Ah, hello, hello, how much do you want for that briefcase?

Bee (TERRY J) Well, I ...

Glans All right then, the briefcase and the umbrella. A fiver down, must be my final offer.

Bee Well, I don't want to sell them. I've come for a job.

Glans Oh, take a seat, take a seat.

Bee Thank you.

Glans I see you chose the canvas chair with the aluminium frame. I'll throw that in and a fiver, for the briefcase and the umbrella . . . no, make it fair, the briefcase and the umbrella and the two pens in your breast pocket and the chair's yours and a fiver and a pair of ex-German U-boat commando's binoculars.

Bee Really, they are not for sale.

Glans Not for sale, what does that mean?

Bee I came about the advertisement for the job of assistant editor.

Glans Oh yeah, right. Ah, OK, ah. How much experience in journalism?

Bee Five years.

Glans Right, typing speed?

Bee Fifty.

Glans O Levels?

Bee Eight.

Glans A Levels?

Bee Two.

Glans Right . . . Well, I'll give you the job, and the chair, and an all-wool ex-army sleeping bag . . . for the briefcase, umbrella, the pens in your breast pocket and your string vest.

Bee When do I start?

Glans Monday.

Bee That's marvellous.

Glans If you throw in the shoes as well. *(presses intercom)* Hello, er . . . Miss Johnson? Could we have two coffees and biscuits please?

Miss Johnson *(over intercom)* One coffee and one biscuit for the two ex-army greatcoats and the alarm clock on the mantelpiece.

Glans Two ex-army greatcoats and the alarm clock and a table lamp, for two coffees and biscuits.

    ANIMATION: *an elderly secretary at a desk in an empty room.*

Miss Johnson Two greatcoats and two table lamps.

    Cut back to real office.

Glans Two greatcoats, one table lamp and a desert boat.

    Cut back to cartoon.

Miss Johnson For two coffees and biscuits?

    Office.

Glans Done.

    Cartoon.

Miss Johnson Done.

Voice Over So Miss Johnson returned to her typing and dreamed her little dreamy dreams, unaware as she was of the cruel trick fate had in store for her. For Miss Johnson was about to fall victim of the dreaded international Chinese Communist Conspiracy. *(lots of little yellow men pour into the office)* Yes, these fanatical thieves under the leadership of the so-called Mao Tse-tung *(who appears in the animation)* had caught Miss Johnson off guard for one brief but fatal moment and destroyed her. *(Miss Johnson is submerged in a tide of yellow men)* Just as they are ready to do anytime free men anywhere waver in their defence of democracy.

A sailing ship with American flag sails in over the yellow men. Zoom in on the flag: Uncle Sam appears in front of it.

Uncle Sam Yes, once again American defence proves its effectiveness against international communism. Using this diagram of a tooth to represent any small country, we can see how international communism works by eroding away from the inside. *(diagram of tooth rotting from inside and collapsing)* When one country or tooth falls victim to international communism, its neighbours soon follow. *(the remaining teeth fall sideways into the gap)* In dentistry, this is known as the Domino Theory. But with American defence the decay is stopped before it starts and that's why nine out of ten small countries choose American defence...

Different Voice Over ... or Crelm toothpaste with the 'miracle ingredient, Fraudulin'! The white car represents Crelm toothpaste with the miracle ingredient, Fraudulin. *(two cars in a bleak landscape)* The not-white car represents *another* toothpaste. *(the cars race off)* Both toothpastes provide 30% protection. *(they pass a banner: '60% protection')* At 60% protection both toothpastes are doing well. And now at 90% protection the ... wait! *(the grey car stops dead at the '90% protection' banner)* The not-white car is out, and the Crelm toothpaste goes on to win with 100% protection! Yes, do like all smart motorists. Choose Crelm toothpaste.

Cut to 'Shrill' advertising man.

'Shrill' Man Or Shrill Petrol with the new additive GLC 9424075. After 6 p.m., 9424047. Using this white card *(half of screen goes white)* to represent engine deposits and this black card *(the other half goes black)* to represent Shrill's new additive GLC 9424075 – after 6 p.m., 9424077 – we can see how the engine deposits are pushed off the face of the earth by the superior forces available to Shrill. *(shot, off)* Aaaagh!

End of animation. Cut to an upper-class drawing room. An elderly man lies dead on the floor. Enter Jasmina and John.

Jasmina (CAROL CLEVELAND) Anyway, John, you can catch the 11.30 from Hornchurch and be in Basingstoke by one o'clock, oh, and there's a buffet car and ... *(sees corpse)* oh! Daddy!

John (ERIC) My hat! Sir Horace!

Jasmina *(not daring to look)* Has he been...
John Yes – after breakfast. But that doesn't matter now... he's dead.
Jasmina Oh! Poor Daddy...
John Looks like I shan't be catching the 11.30 now.
Jasmina Oh no, John, you mustn't miss your train.
John How could I think of catching a train when I should be here helping you?
Jasmina Oh, John, thank you... anyway you could always catch the 9.30 tomorrow – it goes via Caterham and Chipstead.
John Or the 9.45's even better.
Jasmina Oh, but you'd have to change at Lambs Green.
John Yes, but there's only a seven-minute wait now.
Jasmina Oh, yes, of course, I'd forgotten it was Friday. Oh, who could have done this.
Enter Lady Partridge.
Lady Partridge (GRAHAM) Oh, do hurry Sir Horace, your train leaves in twenty-eight minutes, and if you miss the 10.15 you won't catch the 3.45 which means... oh!
John I'm afraid Sir Horace won't be catching the 10.15, Lady Partridge.
Lady Partridge Has he been...?
Jasmina Yes – after breakfast.
John Lady Partridge, I'm afraid you can cancel his seat reservation.
Lady Partridge Oh, and it was back to the engine – fourth coach along so that he could see the gradient signs outside Swanborough.
John Not any more Lady Partridge... the line's been closed.
Lady Partridge Closed! Not Swanborough!
John I'm afraid so.
Enter Inspector Davis.
Inspector (TERRY J) All right, nobody move. I'm Inspector Davis of Scotland Yard.
John My word, you were here quickly, Inspector.
Inspector Yeah, I got the 8.55 Pullman Express from King's Cross and missed that bit around Hornchurch.
Lady Partridge It's a very good train.
All Excellent, very good, delightful.
Tony runs in through the French windows. He wears white flannels and boater and is jolly upper-class.
Tony (MICHAEL) Hello everyone.
All Tony!
Tony Where's Daddy? *(seeing him)* Oh golly! Has he been...?

John and Jasmina Yes, after breakfast.

Tony Then... he won't be needing his reservation on the 10.15.

John Exactly.

Tony And I suppose as his eldest son it must go to me.

Inspector Just a minute, Tony. There's a small matter of... murder.

Tony Oh, but surely he simply shot himself and then hid the gun.

Lady Partridge How could anyone shoot himself and then hide the gun without first cancelling his reservation.

Tony Ha, ha! Well, I must dash or I'll be late for the 10.15.

Inspector I suggest you murdered your father for his seat reservation.

Tony I may have had the motive, Inspector, but I could not have done it, for I have only just arrived from Gillingham on the 8.13 and here's my restaurant car ticket to prove it.

Jasmina The 8.13 from Gillingham doesn't have a restaurant car.

John It's a standing buffet only.

Tony Oh, er... did I say the 8.13, I meant the 7.58 stopping train.

Lady Partridge But the 7.58 stopping train arrived at Swindon at 8.19 owing to annual point maintenance at Wisborough Junction.

John So how did you make the connection with the 8.13 which left six minutes earlier?

Tony Oh, er, simple! I caught the 7.16 Football Special arriving at Swindon at 8.09.

Jasmina But the 7.16 Football Special only stops at Swindon on alternate Saturdays.

Lady Partridge Yes, surely you mean the Holidaymaker Special.

Tony Oh, yes! How daft of me. Of course I came on the Holidaymaker Special calling at Bedford, Colmworth, Fen Ditton, Sutton, Wallington and Gillingham.

Inspector That's Sundays only!

Tony Damn. All right, I confess I did it. I killed him for his reservation, but you won't take me alive! I'm going to throw myself under the 10.12 from Reading.

John Don't be a fool, Tony, don't do it, the 10.12 has the new narrow traction bogies, you wouldn't stand a chance.

Tony Exactly.

Tableau. Loud chord and slow curtain.

Voice Over (JOHN) That was an excerpt from the latest West End hit 'It all happened on the 11.20 from Hainault to Redhill via Horsham and Reigate, calling at Carshalton Beeches, Malmesbury, Tooting Bec, and Croydon West'. The author is Mr Neville Shunt.

Shunt sitting among mass of railway junk, at typewriter, typing away madly.

Shunt (TERRY G) *(typing)* Chuff, chuff, chuff wooooch, wooooch! Sssssssss, sssssssss! Diddledum, diddledum, diddledum. Toot, toot. The train now standing at platform eight, tch, tch, tch, diddledum, diddledum. Chuffff chuffffff eeeeeeeeaaaaaaaa Vooooommmmm.

Cut to art critic.

SUPERIMPOSED CAPTION: 'GAVIN MILLARRRRRRRRRR'

Art Critic (JOHN) Some people have made the mistake of seeing Shunt's work as a load of rubbish about railway timetables, but clever people like me, who talk loudly in restaurants, see this as a deliberate ambiguity, a plea for understanding in a mechanized world. The points are frozen, the beast is dead. What is the difference? What indeed is the point? The point is frozen, the beast is late out of Paddington. The point is taken. If La Fontaine's elk would spurn Tom Jones the engine must be our head, the dining car our oesophagus, the guard's van our left lung, the cattle truck our shins, the first-class compartment the piece of skin at the nape of the neck and the level crossing an electric elk called Simon. The clarity is devastating. But where is the ambiguity? It's over there in a box. Shunt is saying the 8.15 from Gillingham when in reality he means the 8.13 from Gillingham. The train is the same only the time is altered. Ecce homo, ergo elk. La Fontaine knew his sister and knew her bloody well. The point is taken, the beast is moulting, the fluff gets up your nose. The illusion is complete; it is reality, the reality is illusion and the ambiguity is the only truth. But is the truth, as Hitchcock observes, in the box? No there isn't room, the ambiguity has put on weight. The point is taken, the elk is dead, the beast stops at Swindon, Chabrol stops at nothing, I'm having treatment and La Fontaine can get knotted.

Cut to man at desk.

Man (MICHAEL) Gavin Millar...

Cut to another man.

Another Man (TERRY J) ...rrrrrrr...

Cut to first man.

Man ...was not talking to Neville Shunt. From the world of the theatre we turn to the world of dental hygiene. No, no, no, no. From the world of the theatre we turn to the silver screen. We honour one of the silver screen's outstanding writer-dentists... *writer-directors,* Martin Curry who is visiting London to have a tooth out, for the pre-molar, er... *premiere* of his filling, film next Toothday... Tuesday, at the Dental Theatre... *Film* Theatre. Martin Curry talking to Matthew Palate... Padget.

Cut to late-night line-up setting. Interviewer and interviewee.

Padget (TERRY J) Martin Curry, welcome. One of the big teeth... big points that the American critics made about your latest film, 'The Twelve Caesars', was that it was on so all-embracing a topic. What made you undertake so enormous a tusk... task?

We now see that his interviewee has two enormous front teeth.

Curry (GRAHAM) Well I've always been interested in Imperial Rome from Julius Caesar right through to Vethpathian.

Padget Who?

Curry Vethpathian.

Padget Ah! *Vespasian.*

Curry Yes.

Padget When I saw your film it did seem to me that you had taken a rather, um, subjective approach to it.

Curry I'm sorry?

Padget Well, I mean all your main characters had these enormous... well not enormous, these very big... well let's have a look at a clip in which Julius Incisor... *Caesar* talks to his generals during the battle against Caractacus.

Curry I don't see that at all.

Film: interior of a tent; generals around a table.

Labienus (TERRY J) *(with relatively enormous front teeth)* Shall I order the cavalry that they may hide themselves in the wood, O Caesar?

All *(with very large front teeth)* Thus O Caesar.

Julius (GRAHAM) *(with amazingly large front teeth)* Today is about to be a triumph for our native country.

Back to interview set.

Padget Martin Curry, why do all your characters have these very big er... very big um... teeth?

Curry What do you mean?

Padget Well, I mean, er... and even in your biblical epic, 'The Son of Man', John the Baptist had the most enormous... dental appendages... and of course... himself had the most monumental ivories.

Curry No, I'm afraid I don't see that at all. *(picks up glass of water but can't get it to his mouth)* Could I have a straw?

Padget Oh, a straw, yes, yes. Well, while we're doing that perhaps we could take another look at an earlier film, 'Trafalgar'.

Between decks. Nelson lying among others. They all have enormous teeth.

Nelson (ERIC) Cover my coat, Mr Bush, the men must not know of this till victory is ours.

Toad (TERRY J) The surgeon's coming, sir.

Nelson No, tell the surgeon to attend the men that can be saved. He can do little for me, I fear.

Toad Aye, aye, sir.

Nelson Hardy! Hardy!

Hardy (MICHAEL) Sir?

Nelson Hardy ... kiss ... er ... put your hand on my thigh.

Back to interview set. Curry is sitting practically upside down, trying to drink water with much difficulty.

Padget Martin Curry, thank you. Well. We asked the first-night audience what they thought of that film.

Cut to vox pops.

Man With Enormous Ears (JOHN) It wasn't true to life.

Man With Enormous Teeth (TERRY J) Yes it was.

Man With Enormous Nose (ERIC) No it wasn't.

Madly Dressed Man (GRAHAM) I thought it was totally bizarre.

First City Gent (MICHAEL) Well I've been in the city for over forty years and I think the importance of looking after poor people cannot be understressed.

Second City Gent (GRAHAM) Well I've been in the city for twenty years and I must admit – I'm lost.

An Old Gramophone (JOHN) Well, I've been in the city all my life and I'm as alert and active as I've ever been.

Third City Gent (ERIC) Well I've been in the city since I was two and I certainly wouldn't say that I was stuck in a rut ... stuck in a rut ... stuck in a rut ... stuck in a rut ...

Woman (TERRY J) Oh dear, Mr Bulstrode's stuck again.

She runs over and gives him a shove.

Third City Gent I certainly wouldn't say that I was stuck in a rut.

Fourth City Gent (JOHN) Well I've been in the city for thirty years and I've never once regretted being a nasty, greedy, cold hearted, avaricious, money-grubber ... *Conservative.*

Fifth City Gent (TERRY J) Well I've been in the city for twenty-seven years and I would like to see the reintroduction of flogging. Every Thursday, round at my place.

Man (JOHN) *(whose head only is visible above the level of the sea)* Well I've been in the sea for thirty-three years and I've never regretted it.

Camera pulls back to reveal other city gents also with only heads and bowlers visible who say 'quite agree'. Camera pulls back further to reveal an elderly couple sitting in deckchairs.

Man I think it must be a naturalist outing.

Woman I think it must be one of them crackpot religions.

Cut to Arthur Crackpot sitting at a large curved desk on the front of which a sign says 'Crackpot Religions Ltd. Arthur Crackpot President and God (Ltd)'.

Crackpot (ERIC) This is an example of the sort of abuse we get all the time from ignorant people. I inherited this religion from my father, an ex-used-car salesman and part-time window-box, and I am very proud to be in charge of the first religion with free gifts. You get this luxury tea-trolley with every new enrolment. *(pictures of this and the subsequent gifts)* In addition to this you can win a three-piece lounge suite, this luxury caravan, a weekend for two with Peter Bonetti and tonight's star prize, the entire Norwich City Council.

Curtains go up to reveal the council. Terrific 'ooh' from an audience. Bad organ chords played by a nude man (Terry G).

Crackpot And remember with only eight scoring draws you can win a bishopric in a see of your own choice. You see we have a much more modern approach to religion.

Cut to a person in church. They are walking past a pillar. They take out some money and put it in a collecting box. A sign on the box says 'for the rich'. We hear the money going in, then it moves off, along pipes, falling down; eventually it comes down a small pipe and lands with a tinkle in Crackpot's ashtray. He tries the money with his teeth, pops it into his pocket, and finishes reading...

Crackpot Blessed is Arthur Crackpot and all his subsidiaries Ltd. You see, in our Church we have a lot more fun.

Priest (JOHN) *(we see he has a Pepperpot with him)* Oh, Mrs Collins, you did say you were nervous, didn't you? You have eyes on the coffee machine?

Mrs Collins (MICHAEL) I don't mind, I don't mind – it's just nice to be here, Reverend.

Priest *(slaps her)* Archdeacon. You asked for the coffee machine... so let's see what you've won? You chose Hymn no. 437. *(goes to hymn board, removes one of the numbers, and reads what's on the back)* Oh, Mrs Collins, you had eyes on the coffee machine. Well you have won tonight's star prize: the entire Norwich City Council.

Organ music, oohs and applause from audience.

Mrs Collins I've got one already. *(the priest starts to throttle her)*

Cut back to Crackpot in his office.

Crackpot A lot of religions – no names no pack drill – do go for the poorer type of person – face it, there's more of 'em – poor people, thieves, villains, poor people without no money at all – well we don't have none of that tat. Rich people and crumpet over sixteen can enter free: upper middle class quite welcome; lower middle class not under five grand a year. Lower class – I can't touch it. There's no return on it, you see.

Pull back to show interviewer sitting at his side.

Interviewer (CAROL) Do you have any difficulty converting people?

Crackpot Oh no, well we have ways of making them join.

Cut to a photo of a bishop (Graham).

SUPERIMPOSED CAPTION: 'THE BISHOP OF DULWICH'

Crackpot's Voice Norman there does a lot of converting: a lot of protection, that sort of thing. And there's his mate, Bruce Beer.

Photo of Aussie bishop with beer can (John).

SUPERIMPOSED CAPTION: 'THE ARCHBISHOP OF AUSTRALIA'

Crackpot's Voice Brucie has personally converted ninety-two people – twenty-five inside the distance. Then again we're not afraid to use more modern methods.

Cut to 'Daily Mirror' type pin-up of a bikinied lovely in a silly pose, on a beach with a bishop's mitre and Bible. A large headline reads: 'North See Gas'. A subheading says 'Bishop Sarah', then below that, this blurb which is also read voice over.

Voice Over (JOHN) Sarah, today's diocesan lovely is enough to make any chap go down on his knees. This twenty-three-year-old bishop hails appropriately enough from Bishop's Stortford and lists her hobbies as swimming, riding and film producers. What a gas! Bet she's no novice when it comes to converting all in her See.

Cut to Gumby in street.

SUPERIMPOSED CAPTION: 'ARCHBISHOP GUMBY'

Gumby (MICHAEL) *(shouting laboriously)* Basically, I believe in peace and bashing two bricks together. *(he bashes two bricks together)*

Cut to John Lennon.

Lennon (ERIC) I'm starting a war for peace.

Cut to Ken Shabby.

SUPERIMPOSED CAPTION: 'ARCHBISHOP SHABBY'

Shabby (MICHAEL) Cor blimey. I'm raising polecats for peace.

Cut to Arthur Nudge.

SUPERIMPOSED CAPTION: 'ARCHBISHOP NUDGE'

Nudge (ERIC) Peace? I like a peace. Know what I mean? Know what I mean? Say no more. Nudge, nudge.

Cut to a bishop. A sign on the wall says 'Naughty Religion'.

Bishop (JOHN) *(porn-merchant style)* Our religion is the first Church to cater for the naughty type of person. If you'd like a bit of love-your-neighbour – and who doesn't now and again – then see Vera and Ciceley during the hymns.

Cut to wide-boy type, with small moustache and kipper tie. A sign says: 'No Questions Asked Religion'.

Bill (MICHAEL) In our Church we try to help people to help themselves – to cars, washing machines, lead piping, no questions asked. We are the only Church, apart from the Baptists, to do respray jobs.

Cut to loony with a fright wig and an axe in his head. A sign says: 'The Lunatic Religion'.

Ali Byan (TERRY J) We the Church of the Divine Loony believe in the power of prayer to turn the head purple ha, ha, ha.

Cut to a normal looking priest. A sign says: 'The Most Popular Religion Ltd'.

Priest (GRAHAM) I would like to come in here for a moment if I may, and disassociate our Church from these frivolous and offensive religions. We are primarily concerned with what is best . . . *(phone rings; he answers it)* Hello. Oh, well how about Allied Breweries? All right but keep the Rio Tinto *(phone down)* . . . for the human soul.

ANIMATION: *a vicar c/o Terry Gilliam.*

CAPTION: 'CARTOON RELIGIONS LTD'

Voice In our Church we believe first and foremost in you. *(he smiles; the top of his head comes off and the Devil tries to climb out; the vicar replaces his head)* We want you to think of us as your friend. *(as before; the vicar nails the top of his head on)*

Cut to a wide-angle shot of hedgerows, fields and trees.

Voice Over (JOHN) In this picture there are forty people. None of them can be seen. In this film we hope to show you how not to be seen.

CAPTION: 'HM GOVERNMENT, PUBLIC SERVICE FILM NO. 42 PARA 6. "HOW NOT TO BE SEEN"'

Voice Over This is Mr E. R. Bradshaw, of Napier Court, Black Lion Road, SE5. He cannot be seen. Now I'm going to ask him to stand up. Mr Bradshaw will you stand up please?

In the middle distance a smiling holidaymaker in braces, collarless shirt and hankie, stands up. There is a pause. Only the sound of the wind. Then a loud gunshot rings out. Mr Bradshaw crumples to the ground.

Voice Over This demonstrates the value of not being seen.

Cut to another location – this time an empty stretch of scrubland.

Voice Over In this picture we cannot see Mrs B. J. Smegma of 13, The Crescent, Belmont. Mrs Smegma will you stand up please.

There is a pause. Almost on the edge of frame in the distance a Pepperpot stands up, proudly. Immediately a shot rings out and she leaps in the air and dies. Cut to a bush some distance away on open land.

Voice Over This is Mr Nesbitt of Harlow New Town. Mr Nesbitt would you stand up please. *(nothing happens)* Mr Nesbitt has learnt the first lesson of not being seen – not to stand up. However, he has chosen a very obvious piece of cover. *(the bush explodes; cut to a shot of three bushes)* Mr E. V. Lambert, of 'Homeleigh', The Burrows, Oswestry, has presented us with a poser. We do not know which bush he is behind, but we can soon find out. *(the left-hand bush explodes, then the right-hand bush; finally the middle bush explodes; there is a muffled scream; the smoke subsides)* Yes, it was the middle one.

Cut to shot of farmland. There is a waterbutt, a low wall, a big pile of leaves, a bushy tree, a parked car and lots of bushes and trees in the distance.

Voice Over Mr Ken Andrews, of Leighton Road, Slough, has concealed himself extremely well. He could be almost anywhere. He could be behind the wall, inside the water barrel, beneath a pile of leaves, up in the tree, squatting down behind the car, concealed in a hollow, or crouched behind any one of a hundred bushes. However, we happen to know he's in the water barrel.

The water barrel just blows apart in the biggest explosion yet. Cut to a panning shot from beach huts across to beach and sea.

Voice Over Mr and Mrs Watson of 'Ivy Cottage', Worplesdon Road, Hull, chose a very cunning way of not being seen. When we called at their house, we found they had gone away on two weeks' holiday. They had not left any forwarding address, and they had bolted and barred the house to prevent us getting in. However, a neighbour told us where they were.

The camera has come to rest on a very obvious isolated beach hut; it blows up. Cut to a building site in a suburban housing estate. There is a Gumby standing there.

Voice Over And here is the neighbour who told us where they were . . . *(he blows up)* Nobody likes a clever dick. *(cut to stock film of a small house)* And this is where he lived. *(it blows up)* And this is where Lord Langdon lived who refused to speak to us. *(it blows up)* and so did the gentlemen who lived here . . . *(shot of house: it blows up)* . . . and here . . . *(ditto)* and of course here . . . *(series of quick cuts of various atom bombs and hydrogen bomb at moment of impact)* and Manchester and the West Midlands, Spain, China . . . *(mad laugh)*

Cut to a presentation desk. The film is on a screen behind. We see it stop behind him as the presenter speaks.

Presenter (MICHAEL) Ah, well I'm afraid we have to stop the film there, as some of the scenes which followed were of a violent nature which might have proved distressing to some of our viewers. Though not to me, I can tell you. *(cut to another camera; the presenter turns to face it)* In Nova Scotia today, Mr Roy Bent of North Walsham in Norfolk became the first man to cross the Atlantic on a tricycle. His tricycle, specially adapted for the crossing, was ninety feet long, with a protective steel hull, three funnels, seventeen first-class cabins and a radar scanner. *(A head and shoulders picture of Roy Bent comes up on the screen behind him)* Mr Bent is in our Durham studios, which is rather unfortunate as we're all down here in London. And in London I have with me Mr Ludovic Grayson, the man who scored all six goals in Arsenal's 1-0 victory over the Turkish Champions FC Botty. *(he turns)* Ludovic . . . *(pull out to reveal that he is talking to a five-foot-high filing cabinet)* first of all congratulations on the victory.

Voice (TERRY J) *(from inside filing cabinet)* Thank you, David.

Presenter It should send you back to Botty with a big lead.

Voice Oh yes, well we're fairly confident, David.

Presenter Well at the moment, Ludovic, you're crouching down inside a filing cabinet.

Voice Yes that's right, David, I'm trying not to be seen.

Presenter I see. Is this through fear?

Voice Oh no, no, it's common sense really. If they can't see you, they can't get you.

Presenter Ha, ha, ha, but of course they can still hear you. *(the filing cabinet explodes)* Ludovic Grayson, thank you very much for coming on the programme tonight. And we end the show with music. And here with their very latest recording 'Yummy, Yummy, Yummy, I've got love in my tummy' Jackie Charlton and the Tonettes.

Cut to a trendy pop-music set with coloured lights, etc. On the main podium is a large packing crate with a microphone in front of it. The backing vocal is by three more packing crates with microphones. The instrumental group are also in crates. We hear the aforementioned pop song. Roll credits over. Fade out. Cut to BBC 1 caption.

Voice Over (ERIC) For those of you who may have just missed 'Monty Python's Flying Circus', here it is again.

Entire show is recapped in a series of flash clips lasting about twenty seconds.

Twenty-five

Close up of a flag bearing a black eagle on a red background fluttering in the wind. Blue sky behind and scudding clouds. Adventure music as for buccaneer film.

CAPTIONS:

THE BLACK EAGLE
CAST

BLACK EAGLE	THORNTON WELLES
MEG FAIRWEATHER	KATE TAMBLYING
JACK FAIRWEATHER	OWEN TREGOWER
HENRY FAIRWEATHER	RUSS TEMPOLE JNR.
MRS FAIRWEATHER	ALICE SHOEMAKER
DR TENNYSON	MARSHALL M. WEST
LUMPKIN	DINO DE VERE
MR RIVERS	WALTER SCHENKEL
LT STAVEACRE	NORMAN S. HUGHES
A WENCH	MARSHA SUTTON
SECOND WENCH	TINEA PEDIS
THE DOG	KARL

SCREENPLAY BY AL R. SCHROEDER AND WAYNE KOPIT
BASED ON THE NOVEL 'THE BLUE EAGLE' BY RAPHAEL SABATINI

SET DECORATION	CY BORGONI
MAKE-UP	BUNICE DILKES
COSTUMES	JOAN LOUIS
UNIT MANAGER	TREVOR BELOWSKI
CONTINUITY	SUE CARPENTER
SPECIAL EFFECTS	WALTER SCHENKEL

MISS TAMBLYING'S GOWNS BY HEPWORTHS
COLOUR BY CHROMACOLOUR
SOUND RECORDING WCA SYSTEM
COPYRIGHT BY SCHENKEL PRODUCTIONS
ANY SIMILARITY BETWEEN PERSONS LIVING OR DEAD
IS COINCIDENTAL
PRODUCED BY JOSEPH M. SCHLACK
DIRECTED BY LAURENT F. NORDER

Mix through from flag to sea at night. Sound of water lapping. Soft sound of muffled oars drawing nearer. We can see a rowing boat making slowly and silently towards the shore where the camera is. The stirring music continues.

ROLLER CAPTION: 'IN 1742 THE SPANISH EMPIRE LAY IN RUINS. TORN BY INTERNAL DISSENT, AND WRACKED BY NUMEROUS WARS, ITS RICH TRADE ROUTES FELL AN EASY PREY TO BRITISH PRIVATEERS ... AND THE TREASURE OF THE SPANISH MAIN WAS BROUGHT HOME TO THE SHORES OF ENGLAND'

By the time the roller captions have finished the rowing boat has approached much nearer. It stops and they ship their oars. Cut in to close-ups of pirate's face peering into the darkness. Shot from the boat of a deserted cliff top. A light flashes twice. Then there is a pause. Cut back to the boat; the men look uneasy as they wait for the third flash. Cut back to the cliff ... at last the third flash. Cut back to the boat; they start to row again. Cut to them beaching the boat on the shore. They start to unload sacks and chests. Putting them onto their shoulders they start to walk along the shore line. We pan with them for quite some way ... and suddenly between the camera and the pirates we come across the announcer at a desk. He wears a dinner jacket and shuffles some papers in front of him.

Announcer (JOHN) And now for something completely different...

It's Man (MICHAEL) It's...

Animated titles. Cut to a small tobacconist's shop. The tobacconist is handing change to a fireman.

Fireman (MICHAEL) Thank you very much for the change, Mr Tobacconist. *(he exits; then out of vision, very loud)* Was that all right?

Everybody SSSh!

Stirring adventure music of buccaneer film as at the beginning and the roller caption in the same typeface.

ROLLER CAPTION: IN 1970, THE BRITISH EMPIRE LAY IN RUINS, FOREIGN NATIONALS FREQUENTED THE STREETS – MANY OF THEM HUNGARIANS (NOT THE STREETS – THE FOREIGN NATIONALS). ANYWAY, MANY OF THESE HUNGARIANS WENT INTO TOBACCONIST'S SHOPS TO BUY CIGARETTES ...

Enter Hungarian gentleman with phrase book. He is looking for the right phrase.

Hungarian (JOHN) I will not buy this record. It is scratched.

Tobacconist (TERRY J) Sorry?

Hungarian I will not buy this record. It is scratched.

Tobacconist No, no, no. This ... tobacconist's.

Hungarian Ah! I will not buy this tobacconist's. It is scratched.

Tobacconist No, no, no ... tobacco ... er, cigarettes?

Hungarian Yes, cigarettes. My hovercraft is full of eels.

Tobacconist What?

Hungarian *(miming matches)* My hovercraft is full of eels.

Tobacconist Matches, matches? *(showing some)*

Hungarian Yah, yah. *(he takes cigarettes and matches and pulls out loose change; he consults his book)* Er, do you want ... do you want to come back to my place, bouncy bouncy?

Tobacconist I don't think you're using that right.

Hungarian You great pouf.

Tobacconist That'll be six and six please.

Hungarian If I said you had a beautiful body would you hold it against me? I am no longer infected.

Tobacconist *(miming that he wants to see the book; he takes the book)* It costs six and six ... *(mumbling as he searches)* Costs six and six ... Here we are ... Yandelvayasna grldenwi stravenka.

Hungarian hits him between the eyes. Policeman walking along street suddenly stops and puts his hand to his ear. He starts running down the street, round corner and down another street, round yet another corner and down another street into the shop.

Policeman (GRAHAM) What's going on here then?

Hungarian *(opening book and pointing at tobacconist)* You have beautiful thighs.

Policeman What?

Tobacconist He hit me.

Hungarian Drop your panties, Sir William, I cannot wait till lunchtime.

Policeman Right! *(grabs him and drags him out)*

Hungarian My nipples explode with delight.

Cut to a courtroom.

Clerk (ERIC) Call Alexander Yahlt.

Voices Call Alexander Yahlt. Call Alexander Yahlt. Call Alexander Yahlt.

They do this three times finishing with harmony.

Magistrate (TERRY J) Oh shut up.

Alexander Yahlt enters. He is not Hungarian but an ordinary man in a mac.

Clerk You are Alexander Yahlt?

Yahlt (MICHAEL) *(Derek Nimmo's voice [dubbed on])* Oh I am.

Clerk Skip the impersonations. You are Alexander Yahlt?

Yahlt *(normal voice)* I am.

Clerk You are hereby charged that on the 28th day of May 1970 you did wilfully, unlawfully and with malice aforethought publish an alleged English-Hungarian phrasebook with intent to cause a breach of the peace. How do you plead?

Yahlt Not guilty.

Clerk You live at 46, Horton Terrace?

Yahlt I do live at 46, Horton Terrace.

Clerk You are the director of a publishing company?

Yahlt I am the director of a publishing company.

Clerk Your company publishes phrasebooks?

Yahlt My company does publish phrasebooks.

Clerk You did say 46, Horton Terrace didn't you?

Yahlt Yes.

He claps his hand to his mouth; gong sounds – general applause.

Clerk Ha, ha, ha, I got him.

Magistrate Get on with it! Get on with it!

Clerk Yes m'lud, on the 28th of May you published this phrasebook.

Yahlt I did.

Clerk I quote an example. The Hungarian phrase meaning 'Can you direct me to the station' is translated by the English phrase 'Please fondle my bum'.

Yahlt I wish to plead incompetence.

The policeman stands up.

Policeman Please may I ask for an adjournment, m'lud?

Magistrate An adjournment? Certainly not. *(the policeman sits down; there is a loud raspberry; the policeman goes bright red)* Why on earth didn't you say *why* you wanted an adjournment?

Policeman I didn't know an acceptable legal phrase, m'lud.

Cut to stock film of Women's Institute applauding. Cut back to the magistrate.

Magistrate If there's any more stock film of women applauding I shall clear the court.

Clerk Call Abigail Tesler.

Two policemen carry a large photo blow-up the size of a door. It is a photo from a newspaper like the 'Mirror', with a girl in a bikini and the headline across the top: 'Sunshine Sizzler'. Underneath is some small print which is later read out (see below). They prop her up in the witness box.

Defence (JOHN) M'lud – this is Abigail Tesler.

Magistrate Is it?

Defence Yes, m'lud. Twenty-three-year-old Abigail hails from down under, where they're upside down about her. Those Aussies certainly know a thing or two when it comes to beach belles. Bet some life-saver wouldn't mind giving *her* the kiss of life. So watch out for sharks, Abigail!

Cut back to the judge's desk. The judge has turned into a similar photo blow-up of himself, the size of a door. The headline at the top is 'Legal Sizzler'.

Journalist (ERIC) *(voice over)* Is this strictly relevant? quizzed learned lovely, Justice Maltravers. Seventy-eight-year-old Justice hails from Esher, and he's been making a big name for himself at the recent Assizes at Exeter. *(cut back to defence counsel, who has turned into a large photo blow-up of himself headed 'Defence Counsel Sizzler')*

Voice Over (MICHAEL) All will be revealed soon m'lud, quipped tall forty-two-year-old Nelson Bedowes. Cutie QC Nelson's keen on negligence and grievous bodily harm at Gray's Inn. And with cases like he's won we bet Gray's in when Nelson's around.

> ANIMATION: *starting with newspaper photo of judge in dark glasses and full wig and robes with a starlet beside him, walking down London airport departure corridor carrying cases.*

Voice Over (ERIC) Well get on with it, admitted seventy-eight-year-old genial jurisprude Maltravers seen here at London airport, on his way to judge for Britain at the famous International Court in the Hague . . .

Voice Get off!

> CAPTION: 'WORLD FORUM'
>
> *An important-looking current affairs set. On the back wall behind the presenter huge letters say: 'World Forum'*

Presenter (ERIC) Good evening. Tonight is indeed a unique occasion in the history of television. We are very privileged, and deeply honoured to have with us in the studio, Karl Marx, founder of modern socialism, and author of the 'Communist Manifesto'. *(Karl Marx is sitting at a desk; he nods)* Vladimir Ilich Ulyanov, better known to the world as Lenin, leader of the Russian Revolution, writer, statesman, and father of modern communism. *(shot of Lenin also at desk; he nods)* Che Guevara, the Cuban guerrilla leader. *(shot of Guevara)* And Mao Tse-tung, leader of the Chinese Communist Party since 1949. *(shot of Mao; the presenter picks up a card)* And the first question is for you, Karl Marx. The Hammers – the Hammers is the nickname of what English football team? The Hammers? *(shot of Karl Marx furrowing his brow – obviously he hasn't a clue)* No? Well bad luck there, Karl. So we'll go onto you Che. Che Guevara – Coventry City last won the FA Cup in what year? *(cut to Che looking equally dumbfounded)* No? I'll throw it open. Coventry City last won the FA Cup in what year? *(they all look blank)* No? Well, I'm not surprised you didn't get that. It was in fact a trick question. Coventry City have *never* won the FA Cup. So with the scores all equal now we go onto our second round, and Lenin it's your starter for ten. Teddy Johnson and Pearl Carr won the Eurovision Song Contest in 1959. What was the name of the song? . . . Teddy Johnson and Pearl Carr's song in the 1959 Eurovision Song Contest? Anybody? *(buzzer goes à la 'University Challenge': zoom in on Mao Tse-tung)* Yes, Mao Tse-tung?

Mao Tse-tung 'Sing Little Birdie'?

Presenter Yes it was indeed. Well challenged. *(applause)* Well now we come on to our special gift section. The contestant is Karl Marx and the prize this week is a beautiful lounge suite. *(curtains behind the presenter sweep open to reveal a beautiful lounge suite; terrific audience applause; Karl comes out and stands in front of this display; the presenter treats him with Michael Miles' unctuousness)* Now Karl has elected to answer questions on the workers' control of factories so here we go with question number one. Are you nervous? *(Karl nods his head; the presenter reads from a card)* The development of the industrial proletariat is conditioned by what other development?

Karl (TERRY J) The development of the industrial bourgeoisie. *(applause)*

Presenter Yes, yes, it is indeed. You're on your way to the lounge suite, Karl. Question number two. The struggle of class against class is a what struggle? A what struggle?

Karl A political struggle.

Tumultuous applause.

Presenter Yes, yes! One final question Karl and the beautiful lounge suite will be yours ... Are you going to have a go? *(Karl nods)* You're a brave man. Karl Marx, your final question, who won the Cup Final in 1949?

Karl The workers' control of the means of production? The struggle of the urban proletariat?

Presenter No. It was in fact Wolverhampton Wanderers who beat Leicester 3-1.

Cut to stock film of goal being scored in a big football match. Roars from crowd. Stock footage of football crowds cheering.

Voice Over (MICHAEL) and CAPTION: 'IN "WORLD FORUM" TODAY: KARL MARX, CHE GUEVARA, LENIN AND MAO TSE-TUNG. NEXT WEEK, FOUR LEADING HEADS OF STATE OF THE AFRO-ASIAN NATIONS AGAINST BRISTOL ROVERS AT MOLINEUX'

ANIMATION: *sketch leading to a stock drawing of a First World War trench scene – barbed wire against the sky with a helmet stuck on a bayonet.*

Voice Over and CAPTION: 'IN 1914, THE BALANCE OF POWER LAY IN RUINS. EUROPE WAS PLUNGED INTO BLOODY CONFLICT. NATION FOUGHT NATION. BUT NO NATION FOUGHT NATION MORELY THAN THE ENGLISH HIP HIP HOORARY! NICE, NICE! YAH BOO. PHILLIPS IS A GERMAN AND HE HAVE MY PEN'

Different Voice Over and CAPTION: 'START AGAIN'

First Voice Over and CAPTION: 'IN 1914, THE BALANCE OF POWER LAY IN RUINS ...'

Mix through to close up of a harmonica being played by a British Tommy.

CAPTION: 'YPRES 1914'

The camera pulls slowly out, with the plaintive harmonica still playing, to reveal the interior of a bunker in the trenches. Sitting around on old ammunition boxes etc. are the harmonica player, Private Jenkins,

Sergeant Jackson, a padre with no arms, a sheikh, a Viking warrior, a male mermaid, a nun, a milkman and a Greek Orthodox priest. Sounds of warfare throughout, shells thudding, explosions etc.

Sergeant (MICHAEL) *(looking round rather uncomfortably at the strange collection)* Jenkins?

Jenkins (ERIC) *(equally uncomfortable about playing such a tender scene in front of sheiks etc.)* Yes, sir.

Sergeant What are you going to do when you get back to Blighty?

Jenkins I dunno, Sarge . . . I expect I'll be looking after me mum. She'll be getting on a bit now.

Sergeant Got a family of your own 'ave you?

Jenkins No, she's . . . she's all I got left now. My wife, Doreen . . . she . . . I got a letter . . .

Sergeant You don't have to tell me, son.

Jenkins No, sarge, I'd like to tell you, see this place . . .

Cut to long shot of bunker. Floor manager strides on to set.

Floor Manager (TERRY J) Hold it. Hold it. Look, loves . . . can anyone not involved in this scene, please leave the set. *(he starts to herd out anyone not in First War costume)* Now! Come on please. Anyone not concerned in this scene, the canteen's open upstairs. *(sheikh, male mermaid etc. troop off)* Now come on please. *(to soldiers)* Sorry loves. Sorry. We'll have to take it again, from the top. All right. OK . . . Cue!

Back to identical shot of harmonica-playing Tommy; he plays a few bars.

CAPTION: 'KNICKERS 1914'

Cut to long shot. The floor manager rushes on again. The caption remains superimposed.

Floor Manager Hold it. Hold it. Now, who changed the caption? Can whoever changed the caption put the right one back immediately please.

CAPTION: 'YPRES 1914'

Floor Manager Right. All right, we'll take it again from the top. Cue. *(back to identical shot of harmonica-playing Tommy with correct caption superimposed; slow pull out as before; then floor manager rushes on again)* Hold it. Hold it. *(he goes behind some sandbags looking extremely irritated)* Come on. Come on, out of there. *(he hauls a spaceman and hustles him off the set)* You're not in this . . . you're only holding the whole thing up. *(turning to studio as a whole)* Come on please. It's no good, loves. It's no good. We'll have to leave it for now. Come back when everyone's settled down a bit. So that means we go over to the Art Room, all right. So cue camera three! *(cut to Guevara caught in a hot embrace with Karl Marx)* Sorry, camera *four*.

Cut to Art Gallery. A large sign says: 'Italian Masters of the Renaissance'. Two art critics wandering through. They stop in front of a large Titian canvas. The canvas is about ten foot high by six foot wide.

First Critic (MICHAEL) Aren't they marvellous? The strength and boldness... life and power in those colours.

Second Critic (ERIC) This must be Titian's masterpiece.

First Critic Oh indeed – if only for the composition alone. The strength of those foreground figures... the firmness of the line...

Second Critic Yes, the confidence of the master at the height of his powers.

> *At this point a man in a country smock and straw hat and a straw in his mouth comes up to the painting and with a very businesslike manner presses the nipple of a nude in the painting. Ding dong sound of a front doorbell. He stands tapping his feet and whistling soundlessly beside the painting. He nods at the critics. Cut to the top of the painting to see that one of the figures has disappeared leaving a blank. The camera pans down the painting as we hear footsteps, as if coming down a lot of stone steps. Eventually the camera comes to rest beside where the country bumpkin is standing and a door opens in the painting. We do not see who has opened it, but can assume it is the cherub.*

Cherub (TERRY G) Yes?

Bumpkin (TERRY J) Hello sonny, your dad in?

Cherub Yes.

Bumpkin Could I speak to him please? It's the man from 'The Hay Wain'.

Cherub Who?

Bumpkin The man from 'The Hay Wain' by Constable.

Cherub Dad... it's the man from 'The Hay Wain' by Constable to see you.

Solomon (GRAHAM) Coming.

> *Sound of footsteps. Cut to another close up on the painting and we see the main figure disappearing. This figure suddenly puts his head round the door.*

Solomon Hello? How are you? Come on in.

Bumpkin No, no can't stop, just passing by, actually.

Solomon Oh, where are you now?

Bumpkin Well may you ask. We just been moved in next to a room full of Brueghels... terrible bloody din. Skating all hours of the night. Anyway, I just dropped in to tell you there's been a walk-out in the Impressionists.

Solomon Walk-out, eh?

Bumpkin Yeah. It started with the 'Déjeuner Sur L'Herbe' lot, evidently they were moved away from above the radiator or something. Anyway, the Impressionists are all out. Gainsborough's Blue Boy's brought out the eighteenth-century English portraits, the Flemish School's solid, and the German woodcuts are at a meeting now.

Solomon Right. Well I'll get the Renaissance School out.

Bumpkin OK, meeting 4.30 – 'Bridge at Arles'.

Solomon OK, cheerio – good luck, son.

Bumpkin OK.
The door shuts and we hear Solomon's voice over.
Solomon Right – everybody out.
We see various famous paintings whose characters suddenly disappear.
Voices I'm off. I'm off. I'm off, dear. *(etc.)*
Mix through to front room of a suburban house. A man is sawing his – wife in two in the classic long box.
Radio Here is the News . . . *(the man pauses for a moment and looks at radio, then resumes sawing; we zoom in to close up on the radio. There is a window behind it; as the radio talks, a group of paintings with picket signs pass by)* by an almost unanimous vote, paintings in the National Gallery voted to continue the strike that has emptied frames for the last week. The man from Constable's 'Hay Wain' said last night that there was no chance of a return to the pictures before the weekend. Sir Kenneth Clarke has said he will talk to any painting if it can help bring a speedy end to the strike. *(a ghastly scream out of vision; the sawing stops abruptly)* At Sotheby's, prices dropped dramatically as leading figures left their paintings. *(Cut to Sotheby's.)*
Auctioneer (JOHN) What am I bid for Vermeer's 'Lady Who Used to be at a Window'? Do I hear two bob?
Voice Two bob!
Auctioneer Gone. Now what am I bid for another great bargain? Edward Landseer's 'Nothing at Bay'.
Pull out to reveal man standing beside auctioneer with the painting (the stag is missing). Cut to a group of famous characters from famous paintings who are clustered round the camera. Botticelli's Venus is in the centre jabbing her fingers at camera.
Venus All we bloody want is a little bit of bloody consultation.
Fade sound of them all shouting and jostling etc. Bring up sound of radio out of vision.
Radio At a mass meeting at Brentford Football Ground, other works of art voted to come out in support of the paintings. *(still in animation cut to Brentford football ground with famous statues in the stands)* The vote was unanimous. *(they all put their hands up)* with one abstention. *(cut to close up of 'Venus De Milo'; cut to TV Centre and slow zoom in)* Meanwhile, at Television Centre work began again on a sketch about Ypres. A spokesman for the sketch said: he fully expected it to be more sensible this time.
Cut to usual opening shot of close up of harmonica being played by Tommy.
CAPTION: 'YPRES 1914'
Slow zoom out to reveal set-up as before with no extraneous characters.
Sergeant Jenkins.
Jenkins Yes, Sarge?

Sergeant What are you going to do when you get back to Blighty?

Jenkins I dunno, sarge. I expect I'll look after my mum. She'll be getting on a bit now.

Sergeant Got a family of your own have you?

Jenkins No – she's all I got left now. My wife, Doreen... she... I got a letter.

Sergeant You don't have to tell me, son.

Jenkins No, sarge, I'd like to tell you. You see, this bloke from up the street...

Enter a young major – excruciatingly public school.

Major (GRAHAM) OK, chaps, at ease. I've just been up the line...

Sergeant Can we get through, sir?

Major No, I'm afraid we'll have to make a break for it at nightfall.

Sergeant Right, sir. We're all with yer.

Major Yes I know, that's just the problem, Sergeant. How many are there of us?

Sergeant Well there's you, me, Jenkins, Padre, Kipper, there's five, sir.

Major And only rations for...

Sergeant Four, sir.

Major Precisely. I'm afraid one of us will have to take the 'other' way out.

Crash zoom into revolver which the major has brought out. Jarring chord. Close up of faces looking tense from one to the other. Tense music.

Padre (JOHN) I'm a gonner, Major. Leave me, I'm... I'm not a complete man anymore.

Major You've lost both your arms as well.

Padre Yes. Damn silly really.

Major No, no, we'll draw for it. That's the way we do things in the army. Sergeant. The straws!

The sergeant gives him the straws. The major arranges them and hands them round.

Major Right now, the man who gets the shortest straw knows what to do.

They all take the long straws. Including the padre who takes one in his teeth. The major is left with a tiny straw. A pause.

Sergeant Looks like you, sir.

Major Is it? What did we say, the longest straw was it?

Sergeant No, shortest, sir.

Major Well we'd better do it again, there's obviously been a bit of a muddle. *(they do it again and the same thing happens)* Oh dear. Best of three? *(they go through it again and he gets left with it again)* Right, well I've got the shortest straw. So *I* decide what means we use to decide who's going to do . . . to . . . to . . . to er, . . . to do the thing . . . to do the right thing. Now rank doesn't enter into this, but obviously if I should get through the lines, I will be in a very good position to recommend anyone, very highly, for a posthumous VC. *(he looks round to see if there are any takers)* No? Good. Fine. Fine. Fine. Fine. Right. *(counting out)* Dip, dip, dip, my little ship sails on the ocean, you are *(comes back to himself)* . . . no wait, wait a minute, no I, I must have missed out a dip. I'll start again. Dip, dip, dip, dip, my little ship, sails on the ocean, you are . . . *(it's back on him again)* No, this is not working out. It's not working out. What shall we do?

Jenkins How about one potato, two potato, sir?

Major Don't be childish, Jenkins. No, I think, I think fisties would be best. OK, so hands behind backs. After three, OK, one, two, three. *(everyone except the padre who has no arms puts out clenched fist)* Now what's this . . . stone, stone, stone, *(looks down at his hand)* and scissors. Now. Scissors cut everything, don't they?

Sergeant Not stone, sir.

Major They're very *good* scissors. *(then he suddenly sees the padre)* Padre hasn't been!

Sergeant No arms, sir.

Major Oh, I'm terribly sorry, I'm afraid I didn't . . . tell you what. All those people who *don't* want to stay here and shoot themselves raise their arms.

Padre Stop it! Stop it! Stop this . . . this hideous façade.

Sergeant Easy, Padre!

Padre No, no, I must speak. When I, when I came to this war, I had two arms, two good arms, but when the time came to . . . to lose one, I . . . I gave it gladly, I smiled as they cut if off, *(music under: 'There'll Always Be An England)* because I knew there was a future for mankind. I . . . I knew there was hope . . . so long as men were prepared to give their limbs. *(emotionally)* And when the time came for me to give my other arm I . . . I gave it gladly. I . . . I sang as they sawed it off. Because I believed . . . *(hysterically)* Oh you may laugh, but I believed with every fibre of my body, with every drop of rain that falls, a . . . a flower grows. And that flower, that small fragile, delicate flower . . . *(two modern-day ambulance attendants come in with a trolley which they put the padre onto and wheel him away; he is still going on)* . . . shall burst forth and give a new life. New strength! *(cut to a present-day ambulance racing out of TV Centre in speeded-up motion; it roars through the streets, and arrives at the casualty entrance of a hospital; the doors swing open and the padre is rushed out on stretcher (still in fast motion) totally under a blanket; we hear his voice)* . . . freedom. Freedom from fear and freedom from oppression. Freedom from tyranny. *(the camera picks up on sign which reads: 'Royal Hospital for Over-acting)* A world where men and women of all races and creeds can live together in communion and then in the

twilight of this life, our children, and our children's children and . . . *(by this time he has disappeared in through the doors of the hospital)*
Cut to the interior of hospital and see specialist as he walks down a corridor.

Specialist (GRAHAM) All our patients here are suffering from severe over-acting. *(a nurse goes past leading a Long John Silver who keeps going 'Aha! Jim Lad')* When they're brought in they're all really over the top. *(he passes a whole group of Long John Silvers)* And it's our job to try and treat the condition of over-acting . . . *(he passes a group of King Rats, and indicates the worst case)* rather serious. *(he walks on through a door)* This is the Richard III Ward.

Pull out to reveal a crowd of Richard III's. The specialist indicates one who is really over the top.

Richard III (MICHAEL) A horse. A horse. My kingdom for a horse.

Specialist Most of these cases are pretty unpleasant. Nurse . . . *(a nurse comes in and sedates Richard III)* But the treatment does work with some people. This chap came to us straight from the Chichester Festival; we operated just in time, and now he's almost normal.

He walks over to a very ordinary Richard III, who smiles disarmingly and says quite chattily:

Second Richard (ERIC) A horse, a horse, my kingdom for a horse.

Shaking his head sadly, the specialist leaves the ward and opens a door to another one.

Specialist But in here we have some very nasty cases indeed.

ANIMATION: *invoking grotesque Hamlets.*

Hamlets To be or not to be. That is the question. To be . . .

Animation leads to close-up of flowers.

SUPERIMPOSED CAPTION: 'FLOWER ARRANGEMENT'
Pull back to show Gumby in studio with piles of flowers on a table.
SUPERIMPOSED CAPTION: 'INTRODUCED BY D. P. GUMBY'

Gumby (MICHAEL) Good evening. First take a bunch of flowers. *(he grabs flowers from the table)* Pretty begonias, irises, freesias and crymanthesums . . . then arrange them nicely in a vase. *(he thrusts the flowers head downwards into the vase and stuffs them in wildly; he even bangs them with a mallet in an attempt to get them all in)* Get in! Get in! Get in!

Cut to a café. All the customers are Vikings. Mr and Mrs Bun enter-downwards (on wires).

Mr Bun (ERIC) Morning.

Waitress (TERRY J) Morning.

Mr Bun What have you got, then?

Waitress Well there's egg and bacon; egg, sausage and bacon; egg and spam; egg, bacon and spam; egg, bacon, sausage and spam; spam, bacon, sausage and spam; spam, egg, spam, spam, bacon and spam; spam, spam, spam, egg and spam; spam, spam, spam, spam, spam, spam, baked beans, spam, spam, spam, and spam; or lobster thermidor aux crevettes with a mornay sauce garnished with truffle pâté, brandy and a fried egg on top and spam.

Mrs Bun (GRAHAM) Have you got anything without spam in it?

Waitress Well, there's spam, egg, sausage and spam. That's not got *much* spam in it.

Mrs Bun I don't want *any* spam.

Mr Bun Why can't she have egg, bacon, spam and sausage?

Mrs Bun That's got spam in it!

Mr Bun Not as much as spam, egg, sausage and spam.

Mrs Bun Look, could I have egg, bacon, spam and sausage without the spam.

Waitress Uuuuuuggggh!

Mrs Bun What d'you mean uuugggh! I don't like spam.

Vikings *(singing)* Spam, spam, spam, spam, spam . . . spam, spam, spam, spam . . . lovely spam, wonderful spam . . .

Brief stock shot of a Viking ship.

Waitress Shut up. Shut up! Shut up! You can't have egg, bacon, spam and sausage without the spam.

Mrs Bun Why not!

Waitress No, it wouldn't be egg, bacon, spam and sausage, would it.

Mrs Bun I don't like spam!

Mr Bun Don't make a fuss, dear. I'll have your spam. I love it. I'm having spam, spam, spam, spam, spam . . .

Vikings *(singing)* Spam, spam, spam, spam . . .

Mr Bun . . . baked beans, spam, spam and spam.

Waitress Baked beans are off.

Mr Bun Well can I have spam instead?

Waitress You mean spam, spam, spam, spam, spam, spam, spam spam, spam?

Vikings *(still singing)* Spam, spam, spam, spam . . . *(etc.)*

Mr Bun Yes.

Waitress Arrggh!

Vikings . . . lovely spam, wonderful, spam.

Waitress Shut up! Shut up!

The Vikings shut up momentarily. Enter the Hungarian.

Hungarian Great boobies honeybun, my lower intestine is full of spam, egg, spam, bacon, spam, tomato, spam . . .

Vikings *(starting up again)* Spam, spam, spam, spam . . .

Waitress Shut up.

A policeman rushes in and bundles the Hungarian out.

Hungarian My nipples explode...

Cut to a historian.

SUPERIMPOSED CAPTION: 'A HISTORIAN'

Historian (MICHAEL) Another great Viking victory was at the Green Midget café at Bromley. Once again the Viking strategy was the same. They sailed from these fiords here, *(indicating a map with arrows on it)* assembled at Trondheim and waited for the strong north-easterly winds to blow their oaken galleys to England whence they sailed on May 23rd. Once in Bromley they assembled in the Green Midget café and spam selecting a spam particular spam item from the spam menu would spam, spam, spam, spam, spam...

The backdrop behind him rises to reveal the café again. The Vikings Start singing again and the historian conducts them.

Vikings *(singing)* Spam, spam, spam, spam, spam, lovely spam, wonderful spam. Lovely spam wonderful spam...

Mr and Mrs Bun rise slowly in the air.

SUPERIMPOSED CAPTION: 'IN 1970 MONTY PYTHON'S FLYING CIRCUS LAY IN RUINS, AND THEN THE WORDS ON THE SCREEN SAID:'

Fade out and roll credits, which read:

MONTY PYTHON'S FLYING CIRCUS
WAS CONCEIVED, WRITTEN AND SPAM PERFORMED BY
SPAM TERRY JONES
MICHAEL SPAM PALIN
JOHN SPAM JOHN SPAM
JOHN SPAM CLEESE
GRAHAM SPAM SPAM
SPAM CHAPMAN
ERIC SPAM EGG AND
CHIPS IDLE
TERRY SPAM SAUSAGE SPAM
EGG SPAM GILLIAM
ALSO APPEARING ON TOAST
THE FRED TOMLINSON SPAM EGG
CHIPS AND SINGERS
RESEARCH PATRICIA HOULIHAN AND SAUSAGE
MAKE-UP PENNY PENNY PENNY AND SPAM NORTON
COSTUMES EGG BAKED BEANS SAUSAGE AND TOMATO, OH, AND
HAZEL PETHIG TOO
ANIMATIONS BY TERRY (EGG ON FACE) GILLIAM
FILM CAMERAMAN JAMES (SPAM SAUSAGE EGG AND TOMATO)
BALFOUR (NOT SUNDAYS)
FILM EDITOR RAY (FRIED SLICE AND GOLDEN THREE DELICIOUS)
MILLICHOPE (SPAM EXTRA)

SOUND CHIPS SAUSAGE LIVERWURST, PHEASANT, SPAM,
NEWSAGENTS, CHIPS, AND PETER ROSE
LIGHTING OTIS (SPAM'S OFF DEAR) EDDY
DESIGNER ROBERT ROBERT ROBERT ROBERT BERK AND TOMATO
PRODUCED BY IAN (MIXED GRILL) MACNAUGHTON 7/6d
BBC SPAM TV
SERVICE NOT INCLUDED

Voice Over (MICHAEL) Haagbard Etheldronga and his Viking hordes are currently appearing in 'Grin and Pillage it' at the Jodrell Theatre, Colwyn Bay. 'The Dirty Hungarian Phrase Book' is available from Her Majesty's Stationery Office, price – a kiss on the bum.

Fade out. Fade in Karl Marx and Che Guevara lying post-coitally in bed. Karl switches off the light.

Twenty-six

Announcer standing in front of his desk.

Announcer (JOHN) *(reverently)* Ladies and gentlemen, I am not simply going to say 'and now for something completely different' this week, as I do not think it fit. This is a particularly auspicious occasion for us this evening, as we have been told that Her Majesty the Queen will be watching part of this show tonight. We don't know exactly when Her Majesty will be tuning in. We understand that at the moment she is watching 'The Virginian', but we have been promised that we will be informed the moment that she changes channel. Her Majesty would like everyone to behave quite normally but her equerry has asked me to request all of you at home to stand when the great moment arrives, although we here in the studio will be carrying on with our humorous vignettes and spoofs in the ordinary way. Thank you. And now without any more ado and completely as normal, here are the opening titles. *(bows)*

Very regal animated opening titles.

CAPTION: 'ROYAL EPISODE THIRTEEN'

CAPTION: 'FIRST SPOOF'

CAPTION: 'A COAL MINE IN LLANDDAROG CARMARTHEN'

A nice photograph of a typical pit head. Music over this: 'All Through the Night' being sung in Welsh.

Voice Over (JOHN) The coal miners of Wales have long been famed for their tough rugged life hewing the black gold from the uncompromising hell of one mile under. This is *(at this moment across the bottom of the screen comes the following message in urgent teleprinter style, moving right to left, superimposed 'HM THE QUEEN STILL WATCHING 'THE VIRGINIAN')* the story of such men, battling gallantly against floods, roof falls, the English criminal law, the hidden killer carbon monoxide and the ever-present threat of pneumoconiosis which is... a disease miners get.

Cut to coal face below ground where some miners are engaged at their work. They hew away for a bit, grunting and talking amongst themselves. Suddenly two of them square up to one another.

First Miner (GRAHAM) Don't you talk to me like that, you lying bastard. *He hits the second miner and a fight starts.*

Second Miner (TERRY J) You bleeding pig. You're not fit to be down a mine.

First Miner Typical bleeding Rhondda, isn't it. You think you're so bloody clever.

They writhe around on the floor pummelling each other. The foreman comes in.

Foreman (ERIC) You bloody fighting again. Break it up or I'll put this pick through your head. Now what's it all about?

First Miner He started it.
Second Miner Oh, you bleeding pig, you started it.
Foreman I don't care who bloody started it. What's it about?
Second Miner Well . . . he said the bloody Treaty of Utrecht was 1713.
First Miner So it bloody is.
Second Miner No it bloody isn't. It wasn't ratified 'til February 1714.
First Miner He's bluffing. You're mind's gone, Jenkins. You're rubbish.
Foreman He's right, Jenkins. It was ratified September 1713. The whole bloody pit knows that. Look in Trevelyan, page 468.
Third Miner (MICHAEL) He's thinking of the Treaty of bloody Westphalia.
Second Miner Are you saying I don't know the difference between the War of the bloody Spanish Succession and the Thirty bloody Years War?
Third Miner You don't know the difference between the Battle of Borodino and a tiger's bum.
They start to fight.
Foreman Break it up, break it up. *(he hits them with his pickaxe)* I'm sick of all this bloody fighting. If it's not the bloody Treaty of Utrecht it's the bloody binomial theorem. This isn't the senior common room at All Souls, it's the bloody coal face.
A fourth miner runs up.
Fourth Miner (IAN DAVIDSON) Hey, gaffer, can you settle something? Morgan here says you find the abacus between the triglyphs in the frieze section of the entablature of classical Greek Doric temples.
Foreman You bloody fool, Morgan, that's the metope. The abacus is between the architrave and the aechinus in the capital.
Morgan (TERRY G) You stinking liar.
Another fight breaks out. A management man arrives carried in sedan chair by two black flunkies. He wears a colonial governor's helmet and a large sign reading 'frightfully important'. All the miners prostrate themselves on the floor.
Foreman Oh, most magnificent and merciful majesty, master of the universe, protector of the meek, whose nose we are not worthy to pick and whose very faeces are an untrammelled delight, and whose peacocks keep us awake all hours of the night with their noisy lovemaking, we beseech thee, tell thy humble servants the name of the section between the triglyphs in the frieze section of a classical Doric entablature.
Management Man (JOHN) No idea. Sorry.
Foreman Right. Everybody out.
They all walk off throwing down tools. Cut to a newsreader's desk.
Newsreader (MICHAEL) Still no settlement in the coal mine dispute at Llanddarog. Miners refused to return to work until the management

define a metope. Meanwhile, at Dagenham the unofficial strike committee at Fords have increased their demands to thirteen reasons why Henry III was a bad king. And finally, in the disgusting objects international at Wembley tonight, England beat Spain by a plate of braised pus to a putrid heron. And now, the Toad Elevating Moment.

CAPTION: 'THE TOAD ELEVATING MOMENT'

Pompous music. Mix to spinning globe and then to two men in a studio.

Interviewer (TERRY J) Good evening. Well, we have in the studio tonight a man who says things in a very roundabout way. Isn't that so, Mr Pudifoot.

Mr Pudifoot (GRAHAM) Yes.

Interviewer Have you always said things in a very roundabout way?

Mr Pudifoot Yes.

Interviewer Well, I can't help noticing that, for someone who claims to say things in a very roundabout way, your last two answers have very little of the discursive quality about them.

Mr Pudifoot Oh, well, I'm not very talkative today. It's a form of defensive response to intensive interrogative stimuli. I used to get it badly when I was a boy ... well, I say very badly, in fact, do you remember when there was that fashion for, you know, little poodles with small coats ...

Interviewer Ah, now you're beginning to talk in a roundabout way.

Mr Pudifoot Oh, I'm sorry.

Interviewer No, no, no, no. Please do carry on ... because that is in fact why we wanted you on the show.

Mr Pudifoot I thought it was because you were interested in me as a human being. *(gets up and leaves)*

Interviewer Well ... let's move on to our guest who not only lives in Essex but also speaks only the ends of words. Mr Ohn Ith. Mr Ith, good evening.

Enter from back of set (as per Eamonn Andrews) show Mr Ohn Ith. He sits at the desk.

Mr Ith (ERIC) ... ood ... ing.

Interviewer Nice to have you on the show.

Mr Ith ... ice ... o ... e ... ere.

Interviewer Mr Ith, don't you find it very difficult to make yourself understood?

Mr Ith Yes, it is extremely difficult.

Interviewer Just a minute, you're a fraud!

Mr Ith Oh no. I can speak the third and fourth sentences perfectly normally.

Interviewer Oh I see. So your next sentence will be only the ends of words again?

Mr Ith T's ... ight.

Interviewer Well, let's move on to our next guest who speaks only the beginnings of words, Mr J . . . Sm . . . Mr Sm . . . good evening.

Enter Mr Sm.

Mr Sm (JOHN) G . . . e . . .

Interviewer Well, have you two met before?

Mr Sm N . . .

Mr Ith . . . o

Mr Sm N . . .

Mr Ith . . . o

Interviewer Well, this is really a fascinating occasion because we have in the studio Mr . . . oh . . . I . . . who speaks only the middles of words. Good evening.

Enter Scot.

Scot (MICHAEL) . . . oo . . . . . . ni . . .

Interviewer Um, where do you come from?

Scot . . . u . . . i . . . a . . .

Interviewer Dunfermline in Scotland. Well let me introduce you, Mr Ohn Ith . . .

Mr Ith . . . ood . . . ing.

Scot . . . oo . . . . . . ni . . .

Interviewer J . . . Sm . . .

Scot . . . oo . . . . . . ni . . .

Mr Sm G . . . Eve . . .

Interviewer Yes, well, ha, ha, just a moment. Perhaps you would all like to say good evening together.

Mr Sm G . . .

Scot . . . oo . . .

Mr Ith . . . d

Mr Sm Eve . . .

Scot . . . ni . . .

Mr Ith . . . ing.

ANIMATION: *a sketch advertising Crelm toothpaste.*

Cut to a soap powder commercial. Slick adman against neutral background. On his left is an ordinary kitchen table. On his right is a pile of sheets on a stand.

Adman (ERIC) This table has been treated with ordinary soap powder, but these have been treated with new Fibro-Val. *(cut to top shot of interior of washing machine with water spinning round as per ads)* We put both of them through our washing machine, and just look at the difference. *(cut back to the original set-up; the sheets are obviously painted white; the table is smashed up)* The table is broken and smashed, but the sheets, with Fibro-Val, are sparkling clean and white.

Traditional expanding square links to next commercial. Animated countryside with flowers, butterflies and a Babycham animal. A boy and a girl (real, superimposed) wander through hand in hand.

Man's Voice (MICHAEL) I love the surgical garment. Enjoy the delights of the Victor Mature abdominal corset. Sail down the Nile on the Bleed-it Kosher Truss. *(the adman comes into view over the background; he holds a tailor's dummy – pelvis only – with a truss)* And don't forget the Hercules Hold-'em-in, the all-purpose concrete truss for the man with the family hernia.

He throws away the truss. The background changes to blow-up of a fish tank. The adman is sitting at a desk. He pulls a goldfish bowl over.

Adman Well last week on Fish Club we learnt how to sex a pike . . . and this week we're going to learn how to feed a goldfish. Now contrary to what most people think the goldfish has a ravenous appetite. If it doesn't get enough protein it gets very thin and its bones begin to stick out and its fins start to fall off. So once a week give your goldfish a really good meal. Here's one specially recommended by the Board of Irresponsible People. First, some cold consommé or a gazpacho *(pours it in)*, then some sausages with spring greens, sautée potatoes and bread and gravy.

He tips all this into the bowl. An RSPCA man rushes in, grabs the man and hauls him off.

RSPCA Man (IAN DAVIDSON) All right, come on, that's enough, that's enough.

Adman . . . treacle tart . . . chocolate cake and . . .

Voice Over (JOHN) and CAPTION: 'THE RSPCA WISH IT TO BE KNOWN THAT THAT MAN WAS NOT A BONA FIDE ANIMAL LOVER, AND ALSO THAT GOLDFISH DO NOT EAT SAUSAGES. *(the man is still shouting)* SHUT UP! . . . THEY ARE QUITE HAPPY WITH BREADCRUMBS, ANTS' EGGS AND THE OCCASIONAL PHEASANT . . .'

The last four words are crossed out on the caption.

Voice Over Who wrote that?

Mix to a lyrical shot of wild flowers in beautiful English countryside. Gentle pastoral music. The camera begins to pan away from the flowers, moving slowly across this idyllic scene. Mix in the sound of lovers – the indistinct deep voice, followed by a playful giggle from the girl. At first very distant, but as we continue to pan it increases in volume, until we come to rest on the source of the noise – a tape recorder in front of a bush. After a short pause, the camera tracks round behind this bush where are a couple sitting reading a book each. Pan away from them across a field. In the middle of the pan we come across a smooth, moustachioed little Italian head waiter, in tails etc. We do not stop on him.

Waiter (GRAHAM) *(bowing to camera)* I hope you're enjoying the show.

On pans the camera to the end of the field where we pick up a man in a long mac crawling on all fours through the undergrowth. We follow him as he occasionally dodges behind a bush or a tree. He is stealthily tracking something. After a few moments he comes up behind a birdwatcher (in deerstalker and tweeds) who lies at the top of a small rise, with his binoculars trained. With infinite caution the man in the long mac slides up behind the birdwatcher, then he stretches out a hand and opens the flap of the birdwatcher's knapsack. He pulls out a small white paper bag. Holding his breath, he feels inside the bag and produces a small pie, then a tomato and finally two hard-boiled eggs. He pockets the hard-boiled eggs, puts the rest back and creeps away.

Voice Over (ERIC) Herbert Mental collects birdwatchers' eggs. At his home in Surrey he has a collection of over four hundred of them.

Cut to Mental in a study lined with shelves full of hard-boiled eggs.

They all have little labels on the front of them. He goes up and selects one from a long line of identical hard-boiled eggs.

Herbert (TERRY J) 'ere now. This is a very interesting one. This is from a Mr P. F. Bradshaw. He is usually found in Surrey hedgerows, but I found this one in the gents at St Pancras, uneaten. *(he provides the next question himself in bad ventriloquist style)* Mr Mental, why did you start collecting birdwatchers' eggs? *(normal voice)* Oh, well, I did it to get on 'Man Alive'. *(ventriloquially)* 'Man Alive'? *(normal voice)* That's right, yes. But then that got all serious, so I carried on in the hope of a quick appearance as an eccentric on the regional section of 'Nationwide'. *(ventriloquially)* Mr Mental, I believe a couple of years ago you started to collect butterfly hunters. *(normal voice)* Butterfly hunters? *(ventriloquially)* Yes. *(normal voice)* Oh, that's right. Here's a couple of them over here. *(he moves to his left; on the wall behind him are the splayed-out figures of two buttetfly hunters, with pins through their backs and their names on cards underneath)* Nice little chaps. But the hobby I enjoyed most was racing pigeon fanciers.

An open field. A large hamper, with an attendant in a brown coat standing behind it. The attendant opens the hamper and three pigeon fanciers, (in very fast motion) leap out and run off across the field, wheeling in a curve as birds do. Cut to a series of speeded-up close-ups of baskets being opened and pigeon fanciers leaping out. After four or five of these fast close-ups cut to long shot of the mass of pigeon fanciers wheeling across the field like a flock of pigeons. Cut to film of Trafalgar Square. The pigeon fanciers are now running around in the square, wheeling in groups. Cut to Gilliam picture of Trafalgar Square. The chicken man from the opening credits flies past towing a banner which says 'This Space Available, tel. 498 5116'. The head of a huge hedgehog – Spiny Norman – appears above St Martin's-in-the-Fields.

Spiny Norman Dinsdale! Dinsdale!

Animated sequence then leads to:

EXTREMELY ANIMATED CAPTION: 'MONTY PYTHON PROUDLY PRESENTS THE INSURANCE SKETCH'

Interior smooth-looking office. Mr Feldman behind a desk, Mr Martin in front of it. Both point briefly to a sign on the desk: 'Life Insurance Ltd'.

Martin (ERIC) Good morning. I've been in touch with you about the, er, life insurance...

Feldman (JOHN) Ah yes, did you bring the um... the specimen of your um... and so on, and so on?

Martin Yes I did. It's in the car. There's rather a lot.

Feldman Good, good.

Martin Do you really *need* twelve gallons?

Feldman No, no, not really.

Martin Do you test it?

Feldman No.

Martin Well, why do you want it?

Feldman Well, we do it to make sure that you're serious about wanting insurance. I mean, if you're not, you won't spend a couple of months filling up that enormous churn with mmm, so on and so on...

Martin Shall I bring it in?

Feldman Good Lord no. Throw it away.

Martin Throw it away? I was months filling that thing up.

The sound of the National Anthem starts. They stand to attention. Martin and Feldman mutter to each other, and we hear a reverential voice over.

Voice Over (MICHAEL) And we've just heard that Her Majesty the Queen has just tuned into this programme and so she is now watching this royal sketch here in this royal set. The actor on the left is wearing the great grey suit of the BBC wardrobe department and the other actor is... about to deliver the first great royal joke here this royal evening. *(the camera pans, Martin following it part way, to show the camera crew and the audience, all standing to attention)* Over to the right you can see the royal cameraman, and behind... Oh, we've just heard she's switched over. She's watching the 'News at Ten'.

Cries of disappointment. Cut to Reggie Bosanquet (the real one) at the 'News at Ten' set. He is reading.

Reggie ... despite the union's recommendation that the strikers should accept the second and third clauses of the agreement arrived at last Thursday. *(the National Anthem starts to play in the background and Reggie stands, continuing to read)* Today saw the publication of the McGuffie Commission's controversial report on treatment of in-patients in north London hospitals.

A hospital: a sign above door says 'Intensive Care Unit'. A group of heavily bandaged patients with crutches, legs and arms in plaster, etc., struggle out and onto a courtyard.

First Doctor (JOHN) Get on parade! Come on! We haven't got all day, have we? Come on, come on, come on. *(the patients painfully get themselves* *into line)* Hurry up . . . right! Now, I know some hospitals where you get the patients lying around in bed. Sleeping, resting, recuperating, convalescing. Well, that's not the way we do things here, right! No, you won't be loafing about in bed wasting the doctors' time. You – you horrible little cripple. What's the matter with you?

Patient (MICHAEL) Fractured tibia, sergeant.

First Doctor 'Fractured tibia, sergeant'? 'Fractured tibia, sergeant'? Ooh. Proper little mummy's boy, aren't we? Well, I'll tell you something, my fine friend, if you fracture a tibia here you keep quiet about it! Look at him! *(looks more closely)* He's broken both his arms and he don't go shouting about it, do he? No! 'cos he's a man – he's a woman, you see, so don't come that broken tibia talk with me. Get on at the double. One, two, three, pick that crutch up, pick that crutch right up.

The patient hobbles off at the double and falls over.

Patient Aaargh!

First Doctor Right, squad, 'shun! Squad, right turn. Squad, by the left, quick limp! Come on, pick 'em up. Get some air in those wounds.

Cut to second doctor. He is smoking a cigar.

Second Doctor (ERIC) *(to camera)* Here at St Pooves, we believe in ART – Active Recuperation Techniques. We try to help the patient understand that however ill he may be, he can still fulfil a useful role in society. Sun lounge please, Mr Griffiths.

Pull back to show doctor sitting in a wheelchair. A bandaged patient wheels him off

Patient (MICHAEL) I've got a triple fracture of the right leg, dislocated collar bone and multiple head injuries, so I do most of the heavy work, like helping the surgeon.

Interviewer's Voice (ERIC) What does that involve?

Patient Well, at the moment we're building him a holiday home.

Interviewer's Voice What about the nurses?

Patient Well, I don't know about them. They're not allowed to mix with the patients.

Interviewer's Voice Do all the patients work?

Patient No, no, the ones that are really ill do sport.

Cut to bandaged patients on a cross-country run.

Voice Over (MICHAEL) Yes, one thing patients here dread are the runs.

The patients climb over a fence with much difficulty. One falls.

Interviewer's Voice How are you feeling?

Patient (GRAHAM) Much better.

Shots of patients doing sporting activities.

Voice Over But patients are allowed visiting. And this week they're visiting an iron foundry at Swindon, which is crying out for unskilled labour.

('Dr Kildare' theme music; shot of doctors being manicured, having shoes cleaned etc. by patients) But this isn't the only hospital where doctors' conditions are improving.

Sign on wall: 'St Nathan's Hospital For Young, Attractive Girls Who Aren't Particularly Ill'. Pan down to a doctor.

Third Doctor (TERRY J) Er, very little shortage of doctors here. We have over forty doctors per bed – er, patient. Oh, be honest. Bed.

Sign: 'St Gandalf's Hospital For Very Rich People Who Like Giving Doctors Lots Of Money'. Pull back to show another doctor.

Fourth Doctor (GRAHAM) We've every facility here for dealing with people who are rich. We can deal with a blocked purse, we can drain private accounts and in the worst cases we can perform a total cashectomy, which is total removal of all moneys from the patient.

Sign: 'St Michael's Hospital For Linkmen'. Pan down to doctor.

Fifth Doctor (JOHN) Well, here we try to help people who have to link sketches together. We try to stop them saying 'Have you ever wondered what it would be like if' and instead say something like um ... er ... 'And now the mountaineering sketch'.

Cut to a mountaineer hanging on ropes on steep mountain face.

Mountaineer (GRAHAM) I haven't written a mountaineering sketch.

SUPERIMPOSED CAPTION: 'LINK'

Mountaineer But now over to the exploding version of the 'Blue Danube'.

Cut to an orchestra in a field playing the 'Blue Danube'. On each musical phrase, a member of the orchestra explodes. Fade to pitch darkness.

Voice Over (ERIC) And now a dormitory in a girls' public school.

Noise of female snores. Sound of a window sash being lifted and scrabbling sounds. Padding feet across the dorm.

Butch Voice (MICHAEL) Hello, Agnes ... Agnes are you awake? Agnes ...

Sound of waking up. More padding feet.

Butch Voice Agnes ...

Second Butch Voice (ERIC) Who is it ... is that you, Charlie?

First Butch Voice Yeah ... Agnes, where's Jane?

Third Butch Voice (TERRY J) I'm over here, Charlie.

First Butch Voice Jane, we're going down to raid the tuck shop.

Second Butch Voice Oh good oh ... count me in, girls.

Fourth Butch Voice (GRAHAM) Can I come, too, Agnes?

First Butch Voice Yeah, Joyce.

Fifth Butch Voice And me and Avril ...

Third Butch Voice Yeah, rather ... and Suki.

Fourth Butch Voice Oh, whacko the diddle-oh.

First Butch Voice Cave girls... Here comes Miss Rodgers...

Light goes on to reveal a girls' dorm. In the middle of the floor between the beds are two panto geese which run off immediately the light goes on. There is one man in a string vest and short dibley haircut, chest wig, schoolgirl's skirt, white socks and schoolgirl's shoes. Hanging from the middle of the ceiling is a goat with light bulbs hanging from each foot. In the beds are other butch blokes in string vests... and short hair. At the door stands a commando-type Miss Rodgers.

Miss Rodgers (CAROL) All right girls, now stop this tomfoolery and get back to bed, remember it's the big match at St Bridget's tomorrow.

Cut to still of one of them in the uniform as described above.

SUPERIMPOSED CAPTION: 'THE NAUGHTIEST GIRL IN THE SCHOOL'

Voice Over (JOHN) Yes, on your screen tomorrow: 'The Naughtiest Girl in the School' starring the men of the 14th Marine Commandos. *(cut to a picture made up of inch-square photos of various topical subjects e.g. Stalin, Churchill, Eden, White House, atom bomb, map of Western Europe, Gandhi)* And now it's documentary time, when we look at the momentous last years of the Second World War, and tonight the invasion of Normandy performed by the girls of Oakdene High School, Upper Fifth Science.

Stock film of amphibious craft brought up on a beach. The front of the craft crashes down and fifty soldiers rush out. We hear schoolgirl voices. Cut to traditional shot through periscope of ocean, cross-sights scanning the horizon. Submarine-type dramatic noise – motors and asdic.

Cut to interior of submarine. A Pepperpot looks through the periscope, then looks round at her colleagues.

First Pepperpot (GRAHAM) Oh, it's still raining.

Her four companions continue to knit.

Second Pepperpot (ERIC) I'm going down the shops.

First Pepperpot Oh, be a dear and get me some rats' bane for the budgie's boil. Otherwise I'll put your eyes out.

Second Pepperpot Aye, aye, captain. *(goes out)*

Attention noise from the communication tube. A red light flashes by it.

Voice (JOHN) Coo-ee. Torpedo bay.

First Pepperpot Yoo-hoo. Torpedo bay.

Third Pepperpot (TERRY J) She said torpedo bay.

First Pepperpot Yes, she did, she did.

Fourth Pepperpot (MICHAEL) Yes, she said torpedo bay. She did, she did.

Voice Mrs Lieutenant Edale here. Mrs Midshipman Nesbitt's got one of her headaches again, so I put her in the torpedo tube.

First Pepperpot Roger, Mrs Edale. Stand by to fire Mrs Nesbitt.

All Stand by to fire Mrs Nesbitt.

First Pepperpot Red alert, put the kettle on.

Voice Kettle on.

First Pepperpot Engine room, stand by to feed the cat.

Voice Standing by to feed the cat.

First Pepperpot Fire Mrs Nesbitt.

> ANIMATION: *a Pepperpot is fired from a torpedo tube through the water, until she travels head first into a battleship with a loud clang.*

Mrs Nesbitt Oh, that's much better.

Cut to a letter as in the last series, plus voice reading it.

Voice Over (ERIC) As an admiral who came up through the ranks more times than you've had hot dinners, I wish to join my husband O.W.A Giveaway in condemning this shoddy misrepresentation of our modern navy. The British Navy is one of the finest and most attractive and butchest fighting forces in the world. I love those white flared trousers and the feel of rough blue serge on those pert little buttocks...

Cut to a man at a desk.

Presenter (MICHAEL) I'm afraid we are unable to show you any more of that letter. We continue with a man with a stoat through his head.

Cut to man with a stoat through his head. He bows. Cut to film of Women's Institute applauding. Then cut back to man at desk.

Presenter And now...

Cut to a lifeboat somewhere at sea miles from any land. In the lifeboat are five bedraggled sailors, at the end of their tether.

First Sailor (MICHAEL) Still no sign of land... How long is it?

Second Sailor (GRAHAM) That's rather a personal question, sir.

First Sailor You stupid git, I meant how long we've been in the lifeboat. You've spoilt the atmosphere now.

Second Sailor I'm sorry.

First Sailor Shut up! We'll have to start again... Still no sign of land... how long is it?

Second Sailor Thirty-three days, sir.

First Sailor Thirty-three days?

Second Sailor I don't think we can hold out much longer. I don't think I did spoil the atmosphere.

First Sailor Shut up!

Second Sailor I'm sorry, I don't think I did.

First Sailor Of course you did.

Second Sailor *(to third sailor)* Do you think I spoilt the atmosphere?

Third Sailor (ERIC) Well, I think you...

First Sailor Look, shut up! SHUT UP! . . . Still no sign of land . . . how long is it?

Second Sailor Thirty-three days.

Fourth Sailor (TERRY J) Have we started again? *(he is kicked on the leg by the first sailor)* Wagh!

First Sailor Still no sign of land . . . how long is it?

Second Sailor Thirty-three days, sir.

First Sailor Thirty-three days?

Second Sailor Yes. We can't hold out much longer. We haven't had any food since the fifth day.

Third Sailor We're done for. We're done for!

First Sailor Shut up, Maudling. We've just got to keep hoping someone will find us.

Fourth Sailor How are you feeling, captain?

Fifth Sailor (JOHN) Not too good . . . I . . . feel . . . so weak.

Second Sailor We can't hold out much longer.

Fifth Sailor Listen . . . chaps . . . there's one last chance. I'm done for, I've got a gammy leg, I'm going fast, I'll never get through . . . but . . . some of you might . . . so you'd better eat me.

First Sailor Eat you, sir?

Fifth Sailor Yes, eat me.

Second Sailor Uuuuggghhh! With a gammy leg?

Fifth Sailor You don't have to eat the leg, Thompson, there's still plenty of good meat . . . look at that arm.

Third Sailor It's not just the leg, sir . . .

Fifth Sailor What do you mean?

Third Sailor Well sir . . . it's just that . . .

Fifth Sailor Why don't you want to eat me?

Third Sailor I'd rather eat Johnson, sir. *(points at fourth sailor)*

Second Sailor Oh, so would I, sir.

Fifth Sailor I see.

Fourth Sailor Well, that's settled then. Everyone eats me.

First Sailor Well . . . I . . . er . . .

Third Sailor What, sir . . . ?

First Sailor No, no, you go ahead. I won't . . .

Fourth Sailor Nonsense, nonsense, sir, you're starving. Tuck in!

First Sailor No, no, it's not just that . . .

Second Sailor What's the matter with Johnson, sir?

First Sailor Well, he's not kosher.

Third Sailor That depends how we kill him, sir.

First Sailor Yes, yes, I see that . . . well to be quite frank, I like my meat a little more lean. I'd rather eat Hodges.

Second Sailor *(cheerfully)* Oh well . . . all right.

Third Sailor No, I'd still prefer Johnson.

Fifth Sailor I wish you'd all stop bickering and eat me.

Second Sailor Look! I'll tell you what. Why don't those of us who want to, eat Johnson, then you, sir, can eat my leg and then we'll make a stock of the captain and then after that we can eat the rest of Johnson cold for supper.

First Sailor Good thinking, Hodges.

Fourth Sailor And we'll finish off with the peaches. *(picks up a tin of peaches)*

Third Sailor And we can start off with the avocados. *(picks up two avocados)*

First Sailor Waitress! *(a waitress walks in)* We've decided now, we're going to have leg of Hodges . . .

Boos off-screen. Cut to a letter.

Voice Over (JOHN) Dear Sir, I am glad to hear that your studio audience disapproves of the last skit as strongly as I. As a naval officer I abhor the implication that the Royal Navy is a haven for cannibalism. It is well known that we now have the problem relatively under control, and that it is the RAF who now suffer the largest casualties in this area. And what do you think the Argylls ate in Aden. Arabs? Yours etc. Captain B. J. Smethwick in a white wine sauce with shallots, mushrooms and garlic.

ANIMATION: *various really nasty cannibalistic scenes from Terry Gilliam.*

Cut to man.

Man (TERRY J) Stop it, stop it. Stop this cannibalism. Let's have a sketch about clean, decent human beings.

Cut to an undertaker's shop.

Undertaker (GRAHAM) Morning.

Man (JOHN) Good morning.

Undertaker What can I do for you, squire?

Man Well, I wonder if you can help me. You see, my mother has just died.

Undertaker Ah well, we can help you. We deal with stiffs.

Man What?

Undertaker Well, there's three things we can do with your mum. We can bury her, burn her or dump her.

Man *(shocked)* Dump her?

Undertaker Dump her in the Thames.

Man What?

Undertaker Oh, did you like her?

Man Yes!

Undertaker Oh well, we won't dump her, then. Well, what do you think? We can bury her or burn her.

Man Well, which do you recommend?

Undertaker Well, they're both nasty. If we burn her she gets stuffed in the flames, crackle, crackle, crackle, which is a bit of a shock if she's not quite dead, but quick, *(the audience starts booing)* and then we give you a handful of ashes, which you can pretend were hers.

Man Oh.

Undertaker Or if we bury her she gets eaten up by lots of weevils, and nasty maggots, *(the booing increases)* which as I said before is a bit of a shock if she's not quite dead.

Man I see. Well, she's definitely dead.

Voices In Audience Let's have something decent . . . it's disgusting . . .

Undertaker Where is she?

Man She's in this sack.

Undertaker Can I have a look? She looks quite young.

Man Yes, yes, she was.

Increasing protests from audience.

Undertaker *(calling)* Fred!

Fred's Voice (ERIC) Yeah?

Undertaker I think we've got an eater.

Man What?

Another undertaker pokes his head round the door.

Fred Right, I'll get the oven on. *(goes off)*

Man Er, excuse me, um, are you suggesting eating my mother?

Undertaker Er . . . yeah, not raw. Cooked.

Man What?

Undertaker Yes, roasted with a few French fries, broccoli, horseradish sauce . . .

Man Well, I do feel a bit peckish.

Voice From Audience Disgraceful! Boo! *(etc.)*

Undertaker Great!

Man Can we have some parsnips?

Undertaker *(calling)* Fred – get some parsnips.

Man I really don't think I should.

Undertaker Look, tell you what, we'll eat her, if you feel a bit guilty about it after, we can dig a grave and you can throw up in it.

A section of the audience rises up in revolt and invades the set, remonstrating with the performers and banging the counter, etc., breaking up the sketch. Zoom away from them and into caption machine; roll credits. The National Anthem starts. The shouting stops. Mix through credits to show audience and everyone on set standing to attention. As the credits end, fade out.

Twenty-seven Whicker's World

The camera pans across Glencoe. The wind is whistling and climaxes with a great crashing chord, which introduces...
CAPTION: 'NJORL'S SAGA'
        'ICELAND 1126'
The caption fades. Continue the pan until we pick up Icelandic gentleman. He unravels a scroll and starts to read.

Icelandic Gent (MICHAEL) I Eric... um

The camera pans away from him and picks up a man (Terry J) seated at the organ, his back to the camera. He is naked, and he looks identical to the way he did in that deceased classic of our time 'And now for something completely trivial'. He grins at the camera and plays a few chords. Quick cut to the announcer at his desk.

Announcer (JOHN) And now...

Quick cut to close up of 'It's' man.

It's Man (MICHAEL) It's...

Animated titles.

Voice (JOHN) Monty Python's Flying Circus!

Cut to a courtroom. Severe atmosphere.

Judge (TERRY J) Michael Norman Randall, you have been found guilty of the murder of Arthur Reginald Webster, Charles Patrick Trumpington, Marcel Agnes Bernstein, Lewis Anona Rudd, John Malcolm Kerr, Nigel Sinclair Robinson, Norman Arthur Potter, Felicity Jayne Stone, Jean-Paul Reynard, Rachel Shirley Donaldson, Stephen Jay Greenblatt, Karl-Heinz Muller, Belinda Anne Ventham, Juan-Carlos Fernandez, Thor Olaf Stensgaard, Lord Kimberrley of Pretoria, Lady Kimberley of Pretoria, The Right Honourable Nigel Warmsley Kimberley, Robert Henry Noonan and Felix James Bennett, on or about the morning of the 19th December 1972. Have you anything to say before I pass sentence?

Randall (ERIC) Yes, sir. I'm very sorry.

Judge Very sorry!

Randall Yes, sir. It was a very very bad thing to have done and I'm really very ashamed of myself. I can only say it won't happen again. To have murdered so many people in such a short space of time is really awful, and I really am very, very, *very* sorry that I did it, and also that I've taken up so much of the court's valuable time listening to the sordid details of these senseless killings of mine. I would particularly like to say, a very personal and sincere 'sorry' to you, m'lud, my lud for my *appalling* behaviour throughout this trial. I'd also like to say sorry to the police, for putting them to so much trouble *(shot of three heavily bandaged exhausted-looking policemen behind him)* for the literally hours of work they've had to put in, collecting evidence and identifying corpses and so forth. You know I think sometimes we ought to realize the difficult and often dangerous work involved in tracking down violent criminals like myself and I'd just like them to know that their fine work is at least appreciated by me.

The policemen look embarrassed.

First Policeman (GRAHAM) No, no, we were only doing our job.

Second Policeman No, no, no, no.

Randall It's very good of you to say that, but I know what you've been through.

First Policeman No, no, we've had worse.

Third Policeman It was plain sailing apart from the arrest.

Randall I know and I'm grateful. I'd like to apologize too to the prosecuting counsel for dragging him in here morning after morning in such lovely weather.

Counsel (JOHN) Well, I would have had to come in anyway.

Randall Ah good, but what a presentation of a case!

Counsel Oh thank you.

Randall No, no, it's a privilege to watch you in action. I never had a chance.

Counsel Oh yes you did.

Randall Not after that summing up. Great.

Counsel Oh thank you. *(very chuffed)*

Randall And now I must come to the jury. What can I say. I've dragged you in here, day after day, keeping you away from your homes, your jobs, your loved ones, just to hear the private details of my petty atrocities.

Foreman (MICHAEL) No, no, it was very interesting.

Randall But you could have had a much nicer case.

Foreman No, no, murder's much more fun.

First Juryman Yes and so many of them.

Second Juryman Excellent.

Third Juryman We've had a terrific time. *(the jury applauds)*

Randall *(blows his nose, does a Dickie Attenborough)* I'm sorry, I'm very moved. And so, m'lud, it only remains for you to pass the most savage sentence on me that the law can provide.

Judge Well er . . . not necessarily.

Randall No, m'lud, the full penalty of the law is hardly sufficient, I insist I must be made an example of.

Judge Well yes and no. I mean society at large . . .

Randall Oh no, m'lud. Not with mass murder.

Judge But in this case, *(to court)* don't you think?

Court Yes, yes!

Randall Oh, come on, m'lud, you've got to give me life.
Court No, no, no, no.
Randall *(to court at large)* Well, ten years at least.
Judge Ten years!
Court Shame. Shame!
Randall Well five then. Be fair.
Judge No, no. I'm giving you three months.
Randall Oh no, that's *so* embarrassing. I won't hear of it. Give me six . . . please.
Judge Well, all right. Six months.
Randall Thank you, m'lud.
Judge But suspended.
Randall Oh no.
Court Hooray. *(they applaud)*
Foreman Three cheers for the defendant. Hip. Hip.
Court Hooray.
Foreman Hip. Hip.
Court Hooray.
Foreman Hip. Hip.
Court Hooray.
All For he's a jolly good fellow
For he's a jolly good fellow
For he's a jolly good fellow
Voice *(off)* Which nobody can deny.

> ANIMATION: *manhunt inside a man.*
> CAPTION: 'NJORL'S SAGA – PART II'
> *Pan across a bleak landscape.*

Voice Over (JOHN) This little-known Icelandic saga, written by an unknown hand in the late thirteenth century, has remained undiscovered until today. Now it comes to your screens for the first time. Fresh from the leaves of Iceland's history. The terrible 'Njorl's Saga'.
Cut to Viking.
Viking (MICHAEL) It's not *that* terrible.
Cut to landscape. The announcer appears in the corner of the shot.
Announcer No, I meant terribly *violent*.
Cut to Viking.
Viking Oh yeah, yeah.
A Viking hut. A Viking comes out and has great difficulty mounting his horse.

Voice Over (ERIC) Erik Njorl, son of Frothgar, leaves his home to seek Hangar the Elder at the home of Thorvald Nlodvisson, the son of Gudleif, half brother of Thorgier, the priest of Ljosa water, who took to wife Thurunn, the mother of Thorkel Braggart, the slayer of Gudmund the powerful, who knew Howal, son of Geemon, son of Erik from Valdalesc, son of Arval Gristlebeard, son of Harken, who killed Bjortguaard in Sochnadale in Norway over Gudreed, daughter of Thorkel Long, the son of Kettle-Trout, the half son of Harviyoun Half-troll, father of Ingbare the Brave, who with Isenbert of Gottenberg the daughter of Hangbard the Fierce... *(fades and continues under:)*

Another Voice Over (TERRY J) I must apologize for an error in the saga. Evidently Thorgier, the Priest of Ljosa water who took to wife Thurunn, the mother of Thorkel Braggart, the slayer of Gudmund the powerful, who knew Howal, son of Geemon, son of Erik from Vadalesc... *(fades under next speech)*

The Viking has still failed to mount his horse. Both he and the horse look a bit exasperated.

Original Voice Over (JOHN) Well I'm afraid we're having a little trouble getting this very exciting Icelandic saga started. If any of you at home have any ideas about how to get this exciting saga started again here's the address to write to:

Third Voice Over (MICHAEL) Help the Exciting Icelandic Saga, 18b MacNorten Buildings, Oban.

    CAPTION: 'HELP THE EXCITING ICELANDIC SAGA
              C/O MATCH OF THE DAY
              BBC TV
              THE LARCHES
              26 WESTBROOK AVENUE
              FAVERSHAM
              KENT'

Cut to an office: the announcer at a desk. At another desk a secretary applies a deodorant spray to her bust.

Announcer (JOHN) *(to camera)* Hello, well I was the third voice you heard just now. I'm sorry about that terrible mess.

Cut to the Viking at wheel of car.

Viking (MICHAEL) Well it wasn't all that terrible.

Cut back to the office.

Announcer No, no, I meant terrible in the sense of unfortunate.

Cut to the Viking.

Viking Oh.

Cut back to the office.

Announcer Anyway, our plea for assistance has been answered by the North Malden Icelandic Saga Society who've given us some very useful information about the saga and so we carry on now with 'Njorl's Saga' with our thanks going, once again, to the North Malden Icelandic Saga Society.

Cut to the Viking standing by his horse. He is asleep.

Voice Over (ERIC) Erik Njorl, son of Frothgar rode off into the desolate plain. *(the Viking manages to mount the horse; he rides off)* Day and night he rode, looking neither to right nor left. Stopping neither for food nor rest. *(shots of Erik riding through a bleak landscape)* Twelve days and nights he rode. Through rain and storm. Through wind and snow beyond the enchanted waterfall, *(Erik rides past a waterfall)* through the elfin glades until he reached his goal. *(shot of a modern road sign: 'North Malden – please drive carefully')* He had found the rich and pleasant land beyond the mountains, *(shots of Erik riding gently through a modern suburban shopping street)* the land where golden streams sang their way through fresh green meadows. Where there were halls and palaces, an excellent swimming pool and one of the most attractive bonus incentive schemes for industrial development in the city. Only fifteen miles from excellent Thames-side docking facilities and within easy reach of the proposed M25. Here it was that Erik Njorl, son of Frothgar, met the mayor Mr Arthur Huddinut, a local solicitor.

Erik rides up to the town hall and is met by the mayor.

Mayor (MICHAEL) Welcome to North Malden. *(to camera)* Yes, everyone is welcome to North Malden, none more so than the businessmen and investors who shape our society of the future. Here at North Malden ...

His voice fades under the following.

Voice Over (JOHN) And we apologize to viewers of 'Njorl's Saga' who may be confused by some of the references to North Malden. After a frank exchange of views we have agreed to carry on showing this version supplied to us by the North Malden Icelandic Saga Society on the undertaking that future scenes will adhere more closely to the spirit of twelfth-century Iceland.

Film leader countdown (5, 4, 3 . . .) then shot of Erik riding away into bleak landscape.

Voice Over (ERIC) With moist eyes, Erik leaves this happy land to return to the harsh uneconomic realities of life in the land of Ljosa waters. On his way Erik rested a while in the land of Bjornsstrand – the land of dark forces, where Gildor was King. *(Erik comes to a river in a wood; he drinks)* These were the dukes of the land of Bjornsstrand. *(sudden shot of six armoured knights standing in a row)* Proud warriors who bore on their chests the letters of their dread name.

The knights move their shields to reveal on their breastplates the letters MA.L.D.E.N. Shots of Erik battling with the knights. A telephone rings and the following conversation is heard.

Announcer's Voice Hello? Is that the North Malden Icelandic Society?

Voice (MICHAEL) Yes, that's right.

Announcer About this saga.

Voice Oh yes, the Icelandic saga.

Announcer Yes.

Voice Good, isn't it.

Announcer Well er, I don't know, but you promised us that you would stick to the spirit of the original text.

Voice Yes, that's right.

Announcer Well I mean a lot of these things that are happening, well they just don't quite ring true.

One of the knights is carrying a sign: 'Malden, Gateway to Industry'.

Voice Well, it's a new interpretation really.

Another carries a sign, 'ICI thanks Malden'.

Announcer Well we don't want a new . . .

FLASH FRAME CAPTION: 'INVEST IN MALDEN'

Announcer . . . I mean we wanted the proper thing . . . I mean just look what's happening now.

More signs: 'Invest in Malden', 'Malden – 45% Interest Free Loans'.

Voice Banners were a very important part of Icelandic lore, Mr Mills.

Announcer No, no, I'm sorry I, I can't accept that, it's gone too far, I'm very sorry but we'll have to terminate the agreement. You're just trying to cash in on the BBC's exciting Icelandic saga.

The knights are carrying more and more advertising banners and signs.

Voice That's business, Mr Mills.

Announcer Well, that's as maybe but it's not the way the BBC works.

Voice Well I'm sorry you feel that way but er, you know, if you ever want to come to Malden . . .

FLASH CAPTION: 'INVEST IN MALDEN'

Film leader countdown (5, 4, 3 . . .).

CAPTION: 'NJORL'S SAGA – PART III'

Usual dramatic music. Fade music as we come up on a courtroom. A man, Mr Birchenhall, is giving evidence.

Man (GRAHAM) 8 o'clock is a peak viewing hour so naturally we tend to stick to our comedy output – unless of course there's sport – because of course we know this is popular, and popularity is what television is about. Quite frankly I'm sick and tired of people accusing us of being ratings conscious.

Judge (TERRY J) *(to the clerk of the court)* Ratings conscious?

Clerk Transmitting bland garbage, m'lud.

Judge Thank you.

Man Now I'm really cheesed off. I mean it's not your high-brow bleeding plays that pull in the viewers, you know.

Judge *(bored.)* Thank you.

Man *(getting more and more angry)* I mean Joe Public doesn't want to sit down and watch three hours of documentaries every evening.

Judge Thank you.

Man He wants to sit down and he wants to be entertained, he doesn't want a load... *(he is helped out of court by two policemen, still protesting violently)* No really – I'm absolutely fed up with this. I really am.

Judge *(banging gavel)* Case dismissed.

The prosecuting counsel rises anxiously.

Prosecuting Counsel (JOHN) Case *dismissed*, m'lud?

Judge Oh all right, five years.

Prosecuting Counsel Thank you, m'lud. *(he sits)*

Judge Call the next case please.

Prosecuting Counsel Call Erik Njorl, son of Frothgar, brother of Hangnor... (etc.).

Clerk Call Erik Njorl... *(etc.)*.

Voices *(off)* Call Erik Njorl... *(etc.). (all calling at once)*

Erik comes into the dock. He is bandaged almost totally, like a cocoon, including his head. He wears a Viking fur hat. The usher approaches him with the card and Bible.

Usher (ERIC) You are Erik Njorl, son of Frothgar...

Judge Get on with it!

Usher Will you raise your right hand.

Judge He obviously *can't* raise his right hand, you silly usher person... can you raise your right leg Mr Njorl?

Njorl shakes his head.

Usher Can you raise any part of your body, Mr Njorl?

Njorl leans over and whispers in the usher's ear.

Usher I see... well, we'll skip that... well, just take the book in your right hand Mr Njorl without raising any part of your body... Oh...

Judge What is it now, you persistently silly usher?

Usher He can't hold the Bible m'lud.

Judge Well screw the Bible! Let's get on with this bleeding trial, I've got a Gay Lib meeting at 6 o'clock. Superintendent Lufthansa will you please read the charge.

Superintendent (GRAHAM) Is a charge strictly necessary, m'lud?

Judge *(heavy aside)* The press is here.

Superintendent Oh sorry! Right, here we go. You are hereby charged: one, that you did, on or about 1126, conspire to publicize a London Borough in the course of a BBC saga; two, that you were wilfully and persistently a foreigner; three, that you conspired to do things not normally considered illegal; four, that you were caught in possession of an offensive weapon, viz. the big brown table down at the police station.

Judge The big brown table down at the police station?

Superintendent It's the best we could find, m'lud . . . and five . . . all together now . . .

The whole court shout together.

Court Assaulting a police officer!

Prosecuting Counsel Call Police Constable Pan-Am. *(Pan-Am runs into court and starts beating Njorl with a truncheon)* Into the witness box, constable . . . there'll be plenty of time for that later on. *(the policeman gets into box hitting at anyone within range; his colleagues restrain him)* Now, you are Police Constable Pan-Am?

Constable (MICHAEL) No, I shall deny that to the last breath in my body. *(superintendent nods)* Oh. Sorry, yes.

Prosecuting Counsel Police constable, do you recognize the defendant?

Constable No. Never seen him before in my life. *(superintendent nods)* Oh yes, yes he's the one. He done it. I'd recognize him anywhere, sorry, super. *(the superintendent has the grace to look embarrassed)*

Prosecuting Counsel Constable, will you please tell the court in your own words what happened?

Constable Oh yes! *(refers to his notebook)* I was proceeding in a northerly direction up Alitalia Street when I saw the deceased *(points at Njorl)* standing at an upstairs window, baring her bosom at the general public. She then took off her . . . wait a tick. Wrong story. *(refers to his notebook)* Ho yes! There were three nuns in a railway compartment and the ticket inspector says to one of them *(the superintendent shakes his head)* No, anyway I clearly saw the deceased . . .

Clerk Defendant.

Constable Defendant! Sorry. Sorry, super. I clearly saw the defendant . . . doing whatever he's accused of. Red-handed. When kicked . . . *cautioned* he said: 'It's a fair . . . cop, I done it all . . . Right . . . no doubt about . . . that'. Then, bound as he was to the chair, he assaulted myself and three other constables while bouncing around the cell. The end.

Spontaneous applause from the court. Shouts of 'more! more!'. Pan-Am raises his hands and the clapping and shouting dies down.

Constable Thank you, thank you . . . and for my next piece of evidence . . .

Superintendent I think you'd better leave it there, Constable.

Prosecuting Counsel Excellent evidence, Constable *(the constable is removed, flailing his truncheon the while)* . . . Thank you very much. Now then Mr Njorl, will you tell the court please where were you on the night of 1126? *(silence from the bandages)* Move any part of your body if you were north of a line from the Humber to the Mersey.

(silence)

Judge Is he *in* there, d'you think? . . . Hello . . . Hello! Defendant, are you there . . . coo-ee! De-*fend*-ant . . . *(to the clerk of the court)* I think you'd better go and have a look, Maurice.

Clerk Don't call me Maurice in court!

Judge I'm sorry.

The clerk and prosecuting counsel and two policemen look inside Njorl, who is now in fact a framework of bandages with no one inside. From this oh-so zany situation only Terry 'Marty Feldman's Comedy Machine' Gilliam can save us . . .

Animated sketch, leading us into a studio set; a man is sitting in front of a non-animated (but cheap) graph labelled 'Stock Market Report'.

Voice Over (JOHN) And now the Stock Market Report by Exchange Telegraph.

Man (ERIC) Trading was crisp at the start of the day with some brisk business on the floor. Rubber hardened and string remained confident. Little bits of tin consolidated although biscuits sank after an early gain and stools remained anonymous. Armpits rallied well after a poor start. Nipples rose dramatically during the morning but had declined by mid-afternoon, while teeth clenched and buttocks remained firm. Small dark furry things increased severely on the floor, whilst rude jellies wobbled up and down, and bounced against rising thighs which had spread to all parts of the country by mid-afternoon. After lunch naughty things dipped sharply forcing giblets upwards with the nicky nacky noo. Ting tang tong rankled dithely, little tipples pooped and poppy things went pong! Gibble gabble gobble went the rickety rackety roo and . . . *(a bucketful of water descends on him)*

ANIMATION: *ends with an animated woman going into a laundromat. Cut to the interior of a laundromat. Various shabby folk sitting around. Mrs Conclusion approaches Mrs Premise and sits down.*

Mrs Conclusion (GRAHAM) Hello, Mrs Premise.

Mrs Premise (JOHN) Hello, Mrs Conclusion.

Mrs Conclusion Busy day?

Mrs Premise Busy! I've just spent four hours burying the cat.

Mrs Conclusion *Four hours* to bury a cat?

Mrs Premise Yes! It wouldn't keep still, wriggling about howling its head off.

Mrs Conclusion Oh – it wasn't dead then?

Mrs Premise Well, no, no, but it's not at all a well cat so as we were going away for a fortnight's holiday, I thought I'd better bury it just to be on the safe side.

Mrs Conclusion Quite right. You don't want to come back from Sorrento to a dead cat. It'd be so anticlimactic. Yes, kill it now, that's what I say.

Mrs Premise Yes.

Mrs Conclusion We're going to have our budgie put down.

Mrs Premise Really? Is it very old?

Mrs Conclusion No. We just don't like it. We're going to take it to the vet tomorrow.

Mrs Premise Tell me, how do they put budgies down then?

Mrs Conclusion Well it's funny you should ask that, but I've just been reading a great big book about how to put your budgie down, and apparently you can either hit them with the book, or, you can shoot them just there, just above the beak.

Mrs Premise Just there!

Mrs Conclusion Yes.

Mrs Premise Well well well. 'course, Mrs Essence flushed hers down the loo.

Mrs Conclusion Ooh! No! You shouldn't do that – no that's dangerous. Yes, they *breed* in the *sewers,* and eventually you get evil-smelling flocks of huge soiled budgies flying out of people's lavatories infringing their personal freedom. *(life-size cut-out of woman at end of last animation goes by)* Good morning Mrs Cut-out.

Mrs Premise It's a funny thing freedom. I mean how can any of us be really free when we still have personal possessions.

Mrs Conclusion You can't. You can't – I mean, how can I go off and join Frelimo when I've got nine more instalments to pay on the fridge.

Mrs Premise No, you can't. You can't. Well this is the whole crux of Jean-Paul Sartre's 'Roads to Freedom'.

Mrs Conclusion No, it bloody isn't. The nub of that is, his characters stand for all of us in their desire to avoid action. Mind you, the man at the off-licence says it's an everyday story of French country folk.

Mrs Premise What does he know?

Mrs Conclusion Nothing.

Mrs Premise Sixty new pence for a bottle of Maltese Claret. Well I personally think Jean-Paul's masterwork is an allegory of man's search for commitment.

Mrs Conclusion No it isn't.

Mrs Premise Yes it is.

Mrs Conclusion Isn't.

Mrs Premise 'tis.

Mrs Conclusion No it isn't.

Mrs Premise All right. We can soon settle this. We'll ask him.

Mrs Conclusion Do you know him?

Mrs Premise Yes, we met on holiday last year.

Mrs Conclusion In Ibeezer?

Mrs Premise Yes. He was staying there with his wife and Mr and Mr Genet. Oh, I did get on well with Madam S. We were like that.

Mrs Conclusion What was Jean-Paul like?

Mrs Premise Well, you know, a bit moody. Yes, he didn't join in the fun much. Just sat there thinking. Still, Mr Rotter caught him a few times with the whoopee cushion. *(she demonstrates)* Le Capitalisme et La Bourgeoisie ils sont la même chose ... Oooh we did laugh.

Mrs Conclusion Well, we'll give a tinkle then.

Mrs Premise Yes, all right. She said they were in the book. *(shouts)* Where's the Paris telephone directory?

Mrs Inference (ERIC) It's on the drier.

Mrs Premise No, no, that's Budapest. Oh here we are Sartre ... Sartre.

Mrs Varley It's 621036.

Mrs Premise Oh, thank you, Mrs Varley. *(dials)* Hallo. Paris 621036 please and make it snappy, buster ... *(as they wait they sing 'The Girl from Ipanema')* Hallo? Hello Mrs Sartre. It's Beulagh Premise here. Oh, pardon, c'est Beulagh Premise ici, oui, oui, dans Ibeezer. Oui, we met ... nous nous recontrons au Hotel Miramar. Oui, à la barbeque, c'est vrai. Madame S. – est-ce que Jean est chez vous? Oh merde. When will he be free? Oh pardon. Quand sera-t-il libre? Oooooh. Ha ha ha ha. *(to Mrs Conclusion)* She says he's spent the last sixty years trying to work that one out. *(to Madame Sartre)* Très amusant, Madam S. Oui absolument ... à bientôt. *(puts the phone down)* Well he's out distributing pamphlets to the masses but he'll be in at six.

Mrs Conclusion Oh well, I'll ring BEA then.

Cut to them sitting on a raft in mid-ocean.

Mrs Premise Oh look, Paris!

Cut to shot of a notice board on the seashore, it reads 'North Malden Welcomes Careful Coastal Craft'.

Mrs Conclusion That's not Paris. Jean-Paul wouldn't live here. It's a right old dump.

'Alan Whicker', complete with microphone, walks in front of sign.

Whicker (ERIC) But this is where they were wrong. For this was no old dump, but a town with a future, an urban Eldorado where the businessmen of today can enjoy the facilities of tomorrow in the comfort of yesterday. Provided by a go-getting, go-ahead council who know just how loud money can talk. *(a phone off-screen starts to ring)* Interest rates are so low ...

Cut to head of drama's office; he is on the phone.

Head of Drama (JOHN) Well it's none of my business but we had the same trouble with one of our Icelandic sagas. These people are terribly keen but they do rather tend to take over. I think I'd stick to Caribbean

Islands if I were you. *(rings off)* Fine ... and now back to the saga.

CAPTION: 'NJORL'S SAGA – PART IV'

Thundering music. Cut to an Icelandic seashore. Dark and impressive. After a pause the Pepperpots walk into shot.

Mrs Premise Here – this is not Paris, this is Iceland.

Mrs Conclusion Oh, well, Paris must be over there then. *(points out to the sea; they walk back to the raft)*

Stock shot of Eiffel Tower. French accordion music. Mix through to French street thronged by cod Frenchmen with berets and loaves. Mrs Conclusion and Mrs Premise appear and walk up to the front door of an apartment block. On the front door is a list of the inhabitants of the block. They read it out loud.

Mrs Premise Oh, here we are, Number 25 ... *(reads)* Flat 1, Duke and Duchess of Windsor, Flat 2, Yves Montand, Flat 3, Jacques Cousteau, Flat 4, Jean Genet and Friend, Flat 5, Maurice Laroux ...

Mrs Conclusion Who's he?

Mrs Premise Never heard of him. Flat 6, Marcel Marceau, Walking Against the Wind Ltd. Flat 7, Indira Gandhi?

Mrs Conclusion She gets about a bit, doesn't she?

Mrs Premise Yes, Flat 8, Jean-Paul and Betty-Muriel Sartre.

She rings the bell. A voice comes from the intercom.

Voice Oui.

Mrs Premise C'est nous, Betty-Muriel, excusez que nous sommes en retard.

Voice Entrez.

Buzzer sounds.

Mrs Premise Oui, merci.

Interior the Sartres' flat. It is littered with books and papers. We hear Jean-Paul coughing. Mrs Sartre goes to the door. She is a ratbag with a fag in her mouth and a duster over her head. A French song is heard on the radio. She switches it off.

Mrs Sartre (MICHAEL) Oh, rubbish. *(opens the door)* Bonjour.

Mrs Conclusion *(entering)* Parlez vous Anglais?

Mrs Sartre Oh yes. Good day. *(Mrs Premise comes in)* Hello, love!

Mrs Premise Hello! Oh this is Mrs Conclusion from No. 46.

Mrs Sartre Nice to meet you, dear.

Mrs Conclusion Hello.

Mrs Premise How's the old man, then?

Mrs Sartre Oh, don't ask. He's in one of his bleeding moods. 'The bourgeoisie this is the bourgeoisie that' – he's like a little child sometimes. I was only telling the Rainiers the other day – course he's always rude to them, only classy friends we've got – I was saying solidarity with the masses I said ... pie in the sky! Oooh! You're not a

Marxist are you Mrs Conclusion?

Mrs Conclusion No, I'm a Revisionist.

Mrs Sartre Oh good. I mean, look at this place! I'm at my wits' end. Revolutionary leaflets everywhere. One of these days I'll revolutionary leaflets him. If it wasn't for the goat you couldn't get in here for propaganda.

Shot of a goat eating leaflets in corner of room.

Mrs Premise Oh very well. Can we pop in and have a word with him?

Mrs Sartre Yes come along.

Mrs Premise Thank you.

Mrs Sartre But be careful. He's had a few. Mind you he's as good as gold in the morning, I've got to hand it to him, but come lunchtime it's a bottle of vin ordinaire – six glasses and he's ready to agitate.

Mrs Premise and Mrs Conclusion knock on the door of Jean-Paul's room.

Mrs Premise Coo-ee! Jean-Paul? Jean-Paul! It's only us. Oh pardon . . . c'est même nous . . .

They enter. We do not see Jean-Paul although we hear his voice.

Jean-Paul Oui.

Mrs Premise Jean-Paul. Your famous trilogy 'Rues à Liberté', is it an allegory of man's search for commitment?

Jean-Paul Oui.

Mrs Premise I told you so.

Mrs Conclusion Oh coitus.

Stock shot of a plane taking off.

CAPTION: 'THE END'

Then the stock shot of a jet landing which they always use to introduce 'Whicker's World'. This leads us into Whicker Island – a tropical island paradise where all the inhabitants have Alan Whicker suits, glasses and microphones.

CAPTION: 'WHICKER'S WORLD'

Various Whickers pace past the camera.

First Whicker (ERIC) Today we look at a vanishing race. A problem people who are fast disappearing off the face of the earth.

Second Whicker (TERRY J) A race who one might say are losing a winning battle.

Third Whicker (MICHAEL) They live in a sunshine paradise, a Caribbean dream, where only reality is missing.

Fourth Whicker (GRAHAM) For this is Whicker Island.

Fifth Whicker (JOHN) An island inhabited entirely by ex-international interviewers in pursuit of the impossible dream.

First Whicker The whole problem of Whicker Island is here in a nutshell.

Second Whicker There are just too many Whickers.
Third Whicker The light-weight suits.
Fourth Whicker The old school tie.
Fifth Whicker The practised voice of the seasoned campaigner.
First Whicker Cannot hide the basic tragedy here.
Second Whicker There just aren't enough rich people left to interview.
  Cut to a different location.
Third Whicker You can't teach an old dog new tricks and so *(turning to a swimming pool with lots of Whickers around it, wandering with stick mikes and muttering)* you find them . . .
Fourth Whicker *(seated by swimming pool)* Sitting beside elegant swimming pools . . .
Fifth Whicker *(seated at drinks table, with sun umbrella)* . . . sipping Martinis . . .
First Whicker *(standing by the pool)* . . . and waiting for the inevitable interview.
Second Whicker *(standing fully clothed in the pool)* I talked to the island's only white man, Father Pierre.
  Cut to a different location. Feeling of heat. The third Whicker stands beside a priest in a white robe.
Third Whicker Father Pierre, why did you stay on in this colonial Campari-land where the clink of glasses mingles with the murmur of a million mosquitoes, where waterfalls of whisky wash away the worries of a world-weary Whicker, where gin and tonic jingle in a gyroscopic jubilee of something beginning with J – Father Pierre, why *did* you stay on here?
Father Pierre (GRAHAM) *(putting on a pair of Whicker-style glasses)* Well mainly for the interviews.
Fifth Whicker Well there you have it, a crumbling . . .
First Whicker . . . empire in the sun-drenched . . .
Second Whicker Caribbean, where the clichés sparkle on the waters . . .
Third Whicker . . . like the music of repeat fees . . .
First Whicker And so . . .
Fifth Whicker . . . from Whicker Island . . .
First Whicker . . . it's . . .
Second Whicker . . . fare . . .
Third Whicker . . . well and . . .
Fourth Whicker . . . bon . . .
Fifth Whicker . . . voy . . .
First Whicker . . . age.

Cut to film of Whicker plane taking off. Roll credits, which read:
WHICKER'S WORLD WAS CONCEIVED, WRITTEN AND PERFORMED
BY
ALAN WHICKER
JOHN CLEESE WHICKER
GRAHAM WHICKER CHAPMAN
ALAN MICHAEL PALIN WHICKER
ERIC WHICKER WHICKER IDLE
TERRY TERRY WHICKER ALAN GILLIAM
ALSO APPEARING
ALAN WHICKER
MRS IDLE
CONNIE WHICKER BOOTH
RITA WHICKER DAVIES
NIGEL WHICKER JONES
FRANK WILLIAMS AS THE BOY WHICKER
MAKE UP ALAN WHICKER AND MADELAINE GAFFNEY
ALAN WHICKER COSTUMES HAZEL PETHIG
ANIMATIONS BY TERRY WHICKER GILLIAM
MR WHICKER KINDLY PHOTOGRAPHED ON FILM BY ALAN FEATHERSTONE
EDITED ON FILM BY RAY MILLICHOPE
MR WHICKER'S SOUND BY ALAN WHICKER, ALAN WHICKER AND
RICHARD CHUBB
MR WHICKER WAS ENTIRELY LIT BY JIMMY PURDIE
(ASSISTED BY ALAN WHICKER)
MR WHICKER WAS DESIGNED BY ROBERT BERK
PRODUCED BY ALAN WHICKER OH, AND IAN McNAUGHTON
A BBC WHICKER COLOUR PRODUCTION

Twenty-eight

> *Stirring music.*

Voice Over (MICHAEL) and captions:
> 'THE KON TIKI'
> 'RA I'
> 'RA 2'
> 'AND NOW...'
> 'MR AND MRS BRIAN NORRIS'S FORD POPULAR'
> *Pull back from a shot of an old little Ford Popular to reveal Mr and Mrs Norris (Michael and Graham), standing with it outside the front garden of a small suburban semi-detached house.*

Voice Over (ERIC) Who, a year ago, had heard of Mr and Mrs Brian Norris of 37, Gledhill Gardens, Parsons Green? And yet their epic journey in EBW 343 has set them alongside Thor Heyerdahl and Sir Edmund Hillary. Starting only with a theory, Mr Norris set out to prove that the inhabitants of Hounslow could have been descendants of the people of Surbiton who had made the great trek north. No newcomer to this field, Mr Norris's 'A Short History of Motor Traffic Between Purley and Esher' had become a best-selling minor classic in the car-swapping belt. *(shot of Mr Norris gazing into a window, where his book lies; there is a sign saying 'Remaindered')* But why would the people of Surbiton go to Hounslow? Mr Norris had noticed three things. *(split-screen shot of two identical semi-detached houses)* Firstly, the similarity of the houses. Secondly, the similarity of the costume between Hounslow and Surbiton, *(similarly dressed suburbanites on either side of the split screen)* and thirdly, the similarity of speech.
> *Split screen.*

Man on Right (TERRY J) Are you still running the GDBDMDB?

Man on Left (ERIC) Yes, but I've had the excess nipples woppled to remove tamping.

Man on Left Jolly good.

Voice Over Were these just coincidences, or were they, as Mr Norris believed, part of an identical cultural background? One further discovery convinced him. *(cut to two lawnmowers arranged on a table, as if they were exhibits in a museum, with type-written documentation in front of them for the visitor)* The lawnmower. Surely such a gadget could not have been generated independently in two separate areas. Mr Norris was convinced.

Mr Norris's Voice I'm convinced.

Voice Over But how to prove it.

Mr Norris's Voice But how to prove it.

Twenty-eight

Voice Over There was only one way to see if the journey between Surbiton and Hounslow was possible, and that was to try and make it. Months of preparation followed whilst Mr Norris continued his research in the Putney Public Library, *(Mr Norris in a library reading a book titled 'The Lady with the Naked Skin' by Paul Fox Jnr)* and Mrs Norris made sandwiches.

Cut to Mr and Mrs Norris leaving their house.

Voice Over Finally, by April, they were ready. On the 23rd, Mr and Mrs Norris set out from 'Abide-A-Wee' to motor the fifteen miles to Surbiton, watched by a crowd of local well-wishers. *(one tiny child holding a small British flag)* That evening they dined at Tooting. *(quick flash of them sitting in the window of a Golden Egg or Wimpy place)* This would be the last they'd see of civilization. Mr Norris's diary for the 23rd reveals the extraordinary calmness and deep inner peacefulness of his mind.

We see the diary.

Mr Norris's Voice 7.30 Fed cat.
8.00 Breakfast.
8.30 Yes (successfully).
9.00 Set out on historic journey.

Cut to Mr Norris's car driving along a suburban road. A sign says 'You are now leaving Surbiton, gateway to Esher'.

Voice Over On the morning of the 24th, early to avoid the traffic, Mr Norris's historic expedition set out from Surbiton – destination Hounslow. Early on they began to perceive encouraging signs. *(cut to sign saying 'Hounslow 25 miles'; Mr Norris closely examines the sign, as would an archaeologist)* The writing on the sign was almost exactly the same as the writing in the AA book. They were on the right route. During the long hours of the voyage, Mr Norris's wife Betty kept a complete photographic record and made sandwiches. This is some of the unique footage which Mrs Norris got back from the chemists ... *(badly shot pictures of sandwiches, with fingers in the lens, etc.)* Mile succeeded mile and the terrific strain was beginning to tell when suddenly, *(chord; Mr Norris points excitedly, pull back to reveal him standing on a bridge over the Kingston by-pass examining it through field glasses)* by an amazing stroke of luck, Mr Norris had come across the Kingston by-pass. This was something to tell the Round Table. *(cut to a map; it traces the two routes in red as the voice talks)* At this stage, Mr Norris was faced with two major divergent theories concerning his Surbiton ancestors. Did they take the Kingston by-pass, turning left at Barnes, or did they strike west up the A308 via Norbiton to Hampton Wick? Both these theories ran up against one big obstacle – the Thames, *(the car at a river bank; Mr and Mrs Norris puzzling; behind them three or four bridges with traffic pouring over)* lying like a silver turd between Richmond and Isleworth. This was a major setback. How could they possibly cross the river? Several hours of thought produced nothing. There was only one flask of coffee left when suddenly Mr Norris spotted something. *(cut to a sign saying 'Metropolitan Railway)* Could this have been the method used? Hardly daring to believe, Mr Norris led his expedition on to the 3.47. *(cut to them getting on the train)* Forty minutes later, via Clapham, Fulham, Chiswick and Brentford, they approached their goal: Hounslow. *(a sign saying 'Hounslow Central'; Mr Norris sticks a British flag on the platform; he poses for his wife's photos; much hand shaking)* Was this, then, the final proof? Something aroused the accountant's instinct buried deep in Mr Norris's make-up. *(cut to Mr Norris's eyes and furrowed brow)* The journey *was* possible, and yet... *(zoom in on railway timetable on wall saying 'Trains to Surbiton every half hour')* 'Wrong Way' Norris had accidentally stumbled on a piece of anthropological history. It was the inhabitants of Hounslow who had made the great trek south to the sunnier pastures of Surbiton, and *not* vice versa, as he had originally surmised. *This* was the secret of Surbiton! Happy and contented Mr Norris returned to the calmer waters of chartered accountancy, for, in his way, 'Wrong Way' Norris was right.

Music swells, over book title 'The Story of EBW343' by 'Wrong Way' Norris.

CAPTION: 'THE END'

*A music crescendo. Cut to nude organist (*TERRY J*) playing a chord.*

Announcer (JOHN) And now...

It's Man (MICHAEL) It's...

Animated titles.

Voice (JOHN) Monty Python's Flying Circus.

Cut to a headmaster's study.

Headmaster (MICHAEL) Knock, enter and approach. *(knock on door; it opens and three schoolboys in short trousers enter)* Right, it's come to my notice that certain boys have been running a unit-trust linked assurance scheme with fringe benefits and full cash-in endowment facilities. Apparently small investors were attracted by the wide-ranging portfolio and that in the first week the limited offer was oversubscribed eight times.

Stebbins (ERIC) It was Tidwell's idea, sir.

Headmaster Shut up, Stebbins! I haven't finished. Oh, by the way, congratulations on winning the Italian Grand Prix at Monza.

Stebbins Thank you, sir.

Headmaster Shut up. Now then, this sort of extra-curricular capitalist expansion has got to stop! I made it quite clear when Potter tried to go public last term, that these massive stock exchange deals must *not* happen in Big School. Is that clear, Balderston?

Balderston (TERRY G) Yes, sir.

Headmaster Oh, and Balderston, next time you do a 'Panorama' Report on the Black Ghettos you *must* get an exeat form from Mr Dibley.

Balderston Sorry, sir.

Headmaster Shut up, and stop slouching. Now, the reason I called you in here today, is that my wife is having a little trouble with her ... er ... with her waterworks, and I think she needs a bit of attention. Now, which one of you is the surgeon? *(silence)* Come on, I know one of you is, which one is it? *(Tidwell raises hand reluctantly)* Ah! Tidwell. Good. Well, I want you to cut along and have a look at the wife.

Tidwell (TERRY J) Oh, sir! Why don't you ask Stebbins? He's a gynaecologist.

Stebbins Ooh! You rotten stinker, Tidwell!

Headmaster Is this true, Stebbins? Are you a gynaecologist?

Stebbins *(very reluctantly)* Yes, sir.

Headmaster Right, just the man. How much do you charge?

Stebbins *(muttering into his shoes)* Thirty guineas, sir.

Headmaster Excellent. Right. I want you to go along to see the wife. Give her a full examination, and let me know the results by the end of break. And don't pick your nose!

Cut to a sign saying 'How to do it'. Music. Pull out to reveal a 'Blue Peter' type set. Sitting casually on the edge of a dais are three presenters in sweaters – Noel, Jackie and Alan – plus a large bloodhound.

Alan (JOHN) Hello.

Noel (GRAHAM) Hello.

Alan Well, last week we showed you how to become a gynaecologist. And this week on 'How to do it' we're going to show you how to play the flute, how to split an atom, how to construct a box girder bridge, how to irrigate the Sahara Desert and make vast new areas of land cultivatable, but first, here's Jackie to tell you all how to rid the world of all known diseases.

Jackie (ERIC) Hello, Alan.

Alan Hello, Jackie.

Jackie Well, first of all become a doctor and discover a marvellous cure for something, and then, when the medical profession really starts to take notice of you, you can jolly well tell them what to do and make sure they get everything right so there'll never be any diseases ever again.

Alan Thanks, Jackie. Great idea. How to play the flute. *(picking up a flute)* Well here we are. You blow there and you move your fingers up and down here.

Noel Great, great, Alan. Well, next week we'll be showing you how black and white people can live together in peace and harmony, and Alan will be over in Moscow showing us how to reconcile the Russians and the Chinese. So, until next week, cheerio.

Alan Bye.

Jackie Bye.

Children's music. Pull out to reveal that the 'Blue Peter' set is in one corner of a stockbroker-belt sitting room. Two ladies are sitting by the fire looking at a photo album.

Mrs Nigger-Baiter (MICHAEL) Oh, yes, he's such a clever little boy, just like his father.

Mrs S (TERRY J) D'you think so, Mrs Nigger-Baiter?

Mrs Nigger-Baiter Oh yes, spitting image.

The door opens. The son comes in.

Son (JOHN) Good afternoon, mother. Good afternoon, Mrs Nigger-Baiter.

Mrs Nigger-Baiter Ooh, he's walking already!

Mrs S Yes, he's such a clever little boy, aren't you? Coochy coochy coo...

Mrs Nigger-Baiter Hello, coochy coo...

Mrs S Hello, hello... *(they chuck him under the chin)*

Mrs Nigger-Baiter Oochy coochy. *(the son smiles a little tight smile)* Look at him laughing... ooh, he's a chirpy little fellow. Isn't he a chirpy little fellow... eh? eh? Does he talk? Does he talk, eh?

Son Of course I talk, I'm Minister for Overseas Development.

Mrs Nigger-Baiter Ooh, he's a *clever* little boy – he's a *clever* little boy. *(gets out a rattle)* Do you like your rattle? Do you like your rattle? Look at his little eyes following it... look at his iggy piggy piggy little eyeballs eh... oo... he's got a tubby tum-tum. Oh, he's got a tubby tum-tum.

Son *(whilst Mrs Nigger-Baiter is talking)* Mother, could I have a quick cup of tea please. I have an important statement on Rhodesia to make in the Commons at six.

Sound of an explosion out of vision. Cut to reveal Mrs Nigger-Baiter's chair charred and smoking. Mrs Nigger-Baiter is no longer there. The upholstery is smouldering gently.

Mrs S Oh, Mrs Nigger-Baiter's exploded.

Son Good thing, too.

Mrs S She was my best friend.

Son Oh, mother, don't be so sentimental. Things explode every day.

Mrs S Yes, I suppose so. Anyway, I didn't really like her that much.

The doorbell rings. Mrs S goes to the door. A vicar with a suitcase.

Vicar (ERIC) Hello, I'm your new vicar. Can I interest you in any encyclopaedias?

Mrs S Ah, no thank you. We're not Church people, thank you.

The vicar opens his suitcase to reveal it is packed with brushes.

Vicar How about brushes? Nylon or bristle? Strong-tufted, attractive colours.

Mrs S No – really, thank you, vicar.

Vicar Oh dear . . . Turkey? Cup final tickets?

Mrs S No, no really, we're just not religious thank you.

Vicar Oh, well. Bye bye.

Mrs S Bye bye, vicar. *(she shuts the door, as she returns to seat the vicar pops his head round the door again)*

Vicar Remember, if you do want anything . . . jewellery, Ascot water heaters . . .

Mrs S Thank you, vicar. *(he goes)* It's funny, isn't it? How your best friend can just blow up like that? I mean, you wouldn't think it was medically possible, would you?

Cut to a doctor in a posh consulting room.

Doctor (GRAHAM) This is where Mrs Shazam was so wrong. Exploding is a perfectly normal medical phenomenon. In many fields of medicine nowadays, a dose of dynamite can do a world of good. For instance, athlete's foot – an irritating condition – can be cured by applying a small charge of TNT between each toe. *(doorbell)* Excuse me. *(he opens the door)*

Vicar Hello, I'm your new vicar, can I interest you in any of these watches, pens or biros? *(exhibits the collection inside his jacket)*

Doctor No . . . I'm not religious, I'm afraid.

Vicar Oh, souvenirs, badges . . . a little noddy dog for the back of the car?

Doctor No thank you, vicar. Good morning.

Vicar Oh, morning.

He shuts the door.

Doctor Now, many of the medical profession are sceptical about my work. They point to my record of treatment of athlete's foot sufferers – eighty-four dead, sixty-five severely wounded and twelve missing believed cured. But then, people laughed at Bob Hope, people laughed at my wife when she wrapped herself up in greaseproof paper and hopped into the Social Security office, but that doesn't mean that Pasteur was wrong! Look, I'll show you what I mean. *(goes to a wall diagram of two skeletons and taps one with a rod)*

ANIMATION:

Skeleton Watch it, mate. I'm not going to stay round here getting poked and prodded all day. *(clips a face on and moves off the diagram)* I'm off . . . I've got a decent body, all I get is poked and prodded in the chest. *(moving through countryside)* Well, I'm off. I'm going to get another line of work. *(goes past various warning signs)*

Voice Watch it!

Voice Don't go any further!

Voice Turn back!

Voice Stop!

The sprocket holes at the side of the film come into view.

Voice Stop! Oh, please stop!

The skeleton moves past the sprocket holes and falls into blank space.

Voice Oh, my god, he's fallen off the edge of the cartoon.

Voice Well, so much for that link.

Artistic-type set. There is a large screen on back. Stock two-chair set-up as for interview.

Presenter (ERIC) John Cobbley is the Musical and Artistic Director of Covent Garden. He is himself a talented musician, he is a world famous authority on nineteenth-century Russian music and he's come into the studio tonight to talk about Tchaikowsky, which is a bit of a pity as this is 'Farming Club'. On 'Farming Club' tonight we'll be taking a look at the Ministry's *(pigs appear on the screen, Cobbley gets up, looks about him, wanders off rather puzzled)* latest preventative proposals to deal with a possible outbreak of foot and mouth, we'll be talking later to the man who believes that milk yields can be increased dramatically, but first a Farming Club special, the life of Tchaikowsky.

Cue Tchaikowsky's first piano concerto. Stock film of a farmyard with superimposed roller caption.

ROLLER CAPTION: 'FARMING CLUB, IN ASSOCIATION WITH THE POTATO MARKETING BOARD, ALSO IN ASSOCIATION WITH THE BEETROOT, HAM, EGG AND TOMATO MARKETING BOARD, AND ALSO IN ASSOCIATION WITH THE LITTLE GREEN BITS OF CUCUMBER DICED WITH SHALLOTS, GARNISHED WITH CHIVES AND SERVED WITH A ROQUEFORT DRESSING MAKES AN EXCELLENT APPETIZER OR SIDE DISH WITH A STEAK OR A STEW MARKETING BOARD, PRESENTS: THE LIFE OF PETER ILYICH TCHAIKOWSKY, IN ASSOCIATION WITH THE PETER ILYICH TCHAIKOWSKY MARKETING BOARD'

Cut back to the presenter.

Presenter Tchaikowsky. Was he the tortured soul who poured out his immortal longings into dignified passages of stately music, or was he just an old poof who wrote tunes? *(pull back to show a second presenter in the other chair)* Tonight on 'Farming Club' we're going to take an intimate look at Tchaikowsky *(a picture of Tchaikowsky on the screen)* and an intimate look at his friends. *(a picture of a naked sailor on a tiger-skin rug)* Incidentally, BBC Publications have prepared a special pamphlet to go with this programme called 'Hello Pianist', *(it comes up on the screen; on its cover there is a picture of a pig)* and it contains material that some people might find offensive but which is really smashing.

Second Presenter (JOHN) Peter Ilyich Tchaikowsky was born in 1840 in a Ken Russell film just outside St Petersburg. His father (Leo McKern), a freelance bishop, was married to Vern Plachenka (Julie Christie) but secretly deeply in love with Margo Farenka (Shirley Abicair) and the strangely flatulent Madame Ranevsky (Norris McWhirter). Soon, however, the family (Eldridge Cleaver, Moira Lister and Stan the Bat) moved to the neighbouring industrial village of Omsk (Eddie Waring) where they soon found themselves, sadly, quite unable to cope (Anthony Barber). In 1863, however, Tchaikowsky was sent to Moscow to study the piano and, when he'd finished that, the living room. Maurice takes up the story.

Cut to a poofy presenter in really chintzy surroundings.

Maurice (MICHAEL) Well, guess what, the very next thing he did was to go to this extraordinary but *extraordinary* duckety-poos semi-Mondrian house in Robin Russia. Harry here Tammy Tchaikowsky wrote some of the most Sammy super symphonies you've ever Henry heard in the whole of your Lily life.

SUPERIMPOSED CAPTION: 'A FAMOUS MUSIC CRITIC AND HAIRDRESSER'

Maurice She was such a good composer that everybody, but everybody, wanted to know, and quite right too, because she wrote some lovely bits, such as Sally Sleeping Beauty, Patsy Pathetique, Adrian 1812 and lots of Conny concerti for Vera violin and Peter Piano Fanny Forte.

Cut back to second presenter.

Second Presenter But what do we *really* know of this tortured ponce?

Cut to space-programme-type set. Experts at a desk. An Apollo-type monograph behind them says 'Tchaikowsky XII'. The centre motif is a picture of Tchaikowsky.

Expert (GRAHAM) Well, if you can imagine the size of Nelson's Column, which is roughly three times the size of a London bus, then Tchaikowsky was much smaller. His head was about the same size as that of an extremely large dog, that is to say, two very small dogs, or four very large hamsters, or one medium-size rabbit if you count the whole of the body and not just the head. Robin.

He has a model of Tchaikowsky which comes apart.

Second Expert (TERRY J) Thank you. Well here is a three-stage model of Tchaikowsky . . . here you see the legs, used for walking around, and which can be jettisoned at night . . . *(he takes the legs off)* And this is the main trunk, the power house of the whole thing, incorporating of course the naughty bits, which were *extremely* naughty for his time, and the whole thing is subservient to *(takes it off)* this small command module, the, as it were, head of the whole, as it were, body. Robin.

Cut to first expert.

First Expert Peter.

Cut to first presenter.

First Presenter Simon.

Cut to second presenter.

Second Presenter Maurice.

Cut to Maurice.

Maurice Me. Well, poor pet, she was like a lost lamb in an abattoir. Eventually she Dickie died of Colin Cholera in St Patsy Petersburg, in Gertie great Percy pain.

Cut to a piano in a pool of light.

Voice Over (ERIC) Here to play Tchaikowsky's first piano concerto in B Flat Minor is the world-famous soloist Sviatoslav Richter. During the performance he will escape from a sack, three padlocks and a pair of handcuffs.

A chained figure in a sack rolls into shot and starts rolling about and playing the piano concerto. After a minute 'Rita' enters and gestures to him. She is in fish-net tights, etc. – the full conjurer's assistant. He wriggles free from the sack, playing the while. The music stops.

CAPTION: 'SVIATOSLAV RICHTER AND RITA'

Film of an applauding audience in the Royal Albert Hall.

SUPERIMPOSED CAPTION: 'AND NOW'

Jolly showbiz music. A flat goes up, revealing three actors in trim-jeans (which are heavily padded to make you sweat off weight) grouped à la advert. They all have slight Australian accents.

CAPTION: 'TRIM-JEANS THEATRE PRESENTS'

Gary Coover (ERIC) Good evening. This new series of 'Trim-Jeans Theatre Presents' will enable you to enjoy the poetry of T. S. Eliot whilst losing unsightly tummy bulge. Jean.

CAPTION: 'THESE THREE PEOPLE ARE REDUCING THEIR WAIST, THIGHS, HIPS AND ABDOMEN EVEN AS THEY RECOMMEND'

Jean Wennerstrom (GRAHAM) Wow, yes and the inches stay off. Mark.

Mark Edwards (MICHAEL) Terrific! Thrill to Thomas à Becket's Kierkegaardian moment of choice while making your physique tighter, firmer, neater.

Cut to a cathedral interior. There are three priests, four knights and two women, all in trim-jeans. Thomas does not wear one.

Priest (GRAHAM) I am here. No traitor to the King.

First Knight (ERIC) Absolve all those you have excommunicated.

Second Knight (TERRY J) Resign those powers you have arrogated.

Third Knight (MICHAEL) Renew the obedience you have violated.

Fourth Knight (JOHN) Lose inches off your hips, thighs, buttocks and abdomen.

Cut back to Gary and the others.

Gary A terrific product.

All Terrific.

Gary And this comes complete with the most revolutionary guarantee in slenderizing history!

Cut to a man (Terry J) in trim-jeans under a sign saying 'Before'.

Voice Over (MICHAEL) This was Kevin Francis before last season's 'Trim-Jean Play of the Month' production of 'The Seagull' by Anton Chekhov and the Sauna Belt Trim-Jean Company Limited. See Kevin has slipped into his slenderizing garment and is inflating it with the handy little pump provided. Three acts and a few special torso exercises later, Kevin, as Trigorin, the failed writer of sentimental romances, has lost over thirty-three inches. *(same shot but very skinny John Hughman has replaced Terry J)* Wow. What a difference. That Anton Chekhov can certainly write.

Gary Terrific.

Mark Terrific.

Gary Yes, why not join us for a season of classic plays and rapid slenderizing. Enjoy Sir John Gielgud and Sir Ralph Richardson losing a total of fifteen inches in David Storey's 'Home'.

Mark Enjoy the 'The Trim Gentlemen of Verona' and 'Long Day's Journey into Night' while inches melt away.

Jean Enjoy Glenda Jackson with a Constant Snug Fit and Solid Support in all four areas.

Gary Other productions will include... 'Treasure Island'... *(Long John Silver in trim-jeans)* 'Swan Lake' *(cut to a photo of two ballet dancers in a 'lift' position, both wearing tights and trim-jeans)* 'The Life and Loves of Toulouse Lautrec', *(cut to a photo of Toulouse Lautrec, his feet sticking out of the bottom of the trim-jeans)* and the Trim-Jeans version of 'The Great Escape', with a cast of thousands losing well over fifteen hundred inches.

Cut to scrubland, barbed wire à la prison camp in the background. After a few seconds a head appears out of a hole in the ground. He looks around then gets out. He is wearing trim-jeans. He looks back. Satisfied, he beckons. Others start appearing. Three German guards behind the wire muttering.

SUPERIMPOSED CAPTION: 'INCHES LOST SO FAR'

A superimposed counter shows the numbers increasing.

Guard Achtung! Halt! Halt!

A moment's panic. Shooting starts and a siren goes. Men pour out of hole rapidly. Guards pursue them with tracker dogs in trim-jeans. The counter goes berserk.

An animated item ends with a sign saying 'And now, the Fish Slapping Dance'.

Cut to a quayside. John and Michael, dressed in tropical gear and solar topees. John stands still while Michael dances up and down before him to the jolly music of Edward German. Michael holds two tiny fish and from time to time in the course of the dance he slaps John lightly across the cheeks with them. The music ends; Michael stops dancing. John produces a huge great fish and swipes Michael with it. Michael falls off the quay into the water.

ANIMATION: *underwater. We see an animated Michael sinking. He is swallowed by a fish with a swastika on its side.*

Nazi Fish Welcome aboard, Britisher pig. Quite a little surprise, ja? But perhaps you would be so kind as to tell us all you know about certain allied shipping routes, ja? Come on, talk!

The Nazi fish is swallowed by a fish with an RAF emblem.

British Fish Hello, Fritz. Tables seem to have turned, old chap, let's see how you like a bit of your own medicine, eh? Come on, Fritz, now tell us – tell us about...

The British fish is swallowed by a Chinese fish.

Chinese Fish Ah, gleetings, capitalist dog; very sorry but must inform you, you are now prisoner of People's Republic.

Second Voice Am very sorry, comrade commando, but have just picked up capitalist ship on ladar scanner.

The Chinese fish bites the underside of a large ship. Film of big liner sinking in storm. General panic and dramatic music.

Captain (TERRY J) *(over tannoy)* This is your captain speaking. There is no need for panic. Woman and children first. I repeat that, women and children first.

Cut to the ship's bridge. The captain and two or three officers are seen scrambling into ladies' clothing or young children's short trousers and school satchels and caps. The ship pitches and rolls in the gale. The captain is still trying to speak into the PA.

Captain Do not rush for the lifeboats – remember, women and children first.

A first officer is revealed in the corner of the bridge putting a head-dress on a Red Indian outfit.

First Officer (JOHN) And Red Indians!

Captain *(putting his hand over the PA)* What did you have to get dressed up like that for?

First Officer It was the only thing left.

Captain Oh. All right. *(into the PA)* Women, children and Red Indians...

Cut to another officer in astronaut's kit.

Second Officer (TERRY G) And spacemen!

Captain Here is a revised list. Women, children, Red Indians and spacemen. *(hand over PA)* What's *that* meant to be?

Cut to third officer who is putting finishing touches to a medieval outfit.

Third Officer (ERIC) Well it's a sort of impression of what a kind of Renaissance courtier artist might have looked like at the court of one of the great families like the Medicis or the Borgias...

Fourth Officer (GRAHAM) No it's not, it's more Flemish than Italian.

Fifth Officer (MICHAEL) Yes – that's a Flemish merchant of the fifteenth or sixteenth centuries...

Third Officer What! With these tassles...

Fourth Officer Yes, yes. They had those fitted doublets going tapering down into the full hose you know – exactly like that.

Captain *(into the PA)* One moment, please, don't panic. *(puts his hand over the PA)* Now, what is it meant to be? I've got to tell them *something*... is it a Flemish merchant?

Third Officer *No*, it is *not* a Flemish merchant. It's more a sort of idealized version of the complete Renaissance Man...

Captain Oh, all right.

Fourth Officer It's not...

Captain All right! All right! *(into the PA)* This is your captain speaking... do not rush for the lifeboats... women, children, Red Indians, spacemen *(stock film of long shot of sinking vessel, the voice over fading)* and a sort of idealized version of complete Renaissance Men first!

CAPTION: 'A FEW DAYS LATER'

Cut to a police chief's office in an anonymous South American police state. The chief of police at his desk. From outside we hear footsteps approaching the office and voices.

Third Officer's Voice Flemish merchants did not wear hand-embroidered chevrons. They did not!

The door opens and two guards roughly push in the captain in drag, another officer half in drag, half in naval uniform, two officers hastily dressed as children, a complete Renaissance Man, a Red Indian and a spaceman. They stand there for a moment. Then one of the guards pushes his way forward and hands the police chief a piece of paper.

Police Chief (JOHN) Yes, Gomez? *(reads)* Vee found zem valking on zee beach, my capitan. *(the guard nods enthusiastically)* Gomez, why can't you *say* this? *(the guard mouths something)* What? Oh, I see, we can't afford it. *(to camera)* You see the BBC has to pay an actor twenty guineas if he speaks and it makes a bit of a hole in the budget...

Guard (TERRY G) Twenty-*eight* guineas, sir! Ooh, sorry.

Police Chief You fool Gomez – that's twenty-eight guineas...

Second Guard (ERIC) What about me, sir?

Police Chief Are you supposed to speak?

Second Guard No, sir.

Police Chief But you've just spoken!

Second Guard Oh, sorry, sir.

Police Chief You fool, that's, that's fifty-six guineas before we've even started. *(a third guard suddenly rushes up to the window and crashes through it; scream and breaking glass)* What did he do that for?

Second Guard It's a stunt, sir, an extra twenty guineas.

Police Chief *(banging the desk)* Look! We can't afford it! The BBC are short of money as it is.

Cut to a newsreader in a 'News at Nine' set with a bare light bulb hanging in shot. He wears only an old blanket round his shoulders. He is shivering.

Newsreader (ERIC) The BBC wishes to deny rumours that it is going into liquidation. Mrs Kelly, who owns the flat where they live, has said that they can stay on till the end of the month . . . *(he is handed a piece of paper)* and we've just heard that Huw Weldon's watch has been accepted by the London Electricity Board and transmissions for this evening can be continued as planned. *(he coughs and pulls the blanket tighter round his shoulders)* That's all from me so . . . goodnight.

Knocking on the door.

Mr Kelly's Voice (GRAHAM) Are you going to be in there all night?

Newsreader It's just a bulletin, Mr Kelly . . . and now back to the story *(banging)* . . . All right!

Cut back to the same police chief's office. Noises off of people walking down. The door opens and the same crowd is pushed in. No one has any trousers on.

First Guard Ve found ze men, valking on ze beach, my capitain.

Captain We're British Naval Officers, and entitled to be . . .

Enter a pantomime principal boy holding a stuffed cat. All the rest of the group break back in a well-choreographed panto arrowhead and raise their hands toward her.

All It's . . . Puss!

Audience Hello, Puss!

Principal Boy (JULIA BRECK) Hello, children!

Police Chief Stop! Stop this adaptation of 'Puss-in-Boots'! This is the Police Department of the State of Venezuela!

Principal Boy Oh no it isn't!

Police Chief Oh, yes it is!

Principal Boy *(kids joining in voice over)* Oh no it isn't!

All *(plus kids)* Oh yes it is!

Principal Boy *(plus kids)* Oh no it isn't . . .

Police Chief Shut up! Shut up! *(getting up, holding a pistol; he has no trousers; silence)* Now I'm going to ask you some questions, and remember, if you do not give me correct answers, we have ways of making you answer!

Voice From Back Like not paying twenty-eight guineas.

Police Chief Shut up! Now, what ship are you from?

Captain We are from the SS *Mother Goose*, we were twelve days out from Port of Spain, and I . . .

The door is flung open and the second – trouserless – guard rushes in.

Second Guard I got thirty bob for the trousers!

Captain We are from SS *Mother Goose*. We were twelve days out from Port of Spain, and one night I was doing my usual rounds, when I had occasion to pass the forward storage lockers . . .

Slightly eerie music has crept in under his words and the screen goes into a ripple. It gets right out of focus and continues to ripple as it pulls back into focus. Ripple stops and they are still in the same set as they were.

Police Chief Go on!

Captain Well, I noticed something unusual, the main bilge hatches had been opened . . . *(at this point three men in brown coats come in and start taking pictures off the wall, clearing props and chairs from the set, etc.)* and there, crouching amidst the scuppers was the most ghastly creature I'd ever seen in my life. *(the flats start to be flown up, revealing behind a sitting room – so that we can see the police office has been built in the Kelly's sitting room)* As soon as it saw me, its horrible face split aside in a ghastly look of terror. His head, which was like . . .

Scene Shifter Could you sign this please? *(handing the captain a piece of paper)* Thank you.

Captain A small, small rat was ghastly and horrible and befurred . . . its little red eyes glinted in the unaccustomed glare of the midday sun and before I could shut the hatch, it sprang upon me with one almighty . . .

By this time the whole office set has been removed revealing the Kelly's boarding house sitting room. Mr and Mrs Kelly come in through door or put their heads round.

Mrs Kelly (MICHAEL) What's this about doing the 'Horse of the Year Show' in here tonight?

Chief Officer I'm sorry, Mrs Kelly. We don't know, I'm afraid – this is drama.

Mrs Kelly Mr Fox told me, before he went down to the pub, that they were doing 'Horse of the Year Show' in here tonight at 9.10.

Chief of Police This is BBC 2.

Captain I think BBC 1 are in the kitchen.

Mrs Kelly Well, I'm not having Harvey Smith jumping over my binette.

Mr Kelly No, come on. *(they go)*

Captain . . . tearing at my throat, ripping my clothes . . .

Mr Kelly puts his head round the door.

Mr Kelly And turn the gas off before you leave!

Police Chief All right!!

Mr Kelly goes.

Captain I fought it with all my strength, but it was too much for me . . .

Cut to Mr and Mrs Kelly coming through the hall. We can hear the captain's voice growing fainter. Mr and Mrs Kelly go towards the kitchen door and stop and listen. We have lost the captain's voice by now, but from inside the kitchen we hear 'Horse of the Year Show' sound track.

Dorian Williams (voice over) Another clear round for Harvey Smith on 'Omalley'.

Commentator *(voice over on tannoy)* And now it's Mrs David Barker, riding 'Atalanta' Number 3.

Crash of breaking pottery, falling pots and pans, horse neighing.

Mrs Kelly Right! That's it! *(they throw door open and march into the kitchen; a horse plus Pat Hornsby Smith and the commentator and the wreckage of a jump)* Come on now, out! All of you – get out of my kitchen, all of you – come on! Harvey Smith, get out of here!

She chases them out and down the hall.

Paul Fox (TERRY J) *(emerging from another door)* It's one of our most popular programmes.

Mrs Kelly That's what you think, Mr Fox!

She shooshes them all out down the passage and out of the front door. The newsreader with a blanket over him joins them and tries to read off a piece of paper.

Newsreader Well, that's all from BBC Television for this evening . . .

Mrs Kelly *(slamming door on him)* Shove off! Go and find yourself another flat! Get out!

As she slams the door, a piece of paper (obviously a tax return form) is shoved through the door. It has the credits scribbled hurriedly on it; the camera pans into it. After the credits Mrs Kelly stamps on the paper.

Fade out.

Showbiz music, cut to a big sign saying 'It's'. Pull out to reveal glossy, spangly, opulent showbiz set. Two extraordinarily famous guests sitting on sofas.

Announcer's Voice (ERIC) Tonight from London your special guests are Lulu, Ringo Starr and the man you've all been waiting for – your host for tonight . . .

More music. The 'It's' man, tattered and ragged as usual, emerges onto set.

Lulu Love the outfit dear, it's gorgeous.

It's Man Hello, good evening, welcome. It's . . .

The signature tune and opening animated titles start. The 'It's' man, still visible through the titles, tries vainly to stop them. The guests walk off in disgust. The 'It's' man tries to drag them back. Failing, he sits down as the music ends. Fade out.

Twenty-nine

Opening title sequence and signature tune for 'The Money Programme'. Set with presenter and two guests. Close up on presenter.

Presenter (ERIC) Good evening and welcome to 'The Money Programme'. Tonight on 'The Money Programme', we're going to look at money. Lots of it. On film and in the studio. Some of it in nice piles, others in lovely clanky bits of loose change, some of it neatly counted into fat little hundreds, *(starting to get excited)* delicate fivers stuffed into bulging wallets, nice crisp clean cheques, pert pieces of copper coinage thrust deep into trouser pockets, romantic foreign money rolling against the thigh with rough familiarity, *(starting to get over-excited)* beautiful wayward curlicued banknotes, filigree copperplating cheek by jowl with tumbling hexagonal milled edges, rubbing gently against the terse leather of beautifully balanced bank books. *(collects himself)* I'm sorry. But I love money. All money. I've always wanted money. *(getting worked up again)* To handle. To touch. The smell of the rain-washed florin. The lure of the lira. *(standing on the desk)* The glitter and the glory of the guinea. The romance of the rouble. The feel of the franc, the heel of the Deutschmark, the cold antiseptic sting of the Swiss franc, and the sun-burned splendour of the Australian dollar.
(sings to piano accompaniment) I've got ninety thousand pounds in my pyjamas.
I've got forty thousand French francs in my fridge.
I've got lots and lots of lira.
Now the Deutschmark's getting dearer.
And my dollar bills would buy the Brooklyn Bridge.
Five singers (male) in Welsh (women's) national costume come on. A Welsh harpist joins them.

All There is nothing quite as wonderful as money,
There is nothing quite as beautiful as cash,
Some people say it's folly
But I'd rather have the lolly
With money you can make a smash.

Presenter There is nothing quite as wonderful as money
There is nothing like a newly minted pound

All Everyone must hanker
For the butchness of a banker
It's accountancy that makes the world go round.

Presenter You can keep your Marxist ways
For it's only just a phase.

All For its money, money, money,
Makes the world go round.
(a shower of paper notes descends)

Money, money, money, money, money, money!

Cut to side of set where the nude organist (Terry J) plays the final chord and grins at the camera.

Cut to the announcer at his desk.

John And now ...

It's Man It's ...

Animated titles.

Voice Monty Python's Flying Circuses.

Exterior of an Elizabethan palace. Elizabethan music. An Elizabethan messenger on a moped, comes up the drive and drives in through the front door.

SUPERIMPOSED CAPTION: 'ERIZABETH L'

Cut to a long corridor. The messenger appears mopeding along the corridor very fast. He leaps off the moped and hands it to a guard at a door. The guard places the moped on a rack and the messenger enters the door going past three trumpeters who play a fanfare. He approaches a clerical figure, who stands at yet another door.

SUPERIMPOSED CAPTIONS:

'EPISODE THREE'

'THE ALMALDA'

Messenger (MICHAEL) I bling a dispatch flora Prymouth.

Clerk (ERIC) Flom Prymouth?

Messenger Flom Sil Flancis Dlake.

Clerk Entel and apploach the thlone.

The doors open. The messenger leaps on another moped and rides up to the throne on which sits Elizabeth surrounded by her courtiers, all of who are on motorized bicycles.

Queen (GRAHAM) What news flom Prymouth?

Messenger Dlake has sighted the Spanish Freet, youl Majesty.

Queen So! Phirip's garreons ale hele. How many?

Messenger One hundled and thilty-six men of wal.

Leicester (ERIC) Broody herr.

Queen Is Dlake plepaled?

Messenger He has oldeled the whore freet into the Blitish Channer.

Queen So, we must to Tirbuly. Reicestel! Sil Wartel Lareigh! Groucester! We sharr lide to ...

Enter Japanese director.

Japanese (TERRY J) Groucestel! Groucestel! Not Groucester. Come on, ret's get this light. Reicestel!

Leicester Yes.

Japanese That was telliber.

Leicester What?

Japanese Telliber.

Leicester Oh! Solly.

Japanese When you have a rine, ling your berr.

Leicester Ling my berr?

Japanese *(linging his berr for him)* Ling ling. Rike this. And cut the broody herr. Erizabeth!

Queen *(cheesed off)* Yes?

Japanese You should be on a bicycer.

Queen Why?!

Japanese You rook odd rike that.

Queen I do not look odd like this – it's that lot that looks odd. It's bleeding weird having half the Tudor nobility ligging around on motorized bicycles.

Japanese It's vely sullearist.

Queen Horsefeathers!

Leicester Listen mate. I'm beginning to have my doubts about you.

Japanese What do you mean?

Leicester I'm telling you straight, mate. I don't think you're Luchino Visconti at all.

Japanese Of course I am. Me vely impoltant Italian firm dilectol.

Queen You are a Nip.

Japanese Lubbish! Me genuine wop. *(sings)* Alliveldelchi Loma . . .

Leicester He's bluffing.

Japanese *(sings)* Vo-oorale . . . Ooh . . . Is that the time, I must fry.

The door opens. Inspector Leopard runs through the door followed by a copper.

Inspector (JOHN) Not so fast, Yakomoto. *(trumpeters play a fanfare)* Shut up! *(fanfare stops)* Allow me to introduce myself. I am Inspector Leopard of Scotland Yard, Special Fraud Film Director Squad.

Court Leopard of the Yard!

Inspector The same. Only more violent. *(he demonstrates this by kneeing the copper in the balls)* Right, Slit Eyes Yakomoto, I'm arresting you for the impersonation of Signor Luchino Visconti, famous Italian director of such movie classics as 'Ossessione' (1942), 'La Terra Trema' (1948), and 'Bellissima' (1951) – a satisfying ironic slice-of-life drama. 1957 brought to the silver screen his 'I Bianche Notte' adapted by Dostoyevsky, a mannered and romantic melancholy of snow and mist and moonlit encounters on canal bridges. 'Boccaccio 70' followed five years later and the following year saw 'The Leopard'! So impressed was I with this motion picture treatment of the Risorgimento that I went along to Somerset House and changed me own name to

Leopard, preferring it to me original handle, 'Panther' (Aargh). I digress. 1969 saw 'The Damned', a Gotterdammerung epic of political and industrial shennanigans in good old Nazi Germany, starring Helmut Berger as a stinking transvestite what should have his face sawn off, the curvaceous Charlotte Rampling as a bit of tail, and the impeccable Dirk Bogarde as Von Essen. The association of the latter with Signor Visconti fructified with Dirk's magnificent portrayal of the elderly pouf what expires in Venice. And so, Yakomoto . . . blimey, he gone! Never mind. I'll have you instead. *(grabs the queen)*

Queen What?

Inspector I haven't got time to go chasing after him, there's violence to be done.

ANIMATION: *sketch about violence.*

Cut to a kitchen. A man and woman listening to a radio.

Radio Voice I would like to ask the team what they would do if they were Hitler.

Man's Voice Gerald?

Another Voice Well I'd annex the Sudetenland and sign a non-aggression pact with Russia.

First Man's Voice Norman?

Norman's Voice Well I'd do the Reichstag bathroom in purples and golds and ban abortion on demand.

Woman (TERRY J) *(switching the radio off)* Liberal rubbish. Klaus . . . what do you want with your jugged fish?

Man (ERIC) Halibut.

Woman The jugged fish *is* halibut.

Man What fish have you got that isn't jugged, then?

Woman Rabbit.

Man What? Rabbit fish?

Woman Yes. It's got fins.

Man Is it dead?

Woman Well, it was coughing up blood last night.

Man All right I'll have the dead unjugged rabbit fish.

CAPTION: 'ONE DEAD UNJUGGED RABBIT FISH LATER'

Man Well that was really horrible.

Woman You're always complaining.

Man What's for afters?

Woman Well there's rat cake . . . rat sorbet . . . rat pudding . . . or strawberry tart.

Man Strawberry tart?!

Woman Well it's got *some* rat in it.

Man How much?
Woman Three (rather a lot really).
Man ... well, I'll have a slice without so much rat in it.
 CAPTION: 'ONE SLICE OF STRAWBERRY TART WITHOUT SO MUCH RAT IN IT LATER'
Man Appalling.
Woman Moan, moan, moan.
 Enter their son.
Son (GRAHAM) Hello, Mum, hello, Dad.
Man Hello, son.
Son There's a dead bishop on the landing.
Woman Where did that come from?
Son What do you mean?
Woman What's its diocese?
Son Well it looked a bit Bath and Wellsish to me.
Man I'll go and have a look. *(goes out)*
Woman I don't know who keeps bringing them in here.
Son Well it's not me.
Woman I've put three out by the bin and the dustmen won't touch 'em.
Man *(coming back)* Leicester.
Woman How do you know?
Man Tattooed on the back of his neck. I'm going to call the police.
Woman Shouldn't you call the Church?
Son Call the Church police.
Man ... all right. *(shouts)* The Church police!
 Enter two policemen with ecclesiastical accoutrements.
Church Policeman (MICHAEL) Yus?
Woman There's another dead bishop on the landing.
Church Policeman Suffragan or diocesan?
Woman How should I know?
Church Policeman It's tattooed on the back of their necks. 'ere! Is that rat tart?
Woman Yes.
Church Policeman Disgusting. Right! The hunt is on. *(kneels)* Oh Lord we beseech thee tell us who croaked Leicester.
 Organ music. A huge hand descends and points at the man.
Man All right, it's a fair cop, but society is to blame.
Church Policeman Agreed.
Man I would like the three by the bin to be taken into consideration.

Church Policeman Right. And now, I'd like to conclude this arrest with a hymn.

All *(singing)* And did those feet in ancient times walk upon England's mountains green. *(policemen escort the man out)* And was the holy lamb of God on England's pleasant pastures seen.

ANIMATION: *bouncing Queen Victoria.*

Voice Over Meanwhile in the jungle next door.

A steamy tropical jungle. A native guide leads four explorers in pith helmets and old-fashioned long shorts through the jungle. Cicada sounds and shrieks of predatory jungle birds. Intercut close-ups of perspiring foreheads etc. The native guide keeps beckoning them to hurry. The jungle appears to get thicker: they have to push their way through the undergrowth. Finally the guide stops and points, with eyes staring. The four explorers cluster round and look over his shoulder. A neat clearing in the thick of the jungle. Tables set as in a London bistro with check cloths and big wooden pepper mills, candles and menus standing on each table. Sitting at the tables are six other explorers in pith helmets etc., eating and chatting. Clink of coffee cups.

First Explorer (JOHN) What a simply super little place!

Second Explorer (ERIC) Yes, they've done wonders with it. You know this used to be one of the most swampy disease-infested areas of the whole jungle, and they've turned it into this smashing little restaurant. *(across the restaurant the head waiter appears, dressed in black tie and tails just a bit too big for him; he beckons them to a table)* Here you are Omkami, thank you. Hello, Mr Akwekwe.

Akwekwe (MICHAEL) Hello, Mr Spare-Buttons-Supplied-With-The-Shirt. Nice to see you again.

Second Explorer These are some of my fellow explorers: Sir Charles Farquarson, Brian Bailey, Betty Bailey and this is Mr Akwekwe, who started the whole place.

Third Explorer (GRAHAM) It really is super.

Fourth Explorer (CAROL) *(who is dressed as a man and has a moustache)* Terrific idea.

Akwekwe May I recommend the alligator purées.

Suddenly there is a hideous scream. We see a gorilla tear a man from his table at the back of the restaurant, in front of a tree and drag him back into the jungle. Awful shrieks are heard. Akwekwe runs into the jungle shouting. Terrible sounds of the unseen fight. Thrashing about of bushes in the distance. A shot rings out. Then silence also rings out. Akwekwe emerges, dragging the inert body of the cash customer whom he puts back in his chair. He slumps forward. Akwekwe comes back to the table in the foreground which has remained in the foreground throughout this preceding shot, with cut ins of the four explorers looking through the menu. Akwekwe has a bloodstained claw mark right across his face and chest and his dicky is torn and bloodstained.

Akwekwe Now then, have you decided?

He produces a notepad such as waiters always carry.

Second Explorer Ye-es... Well there's two avocado vinaigrette here and what are you going to have Brian?

Fourth Explorer Er quiche Lorraine for me, please.

Akwekwe Right, so that's two avocado, one quiche...

Cut to close up of pigmy's evil face parting leaves and firing a blow-pipe. Cut to another table where two explorers are having coffee and cigars. One of them stiffens and then slumps forward. Cut to Akwekwe at the main table registering what has happened. We pan with him as he rushes over to the bushes. Sound of pigmies retreating into the bushes. Akwekwe shouts after him. We pan with Akwekwe as he walks over to the table where the customer has slumped forward. He pulls him up, looks at dart sticking out of his chest, tut tuts with annoyance and lets him slump back on to the table again. He returns to the main table.

Akwekwe So, that's two avocado, one quiche...

Third Explorer And a soup of the day.

Akwekwe Right. *(sinister sound of jungle drums in distance; close up of look of fear in Akwekwe's eyes)* And to follow?

Second Explorer Two chicken à la Reine, with sauce provençale.

First Explorer And one scampi desirée.

Third Explorer And boeuf bourguignon with a green salad.

Jungle drums getting louder. Akwekwe shouts off towards the back of the clearing where we assume the kitchens must be.

Akwekwe Right on. Two chicken! One scampi! One boeuf with green salad!

He casts yet another fearful glance in the direction of the ever-increasing drum beats.

Akwekwe There may be... a little delay.

Second Explorer That's fine but we have to be out by three.

Akwekwe Yes, sir. Yes, we'll try.

The drum beats get louder. Shot of forest, rustling of bushes. Close-up of Akwekwe's eyes. Another shot of forest. Drum beats louder. More rustling. Close up of Akwekwe's eyes and sweating forehead. Forest again and more noise. Close up of Akwekwe; he now has blood on his face, his eyes dilate with fear, the drum beats become deafening. Sudden cut to BBC world symbol.

Voice Over (ERIC) The BBC would like to announce that the next scene is not considered suitable for family viewing. It contains scenes of violence, involving people's heads and arms getting chopped off, their ears nailed to trees, and their toenails pulled out in slow motion. There are also scenes of naked women with floppy breasts, and also at one point you can see a pair of buttocks and there's another bit where I'll swear you can see everything, but my friend says it's just the way he's holding the spear. *(pulling himself together)* Because of the unsuitability of the scene, the BBC will be replacing it with a scene from a repeat of 'Gardening Club' for 1958.

A beautiful well-stocked garden bed. 'Gardening Club' music. After two seconds there are shrieks of licentious and lustful laughter. A nude woman pursues a city gent, both screaming with pleasure, into the middle of the flowerbed and they roll around smashing up the flowers in unbridled erotic orgy. Immediately two nuns run in to join the fun, followed by two Vikings, a Gumby, a pantomime goose, etc. The whole of this orgy is speeded up.

CAPTION: 'KEN RUSSELL'S GARDENING CLUB (1958)'

Voice Over And now back to the story.

Cut to the edge of the jungle. Emerging from the dense undergrowth are two pigmy warriors pulling the four explorers who are roped together. The pigmies carry spears. We lose the pigmies and hold just the explorers in frame, and track with them.

Third Explorer That was a nasty business back at the restaurant.

First Explorer Yes, I thought most places took Barclaycard nowadays.

Second Explorer Where do you think they're taking us, Brian?

Fourth Explorer God knows!

Third Explorer *(pointing, eyes wide with amazement)* Look!

Cut to a stock shot of a volcano. Thrilling chord. Cut back to explorers.

Second Explorer *(filled with awe)* The sacred volcano Andu! Which no man has seen before.

Third Explorer No, no, no, next to that.

Cut to stock shot of collection of big chimneys in a brickworks. Another thrilling chord. Cut back to explorers.

First Explorer The London Brick Company?

Third Explorer No, no, no, no – *next* to that.

Cut to stock shot of plateau of Roiurama. Yet another thrilling chord. Cut back to explorers.

First Explorer The forbidden plateau of Roiurama, the Lost World, thrown up by mighty earth movements thousands of millions of years ago, where strange primeval creatures defying evolution, lurk in the dark, impenetrable forests, cut off forever from the outside world.

Second Explorer I still can't see it.

Fourth Explorer You don't think that's where they're taking us?

Third Explorer Yes, and God knows what we'll find there.

A pigmy native rushes up from behind them, holding a script.

Native (MICHAEL) What page please?

Second Explorer What?

Native *(with a trace of irritation)* What page in the script?

Second Explorer *(whispered)* Page 7.

Native *(he speaks the lines over to himself)* 'Come on, you dogs, we have far to go. We must lose no time'. *(tries with eyes shut)* 'Come on, you dogs, we have far to go. We must lose no time'. 'Come on you dogs'. *(throws away the script, starts to push them roughly)* Come on you dogs, we have time to lose, this has gone too far.

Stock film of Houses of Parliament from across the Thames.

Voice Over (GRAHAM) Meanwhile back in London ... at the British Explorers' Club in the Mall ...

Cut to the leather-armchaired hallway of a London club. In four of the chairs sit men in polar explorers' kit – furs, iced-over goggles, etc. – reading newspapers. At one chair sits a man in Norfolk jacket and plus fours. Around his neck he wears a sign saying 'Our Hero'. He is reading a newspaper but obviously has something else on his mind. Suddenly he throws the paper down and gets up. He walks over to the porter's desk. As he does this a polar expedition with four huskies, a sled, and two explorers pass him. Our Hero goes up to the desk. A whiskery old porter stands behind it.

Our Hero (TERRY J) Any news of Betty Bailey's expedition, Hargreaves?

Hargreaves (MICHAEL) Er ... um ... er ...

Our Hero *(through clenched teeth)* Page 9 ...

Hargreaves *(thumbing ower page of script beneath counter)* 'The Lost World of Roiurama'.

Our Hero That's my line.

Hargreaves Oh, sorry. 'Where were they going, sir'?

Our Hero The Lost World of Roiurama.

Hargreaves Yes sir, we've got a telegram.

Our Hero Oh!

Hargreaves *(reads it)* Reads it. Expedition superb. Weather excellent. Everything wonderful.

Our Hero I wonder what's gone wrong.

Hargreaves For God's sake be careful ...

Our Hero *(irritably)* Wait a minute ... I'm going to go ... after them.

Hargreaves For God's sake be careful, sir.

Cut to film of the lost world. Tropical South American vegetation. Our four explorers limp along exhaustedly.

Second Explorer My God, Betty, we're done for ...

Third Explorer We'll never get out of here ... we're completely lost, lost. Even the natives have gone.

First Explorer Goodbye Betty, Goodbye Farquarson. Goodbye Brian. It's been a great expedition ...

Music. Cut to engraving of Crystal Palace.

SUPERIMPOSED CAPTION: 'CRYSTAL PALACE 1851'
Cut immediately back to jungle.
First Explorer Great *expedition* . . .
Third Explorer All that'll be left of us will be a map, a compass and a few feet of film, recording our last moments . . .
First Explorer Wait a moment!
Fourth Explorer What is it?
First Explorer If we're on film, there must be someone filming us.
Second Explorer My God, Betty, you're right!
They all look around, then gradually all notice the camera. They break out in smiles of relief, come towards the camera and greet the camera crew.
Third Explorer Look! Great to see you!
First Explorer What a stroke of luck!
Camera Crew Hello! . . .
First Explorer Wait a minute!
Fourth Explorer What is it again?
First Explorer If this is the crew who *were* filming us . . . who's filming us now? Look!
Cut to another shot which includes the first camera crew and yet another camera crew with all their equipment. The director is dressed the same as Yakomoto, the director in 'Erizabeth L' only he is blacked up.
Director (TERRY J) *(African accent)* Cut there man! No! No good! How we going to get feeling of personal alienation of self from society with this load of Bulldog Drummond crap? When I was doing 'La Notte' wi' dat Monica Vitti gal she don't gimme none of this empire building shit, man . . .
Camera pans slightly to reveal a door in jungle. It opens and an inspector enters.
Inspector (ERIC) Not so fast, Akarumba! Allow me to introduce myself. I'm Inspector Baboon of Scotland Yard's Special Fraud Film Director Squad, Jungle Division.
Fourth Explorer Baboon of the Yard!
Inspector Shut up! *(shoots her)* Right, Akarumba! I'm arresting you for impersonating Signor Michelangelo Antonioni, an Italian film director who co-scripts all his own films, largely jettisoning narrative in favour of vague incident and relentless character study . . . *(during this harangue the credits start to roll, music very faint beneath his words)* . . . In his first film: 'Cronaca Di Un Amore' (1950), the couple are brought together by a shared irrational guilt. 'L'Amico' followed in 1955, and 1959 saw the first of Antonioni's world-famous trilogy, 'L'Avventura' – an acute study of boredom, restlessness and the futilities and agonies of purposeless living. In 'L'Eclisse', three years

later, this analysis of sentiments is taken up once again. 'We do not have to know each other to love', says the heroine, 'and perhaps we do not have to love . . .' The 'Eclipse' of the emotions finally casts its shadow when darkness descends on a street corner. *(the credits end; voice and picture start to fade)* . . . Signor Antonioni first makes use of colour to underline . . .

Fade to black and cut to BBC world symbol.

Continuity Voice (ERIC) And now on BBC 1 another six minutes of Monty Python's Flying Circus.

A reception desk in a sort of office building.

Receptionist (RITA DAVIES) Yes, sir?

Man I'd like to have an argument please.

Receptionist Certainly sir, have you been here before . . . ?

Man No, this is my first time.

Receptionist I see. Do you want to have the full argument, or were you thinking of taking a course?

Man Well, what would be the cost?

Receptionist Yes, it's one pound for a five-minute argument, but only eight pounds for a course of ten.

Man Well, I think it's probably best if I start with the one and see how it goes from there. OK?

Receptionist Fine. I'll see who's free at the moment . . . Mr Du-Bakey's free, but he's a little bit conciliatory . . . Yes, try Mr Barnard – Room 12.

Man Thank you.

The man walks down a corridor. He opens door 12. There is a man at a desk.

Mr Barnard (GRAHAM) *(shouting)* What do you want?

Man Well I was told outside . . .

Mr Barnard Don't give me that you snotty-faced heap of parrot droppings!

Man What!

Mr Barnard Shut your festering gob you tit! Your type makes me puke! You vacuous toffee-nosed malodorous pervert!!

Man Look! I came in here for an argument.

Mr Barnard *(calmly)* Oh! I'm sorry, this is abuse.

Man Oh I see, that explains it.

Mr Barnard No, you want room 12A next door.

Man I see – sorry. *(exits)*

Mr Barnard Not at all. *(as he goes)* Stupid git.

Outside 12A. The man knocks on the door.

Mr Vibrating (JOHN) *(from within)* Come in.

The man enters the room. Mr Vibrating is sitting at a desk.

Man Is this the right room for an argument?
Mr Vibrating I've told you *once*.
Man No you haven't.
Mr Vibrating Yes I have.
Man When?
Mr Vibrating Just now!
Man No you didn't.
Mr Vibrating Yes I did!
Man Didn't.
Mr Vibrating Did.
Man Didn't.
Mr Vibrating I'm telling you I did!
Man You did not!
Mr Vibrating I'm sorry, is this a five-minute argument, or the full half-hour?
Man Oh . . . Just a five-minute one.
Mr Vibrating Fine *(makes a note of it; the man sits down)* thank you. Anyway I did.
Man You most certainly did not.
Mr Vibrating Now, let's get one thing *quite* clear. I most definitely told you!
Man You did not.
Mr Vibrating Yes I did.
Man You did not.
Mr Vibrating Yes I did.
Man Didn't.
Mr Vibrating Yes I did.
Man Didn't.
Mr Vibrating Yes I did!!
Man Look this isn't an argument.
Mr Vibrating Yes it is.
Man No it isn't, it's just contradiction.
Mr Vibrating No it isn't.
Man Yes it is.
Mr Vibrating It is not.
Man It is. You just contradicted me.
Mr Vibrating No I didn't.
Man Ooh, you did!
Mr Vibrating No, no, no, no, no.
Man You did, just then.
Mr Vibrating No, nonsense!

Man Oh, look this is futile.
Mr Vibrating No it isn't.
Man I came here for a good argument.
Mr Vibrating No you didn't, you came here for an *argument*.
Man Well, an argument's not the same as contradiction.
Mr Vibrating It can be.
Man No it can't. An argument is a connected series of statements to establish a definite proposition.
Mr Vibrating No it isn't.
Man Yes it is. It isn't just contradiction.
Mr Vibrating Look, if I argue with you I must take up a contrary position.
Man But it isn't just saying 'No it isn't'.
Mr Vibrating Yes it is.
Man No it isn't, argument is an intellectual process . . . contradiction is just the automatic gainsaying of anything the other person says.
Mr Vibrating No it isn't.
Man Yes it is.
Mr Vibrating Not at all.
Man Now look!
Mr Vibrating *(pressing the bell on his desk)* Thank you, good morning.
Man What?
Mr Vibrating That's it. Good morning.
Man But I was just getting interested.
Mr Vibrating Sorry the five minutes is up.
Man That was never five minutes just now!
Mr Vibrating I'm afraid it was.
Man No it wasn't.
Mr Vibrating I'm sorry, I'm not allowed to argue any more.
Man What!?
Mr Vibrating If you want me to go on arguing you'll have to pay for another five minutes.
Man But that was never five minutes just now . . . oh come on! *(Vibrating looks round as though man was not there)* This is ridiculous.
Mr Vibrating I'm very sorry, but I told you I'm not allowed to argue unless you've paid.
Man Oh. All right. *(pays)* There you are.
Mr Vibrating Thank you.
Man Well?
Mr Vibrating Well what?

Man That was never five minutes just now.
Mr Vibrating I told you I'm not allowed to argue unless you've paid.
Man I've just paid.
Mr Vibrating No you didn't.
Man I did! I did! I did!
Mr Vibrating No you didn't.
Man Look I don't want to argue about that.
Mr Vibrating Well I'm very sorry but you didn't pay.
Man Aha! Well if I didn't pay, why are you arguing... got you!
Mr Vibrating No you haven't.
Man Yes I have... if you're arguing I must have paid.
Mr Vibrating Not necessarily. I could be arguing in my spare time.
Man I've had enough of this.
Mr Vibrating No you haven't.
Man Oh shut up! *(he leaves and sees a door marked complaints; he goes in)* I want to complain.
Man in Charge (ERIC) *You* want to complain... look at these shoes... I've only had them three weeks and the heels are worn right through.
Man No, I want to complain about...
Man in Charge If you complain nothing happens... you might just as well not bother. My back hurts and... *(the man exits, walks down the corridor and enters a room)*
Man I want to complain. *('Spreaders' who is just inside door hits man on the head with a mallet)* Ooh!
Spreaders (TERRY J) No, no, no, hold your head like this, and then go 'waaagh'! Try it again. *(he hits him again)*
Man Waaghh!
Spreaders Better. Better. But 'waaaaagh'! 'Waaaagh'! Hold your hands here...
Man No!
Spreaders Now. *(hits him)*
Man Waagh!
Spreaders That's it. That's it. Good.
Man Stop hitting me!
Spreader What?
Man Stop hitting me.
Spreaders Stop hitting you?
Man Yes.
Spreaders What did you come in here for then?
Man I came here to complain.

Spreaders Oh I'm sorry, that's next door. It's being hit on the head lessons in here.
Man What a stupid concept.
Detective Inspector Fox enters.
Fox (GRAHAM) Right. Hold it there.
Man and Spreaders What?
Fox Allow me to introduce myself. I'm Inspector Fox of the Light Entertainment Police, Comedy Division, Special Flying Squad.
Man and Spreaders Flying Fox of the Yard.
Fox Shut up! *(he hits the man with a truncheon)*
Man Ooooh!
Spreaders No, no, no – Waagh!
Fox And you. *(he hits Spreaders)*
Spreaders Waagh!
Fox He's good! You could learn a thing or two from him. Right now you two me old beauties, you are nicked.
Man What for?
Fox I'm charging you two under Section 21 of the Strange Sketch Act.
Man The what?
Fox You are hereby charged that you did wilfully take part in a strange sketch, that is, a skit, spoof or humorous vignette of an unconventional nature with intent to cause grievous mental confusion to the Great British Public. *(to camera)* Evening all.
Spreaders It's a fair cop.
Fox And you tosh. *(hits the man)*
Man WAAAGH!
Fox That's excellent! Right, come on down the Yard.
Another inspector arrives.
Inspector (ERIC) Hold it. Hold it. Allow me to introduce myself. I'm Inspector Thompson's Gazelle of the Programme Planning Police, Light Entertainment Division, Special Flying Squad.
Fox Flying Thompson's Gazelle of the Yard!
Inspector Shut up! *(he hits him)*
Fox Waaaagh!
Spreaders He's good.
Inspector Shut up! *(hits Spreaders)*
Spreaders WAAGH!
Man Rotten. *(he gets hit)* WAAAGH!
Inspector Good. Now I'm arrestin' this entire show on three counts: one, acts of self-conscious behaviour contrary to the 'Not in front of the

children' Act, two, always saying 'It's so and so of the Yard' every time the fuzz arrives and, three, and this is the cruncher, offences against the 'Getting out of sketches without using a proper punchline' Act, four, namely, simply ending every bleedin' sketch by just having a policeman come in and . . . wait a minute.

Another policeman enters.

Policeman (JOHN) Hold it. *(puts his hand on Inspector Thompson's Gazelle's shoulder)*

Inspector It's a fair cop.

A large hairy hand appears through the door and claps him on the shoulder.

CAPTION: 'THE END'

Cut to BBC world symbol.

Announcer's Voice (ERIC) And now on BBC 1, one more minute of Monty Python's Flying Circus.

Thirty

Stock colour film of vivid explosive action for fifteen seconds: dog fight RAF style; trains crashing; Spanish hotel blowing up; car crashing and exploding; train on collapsing bridge; volcano erupting; Torrey Canyon burning; forest fire blazing. From this we zoom the following words individually:
CAPTION: 'BLOOD, DEATH, WAR, HORROR'
Cut to an interviewer in a rather dinky little set. On the wall there is a rather prettily done sign, not too big, saying 'Blood, Devastation, Death, War and Horror', as if it were a show's title.

Interviewer (MICHAEL) Hello, good evening and welcome to another edition of 'Blood, Devastation, Death, War and Horror', and later on we'll be talking to a man who *does* gardening. But our first guest in the studio tonight is a man who talks entirely in anagrams.

Man (ERIC) Taht si crreoct.

Interviewer Do you enjoy this?

Man I stom certainly od. Revy chum so.

Interviewer And what's your name?

Man Hamrag, Hamrag Yatlerot.

Interviewer Well, Graham, nice to have you on the show. Now where do you come from?

Man Bumcreland.

Interviewer Cumberland?

Man Staht sit sepreicly.

Interviewer And I believe you're working on an anagram version of Shakespeare...

Man Sey sey, taht si crreoct, er. Ta the mnemot I'm wroking on 'The Mating of the Wersh'.

Interviewer 'The Mating of the Wersh'. By William Shakespeare?

Man Nay, by Malliwi Rapesheake.

Interviewer And er, what else?

Man 'Two Netlemeg of Verona', 'Twelfth Thing', 'The Chamrent of Venice'...

Interviewer Have you done 'Hamlet'?

Man 'Thamle'. 'Be ot or bot ne ot, tath is the nestquie'.

Interviewer And what is your next project?

Man 'Ring Kichard the Thrid'.

Interviewer I'm sorry?

Man 'A shroe! A shroe! My dingkome for a shroe!'

Interviewer Ah, Ring Kichard, yes . . . but surely that's not an anagram, that's a spoonerism.

Man If you're going to split hairs I'm going to piss off. *(he leaves)*

Cut to the naked organist (Terry J), then to the announcer.

Announcer (JOHN) And now . . .

It's Man (MICHAEL) It's . . .

Animated titles, title given as:

Voice Over (JOHN) Tony M. Nyphot's Flying Risccu.

CAPTION: 'CHAMRAN KNEBT'

Pull out a little. The board has little green curtains and there is a Pepperpot standing in front of it.

Presenter (JOHN) Mrs Scab, you have twelve hours to beat the clock.

A gong goes. A superimposed clock starts to move incredibly fast. It has a minute hand and an hour hand. Twelve hours pass very quickly. The Pepperpot starts to rearrange the letters, very quickly. She gets it right. It reads: 'merchant bank'. The gong goes, and the clock stops.

Presenter Correct!

Pepperpot I've done it. I've done it. Ha, ha, ha!

An enormous head of a large cartoon-type hammer hits her and she goes down very fast.

Cut to a city gent in his office. A sign on his desk says a 'Chamran Knebter'. He is waiting to answer his phone. It rings; he answers.

City Gent (JOHN) Hello? Ah, Mr Victim, I'm glad to say that I've got the go-ahead to lend you the money you require. Yes, of course we will want as security the deeds of your house, of your aunt's house, of your second cousin's house, of your wife's parents' house, and of your grannie's bungalow, and we will in addition need a controlling interest in your new company, unrestricted access to your private bank account, the deposit in our vaults of your three children as hostages and a full legal indemnity against any acts of embezzlement carried out against you by any members of our staff during the normal course of their duties . . . no, I'm afraid we couldn't accept your dog instead of your youngest child, we would like to suggest a brand new scheme of ours under which 51 % of both your dog and your wife pass to us in the event of your suffering a serious accident. Fine. No, not at all, nice to do business with you. *(puts the phone down, speaks on intercom)* Miss Godfrey, could you send in Mr Ford please. *(to himself)* Now where's that dictionary – ah yes – here we are, inner life . . . inner life . . . *(a knock on the door)* Come in. *(Mr Ford enters, he is collecting for charity with a tin)* Ah, Mr Ford isn't it?

Mr Ford (TERRY J) That's right.

City Gent How do you do. I'm a merchant banker.

Mr Ford How do you do Mr . . .

City Gent Er... I forget my name for the moment but I *am* a merchant banker.

Mr Ford Oh. I wondered whether you'd like to contribute to the orphan's home. *(he rattles the tin)*

City Gent Well I don't want to show my hand too early, but actually here at Slater Nazi we are quite keen to get into orphans, you know, developing market and all that... what sort of sum did you have in mind?

Mr Ford Well... er... you're a rich man.

City Gent Yes, I am. Yes. Yes, very very rich. Quite phenomenally wealthy. Yes, I do own the most startling quantities of cash. Yes, quite right... you're rather a smart young lad aren't you. We could do with somebody like you to feed the pantomime horse. Very smart.

Mr Ford Thank you, sir.

City Gent Now, you were saying. I'm very, very, very, very, very, very, very, very, very, very, very rich.

Mr Ford So er, how about a pound?

City Gent A pound. Yes, I see. Now this loan would be secured by the...

Mr Ford It's not a *loan*, sir.

City Gent What?

Mr Ford It's not a loan.

City Gent Ah.

Mr Ford You get one of these, sir. *(he gives him a flag)*

City Gent It's a bit small for a share certificate isn't it? Look, I think I'd better run this over to our legal department. If you could possibly pop back on Friday.

Mr Ford Well do you have to do that, couldn't you just give me the pound?

City Gent Yes, but you see I don't know what it's *for*.

Mr Ford It's for the orphans.

City Gent Yes?

Mr Ford It's a gift.

City Gent A what?

Mr Ford A gift?

City Gent Oh a *gift*!

Mr Ford Yes.

City Gent A tax dodge.

Mr Ford No, no, no, no.

City Gent No? Well, I'm awfully sorry I don't understand. Can you just explain exactly what you want.

Mr Ford Well, I want you to give me a pound, and then I go away and give it to the orphans.

City Gent Yes?

Mr Ford Well, that's it.

City Gent No, no, no, I don't follow this at all, I mean, I don't want to seem stupid but it looks to me as though I'm a pound down on the whole deal.

Mr Ford Well, yes you are.

City Gent I am! Well, what is my incentive to give you the pound?

Mr Ford Well the incentive is – to make the orphans happy.

City Gent *(genuinely puzzled)* Happy? . . . You quite sure you've got this right?

Mr Ford Yes, lots of people give me money.

City Gent What, just like that?

Mr Ford Yes.

City Gent Must be sick. I don't suppose you could give me a list of their names and addresses could you?

Mr Ford No, I just go up to them in the street and ask.

City Gent Good lord! That's the most exciting new idea I've heard in years! It's so simple it's brilliant! Well, if that idea of yours isn't worth a pound I'd like to know what is. *(he takes the tin from Ford)*

Mr Ford Oh, thank you, sir.

City Gent The only trouble is, you gave me the idea before I'd given you the pound. And that's not good business.

Mr Ford Isn't it?

City Gent No, I'm afraid it isn't. So, um, off you go. *(he pulls a lever opening a trap door under Ford's feet and Ford falls through with a yelp)* Nice to do business with you.

Cut briefly to a Mongol.

Mongol (MICHAEL) Anyway.

Cut back to the banker.

City Gent And off we go again. *(he goes to the intercom)* Ah Miss Godfrey could you send in the pantomime horses please.

The door opens and two pantomime horses run in. Pantomime music.

They do a routine including running round the room and bumping into each other. They then stand in front of the city gent crossing their legs and putting their heads on one side.

City Gent Now I've asked you to . . . *(they repeat the routine)* Now I've asked you . . . *(they start again)* Shut up! *(they stop)* Now I've asked you in here to see me this morning because I'm afraid we're going to have to let one of you go. *(the pantomime horses heads go up, their ears waggle and their eyes go round)* I'm very sorry but the present rationalization of this firm makes it inevitable that we hive one of you off. *(water spurts out of their eyes in a stream)* Now you may think that this is very harsh behaviour but let me tell you that our management consultants actually queried the necessity for us to employ a pantomime horse at all. *(the horses register surprise and generally behave ostentatiously)* And so the decision has to be made which one of you is to go. Champion . . . how many years have you been with this firm? *(Champion stamps his foot three times)* Trigger? *(Trigger stamps his front foot twice and rear foot once)* I see. Well, it's a difficult decision. But in accordance with our traditional principles of free enterprise and healthy competition I'm going to ask the two of you to fight to the death for it. *(one of the horses runs up to him and puts his head by the city gent's ear)* No, I'm afraid there's no redundancy scheme.

The horses turn and start kicking each other on the shins. After a few blows:

Voice Over (JOHN) *(German accent)* In the hard and unrelenting world of nature the ceaseless struggle for survival continues. *(one of the pantomime horses turns tail and runs out)* This time one of the pantomime horses concedes defeat and so lives to fight another day. *(cut to stock film of sea lions fighting)* Here, in a colony of sea lions, we see a huge bull sea lion seeing off an intruding bull who is attempting to intrude on his harem. This pattern of aggressive behaviour is typical of these documentaries. *(cut to shot of two almost stationary limpets)* Here we see two limpets locked in a life or death struggle for territory. The huge bull limpet, enraged by the rock, endeavours to encircle its sprightly opponent. *(shot of wolf standing still)* Here we see an ant. This ant is engaged in a life or death struggle with the wolf. You can see the ant creeping up on the wolf on all sixes. *(a moving arrow is superimposed)* Now he stops to observe. Satisfied that the wolf has not heard him, he approaches nearer. With great skill he chooses his moment and then, quick as a limpet, with one mighty bound *(the arrow moves to the wolf's throat; the wolf does not move)* buries his fangs in the wolf's neck. The wolf struggles to no avail. A battle of this kind can take anything up to fifteen years because the timber ant has such a tiny mouth. *(distant shot of two men fighting violently)* Here we see Heinz Sielmann engaged in a life or death struggle with Peter Scott. They are engaged in a bitter punch-up over repeat fees on the overseas sales of their nature documentaries. *(another man joins in)* Now they have been joined by an enraged Jacques Cousteau. This is typical of the harsh and bitchy world of television features. *(shot of honey bear sitting about aimlessly)* Here we see a honey bear not engaged in a life or death struggle about anything. These honey bears are placid and peaceful creatures and consequently bad television. *(shot of pantomime horse running along in a wood)* Here we see a pantomime horse. It is engaged in a life or death struggle for a job with a merchant bank. However, his rival employee, the huge bull pantomime horse, is lying in wait for him. *(pantomime horse behind tree drops sixteen-ton weight on the horse* *running under the tree)* Poor pantomime horse. *(shot of pantomime goose behind a small tree with a bow and arrow)* Here we see a pantomime goose engaged in a life or death struggle with Terence Rattigan. *(we see Terence walking along)* The enraged goose fires. *(the goose fires and hits Terence in the neck; Terence looks amazed and dies)* Poor Terence. Another victim of this silly film. *(shot of an amazing-looking large woman with a crown waiting in the undergrowth by the side of a path)* Here we see an enraged pantomime Princess Margaret, she is lying in wait for her breakfast. *(a breakfast tray appears being pulled along the path by a length of wire)* The unsuspecting breakfast glides over closer to its doom. The enraged pantomime royal person is poised for the kill. She raises her harpoon and fires. *(the pantomime Princess Margaret does so, hurling the harpoon at the moving tray)* Pang! Right in the toast. A brief struggle and all is over. Poor breakfast! Another victim of the ... aargh!

ANIMATION: *which begins by showing the sudden demise of the previous voice over and continues with the story of a carnivorous house.*

CAPTION: 'THE MAKERS OF THIS FILM WOULD LIKE TO THANK THE FOLLOWING PEOPLE WHO GAVE US LOTS OF MONEY TO SEE THEIR NAMES IN LIGHTS: VICTOR – HIS FRIEND BOBBY – AND – MARY'

Pull back to show that 'Mary' is part of a sign saying: 'Mary Recruitment Office'. Pull out to reveal that it is a sign over a shop as for army recruiting office. An RSM with waxed moustache and snappy straight-against-the-forehead peaked cap comes out of the shop. He hangs a clearly printed sign on a nail on the door. It reads: 'Sketch just starting – actor wanted'.

Voice Over (JOHN) Sketch just starting, actor wanted.

The RSM looks up and down the road, glances up at the sign above his shop without noticing it. He goes inside again. A man walk up, reads the sign and enters. He is Mr Man.

Mr Man (ERIC) Good morning.

RSM (GRAHAM) Morning, sir.

Mr Man I'd like to join the army please.

RSM I see, sir. Short service or long service commission, sir?

Mr Man As long as possible please.

RSM Right well I'll just take a few particulars and then ...

Suddenly he looks as though a dim memory has penetrated his skull. He breaks off, looking thoughtful, walks towards the door and exits. He comes out of shop, looks up at word 'Mary' tuts and changes the letters round to read 'Army'. He suddenly looks round and we see a queue of nuns.

RSM Shove off! *(he goes back inside)* Then there'll be a few forms to sign, and of course we'll need references and then a full medical examination by the ...

Mr Man Yes. Yes, yes I see. *(diffidently)* I was just wondering whether it would be possible for me to join . . . the women's army?

RSM The Women's Royal Army Corps, sir?

Mr Man Yes. I was just thinking, you know, if it was possible for me to have my choice . . . I'd prefer to be in the Women's Royal Army Corps.

RSM Well, I'm afraid that the people that recruit here normally go straight into the Scots Guards.

Mr Man Which is all . . . men . . . I suppose?

RSM Yes it is.

Mr Man Yes. Are there any regiments which are more effeminate than others?

RSM Well, no sir. I mean, apart from the Marines, they're all dead butch.

Mr Man You see, what I really wanted was a regiment where I could be really quiet and have more time to myself to work with fabrics, and creating new concepts in interior design.

RSM Working with fabrics and experimenting with interior design!

Mr Man Yes.

RSM Oh well you want the Durham Light Infantry then, sir.

Mr Man Oh.

RSM Oh yes. That's the only regiment that's really doing something *new* with interior design, with colour, texture, line and that.

Mr Man I see.

RSM Oh yes, I mean their use of colour with fabrics is fantastic. I saw their pattern book the other day – beautiful, beautiful. Savage tans, great slabs of black, set against aggressive orange. It really makes you want to shout out, this is good! This is real!

Mr Man Really?

RSM Oh yes. I mean the Inniskillin Fusiliers and the Anglian Regiment are all right if you're interested in the art nouveau William Morris revival bit, but if you really want a regiment of the line that is really saying something about interior decor, then you've *got* to go for the Durham Light Infantry.

Mr Man Oh, I've had enough of this. I'm handing in my notice.

RSM What do you mean?

Mr Man Well I mean, when I applied for this job I thought I'd get a few decent lines but you end up doing the whole thing. I mean my last five speeches have been 'really, really – I see – I see' and 'really'. I wouldn't give those lines to a dog.

RSM All right, all right, all right, sonny. I'll tell you what. We'll do something different. I'll be a bus conductor, and you can be a really funny passenger on a bus.

Cut to a bus set. This is a very bad backcloth of the interior of the top deck of a bus. It looks like the set for a rather tatty revue. On the cut

> *Mr Man is standing in exactly the same place as he was – so that it looks as if the scene has changed around him. The RSM appears from one side. He is still dressed basically as an RSM but has a few bus conductor things such as a ticket machine, money satchel and a big arrow through his neck. He talks like a music-hall comedian.*

RSM Any more fares please? I've got a chauffeur and every time I go to the lavatory he drives me potty! Boom-boom! One in a row. *(sings)* I'm not unusual. I'm just . . .

Mr Man Fivepenny please.

RSM Five beautiful pennies going in to the bag . . . and you are the lucky winner of . . . one fivepenny ticket! *(hands him a ticket)* What's the Welshman doing under the bed? He's having a leak! Oh they're all in here tonight. *(brief film clip of audience laughing)*

Mr Man Look!

RSM I am looking – it's the only way I keep my eyelids apart! Boom-boom! Every one a Maserati!

Mr Man Look! You said I was going to be a funny passenger.

RSM *(snapping out of music-hall manner)* What do you mean?

Mr Man I mean, all I said was, fivepenny please. You can't call that a funny line.

RSM Well it's the way you said it.

Mr Man No it isn't. *Nobody* can say 'fivepenny please' and make it funny.

> *Cut to vox pop of city gent in a busy street.*

City Gent (TERRY J) Fivepenny please.

> *Cut to stock film of audience rolling about with laughter and clapping. Cut back to vox pop of city gent in street. He looks rather bewildered. He shrugs, turns and as he starts to walk away the camera pulls out. We see the city gent pass two colleagues.*

City Gent Morning.

> *They collapse laughing and roll about on the pavement. The city gent hurries on, and turns into the door of a big office block. Cut to the foyer. A hall porter is standing behind a counter.*

City Gent Not so warm today, George.

> *A shriek of mirth from the porter who collapses behind the counter. The city gent continues walking into the lift. There are two other city gents and one secretary already in the lift. The doors shut.*

Man's Voice Good morning.

Secretary's Voice Good morning.

City Gent's Voice Good morning.

> *Shrieks of laughter. Cut to the doors of the lift on the third floor. Lift doors open and the city gent steps out rather quickly looking embarrassed. Behind him he leaves the three collapsed with mirth on the floor. The lift doors shut and the lift goes down again. Cut to interior*

of boss's office. A knock on the door. The boss is standing with his back to the door desperately preparing himself to keep a straight face.

Boss (MICHAEL) Come in, Mr Horton.

The city gent enters.

City Gent Morning, sir.

Boss Do – do sit down. *(he indicates chair, trying not to look at the city gent as he does so)*

City Gent Thank you, sir.

The boss starts to snigger but suppresses it with feat of self-control.

Boss Now then Horton, you've been with us for twenty years, and your work in the accounts department has been immaculate. *(the city gent starts to speak; the boss suppresses another burst of laughter)* No no – please don't say anything. As I say, your work has been beyond reproach, but unfortunately the effect you have on your colleagues has undermined the competence *(almost starts laughing)* . . . has undermined the competence of this firm to such a point that I'm afraid that I've got no option but to sack you.

City Gent *(in a broken voice)* I'm sorry to hear that, sir. *(the boss giggles, gets up hastily and turning his back on city gent leans against the mantelpiece; his desire to laugh mounts through the next speech)* It couldn't have come at a worse time. There's school fees for the two boys coming up, and the wife's treatment costing more now . . . I don't know where the money's coming from as it is. And now I don't see any future . . . I'd been hoping I'd be able to hang on here just for the last couple of years but . . . now . . . I just want to go out and end it all.

The boss cannot control himself any longer. He collapses in helpless mirth, falling all over the room. Immediately we cut to stock film of terrific audience laughter.

Cut to backdrop of a circus ring. In front of it, as if in the ring, stand the RSM and Mr Man. Mr Man is as before. The RSM is dressed the same except that over his uniform he wears baggy trousers and braces and a funny nose. He is responding to the audience applause. Mr Man has obviously just been drenched with hot water – he is soaked and steam is rising.

RSM Thank you! Thank you! Thank you! Thank you and now for the fish – the fish down the trousers. *(the RSM picks up fish and puts it down Mr Man's trousers)* It's your laugh mate it's not mine. It's your trousers – not my trousers – it's your trousers – and now for the whitewash. *(the RSM pours a bucket of whitewash over him)* The whitewash over you – not over me. It's over you. You get the laugh. You get all the laughs. And now for the custard pie in the mush. *(more laughter, the RSM puts custard pie in his face and knees him in the balls)* It's not my mush – it's your mush. It's your laugh – it's your laugh mate – not mine. It's your bleeding laugh.

Cut to stock film of Mr Heath laughing followed by stock film of Women's Institute applauding.

CAPTION: 'THE BOLS STORY'

CAPTION: 'THE STORY OF HOLLAND'S MOST FAMOUS APERITIF'

Mr Orbiter-5 is sitting in a swivel chair facing camera in a TV presentation set. Behind him is a flat with enormous lettering which says 'Is the Queen sane?' Zoom in on Mr Orbiter-5. He starts talking immediately.

Mr Orbiter (MICHAEL) Good evening. Well tonight, we are going to talk about... well that is... *I* am going to talk about... well actually I *am* talking about it now... well I'm not talking about it *now*, but l am talking... I know I'm pausing occasionally, and not talking during the pauses, but the pauses are part of the whole process of talking... when one *talks* one has to *pause*... er... like then! I paused... but I was still talking... and again there! No the real point of what I'm saying is that when I appear *not* to be talking don't go nipping out to the kitchen, putting the kettle on... buttering scones... or getting crumbs and bits of food out of those round brown straw mats that the teapot goes on... because in all probability I'm *still* talking and what you heard was a pause er... like there again. Look! To make it absolutely easier, so there's no problem at all, what I'll do, I'll give you some kind of sign, like this *(makes a gesture)* while I'm *still* talking, and only pausing in between words... and when I've finished altogether I'll do this. *(he sits upright and folds his arms)* All right?

SUPERIMPOSED CAPTION: 'THE END'

Mr Orbiter No, no! No sorry – just demonstrating... haven't finished. Haven't started yet. *(the caption is removed; he sits and tries to gather his thoughts then suddenly remembers)* Oh dear. *(does the gesture hastily)* Nearly forgot the gesture. Hope none of you are nipping out into the kitchen, getting bits of food out of those round brown mats which the teapot... Good evening *(gesture)* Tonight I want to talk about...

Cut to the BBC world symbol.

Adrian (ERIC) *(voice over)* We interrupt this programme to annoy you and make things generally irritating for you.

Cut back to Mr Orbiter-5.

Mr Orbiter ... with a large piece of wet paper. *(gesture)* Turn the paper over – turn the paper over keeping your eye *on* the camel, and paste down the *edge* of the sailor's uniform, until the word 'Maudling' is almost totally obscured. *(gesture)* Well, that's one way of doing it. *(gesture)*

Cut to the BBC world symbol again and hold throughout the following dialogue.

Adrian *(voice over)* Good evening, we interrupt this programme again, a, to irritate you and, b, to provide work for one of our announcers.

Jack (JOHN) *(voice over)* Good evening, I'm the announcer who's just been given this job by the BBC and I'd just like to say how grateful I am *to* the BBC for providing me with work, particularly at this time of year, when things are a bit thin for us announcers... um... I don't know whether I should tell you this, but, well, I have been going through a rather tough time recently. Things have been pretty awful at home. My wife, Josephine... 'Joe-jums' as I call her... who is also an announcer...

Joe-jums (CAROL) Hello.

Jack ... has not been able to announce since our youngest, Clifford, was born, and, well, *(tearfully)* I've just got no confidence left... I can't get up in the morning... I feel there's nothing worth living for...
(he starts to sob)

Dick (MICHAEL) Hello, I'm another announcer, my name's Dick. Joe-jums just rang me and said Jack was having a bad time with this announcement, so I've just come to give him a hand. How is he, Joe-jums?

Joe-jums Pretty bad, Dick.

Dick Jack... it's Dick... Do you want me to make the announcement?

Jack No, no Dick. I must do it myself... *(emotionally)* it's my last chance with the BBC, I can't throw it away... I've got to do it... for Joe-jums... for the kids... I've got to go through with it...

Dick Good man. Now remember your announcer's training: deep breaths, and try not to think about what you're saying...

Jack Good evening. This *(a trace of superhuman effort in his voice)* is BBC 1...

Joe-jums Good luck, Jack.

Dick Keep going, old boy.

Jack It's... nine o'clock... and... time... for... the News... read by... Richard Baker...

Cut to start of the 'Nine O'Clock News'.

Joe-jums You've done it.

Dick Congratulations, old man!

Richard Baker is sitting at a desk. As Richard Baker speaks we hear no sounds apart from the sounds of celebration of the announcers – champagne corks popping, etc. At the beginning of the news Baker uses the gesture between sentences that we have seen Mr Orbiter-5 use, plus other gestures. Behind him on the screen a collage of photos appear one after the other: Richard Nixon, Tony Armstrong-Jones, the White House, Princess Margaret, parliament, naked breasts, a scrubbing brush, a man with a stoat through his head, Margaret Thatcher, a lavatory, a Scotsman lying on his back with his knees drawn up, a corkscrew, Edward Heath, a pair of false teeth in a glass. Whilst these have been going on Baker has been making gestures starting with elbow-up gesture and getting progressively more obscure and intriguing. We don't hear him at all, we hear all the announcers having a party and congratulating Jack.

Joe-jums Fantastic darling, you were brilliant. No, no, it was the best you ever did.

Jack Thank God.

Joe-jums It was absolutely super.

Dick ... have a drink. For God's sake drink this ...

Jack Fantastic.

Dick The least I could do – super – I must come over.

Jack I can't tell you how much that means. *(etc.)*

Eventually the voices stop and for the first time we hear Richard Baker's voice.

Baker ... until the name Maudling is almost totally obscured. That is the ned of the nicro-not wens. And now it's time for the late night flim.

James Bond style opening titles with pictures of a pantomime horse.

THE PANTOMIME HORSE IS A SECRET AGENT FILM.

WRITTEN BY TALBOT ROTHWELL AND MIREILLE MATHIEU.

BASED ON AN IDEA BY EDWARD VII.

DIRECTED BY QUEEN JULIANA OF THE NETHERLANDS.

PRODUCED BY SIR ALEC DOUGLAS-HOME AND KING HAAKON OF NORWAY.

A CORPSE-HAAKON PRODUCTION.

Cut to an idyllic scene – a boat drifting serenely on a river. A beautiful girl lies reclining in one end of the boat. A hoof appears round Carol's shoulders.

Girl (CAROL) Oh pantomime horse, that was wonderful.

Dobbin Would you like another glass?

Girl No, no, I mustn't. It makes me throw up ... oh, I'm so bleeding happy.

Dobbin Oh, Simone!

Girl Oh, pantomime horse.

Cut to Graham in loony get-up.

Loony Then ...

The pantomime horse spins round and fires his revolver towards some trees overhanging the water. Another pantomime horse falls out of the tree into the water. A third pantomime horse scurries out from behind a bush and runs off into the undergrowth. Dobbin leaps out of the boat. The girl jumps after him. A car drives out of some bushes on to the road and accelerates away. The pantomime horse is in it. Dobbin and the girl leap into their own expensive sports car and give chase. Shots of exciting chase. After two or three shots of the cars chasing, the two pantomime horses are seen on two tandems, continuing the chase. Cut to them chasing each other on horseback. Cut to them chasing each other on rickshaws. Cut to them chasing each other on foot.

Voice Over (JOHN) And now the English pantomime horse has very nearly caught up with the Russian pantomime horse, I think he's going to take him any moment now but what is this? What is this? *(round the corner are waiting a pantomime goose and a pantomime Princess Margaret; the Russian pantomime horse runs past them and they leap on the English pantomime horse and a fight starts)* Yes it's pantomime Princess Margaret and the pantomime goose and they're attacking the English pantomime horse and the Russian pantomime horse has got away. But who is this? *(a car draws up and Terence Rattigan and the Duke of Kent and the RSM run up and join in the fighting; the Russians are joined by Heinz Sielmann and Peter Scott and Jacques Cousteau)* My goodness me it's the Duke of Kent to the rescue ...

The fighting continues, behind, while the credits roll in front, reading as follows:

TONY M. NYPHOT'S FLYING RISCCU
SAW CODVENICE, TWITNER
DNA FORDEPERM YB
HAMRAG PACHMAN
JOHN ECLES
RICE LIED
TORN JERSEY (5.5)
MICHAEL LAPIN
MARTY RIGELLI
SOLA GAERAPPIN
CAROL CLEVELAND
ARCHSEER YB
SUZAN DAVIES
KAME PU
MADELAINE GAFFNEY
MUTESOCS
HAZEL PETHIG
MAINATIONS YB
TERRY GILLIAM
CUFFS LAVISEET
BERNARD WILKIE
PISHCARG
BOB BLAGDEN
MALE FANCIMARM
ALAN FEATHERSTONE
MOLE TRIFID
RAY MILLICHOPE
DOSUN
RICHARD CHUBB
LIGHTGIN
JIMMY PURDIE
REDENSIG
IAN WATSON
DECODURP YB
IAN MACNAUGHTON
B. B. LURCOO

Voice Over (JOHN) *(German accent)* Here you see some English comic actors engaged in a life or death struggle with a rather weak ending. This is typical of the zany madcap world of the irresistible kooky funsters. The English pantomime horse wins and so is assured of a place in British history and a steady job in a merchant bank. Unfortunately, before his pension rights are assured, he catches bronchitis and dies, another victim of the need to finish these shows on time.

Shot of pantomime horse in bed with his legs sticking in the air.

CAPTION: 'ETH NED'

Thirty-one The All-England Summarize Proust Competition

Nude man at the organ plays chords.
Announcer (JOHN) And now...
It's Man (MICHAEL) It's...
Animated titles.
Voice Over (JOHN) Monty Python's Flying Circuses...
The hall of the Memorial Baths, Swansea, done up for a gala occasion. There is a stage with flags, bunting and flowers. Echoing noise of audience anticipation. Muffled tannoy announcements in background.
Voice Over (ERIC) Good evening, and welcome to the Arthur Ludlow Memorial Baths, Newport, for this year's finals of the All-England Summarize Proust Competition. *(pull back slightly to reveal big banner across the top of the stage: 'All-England Summarize Proust Competition')* As you may remember, each contestant has to give a brief summary of Proust's 'A La Recherche du Temps Perdu', once in a swimsuit and once in evening dress. The field has now narrowed to three finalists and your judges tonight are... *(cut to panel of judges at long desk; they are all cut-outs of smiling photos of the following)* Alec and Eric Bedser, ex-Surrey cricketers, Stewart Surridge, ex-captain of Surrey, Omar Sharif, Laurie Fishlock, ex-Surrey opening batsman, Peter May, the former Surrey and England Captain, and Yehudi Menuhin, the world-famous violinist and the President of the Surrey Cricket Club. And right now it's time to meet your host for tonight – Arthur Mee!

Showbiz music, applause, and Arthur Mee appears from the back of the stage; he wears the now traditional spangly jacket. He comes forward and speaks into the mike (the sound is rather hollow and strident as in big halls with a hastily rigged PA).

Mee (TERRY J) Good evening and welcome, whereas Proust would say, 'la malade imaginaire de recondition et de toute surveillance est bientôt la même chose'. *(roars of applause; quick shot of grinning faces of the jury)* Remember each contestant this evening has a maximum of fifteen seconds to sum up 'A La Recherche du Temps Perdu' and on the Proustometer over here... *(curtain pulls back at back of stage to reveal a truly enormous, but cheap, audience appreciation gauge; it lists the seven books of Proust's masterwork in the form of a thermometer)* you can see exactly how far he gets. So let's crack straight on with our first contestant tonight. He's last year's semi-finalist from Luton – Mr Harry Bagot. *(Harry Bagot, in evening dress, comes forward from back of stage, he has a number three on his back; Mee leads the applause for him)* Hello Harry. Now there's the summarizing spot, you're on the summarizing spot, fifteen seconds from *now*.

Music starts, continuity-type music. The needle of the Proustometer creeps up almost imperceptibly to a tiny level.

Harry (GRAHAM) Proust's novel ostensibly tells of the irrevocability of time lost, the forfeiture of innocence through experience, the reinstatement of extra-temporal values of time regained, ultimately the novel is both optimistic and set within the context of a humane religious experience, re-stating as it does the concept of intemporality. In the first volume, Swann, the family friend visits . . .

Gong goes, chord of music, applause. The meter has hardly risen at all.

Mee Well tried, Harry.

Voice Over A good attempt there but unfortunately he chose a general appraisal of the work, before getting on to the story and as you can see *(close up of Proustometer)* he only got as far as page one of 'Swann's Way', the first of the seven volumes. A good try though and very nice posture.

Cut back to the stage.

Mee Harry Bagot, you're from Luton?

Harry Yes, Arthur, yeah.

Mee Now Harry what made you first want to try and start summarizing Proust?

Harry Well I first entered a seaside Summarizing Proust Competition when I was on holiday in Bournemouth, and my doctor encouraged me with it.

Mee And Harry, what are your hobbies outside summarizing?

Harry Well, strangling animals, golf and masturbating.

Mee Well, thank you Harry Bagot.

Harry walks off-stage. Music and applause.

Voice Over Well there he goes. Harry Bagot. He must have let himself down a bit on the hobbies, golf's not very popular around here, but never mind, a good try.

Mee Thank you ladies and gentlemen. Mr Rutherford from Leicester, are you ready Ronald? *(Ronald is a very eager man in tails)* Right. On the summarizing spot. You have got fifteen seconds from now.

Ronald (MICHAEL) Er, well, Swann, Swann, there's this house, there's this house, and er, it's in the morning, it's in the morning – no, it's the evening, in the evening and er, there's a garden and er, this bloke comes in – bloke comes in – what's his name – what's his name, er just said it – big bloke – Swann, Swann . . .

The gong sounds. Mee pushes Ronald out.

Mee And now ladies and gentlemen, I'd like you to welcome the last of our all-England finalists this evening, from Bingley, the Bolton Choral Society and their leader Superintendent McGough. *(a big choir comes on, immaculately drilled, each holding a score, with Fred Tomlinson as superintendent McGough)* All right Bingley, remember you've got fifteen seconds to summarize Proust in his entirety starting from now.

First Soloist Proust, in his first book wrote about . . . fa la la . . .

Second Soloist Proust in his first book wrote about . . .

Tenors He wrote about. . .

They continue contrapuntally, in madrigal, never getting beyond these words until they rallentando to say . . .

All Proust in his first book wrote about the . . . *(gong sounds)*

Voice Over Very ambitious try there, but in fact the least successful of the evening, they didn't even get as far as the first volume. *(the singers leave the stage)*

Mee Well ladies and gentlemen, I don't think any of our contestants this evening have succeeded in encapsulating the intricacies of Proust's masterwork, so I'm going to award the first prize this evening to the girl with the biggest tits.

Applause and music. A lady with enormous knockers comes on to the side of the stage. Roll credits:

THE ALL-ENGLAND SUMMARIZE PROUST COMPETITION A BBC PRODUCTION

WITH MR I. T. BRIDDOCK, 2379, THE TERRACE, HODDESDON.

IT WAS CONCEIVED, WRITTEN AND PERFORMED BY . . .

Roll usual Monty Python credits and music. Behind them the lady accepts the cup and the singers come back on stage and admire her. Fade out. Slight pause. Fade up on stock film of Everest. Whistling wind, stirring music.

Voice Over (MICHAEL) Mount Everest. Forbidding. Aloof. Terrifying. The mountain with the biggest tits in the world.

Sound of gong.

Second Voice (ERIC) Start again.

A very silly loony leans into shot, on overlay (i.e. in front of picture), and waves to the camera. He goes out of shot again.

Voice Over Mount Everest. Forbidding. Aloof. Terrifying. This year this remote Himalayan mountain, this mystical temple, surrounded by the most difficult terrain in the world repulsed yet another attempt to conquer it. This time by the International Hairdressers' Expedition. *(cut to shot of pup tent in a blizzard)* In such freezing adverse conditions man comes very close to breaking point. What was the real cause of the disharmony which destroyed their chances of success?

Cut to three head-and-shoulders shots. They look like typical mountaineers: frost in their beards, tanned, with snow glasses on their foreheads and authentic Everest headgear.

First Climber (MICHAEL) Well, people would keep taking my hairdryer and never returning it.

Second Climber (GRAHAM) There was a lot of bitching in the tents.

Third Climber (ERIC) You couldn't get near the mirror.

Cut to a colonel figure, digging in a garden in Jersey.

Voice Over The leader of the expedition was Colonel Sir John 'Teasy Weasy' Butler, veteran of K2, Annapurna, and Vidals. His plan was to ignore the usual route round the South Col and to make straight for the top.

Cut to a photo of Everest with dots superimposed, showing the route.

Colonel (GRAHAM) Well we established base salon here. *(on the photo, we see the words 'base salon')* And climbed quite steadily up to Mario's here. *(at the top of the route we see 'Mario's')* From here using crampons and cutting ice steps as we went, we moved steadily up the Lhotse Face to the North Ridge, establishing camp three where we could get a hot meal, a manicure and a shampoo and set.

Cut to stock film of people actually climbing Everest.

Voice Over Could it work? Could this eighteen-year-old hairdresser from Brixton succeed where others had failed? The situation was complicated by the imminent arrival of the monsoon storms. Patrice takes up the story.

Cut to interior of hairdresser's salon. Patrice speaks into the mirror, as he is blow-drying and curling a lady's hair.

Patrice (ERIC) Well, we knew as well as anyone that the monsoons were due, but the thing was, Ricky and I had just had a blow dry and rinse, and we couldn't go out for a couple of days.

Cut to stock film of some people leaving a little tent on a mountain.

Voice Over After a blazing row the Germans and the Italians had turned back, taking with them the last of the hair nets. On the third day a blizzard blew up. *(close up on the tent in a blizzard; no people in shot)* Temperatures fell to minus thirty centigrade. Inside the little tent things were getting desperate.

We cut inside the tent. The wind is banging against the side of the material, sounds of a vicious blizzard. Ricky is sitting next to another member of the expedition. Both are under hairdryers, in full climbing gear up to their necks. One is reading 'Vogue', Ricky is doing his nails.

Ricky (MICHAEL) Well, things have got so bad that we've been forced to use the last of the heavy oxygen equipment just to keep the dryers going.

Woman *(off-screen)* Cup of Milo, love.

Ricky Oh she's a treas. *(he takes the drink)*

Cut to a wide shot of Everest.

Voice Over But a new factor had entered the race. A team of French chiropodists, working with brand new cornplasters and Doctor Scholl's Mountaineering Sandals, were covering ground fast. The Glasgow Orpheus Male Voice Choir were tackling the difficult North Col. *(quick cut to film of lots of people climbing up Everest; dubbed over is the 'Proust' song as in 'Proust Competition' item)* Altogether fourteen expeditions *(cut to diagram with hundreds of dotted lines over it, fourteen different routes)* were at his heels. This was it. Rick had to make a decision.

Cut back to Patrice in the salon.

Patrice Well, he decided to open a salon.

As Patrice continues, his hairdresser voice over starts over this picture.

Voice Over It was a tremendous success.

Cinema-style advert with still photos.

Advert Voice (ERIC) Challenging Everest? Why not drop in at Ricky Pules' – only 24,000 feet from this cinema. Ricky and Maurice offer a variety of styles for the well-groomed climber. Like Sherpa Tensing and Sir Edmund Hillary be number one to the top when you're Number One on Top. *(just their heads turn to show off the hair-do)*

Animated sketch leads to little old Mrs Little on the phone in her hall. She is a dear little old lady and lives in a rather fussy ducks-on-wall house.

Mrs Little (TERRY J) Hello, is that the fire brigade?

Cut to the fire station.

First Fireman (MICHAEL) No, sorry, wrong number.

He puts the phone back. Pull out to reveal four or five firemen in full gear, surrounded by fire-fighting equipment and a gleaming fire engine. The firemen are engaged in a variety of homely pursuits: one is soldering a crystal set, another is cooking at a workbench, another is doing embroidery, another is at a sewing machine. The first fireman is at the phone on the wall. He goes back to clearing up a budgie's cage.

Second Fireman (ERIC) That phone's not stopped ringing all day.

Third Fireman What happens when you've mixed the batter, do you dice the ham with the coriander?

First Fireman No, no, you put them in separately when the vine leaves are ready.

The phone rings.

Second Fireman Oh, no, not again.

Third Fireman Take it off the hook.

The first fireman takes the phone off the hook. Cut back to Mrs Little on phone. She looks at the receiver then listens again.

Mrs Little I can't get the fire brigade Mervyn.

Mervyn, her 38-year-old, 6' 8" son appears.

Mervyn (JOHN) Here, let me try, dear. You go and play the cello.

Mrs Little Oh it doesn't do any good, dear.

Mervyn Look. Do you want the little hamster to live or not?

Mrs Little Yes I do, Mervyn.

Mervyn Well go and play the cello!

She looks helplessly at him, then goes into the sitting room. Mervyn dials.

Mervyn Hello, hello, operator? Yes we're trying to get the fire brigade . . . No, the fire brigade. Yes, yes, yes, yes, yes, yes, yes, yes, yes, yes, what? . . . *(he takes one of his shoes off and looks in it)* Size eight. Yes, yes, yes, yes, yes, yes, no of course not. Yes . . .

Mrs Little appears, dabbing at her eyes with a handkerchief.

Mrs Little *(touching Mervyn gently on the arm)* He's gone, dear.

Mervyn What?

Mrs Little He's slipped away.

Mervyn What?

Mrs Little The sodding hamster's dead!

Mervyn *(broken)* Oh no!! What were you playing?

Mrs Little Some Mozart concertos, dear.

Mervyn What . . . How did he . . . ?

Mrs Little His eyes just closed, and he fell into the wastepaper basket. I've covered him with a copy of the 'Charlie George Football Book'.

Mervyn *(handing her the phone)* Right, you hang on. I must go and see him.

Mrs Little There was nothing we could do, Mervyn. If we'd have had the whole Philharmonic Orchestra in there, he'd still have gone.

Mervyn I'm going upstairs, I can't bear it.

Mrs Little *(restraining him)* There isn't an upstairs dear, it's a bungalow.

Mervyn Damn. *(he storms off)*

Mrs Little *(into the phone)* Hello, I'm sorry to keep you waiting, it's just that . . . *(she takes her shoe off and looks inside)* size three, yes it's just – we've lost a dear one and my son was . . . yes, that's right, size eight, yes and . . . Oh I see . . . yes, yes, yes, yes, yes, yes, yes, I see, yes, yes. I, I . . . Yes, yes. No . . . no . . . yes, I see. They can't get the fire brigade Mervyn – will the Boys' Brigade do.

Mervyn *(off)* No! They'd be useless!

Mrs Little No, he doesn't want anyone at the moment, thank you. No, yes, yes, no thank you for trying, yes, yes, . . . no, Saxones, yes, yes thank you, bye, bye.

As she puts the phone down the front door beside her opens and there stands a huge African warrior in warpaint and with a spear and shield. At his feet are several smart suitcases.

Eamonn (GRAHAM) Mummy.

Mrs Little Eamonn. *(he brings in the cases and closes the front door)* Mervyn! Look it's our Eamonn – oh let me look at you, tell me how . . . how is it in Dublin?

Eamonn Well, things is pretty bad there at the moment but there does seem some hope of a constitutional settlement.

Mrs Little Oh don't talk. Let me just look at you.

Eamonn Great to be home, Mummy. How are you?

Mrs Little Oh, I'm fine. I must just go upstairs and get your room ready.

Eamonn It's a bungalow, Mummy.

Mrs Little Oh damn, yes. Mervyn, Mervyn – look who's here, it's our Eamonn come back to see us.

Mervyn appears. He still looks shattered by the death of the hamster.

Mervyn Hello, Eamonn.

Eamonn Hello, Merv.

Mervyn How was Dublin?

Eamonn Well as I was telling Mummy here, things is pretty bad there at the moment but there does seem some hope of a constitutional settlement.

The phone rings.

Mervyn *(answering phone)* Hello, yes, yes, yes, yes, yes – what? what? . . . *(looking at Eamonn's bare foot)* Size seven. Yes, yes, yes, yes, yes, . . . it's the fire brigade, they want to know if they can come round Thursday evening.

Mrs Little Oh no, Thursday's the Industrial Relations Bill Dinner Dance. Can't they make it another day?

Mervyn *(into the phone)* Hello, no Thursday's *right out*. Yes, yes, yes, yes . . . *(fade out)*

Fade up on a dinner-jacketed announcer sitting at a table with a bowl of flowers on it. A hand waves from inside the bowl of flowers.

Announcer (MICHAEL) And so it was the fire brigade eventually came round on Friday night.

Cut to fire engines skidding out of the fire station and roaring away – speeded up. They skid to a halt outside the Littles' suburban house. Firemen pour out of the fire engine and start to swarm in through the windows. Cut to interior of Littles' sitting room. It is laid out for a cocktail party. Mervyn is in evening dress and is sitting on the sofa looking very depressed. Mrs Little in a faded cocktail dress. Eamonn still in warpaint with spear and shield. The firemen appear.

Mrs Little Oh, so glad you could come. What would you like to drink? Gin and tonic? Sherry?

Firemen *(in unison)* A drop of sherry would be lovely. *(as she starts to pour drinks the firemen confide in unison)* We do like being called out to these little parties, they're much better than fires.

The phone rings. Half the firemen go to answer it.

A Fireman *(off)* Yes, yes yes.

Firemen Well, how was Dublin, Eamonn?

Eamonn Well, as I was telling Mummy and Mervyn earlier, things is pretty bad there at the moment but there does seem some hope of a constitutional . . .

Mrs Little *(to camera)* Look at them enjoying themselves. *(shot of party in the hall; we can just see the fireman on phone; they keep looking at their shoe sizes)* You know I used to dread parties until I watched 'Party Hints by Veronica'. I think it's on now . . .
Panning shot across mountains in CinemaScope format.
SUPERIMPOSED ROLLER CAPTION:
THE BRITISH BROADCASTING CORPORATION
IN ASSOCIATION WITH TRANSWORLD INTERNATIONAL
AND NIMROD PRODUCTIONS PRESENT
AN ARTHUR E. RICEBACHER
AND DAVID A. SELTZER PRODUCTION
FOR HASBACH ENTERPRISES
OF CHARLES D. ORTIZ' ADAPTATION
OF THE PULITZER PRIZEWINNING IDEA
BY DANIEL E. STOLLMEYER
BROUGHT TO THE SCREEN FROM ROBERT HUGHES'S NOVEL
BY LOUIS H. TANNHAUSER AND VERNON D. LARUE
PARTY HINTS BY VERONICA SMALLS
A SELZENBACH-TANSROD PRODUCTION
IN ASSOCIATION WITH
VICTOR A. LOUNGE
ROLO NICE SWEETIES
FISON'S FERTILIZERS
TIME LIFE INNIT-FOR-THE-MONEY LIMITED
THE TRUSTEES OF ST PAUL'S CATHEDRAL
THAT NICE MR ROBINSON AT THE VET'S
RALPH READER
RALPH NADER
THE CHINESE GOVERNMENT
MICHAEL'S AUNTIE BETTY IN AUSTRALIA
A CINEMASCOPE PRODUCTION
Cut to Veronica in the 'Party Hints' set – a chintzy kitchen.
Veronica (ERIC) Hello, last week on 'Party Hints' I showed you how to make a small plate of goulash go round twenty-six people, how to get the best, out of your canapés, and how to unblock your loo. This week I'm going to tell you what to do if there is an armed communist uprising near your home when you're having a party. Well obviously it'll depend how far you've got *with* your party when the signal for Red Revolt is raised. If you're just having preliminary aperitifs – Dubonnet, a sherry or a sparkling white wine – then the guests will obviously be in a fairly formal mood and it will be difficult to tell which are the communist agitators. So the thing to do is to get some cloth and some bits of old paper, put it down on the floor and shoot everybody. This will deal with the Red Menace on your own doorstep. If you're having canapés, as I showed you last week, or an outdoor barbecue, then the thing to do is set fire to all houses in the street. This will stir up anti-communist hatred and your neighbours

will be right with you as you organize counter-revolutionary terror. So you see, if you act promptly enough, any left-wing uprising can be dealt with by the end of the party. Bye...

ANIMATION: *one dozen communist revolutions.*

Then cut to a language laboratory. Mr Mann is showing Tick round. There is a line of booths, each lined with pegboard. Each has a person with a pair of earphones on with attached microphones, a tape recorder and a swivel chair.

First Booth (ERIC) Bleck people. Bleck people. Rrrhodesian. Kill the blecks. Rrhodesian. Smith. Smith. Kill the blecks within the five principles.

He starts to rewind the tape recorder. Nods at Mr Mann. They come to the second booth.

Second Booth (TERRY J) I'm afraid I cannot comment on that until it's been officially hushed up.

Mr Mann (GRAHAM) This is our politicians' booth.

Second Booth While there is no undue cause for concern, there is certainly no room for complacency. Ha, ha, ha. He, he, he.

They pass on to the next booth.

Third Booth (MICHAEL) Well I'll go, I'll go to the foot of our stairs. Ee ecky thump. Put wood in 'ole, muther.

Mr Mann taps him. He removes his earphones.

Third Booth *(normal)* Yes?

Mr Mann Ee ecky thump.

Third Booth *(trying it)* Ee ecky thump.

Mr Mann Ee ecky thump! *(indicates more power)*

Third Booth Ee ecky thump!

Mr Mann Excellent.

Third Booth Thank you, sir. *(puts earphones on, listens)*

Mr Mann It's a really quick method of learning.

Third Booth Can you smell gas or is it me?

Tick (JOHN) *(who is very diffident)* Looks jolly good.

They come to the fourth booth where sits a very city-type gent.

Fourth Booth Hello, big boy. *(very breathy)* Oo varda the ome. D'you want a nice time?

Mr Mann Very good.

Fourth Booth *(butch)* Thank you very much, sir.

They pass the fifth booth, whose occupant is making silly noises.

Mr Mann And we control everything from here. *(indicating the control desk)*

Tick Superb.

Mr Mann Well then what sort of thing were you looking for?

Tick Well, er, really something to make me a little less insignificant?

Mr Mann Oh, I see sort of 'Now look here, you may be Chairman but your bloody pusillanimous behaviour makes me vomit!' That sort of thing? ...

Tick Oh no, no, no, not really no.

Mr Mann Oh I see, well perhaps something a bit more sort of Clive Jenkins-ish? Perhaps – sort of *(Welsh accent)* 'Mr Smarmy so-called Harold Wilson can call himself pragmatic until he's blue in the breasts'.

Tick Oh no, I really want something that will make people be attracted to me like a magnet.

Mr Mann I see, well, you want our 'Life and Soul of the Party' tape then, I think.

Tick What's that?

Mr Mann Well it's sort of "ello squire, haven't seen you for a bit, haven't seen you for a bit either, Beryl. Two pints of wallop please, love. Still driving the Jensen then? Cheer up Jack it may never happen, what's your poison then?'

Tick Fantastic, yes.

Mr Mann Right, I'll just see if we've got the tape.

> *He puts the headphones on. Whilst he looks away, the whole of the back wall of people in booths, swing round on their chairs and do a little thirties routine, with their earphones on, kicking their legs, etc., they sing.*
>
> SUPERIMPOSED CAPTION: 'SANDY WILSON'S VERSION OF "THE DEVILS"'

All Boo boopee doo
Boo boopee doo
Scuby duby duby doo-oo!
Hello Operator
Is that the Central Line
Give me the Piccadilly number
Nine one o nine
Mr Operator now that number's wrong
So come on everybody Let's sing this song ...
... Proust in his first book wrote about ... etc. ...

Gong sounds.

Voice Over (ERIC) Start again.

> *The loony leans into shot and waves. Fade to black. Fade up on close up of picture of Everest. Pull back to reveal travel agent's office.*

Bounder (MICHAEL) Mount Everest, forbidding, aloof, terrifying. The highest place on earth. No I'm sorry we don't go there. No.

> *By the time Bounder is saying his last sentence the camera has revealed the office and Bounder himself sitting at a desk. Bounder now replaces the telephone into which he has been speaking. After a pause the tourist – Mr Smoke-Too-Much – enters the office and approaches Mr Bounder's secretary.*

Tourist (ERIC) Good morning.

Secretary (CAROL) Oh good morning. *(sexily)* Do you want to go upstairs?

Tourist What?

Secretary *(sexily)* Do you want to go upstairs? *(brightly)* Or have you come to arrange a holiday?

Tourist Er . . . to arrange a holiday.

Secretary Oh, sorry.

Tourist What's all this about going upstairs?

Secretary Oh, nothing, nothing. Now, where were you thinking of going?

Tourist India.

Secretary Ah one of our adventure holidays!

Tourist Yes!

Secretary Well you'd better speak to Mr Bounder about that. Mr Bounder, this gentleman is interested in the India Overland.

Walks over to Bounder's desk where he is greeted by Bounder.

Bounder Ah. Good morning. I'm Bounder of Adventure.

Tourist My name is Smoke-Too-Much.

Bounder What?

Tourist My name is Smoke-Too-Much. Mr Smoke-Too-Much.

Bounder Well, you'd better cut down a bit then.

Tourist What?

Bounder You'd better cut down a bit then.

Tourist Oh I see! Cut down a bit, for Smoke-Too-Much.

Bounder Yes, ha ha . . . I expect you get people making jokes about your name all the time, eh?

Tourist No, no actually. Actually, it never struck me before. Smoke . . . too . . . much!

Bounder Anyway, you're interested in one of our adventure holidays, eh?

Tourist Yes. I saw your advert in the bolour supplement.

Bounder The what?

Tourist The bolour supplement.

Bounder The colour supplement?

Tourist Yes. I'm sorry I can't say the letter 'B'.

Bounder C?

Tourist Yes that's right. It's all due to a trauma I suffered when I was a spoolboy. I was attacked by a bat.

Bounder A cat?

Tourist No a bat.

Bounder Can you say the letter 'K'.

Tourist Oh yes. Khaki, king, kettle, Kuwait, Keble Bollege Oxford.

Bounder Why don't you say the letter 'K' instead of the letter 'C'?

Tourist What you mean ... spell bolour with a 'K'?

Bounder Yes.

Tourist Kolour. Oh, that's very good, I never thought of that.

Bounder Anyway, about the holiday.

Tourist Well I saw your adverts in the paper and I've been on package tours several times, you see, and I decided that this was for me.

Bounder Ah good.

Tourist Yes I quite agree with you, I mean what's the point of being treated like a sheep, I mean I'm fed up going abroad and being treated like sheep, what's the point of being carted round in buses, surrounded by sweaty mindless oafs from Kettering and Boventry in their cloth caps and their cardigans and their transistor radios and their 'Sunday Mirrors', complaining about the tea, 'Oh they don't make it properly here do they not like at home' stopping at Majorcan bodegas, selling fish and chips and Watney's Red Barrel and calamares and two veg and sitting in cotton sun frocks squirting Timothy White's suncream all over their puffy raw swollen purulent flesh cos they 'overdid it on the first day'!

Bounder *(agreeing patiently)* Yes. Absolutely, yes, I quite agree ...

Tourist And being herded into endless Hotel Miramars and Bellevueses and Bontinentals with their international luxury modern roomettes and their Watney's Red Barrel and their swimming pools full of fat German businessmen pretending to be acrobats and forming pyramids and frightening the children and barging in to the queues and if you're not at your table spot on seven you miss your bowl of Campbell's Cream of Mushroom soup, the first item on the menu of International Cuisine, and every Thursday night there's bloody cabaret in the bar featuring some tiny emaciated dago with nine-inch hips and some big fat bloated tart with her hair Brylcreemed down and a big arse presenting Flamenco for Foreigners.

Bounder *(beginning to get fed up)* Yes, yes, now ...

Tourist And then some adenoidal typists from Birmingham with diarrhoea and flabby white legs and hairy bandy-legged wop waiters called Manuel, and then, once a week there's an excursion to the local Roman ruins where you can buy cherryade and melted ice cream and bleedin' Watney's Red Barrel, and then one night they take you to a local restaurant with local colour and colouring and they show you there and you sit next to a party of people from Rhyl who keeps singing 'Torremolinos, Torremolinos', and complaining about the food, 'Oh! It's so greasy isn't it?' and then you get cornered by some drunken greengrocer from Luton with an Instamatic and Dr Scholl sandals and Tuesday's 'Daily Express' and he drones on and on and on about how Mr Smith should be running this country and how many languages Enoch

Powell can speak and then he throws up all over the Cuba Libres.

Bounder Will you be quiet please.

Tourist And sending tinted postcards of places they don't know they haven't even visited, 'to all at number 22, weather wonderful our room is marked with an "X". Wish you were here.'

Bounder Shut up.

Tourist 'Food very greasy but we have managed to find this marvellous little place hidden away in the back streets.'

Bounder Shut up!

Tourist 'Where you can even get Watney's Red Barrel and cheese and onion . . .'

Bounder Shut up!!!

Tourist '. . . crisps and the accordionist plays "Maybe its because I'm a Londoner"' and spending four days on the tarmac at Luton airport on a five-day package tour with nothing to eat but dried Watney's sandwiches . . .

Bounder Shut your bloody gob! I've had enough of this, I'm going to ring the police.

He dials and waits. Cut to a corner of a police station. One policeman is knitting, another is making a palm tree out of old newspapers. The phone rings.

Knitting Policeman Oh . . . take it off the hook. *(they do so)*

Cut back to travel agent's office. The man is still going on, the travel agent looks crossly at the phone and puts it down. Then picks it up and dials again.

Bounder Hello operator, operator . . . I'm trying to get the police . . . the police yes, what? *(takes his shoe off and looks inside)* nine and a half, nine and a half, yes, yes . . . I see . . . well can you keep trying please . . .

Through all this the tourist is still going on:

Tourist . . . and there's nowhere to sleep and the kids are vomiting and throwing up on the plastic flowers and they keep telling you it'll only be another hour although your plane is still in Iceland waiting to take some Swedes to Yugoslavia before it can pick you up on the tarmac at 3 a.m. in the bloody morning and you sit on the tarmac till six because of 'unforeseen difficulties', i.e. the permanent strike of Air Traffic Control in Paris, and nobody can go to the lavatory until you take off at eight, and when you get to Malaga airport everybody's swallowing Enterovioform tablets and queuing for the toilets and when you finally get to the hotel there's no water in the taps, there's no water in the pool, there's no water in the bog and there's only a bleeding lizard in the bidet, and half the rooms are double-booked and you can't sleep anyway . . .

The secretary comes up and looks into the camera.

Secretary Oh! Sorry to keep you waiting... will you come this way please...

The camera follows her as she leads us out of the office, with agent and client still rabbiting on, down a short passage to a documentary interview set where the two participants are sitting waiting. We follow her into the set.

Secretary Here they are. *(she turns to the camera again, which moves a little towards her, as if waiting to be summoned)* Just here will do fine! Goodbye.

A presenter sitting with a guest in the usual late-night line-up set.

Presenter (GRAHAM) Good evening.

CAPTION: 'THRUST – A QUITE CONTROVERSIAL LOOK AT THE WORLD AROUND US'

Presenter I have with me tonight Anne Elk. Mrs Anne Elk.

Miss Elk (JOHN) Miss.

SUPERIMPOSED CAPTION: 'ANNE ELK'

Presenter You have a new theory about the brontosaurus.

Miss Elk Can I just say here Chris for one moment that I have a new theory about the brontosaurus.

Presenter Exactly. *(he gestures but she does not say anything)* What is it?

Miss Elk Where? *(looks round)*

Presenter No, no your new theory.

Miss Elk Oh, what is my theory?

Presenter Yes.

Miss Elk Oh what is my theory that it is. Well Chris you may well ask me what is my theory.

Presenter I *am* asking.

Miss Elk Good for you. My word yes. Well Chris, what is it that it is – this theory of mine. Well, this is what it is – my theory that I have, that is to say, which is mine, is mine.

Presenter *(beginning to show signs of exasperation)* Yes, I know it's yours, what is it?

Miss Elk Where? Oh, what is my theory? This is it. *(clears throat at some length)* My theory that belongs to me is as follows. *(clears throat at great length)* This is how it goes. The next thing I'm going to say is my theory. Ready?

Presenter Yes.

Miss Elk My theory by A. Elk. Brackets Miss, brackets. This theory goes as follows and begins now. All brontosauruses are thin at one end, much much thicker in the middle and then thin again at the far end. That is my theory, it is mine, and belongs to me and I own it, and what it is too.

Presenter That's *it*, is it?

Miss Elk Spot on, Chris.

Presenter Well, er, this theory of yours appears to have hit the nail on the head.

Miss Elk And it's mine.

Presenter Yes, thank you very much for coming along to the studio. Thank you.

Miss Elk My pleasure, Chris...

Presenter Next week Britain's newest wasp farm...

Miss Elk It's been a lot of fun.

Presenter Yes, thank you very much.

Miss Elk Saying what my theory is.

Presenter Yes, thank you.

Miss Elk And whose it is.

Presenter Yes, thank you – that's all – thank you... opens next week.

Miss Elk I have another theory.

Presenter Yes.

Miss Elk Called my second theory, or my theory number two.

Presenter Thank you. Britain's newest wasp farm...

Miss Elk This second theory which was the one that I had said...

Presenter *(the phone rings; he answers)* Yes, no I'm trying...

Miss Elk Which I could expound without doubt. This second theory which, with the one which I have said, forms the brace of theories which I own and which belong to me, goes like this...

Presenter *(looking at his shoe)* nine and a half, wide fitting... Baileys of Bond Street. What? No, sort of brogue.

Miss Elk This is what it is. *(clears throat)*

Presenter Eight and a half.

Miss Elk This is it... *(lots of noisy throat clearing)*

He rises and leaves the set to go next door to the travel agent set, leaving Miss Elk behind for a moment. Bounder is still on the phone. His other phone rings; he answers it.

Bounder Hello, yes... yes...

The presenter enters the travel set. The tourist is still droning on as before and Bounder is still on the phone.

Tourist *(carrying on all through the scene below)* ... and the Spanish Tourist Board promises you that the raging cholera epidemic is merely a case of mild Spanish tummy, like the last outbreak of Spanish tummy in 1660 which killed half London and decimated Europe, and meanwhile the bloody Guardia are busy arresting sixteen-year-olds for kissing in the streets and shooting anyone under nineteen who doesn't like Franco...

The presenter approaches Bounder.

Presenter The fire brigade are here. They're coming!

Bounder Hello! No, no, no I think they are all part of the British Shoe Corporation now.

Miss Elk follows the presenter in.

Miss Elk Chris, this other theory of mine which is mine like the other one I also own. The second theory...

The fire brigade enter and the secretary goes to greet them. They speak to her and she takes off her shoe to check the size. Meanwhile...

Miss Elk My second theory states that fire brigade choirs seldom sing songs about Marcel Proust.

With only a half-beat pause the fire brigade start singing the Proust song. After the usual number of lines we hear the gong.

Voice Over (ERIC) Start again.

The loony looks into the scene on overlay and waves at the camera just as we fade to black. We hold black for a few seconds and then the loony leans in to the black and waves again before fading away.

Thirty-two

Newsreel footage.

Voice Over (ERIC) *(newsreel voice)* In the modern Britain, united under a great leader, it's the housewives of Britain who are getting things moving. *(Red Devils flying; picture of Edward Heath)* Here a coachload of lovely ladies are on their way to speed up production in a car factory. *(coach load of Pepperpots, middle class, grey hair, Mary Whitehouse glasses; the coach says 'Tory Tours')* And here we are boys, it's the no-hurry brigade hanging about for endless overtime. And just watch these gallant girls go into action... *(cut to a factory yard; some workers in brown overalls are eating sandwiches out of tins; the clock says 1.15; the coach comes swinging in in undercrank, the ladies pour out about to belt the men with umbrellas and handbags; the men flee back into factories)* Not working fast enough? Well, there's an answer for that. *(a man at a machine, producing something incredibly fast; a Pepperpot holds an enormous sledgehammer)* Yes, this is certainly the way to speed up production. *(wide shot of factory interior; three Pepperpots stand on a gantry above work floor, wearing armbands, saying 'P.P.' and dark Mary Whitehouse glasses)* This is the recipe for increased productivity to meet the threat of those nasty foreigners when Britain takes her natural place at the head of the British Common Market. *(a group of strikers, picketing with slogans, 'Fair Pay', 'Less Profits', 'Parity', 'No Victimization')* And how's this for a way to beat strikers. *(Pepperpots arrive, clinging to side of old Buick; they race in and start beating the strikers with the banners)* Those spotty continental boys will soon have to look out for Mrs Britain, and talking of windmills, these girls aren't afraid to tilt at the permissive society. *(art gallery exterior; Pepperpots run in with bundles and ladders)* Business is booming in the so-called arts, but two can play at that game, chum. *(cut to art gallery interior; pan around paintings 'cleaned up' – trousers and cardigans being added to nude pictures and statues, Bermuda shorts on David, shorts on tubular structure, an attendant in shorts too).* And it's not just the modern so-called plastic arts that get the clean-up treatment.

Cut to a theatre stage. Desdemona on a bed. Othello with her.

Othello Oh Desdemona, Desdemona.

The Pepperpots race on to the stage and pull him off.

Voice Over And those continentals had better watch out for their dirty foreign literature. Jean-Paul Sartre and Jean Genet won't know what's hit them. Never mind the foulness of their language – come '73 they'll all have to write in British. *(Pepperpots burning books: 'Bertrand Russell', 'Das Kapital', the 'Guardian', 'Sartre', 'Freud')* You can keep your fastidious continental bidets Mrs Foreigner – Mrs Britain knows how to keep *her* feet clean... but she'll battle like bingo boys when it comes to keeping the television screen clean...

Cut to the BBC TV Centre. The Pepperpots parade in carrying signs: 'Clean TV Centre', 'God Says No To Filth', 'To The Cells'. Another Pepperpot in the background holds a sign: 'Wanted Dead Or Alive' and photo of Robert Robinson.

Voice Over Better watch out for those nasty continental shows on the sneaky second channel. *(armed Pepperpots escorting people out of TV Centre)* But apart from attacking that prurient hot-bed of left-wing continentalism at Shepherds Bush, what else do these ordinary mums think? Do they accept Hegelianism?

Pepperpot (GRAHAM) No!

Voice Over Do they prefer Leibnitz to Wittgenstein?

Pepperpot (TERRY J) No! No!

Voice Over And where do they stand on young people?

Pepperpot (ERIC) Just here, dear. *(Pepperpot standing on long-haired youth's head)*

Voice Over And their power is growing daily and when these girls roll their sleeves up its arms all the way. *(Pepperpots standing on the turret of an armoured vehicle; four Pepperpots on motor bikes flank it)* Yes, this is the way to fight the constant war against pornography.

Machine guns chatter. Two Pepperpots in a trench firing. Mortar bombs, reloading and firing. Bombs and smoke. At the end of the film we pick up on the nude organist (Terry J), sitting amongst the explosions. He plays his chords.

Announcer (JOHN) And now...

It's Man (MICHAEL) It's...

Animated titles.

Voice (JOHN) Monty Python's Flying Circus.

Close up on a sign saying 'Harley Street'. Stirring music. Mix through to interior of a smart, plush, ever so expensive Harley Street consulting room. The music swells and fades. Knocking at door, a short pause, then T. F. Gumby enters, backwards.

T. F. Gumby (MICHAEL) Doctor! Doctor! DOCTOR! *(he goes up to the antique desk and bangs the bell violently; he smashes the intercom and generally breaks the desk up)* Doctor! Doctor! DOCTOR! DOCTOR! Doctor! Doctor! Where is the Doctor?

A pause. Then another door opens and another Gumby appears.

Gumby Specialist (JOHN) Hello!

T. F. Gumby Are you the brain specialist?

Specialist Hello!

T. F. Gumby Are you the brain specialist?

Specialist No, no, I am not the brain specialist. No, no, I am not... Yes. Yes I am.

T. F. Gumby My brain hurts!

Specialist Well let's take a look at it, Mr Gumby.

Gumby specialist starts to pull up Gumby's sweater.

T. F. Gumby No, no, no, my brain in my head. *(specialist thumps him on the head)*

Specialist It will have to come out.

T. F. Gumby Out? Of my head?

Specialist Yes! All the bits of it. Nurse! Nurse! *(a nurse enters)* Nurse, take Mr Gumby to a brain surgeon.

Nurse Yes doctor . . .

She leads Gumby out. In the background the specialist is grunting and shouting.

Specialist Where's the 'Lancet'?

Nurse *(to T. F. Gumby)* He's brilliant you know.

Specialist Where's the bloody 'Lancet'? My brain hurts too.

Ambulance racing. 'Dr Kildare' theme. Cut to operating theatre. The surgeon is not a Gumby.

Surgeon (GRAHAM) *(putting on Gumby props)* Gloves . . . glasses . . . moustache . . . handkerchief. . . *(Gumby voice)* I'm going to operate!!

We now see he is surrounded by Gumbys. T. F. Gumby is on operating table.

All Let's operate.

They begin to use woodworking implements on T. F. Gumby.

T. F. Gumby Hello!

Surgeon Gumby Ooh! We forgot the anaesthetic!

Operating Gumbys The anaesthetic! The anaesthetic!!

At that moment a Gumby anaesthetist comes crashing through the wall with two gas cylinders.

Gumby Anaesthetist I've come to anaesthetize you!!

He raises a gas cylinder and strikes Gumby hard over the head with it. Bong. Blackness. Into the oblivion of animation.
Then cut to an ordinary suburban living room. Mr and Mrs Jalin are sitting on a sofa. The previous item in the show is visible on their TV set. Mrs Jalin is stuffing a chicken. Mr Jalin is reading the telephone directory. The picture changes and we hear voice from TV.

Voice (ERIC) The 'Nine O'Clock News' which was to follow has been cancelled tonight so we can bring you the quarter finals of the All Essex Badminton Championship. Your commentator as usual is Edna O'Brien.

Commentator (MICHAEL) *(Irish accent)* Hullo fans. Begorra an' to be sure there's some fine badminton down there in Essex this afternoon. We really . . .

Mr Jalin picks up a jousting ball and chain and smashes the TV set.

There is a ring from the doorbell. Mr Jalin sits. Mrs Jalin goes to the door, exits and comes back.

Mrs Jalin (GRAHAM) George.

Mr Jalin (TERRY J) Yes, Gladys.

Mrs Jalin There's a man at the door with a moustache.

Mr Jalin Tell him I've already got one. *(Mrs Jalin hits him hard with a newspaper)* All right, all right. What's he want then?

Mrs Jalin He says do we want a documentary on molluscs.

Mr Jalin Molluscs!

Mrs Jalin Yes.

Mr Jalin What's he mean, molluscs?

Mrs Jalin MOLLUSCS!! GASTROPODS! LAMELLIBRANCHS! CEPHALOPODS!

Mr Jalin Oh molluscs, I thought you said bacon. *(she hits him again)* All right, all right. What's he charge then?

Mrs Jalin It's free.

Mr Jalin Ooh! Where does he want us to sit.

Mrs Jalin *(calling through the door)* He says yes.

Mr Zorba enters carrying plywood flat with portion cut out to represent TV. He stands behind flat and starts.

Zorba (JOHN) Good evening. Tonight molluscs. The mollusc is a soft-bodied, unsegmented invertebrate animal usually protected by a large shell. One of the most numerous groups of invertebrates, it is exceeded in number of species only by the arthropods... viz. *(he holds up a lobster)*

Mrs Jalin Not very interesting is it?

Zorba What?

Mrs Jalin I was talking to him.

Zorba Oh. Anyway, the typical mollusc, viz, a snail *(holds one up)* consists of a prominent muscular portion... the head-foot... a visceral mass and a shell which is secreted by the free edge of the mantle.

Mrs Jalin Dreadful isn't it?

Zorba What?

Mrs Jalin I was talking to him.

Zorba Oh. Well anyway... in some molluscs, however, viz, slugs, *(holds one up)* the shell is absent or rudimentary...

Mr Jalin Switch him off.

Mrs Jalin gets up and looks for the switch unsuccessfully.

Zorba Whereas in others, viz, cephalopods the head-foot is greatly modified and forms tentacles, viz, the squid. *(looking out)* What are you doing?

Mrs Jalin Switching you off.

Zorba Why, don't you like it?

Mrs Jalin Oh it's dreadful.
Mr Jalin Embarrassing.
Zorba Is it?
Mrs Jalin Yes, it's perfectly awful.
Mr Jalin Disgraceful! I don't know how they've got the nerve to put it on.
Mrs Jalin It's so boring.
Zorba Well . . . it's not much of a subject is it . . . be fair.
Mrs Jalin What do you think, George?
Mr Jalin Give him another twenty seconds.
Zorba Anyway the majority of the molluscs are included in three large groups, the gastropods, the lamellibranchs and the cephalopods . . .
Mrs Jalin We knew that. *(she gets up and goes to the set)*
Zorba However, what is more interesting, er . . . is the molluscs's er . . . sex life.
Mrs Jalin *(stopping dead)* Oh!
Zorba Yes, the mollusc is a randy little fellow whose primitive brain scarcely strays from the subject of the you know what.
Mrs Jalin *(going back to sofa)* Disgusting!
Mr Jalin Ought not to be allowed.
Zorba The randiest of the gastropods is the limpet. This hot-blooded little beast with its tent-like shell is always on the job. Its extra-marital activities are something startling. Frankly I don't know how the female limpet finds the time to adhere to the rock-face. How am I doing?
Mrs Jalin Disgusting.
Mr Jalin But more interesting.
Mrs Jalin Oh yes, tch, tch, tch.
Zorba Another loose-living gastropod is the periwinkle. This shameless little libertine with its characteristic ventral locomotion . . . is *not* the marrying kind: Anywhere anytime is its motto. Up with the shell and they're at it.
Mrs Jalin How about the lamellibranchs?
Zorba I'm coming to them . . . the great scallop *(holds one up)* . . . this tatty, scrofulous old rapist, is second in depravity only to the common clam. *(holds up a clam)* This latter is a right whore, a harlot, a trollop, a cynical bed-hopping firm-breasted Rabelaisian bit of sea food that makes Fanny Hill look like a dead Pope . . . and finally among the lamellibranch bivalves, that most depraved of the whole sub-species – the whelk. The whelk is nothing but a homosexual of the worst kind. This gay boy of the gastropods, this queer crustacean, this mincing mollusc, this screaming, prancing, limp-wristed queen of the deep makes me sick.
Mrs Jalin Have you got one?
Zorba Here! *(holds one up)*

Mrs Jalin Let's kill it. Disgusting.
  Zorba throws it on the floor and Mr and Mrs Jalin stamp on it.
Mr Jalin That'll teach it. Well thank you for a very interesting programme.
Zorba Oh, not at all. Thank you.
Mrs Jalin Yes, that was very nice.
Zorba Thank you. *(he shakes hands with her)*
Mrs Jalin Oh, thank you.
  Cut to a studio presenter at a desk.
Presenter (TERRY G) And now a word from the man in the . . .
  Cut to Glencoe vox pop: a loony.
Loony (GRAHAM) . . . street.

  ANIMATION: *high-suction baby.*
  Cut to a 'Nine O'clock News' set. A newsreader is at a desk. Photos come up on inlay screen behind him. An anonymous minister's photo is on screen.
Newsreader (MICHAEL) The Minister for not listening to people toured Batley today to investigate allegations of victimization in home-loan improvement grants, made last week *(photo behind changes to close up of another faceless minister)* by the Shadow Minister for judging people at first sight to be marginally worse than they actually are. *(photo changes to exterior of the Home Office)* At the Home Office, the Minister for inserting himself in between chairs and walls in men's clubs, was at his desk after a short illness. He spent the morning dealing with the Irish situation and later in the day had long discussions with the Minister for running upstairs two at a time, flinging the door open and saying 'Ha, ha! Caught you, Mildred'. *(photo of the Houses of Parliament)* In the Commons there was another day of heated debate on the third reading of the Trade Practices Bill. Mr Roland Penrose, the Under-Secretary for making deep growling noises grrr, launched a bitter personal attack on the ex-Minister for delving deep into a black satin bag and producing a tube of Euthymol toothpaste. Later in the debate the Junior Minister for being frightened by any kind of farm machinery, challenged the Under-Secretary of State for hiding from Terence Rattigan to produce the current year's trading figures, as supplied by the Department of stealing packets of bandages from the self-service counter at Timothy Whites and selling them again at a considerable profit. Parliament rose at 11.30, and, crawling along a dark passageway into the old rectory *(the camera starts to track slowly into the newsreader's face so that it is eventually filling the screen)* broke down the door to the serving hatch, painted the spare room and next weekend I think they'll be able to make a start on the boy's bedroom, while Amy and Roger, up in London for a few days, go to see the mysterious Mr Grenville.
  SUPERIMPOSED CAPTION: 'TODAY IN PARLIAMENT HAS NOW BECOME THE CLASSIC SERIAL'

Newsreader He in turn has been revealed by D'Arcy as something less than an honest man. Sybil feels once again a resurgence of her old affection and she and Balreau return to her little house in Clermont-Ferrand, the kind of two-up, two-down house that most French workers throughout the European Community are living in today.
SUPERIMPOSED CAPTION: 'THE CLASSIC SERIAL HAS NOW BECOME THE TUESDAY DOCUMENTARY'

Cut to a photo of a French construction site. The camera tracks over the photo.

Presenter (ERIC) The ease of construction, using on-site prefabrication facilities *(the camera starts to pull out slowly from the photo to reveal the photo is part of the backdrop of a documentary set about the building trade; the documentary presenter is sitting in a chair)* makes cheap housing a reality. The walls of these houses are lined with prestressed asbestos which keeps the house warm and snuggly and ever so safe from the big bad rabbit, who can scratch and scratch for all he's worth, but he just can't get into Porky's house.
SUPERIMPOSED CAPTION: 'THE TUESDAY DOCUMENTARY HAS BECOME "CHILDREN'S STORY"'

Presenter Where is Porky? Here he is. What a funny little chap. *(cut to animated Porky doing little dance)* But Porky's one of the lucky ones – he survived the urban upheaval of the Thirties and Forties. For him, Jarrow is still just a memory. *(zoom out to see Porky as part of documentary-type graph)* The hunger marches, the East End riots, the collapse of the Labour Government in 1931 . . . *(stock film of Ramsay MacDonald)*
SUPERIMPOSED CAPTION: 'THE CHILDREN'S STORY HAS GONE BACK INTO THE TUESDAY DOCUMENTARY'

Presenter . . . are dim reminders of the days before a new-found affluence swept the land, *(stock shots of Christmas lights in Regent Street, shopping crowds, tills and consumer goods ending up with toys)* making it clean and tidy and making all the shops full of nice things, lovely choo-choo trains . . .
SUPERIMPOSED CAPTION: 'NO IT HASN'T'

Presenter . . . and toys and shiny cars that go brrm, brim brrm, *(shots of toys)* and everybody was happy and singing all the day long *(cut to the presenter; by now he has a big kiddies' book which he shuts)* and nobody saw the big bad rabbit ever again.

Cut to a politician giving a party political broadcast in one of those badly lit sets that they use for broadcasts of that nature.

Politician (TERRY J) But you know it's always very easy to blame the big bad rabbit . . .
SUPERIMPOSED CAPTION: 'NOW IT'S BECOME A PARTY POLITICAL BROADCAST'

Politician ... when by-elections are going against the Government. *(he turns and we cut to side camera which reveals a cross behind him as for religious broadcast)* Do you think we should really be blaming ourselves?

SUPERIMPOSED CAPTION: 'NO, SORRY, "RELIGION TODAY"'

Politician Because you know, that's where we really ought to start looking.

A football comes in, he heads it neatly out of shot.

SUPERIMPOSED CAPTION: 'MATCH OF THE DAY'

Cut to stock film of ball flying into net and shot of Wembley crowd roaring. Then cut into short sequence of footballers in slow-motion kissing each other.

SUPERIMPOSED CAPTION: 'POLITICIANS – AN APOLOGY'

The camera pans across a landscape. Roller caption starts to come up, superimposed. The words are quite large and easily readable, but well spaced so that the roller will seem to go on for quite some time. Voice over reads.

Voice Over (ERIC) and CAPTION: 'WE WOULD LIKE TO APOLOGIZE FOR THE WAY IN WHICH POLITICIANS ARE REPRESENTED IN THIS PROGRAMME. IT WAS NEVER OUR INTENTION TO IMPLY THAT POLITICIANS ARE WEAK-KNEED, POLITICAL TIME-SERVERS WHO ARE CONCERNED MORE WITH THEIR PERSONAL VENDETTAS AND PRIVATE POWER STRUGGLES THAN THE PROBLEMS OF GOVERNMENT, NOR TO SUGGEST AT ANY POINT THAT THEY SACRIFICE THEIR CREDIBILITY BY DENYING FREE DEBATE ON VITAL MATTERS IN THE MISTAKEN IMPRESSION THAT PARTY UNITY COMES BEFORE THE WELL-BEING OF THE PEOPLE THEY SUPPOSEDLY REPRESENT, NOR TO IMPLY AT ANY STAGE THAT THEY ARE SQUABBLING LITTLE TOADIES WITHOUT AN OUNCE OF CONCERN FOR THE VITAL SOCIAL PROBLEMS OF TODAY. NOR INDEED DO WE INTEND THAT VIEWERS SHOULD CONSIDER THEM AS CRABBY ULCEROUS LITTLE SELF-SEEKING VERMIN WITH FURRY LEGS AND AN EXCESSIVE ADDICTION TO ALCOHOL AND CERTAIN EXPLICIT SEXUAL PRACTICES WHICH SOME PEOPLE MIGHT FIND OFFENSIVE. WE ARE SORRY IF THIS IMPRESSION HAS COME ACROSS.

Cut to a similar landscape. Preparations for an expedition are underway: equipment being piled into Land Rovers etc. An interviewer walks into shot.

Interviewer (JOHN) Hello. All the activity you can see in progress here is part of the intricate ... aah! *(he steps into a man-trap, but continues bravely)* preparations for the British Naval Expedition to Lake Pahoe. The leader of the expedition is Sir Jane Russell. *(the interviewer in slightly different spot with the admiral; we now see that the interviewer has a wooden leg and a crutch)* Sir Jane, what is the purpose of your expedition?

Sir Jane (GRAHAM) Well this is a completely uncharted lake with like hitherto unclassified marine life man, so the whole scene's wide open for a scientific exploration.

Interviewer *(now with a parrot on his shoulder)* One can see the immense amount of preparation involved. Have there been many difficulties in setting up this venture?

Sir Jane *(with 'naval-lib' badge)* Well the real hang-up was with the bread man but when the top brass pigs came through we got it together in a couple of moons. Commodore Betty Grable, who's a real sub-aqua head, has got together diving wise and like the whole gig's been a real gas man.

Interviewer *(now with Long John Silver hat)* Thank you. *(and eyepatch)* Lieutenant Commander Dorothy Lamour.

Parrot Pieces of eight.

Interviewer *(now with Long John Silver jacket)* Dorothy you're in charge of security and liaison for this operation.

Dorothy Lamour (ERIC) Right on. *(he is smoking something and is really cool)*

Interviewer You've kept this all rather hush-hush so far shipmate.

Dorothy Lamour Yeah, it's been really heavy man with all these freaks from the fascist press trying to blow the whole scene.

Interviewer *(to camera)* There's no doubt about it, this expedition does have some rather unusual aspects, Jim lad. For a first, why does the senior personnel all bear the names of Hollywood film stars of the forties ... and female ones at that, shiver me timbers 'tis the black spot, and secondly, I be not afraid of thee Blind Pugh ... why do they talk this rather strange stilted, underground jargon, belay the mainbrace Squire Trelawney this be my ship now. *(he is hit by a dart)* Argh! A tranquillizing dart fired by the cowardly BBC health department dogs ... they've done filled me full of chlorpromazine damn!

He falls. A second interviewer comes into shot and catches the microphone.

Second Interviewer (TERRY J) I'm sorry about my colleague's rather unconventional behaviour.

Sir Jane *(running towards the camera)* The navy's out of sight man come together with the RN it's really something other than else.

Animated psychedelic advert for the Royal Navy.

Animated Voice You dig it, man?

Cut back to second interviewer.

Second Interviewer Hello. I'm sorry about my colleague's rather unconventional behaviour just now, but things haven't been too easy for him recently, trouble at home, rather confidential so I can't give you all the details ... interesting though they are ... three bottles of rum with his Weetabix, and so on, anyway ... apparently the girl wasn't even ... anyway the activity you see behind me ... it's the mother I feel sorry for. I'll start again. The activity you see behind me is part of the preparations for the new Naval Expedition to Lake Pahoe. The man in charge of this expedition is Vice Admiral Sir John Cunningham. Sir John, hello there.

Sir John (GRAHAM) Ah, hello. Well first of all I'd like to apologize for the behaviour of certain of my colleagues you may have seen earlier, but they are from broken homes, circus families and so on and they are in no way representative of the new modern improved British Navy. They are a small vociferous minority; and may I take this opportunity of emphasizing that there is no cannibalism in the British Navy. Absolutely none, and when I say none, I mean there is a certain amount, more than we are prepared to admit, but all new ratings are warned that if they wake up in the morning and find toothmarks at all anywhere on their bodies, they're to tell me immediately so that I can immediately take every measure to hush the whole thing up. And, finally, necrophilia is *right out. (the interviewer keeps nodding but looks embarrassed)* Now, this expedition is primarily to investigate reports of cannibalism and necrophilia in... this expedition is primarily to investigate reports of unusual marine life in the as yet uncharted Lake Pahoe.

Interviewer And where exactly is the lake?

Sir John Er 22A, Runcorn Avenue, I think. Yes, that's right, 22A.

Interviewer Runcorn Avenue?

Sir John Yes, it's just by Blenheim Crescent... do you know it.

Interviewer You mean it's in an ordinary street?

Sir John Of course it's not an ordinary street! It's got a lake in it!

Interviewer Yes but I...

Sir John Look, how many streets do you know that have got lakes in them?

Interviewer But you mean... is it very large?

Sir John Of *course* it's not large, you couldn't get a large lake *in* Runcorn Avenue! You'd have to knock down the tobacconist's! *(looking off camera)* Jenkins... no!

We see a rather sheepish rating about to sink his teeth into a human leg. Sir John puts his hand in front of the lens. Cut to Runcorn Avenue, an ordinary street with houses now turned into flats. The Land Rover arrives with the equipment.

Interviewer I'm now standing in Runcorn Avenue. Sir John... where exactly is the lake?

Sir John Er, well let's see, that's 18... that's 20 so this must be the one.

Interviewer Er, excuse me...

Sir John Yes, that's the one all right.

Interviewer But it's an ordinary house.

Sir John Look, I'm getting pretty irritated with this line of questioning.

Interviewer But it doesn't even look like a lake...

Sir John Look, your whole approach since this interview started has been to mock the Navy. When I think that it was for the likes of you that I had both my legs blown off...

Interviewer *(pointing at perfectly healthy legs)* You haven't had both your legs blown off!

Sir John I was talking metaphorically you fool. Jenkins – put that down. *(Jenkins returns the leg to the Land Rover)* Right, is the equipment ready?

Rating (ERIC) Diving equipment all ready man. *(gives hippy salute)*

Sir John *(warning finger)* Right. Now quite simply the approach to Lake Pahoe is up the steps, and then we come to the shores of the lake. Now, I'm going to press the bell just to see if there's anyone in.

Man (MICHAEL) *(answering)* Hello?

Sir John Good morning – I'm looking for a Lake Pahoe.

Man There's a Mr Padgett.

Sir John No, no a *lake*.

Man There's no lake here, mate. This is Runcorn Avenue. What's the camera doing?

Woman (ERIC) *(coming out)* Camera? What's he want? Oooh, are we on the telly? *(grins at the camera)*

Man He's looking for a lake.

Sir John Lake Pahoe.

Woman Oh, you want downstairs, 22A the basement.

Sir John Ah! Thank you very much. Good morning. Come on men, downstairs.

They walk down to the basement. The interviewer intercepts Sir John.

Interviewer Were you successful, Sir John?

Sir John It's in the basement.

Interviewer In the basement?

He sees a parrot on his shoulder.

Parrot Pieces of eight.

Interviewer Eugh! *(he knocks it off)*

Sir John goes to the front door of 22A and rings. Then he looks into the living room through the window. A middle-aged couple are sitting inside. The room is full of water. The man reads the paper and the woman knits. Both wear breathing apparatus. Sir John knocks on the window. The woman looks up.

Sir John Hello.

Woman Ooooh. I think it's someone about the damp.

Sir John Hello.

Man Tell 'em about the bleeding rats, too.

Woman I'll go. *(she swims to window and shouts out)* Yes?

Sir John Good morning, is this Lake Pahoe?

Woman Well, I don't know about that, but it's bleeding damp. Are you from the council?

Sir John No. We are the official British Naval Expedition to this lake. May we come in?

Woman Hang on.

She submerges and picks up a big sign showing it to the man. The sign reads 'It's not the council, it's a British Naval Expedition to Lake Pahoe or something and can they come in'. The man reads the card. An enormous shark looks over his shoulder appearing from a cupboard. The man sees it and hits it with a newspaper.

Man Bloody sharks.

Woman Get in.

He holds up a sign reading 'Tell them to go away'. The woman swims to the window and gives a V-sign to Sir John.

Sir John Well um . . . that would appear to be the end of the expedition.

Cut to an interview set.

Interviewer (JOHN) The Magna Carta – was it a document signed at Runnymede in 1215 by King John pledging independence to the English barons, or was it a piece of chewing gum on a bedspread in Dorset? The latter idea is the brainchild of a man new to the field of historical research. Mr Badger, why – why are you on this programme?

Pull back to show Mr Badger. He wears a flat cap and has a Scots accent.

Badger (ERIC) Well, I think I can answer this question most successfully in mime. *(mimes incomprehensibly)*

Interviewer But why Dorset?

Badger Well, I have for a long time been suffering from a species of brain injury which I incurred during the rigours of childbirth, and I'd like to conclude by putting my finger up my nose.

Interviewer Mr Badger, I *think* you're the silliest person we've ever had on this programme, and so I'm going to ask you to have dinner with me.

CAPTION: 'LATER THE SAME SKETCH'

Cut to them sitting at a restaurant table.

Badger My wife Maureen ran off with a bottle of Bell's whisky during the Aberdeen versus Raith Rovers match which ended in a goalless draw. Robson particularly, in goal, had a magnificent first half, his fine positional sense preventing the build-up of any severe pressure on the suspect Aberdeen defence. McLoughlan missed an easy chance to clinch the game towards the final whistle but Raith must be well satisfied with their point.

Interviewer Do please go on. This is the least fascinating conversation I've ever had.

A waiter comes in.

Waiter (MICHAEL) Would you like to order sir?

Interviewer Yes, Mr Badger, what would you like to start with?

Badger Er, I'll have a whisky to start with.

Waiter For first course, sir?

Badger Aye.

Waiter And for main course, sir?

Badger I'll have a whisky for main course and I'll follow that with a whisky for pudding.

Waiter Yes sir, and what would you like with it, sir? A whisky?

Badger No, a bottle of wine.

Waiter Fine, sir, he said between clenched teeth knowing full well it was a most unrewarding part.

Interviewer This is the silliest sketch I've ever been in.

Badger Shall we stop it?

Interviewer Yeah, all right. *(they get up and walk out)*

    CAPTION: 'THE END'

    CREDITS

Thirty-three

A light comes up on an organ in the centre of a concert-hall stage. Applause. The organist with wild hair (Terry J) appears from left. He walks fully clothed across to the organ looking pleased with himself. He sits at the organ and raises his hands ... his clothes fly up into the air so that, as per normal, he is naked. He plays the usual chords. Cut on the last note to a naked quartet with identical grins, fright wigs and blacked-out teeth staring maniacally at the camera.

Announcer (JOHN) And now ...

It's Man (MICHAEL) It's ...

Animated titles.

Voice Over (JOHN) Monty Python's Flying Circus.

Cut to stock film of First World War fighter planes in a dog-fight. Heroic war music.

Voice Over (JOHN) The Adventures of Biggles. Part one – Biggles dictates a letter.

Mix through to Biggles and secretary in an office.

Biggles (GRAHAM) Miss Bladder, take a letter.

Secretary (NICKI HOWORTH) Yes, Señor Biggles.

Biggles Don't call me señor! I'm not a Spanish person. You must call me Mr Biggles, or Group Captain Biggles, or Mary Biggles if I'm dressed as my wife, but never señor.

Secretary Sorry.

Biggles I've never even been to Spain.

Secretary You went to Ibiza last year.

Biggles That's still not grounds for calling me señor, or Don Beeg-les for that matter. Right, Dear King Haakon ...

Secretary Of Norway, is that?

Biggles Just put down what I say.

Secretary Do I put that down?

Biggles Of course you don't put that down.

Secretary Well what about that?

Biggles Look. *(she types)* Don't put that down. Just put down – wait a mo – wait a mo. *(puts on antlers)* Now, when I've got these antlers on – when I've got these antlers on I *am* dictating and when I take them off *(takes them off)* I am *not* dictating.

Secretary *(types)* I am not dictating.

Biggles What? *(she types; puts the antlers on)* Read that back.

Secretary Dear King Haakon, I am not dictating what?

Biggles No, no, no, you loopy brothel inmate.

Secretary I've had enough of this. I am not a courtesan. *(moves round to front of the desk, sits on it and crosses her legs provocatively)*

Biggles Oh, oh, 'courtesan', oh aren't we grand. Harlot's not good enough for us eh? Paramour, concubine, fille de joie. That's what we are not. Well listen to me my fine fellow, you are a bit of tail, that's what you are.

Secretary I am not, you demented fictional character.

Biggles Algy says you are. He says you're no better than you should be.

Secretary And how would *he* know?

Biggles And just what do you mean by that? Are you calling my old fictional comrade-in-arms a fairy?

Secretary Fairy! Poof's not good enough for Algy, is it. He's got to be a bleedin' fairy. Mincing old RAF queen. *(sits at the desk)*

Biggles *(into the intercom)* Algy, I have to see you.

Algy (MICHAEL) Right ho. *(he enters)* What ho everyone.

Biggles Are you gay?

Algy I should bally well say so, old fruit.

Biggles Ugh! *(he shoots him)* Dear King Haakon . . . oh . . . *(takes the antlers off)* Dear King Haakon. *(the secretary types)* Just a line to thank you for the eels. Mary thought they were really scrummy, comma, so did I full stop. I've just heard that Algy was a poof, exclamation mark. What would Captain W. E. Johns have said, question mark. Sorry to mench, but if you've finished with the lawn-edger could you pop it in the post. Love Biggles, Algy deceased and Ginger. Ginger! *(puts the antlers on)*

Secretary What?

Biggles Rhyming slang – ginger beer.

Secretary Oh.

Biggles *(into the intercom)* Ginger.

Ginger Hello, sweetie.

Biggles I have to see you.

The door opens, Ginger enters as a terrible poof in camp flying gear, sequins, eye make-up, silver stars on his cheeks.

Ginger (TERRY G) Yes, Biggles?

Biggles Are you a poof?

Ginger *(camp outrage)* I should say not.

Biggles Thank God for that. Good lad. *(Ginger exits)* Stout fellow, salt of the earth, backbone of England. Funny, he *looks* like a poof. *(takes off the antlers)* Dear Princess Margaret.

Pantomime Princess Margaret enters from cupboard.

Margaret Hello.

Biggles Get back in the cupboard you pantomimetic royal person. *(she goes)* Quick cut to a loony.

Loony (GRAHAM) Lemon curry?

Cut back to Biggles.

Biggles Dear *real* Princess Margaret, thank you for the eels, full stop. They were absolutely delicious and unmistakably regal, full stop. Sorry to mench but if you've finished with the hairdryer could you pop it in the post. Yours fictionally Biggles, Oh, PS see you at the Saxe-Coburgs' canasta evening. *(puts the antlers on)* That should puzzle her.

Secretary *(sexily)* Si Señor Biggles.

Biggles Silence, naughty lady of the night!

Bring up heroic music and mix through to stock film of fighter planes in dog-fight.

Voice Over (JOHN) Next week part two – 'Biggles Flies Undone'.

Then a very noisy and violent animation sketch.

Voice Over Meanwhile not very far away.

Cut to mountain climbers, with all the accoutrements: ropes, carabino's helmets, pitons, hammers, etc. They are roped together, apparently climbing a mountain.

Voice Over (MICHAEL) Climbing. The world's loneliest sport, where hardship and philosophy go hand in glove. And here, another British expedition, attempting to be the first man to successfully climb the north face of the Uxbridge Road. *(Pull out to reveal that they are climbing along a wide pavement; a shopper pushing a pram comes into shot)* This four-man rope has been climbing tremendously. BBC cameras were there to film every inch.

Cut to a BBC cameraman clinging to a lamppost, filming. He is wearing climbing gear too. Cut to papier mâché model of the Uxbridge Road, with the route all neatly marked out in white, and various little pins for the camps.

Chris (ERIC) *(voice over)* The major assault on the Uxbridge Road has been going on for about three weeks, really ever since they established base camp here at the junction of Willesden Road, and from there they climbed steadily to establish camp two, outside Lewis's, and it's taken them another three days to establish camp three, here outside the post office. *(cut to a pup tent being firmly planted on the side of a large post-box; it has a little union jack on it)* Well they've spent a good night in there last night in preparation for the final assault today. The leader of the expedition is twenty-nine-year-old Bert Tagg – a local headmaster and mother of three.

Cut to Bert crawling along the pavement. The interviewer is crouching down beside him.

Interviewer (JOHN) Bert. How's it going?

Bert (GRAHAM) Well, it's a bit gripping is this, Chris. *(heavy breathing interspersed)* I've got to try and reach that bus stop in an hour or so and I'm doing it by . . . *(rearranging rope)* damn . . . I'm doing it, er, by laying back on this gutter so I'm kind of guttering and laying back at the same time, and philosophizing.

Interviewer Bert, some people say this is crazy.

Bert Aye, well but they said Crippen was crazy didn't they?

Interviewer Crippen *was* crazy.

Bert Oh, well there you are then. *(shouts)* John, I'm sending you down this carabine on white. *(there is a white rope between Bert and John)*

Quick cut to Viking.

Viking (MICHAEL) Lemon curry?

Cut back to the street.

Bert Now you see he's putting a peg down there because I'm quite a way up now, and if I come unstuck here I go down quite a long way.

Interviewer *(leaving him)* Such quiet courage is typical of the way these brave chaps shrug off danger. Like it or not, you've got to admire the skill that goes into it.

By the miracle of stop action, they all fall off the road, back down the pavement. Passers-by, also in stop action, walk by normally, ignoring the fall.

Cut to an ordinary kitchen. A Mrs Pinnet type lady with long apron and headscarf is stuffing a chicken with various unlikely objects. The door opens. Sound of rain, wind and storm outside. A lifeboatman enters, soaked to the skin. He shuts the door.

Lifeboatman (MICHAEL) *(taking off his sou'wester and shaking the water off it)* Oh it's terrible up on deck.

Mrs Neves (TERRY J) Up on deck?

Lifeboatman Yes on deck. It's diabolical weather.

Mrs Neves What deck, dear?

Lifeboatman The deck. The deck of the lifeboat.

Mrs Neves This isn't a lifeboat, dear. This is 24, Parker Street.

Lifeboatman This is the Newhaven Lifeboat.

Mrs Neves No it's not, dear.

The lifeboatman puts on his sou'wester, goes over to the back door and opens it. He peers out. Sound of wind and lashing rain. Cut to the back door at the side of a suburban house, the lifeboatman looking out over the lawns, flowers and windless, rainless calm across to similar neat suburban houses. The noise cuts. The lifeboatman withdraws his head from the door. Sound of wind and rain again which cease abruptly as he withdraws his head and shuts the door.

Lifeboatman You're right. This isn't a lifeboat at all.

Mrs Neves No, I wouldn't live here if it was.

Lifeboatman Do you mind if I sit down for a minute and collect my wits?

Mrs Neves No, you do that, I'll make you a nice cup of tea.

Lifeboatman Thanks very much.

> *The door flies open. More sound of wind and rain. Two other rain-soaked lifeboatmen appear.*

Second Lifeboatman (GRAHAM) Oooh, it's a wild night up top.

Third Lifeboatman (TERRY G) Your turn on deck soon, Charlie.

First Lifeboatman It's not a lifeboat, Frank.

Third Lifeboatman What?

Second Lifeboatman What do you mean?

First Lifeboatman It's not a lifeboat. It's this lady's house.

> *The two lifeboatmen look at each other, then turn and open the door. Sound of wind and rain as usual. They peer out. Cut to the back door – the two lifeboatmen are peering out. They shout.*

Second and Third Lifeboatmen Captain! Captain! Ahoy there! Ahoy there! Captain!!

> *Their voices carry over the following shot or two. Cut to reverse angle of window across the road. A net curtain moves and an eye peers out. We still hear the shouts. Close up on an elderly spinster (Gladys) holding the net curtain discreetly ajar.*

Enid (ERIC) Who's that shouting?

> *We pull out to reveal a sitting room full of high-powered eavesdropping equipment, i.e. an enormous telescope on wheels with a controller's chair attached to it, several subsidiary telescopes pointing out of the window, radar scanners going round and round, two computers with flashing lights, large and complex tape and video recorders, several TV monitors, oscilloscopes, aerials, etc. All these have been squeezed in amongst the furniture of two retired middle-class old ladies. Enid, a dear old lady with a bun, sits at the control seat of an impressive-looking console, pressing buttons. She also has some knitting.*

Gladys (JOHN) It's a man outside Number 24.

Enid Try it on the five-inch, Gladys.

Gladys *(looking at the array of telescopes)* I can't. I've got that fixed on the Baileys at Number 13. Their new lodger moves in today.

Enid All right, hold 13 on the five-inch and transfer the Cartwrights to the digital scanner.

> *Gladys leaps over to the tape deck, presses levers and switches. Sound of tape reversing. There is a hum and lights flash on and off. A blurred image of a lady in the street comes up on one of the monitors.*

Enid Hold on, Mrs Pettigrew's coming back from the doctor's.

Gladys All right, bring her up on two. What's the duration reading on the oscillator?

Enid 48.47.

Gladys Well that's a long time for someone who's just had a routine checkup.

Enid *(reading a graph on a computer)* Yes, her pulse rate's 146!

Gladys Zoom in on the 16mm and hold her, Enid.

Enid Roger, Gladys.

Gladys I'll try and get her on the twelve-inch. *(she climbs into the control seat of the huge mobile telescope; we cut to the view through Gladys's telescope – out of focus at first, but then sharper as she zooms in towards the side door of Number 24)* Move the curtain, Enid. *(the curtain is opened a little)* Thank you, love.

Cut to the interior of Mrs Neves's kitchen once again. It is absolutely full of lifeboatmen. They are all talking happily and drinking cups of tea. We pick up the conversation between two of them.

First Lifeboatman Yes, it's one of those new self-righting models. Newhaven was about the first place in the country to get one.

Second Lifeboatman What's the displacement on one of them jobs then?

First Lifeboatman Oh it's about 140-150 per square inch.

Mrs Neves Who's for fruit cake?

All Oh yes, please, please.

Mrs Neves Yes, right, macaroons, that's two dozen fruit cakes, half a dozen macaroons. Right ho. Won't be a jiffy then.

She puts a scarf on, pick up a basket and goes out of the front door. As she opens door, we hear the sound of a storm which carries us into the next shot. Cut to the deck of a lifeboat; rain-lashed, heaving, wind-tossed. Mrs Neves struggles against the gale force winds along the deck. She hammers on a hatch in the forward part of the lifeboat.

Mrs Neves Yoohoo! Mrs Edwards!

The hatch opens and a cosy shop-keeping Pepperpot sticks her head out.

Mrs Edwards (GRAHAM) Hello.

Mrs Neves Hello, two dozen fruit cakes and half a dozen macaroons.

Mrs Edwards Sorry love, no macaroons. How about a nice vanilla sponge.

Mrs Neves Yes, that'll be lovely.

Mrs Edwards Right ho. *(sound of a ship's horn; they both look)* There's that nice herring trawler come for their Kup Kakes. Excuse me. *(she produces a loudhailer)* Hello, Captain Smith?

Voice Hallooooo!

Mrs Edwards hurls a box of Kup Kakes off deck.

Mrs Edwards Kup Kakes to starboard.

Voice Coming.

Mrs Neves I'll pay you at the end of the week, all right?

Mrs Edward OK, right ho.

Mrs Neves struggles back along the deck. Cut to stock film of Ark Royal in a storm.

Mrs Neves Here, it's the *Ark Royal*, Doris. Have you got their rock buns ready?

Sound of a ship's horn.

Mrs Edwards Hang on!

Doris appears at the hatch, and hands over two cake boxes.

Doris (JOHN) Here we are, five for them and five for HMS *Eagle*.

Mrs Edwards Right ho. *(takes them and throws them both overboard; an officer climbs up the side of the boat)* Yes?

Officer (MICHAEL) HMS *Defiant*? Two set teas please.

Mrs Edwards Two set teas, Doris. Forty-eight pence. There we are, thank you.

Money is handed over. The teas emerge on two little trays with delicate crockery, little teapots, milk jugs, etc.

Officer By the way, do you do lunches?

Mrs Edwards No, morning coffee and teas only.

Officer Right ho. *(holding the teas he goes up to edge and jumps overboard)*

Cut to very quick series of stills of storage jars.

CAPTION: 'STORAGE JARS'

Urgent documentary music. Mix through to an impressive documentary set. Zoom in fast to presenter in a swivel chair. He swings round to face the camera.

Presenter (ERIC) Good evening and welcome to another edition of 'Storage Jars'. On tonight's programme Mikos Antoniarkis, the Greek rebel leader who seized power in Athens this morning, tells us what he keeps in storage jars. *(quick cut to photo of a guerrilla leader with a gun; sudden dramatic chord; instantly cut back to the presenter)* From strife-torn Bolivia, Ronald Rodgers reports on storage jars there. *(still of a Bolivian city and again dramatic chord and instantly back to the presenter)* And closer to home, the first dramatic pictures of the mass jail-break near the storage jar factory in Maidenhead. All this and more in storage jars!

Cut to a road in front of a heap of smouldering rubble. Dull thuds of mortar. Reporter in short sleeves standing in tight shot. Explosions going off behind him at intervals.

Rodgers (TERRY J) This is La Paz, Bolivia, behind me you can hear the thud of mortar and the high-pitched whine of rockets, as the battle for control of this volatile republic shakes the foundations of this old city. *(slowly we pull out during this until we see in front of him a fairly long trestle table set out with range of different-sized storage jars)* But whatever their political inclinations these Bolivians are all keen users of storage jars. *(the explosions continue behind him)* Here the largest size is used for rice and for mangoes – a big local crop. Unlike most revolutionary

South American states they've an intermediary size in between the 2lb and 5lb jars. This gives this poor but proud people a useful jar for apricots, plums and stock cubes. The smallest jar – this little 2oz jar, for sweets, chocolates and even little shallots. No longer used in the West it remains here as an unspoken monument to the days when La Paz knew better times. Ronald Rodgers, 'Storage Jars', La Paz.

ANIMATION: *television is bad for your eyes.*

Voice Over and CAPTION: 'THE SHOW SO FAR'

Cut to a man sitting at a desk with a script.

Mr Tussaud (TERRY J) Hello, the, er, show so far . . . well it all started with the organist losing his clothes as he sat down at the organ, and after this had happened and we had seen the titles of the show, we saw Biggles dictating a letter to his secretary, who thought he was Spanish, and whom he referred to as a harlot and a woman of the night, although she preferred to be called a courtesan. Then we saw some people trying to climb a road in Uxbridge. And then there were some cartoons and then some lifeboatmen came into a woman's sitting room and after a bit the woman went out to buy some cakes on a lifeboat and then a naval officer jumped into the sea. Then we saw a man telling us about storage jars from Bolivia, then there were some more cartoons and then a man told us about what happened on the show so far and a great hammer came and hit him on the head. *(he frowns)* I don't remember that? *(a big hammer hits him on the head)*

Quick cut to 'It's' man.

It's Man Lemon curry?

A montage of arty photographs. The cutting from photo to photo is pretty fast. Greek music is heard. Starting with: a close up of Mousebender, who is respectable and wears smart casual clothes; various photos of Mousebender walking along the pavement, again very artily shot from show-off angles; Mousebender pausing outside a shop; Mousebender looking up at the shop; Edwardian-style shop with large sign above it reading 'Ye Olde Cheese Emporium'; another sign below the first reading 'Henry Wensleydale, Purveyor of Fine Cheese to the Gentry and the Poverty Stricken Too'; another sign below this reading 'Licensed for Public Dancing'; close up of Mousebender looking pleased; shot of Mousebender entering the shop. Music cuts dead. Cut to interior of the cheese shop. Greek music playing as Mousebender enters. Two men dressed as city gents are Greek dancing in the corner to the music of a bouzouki. The shop itself is large and redolent of the charm and languidity of a bygone age. There is actually no cheese to be seen either on or behind the counter but this is not obvious. Mousebender approaches the counter and rings a small handbell. Wensleydale appears.

Wensleydale (MICHAEL) Good morning, sir.

Mousebender (JOHN) Good morning. I was sitting in the public library in Thurmond Street just now, skimming through 'Rogue Herries' by Horace Walpole when suddenly I came over all peckish.

Wensleydale Peckish, sir?

Mousebender Esurient.

Wensleydale Eh?

Mousebender *(broad Yorkshire)* Eee I were all hungry, like.

Wensleydale Oh, hungry.

Mousebender *(normal accent)* In a nutshell. So I thought to myself 'a little fermented curd will do the trick'. So I curtailed my Walpolling activities, sallied forth and infiltrated your place of purveyance to negotiate the vending of some cheesy comestibles. *(smacks his lips)*

Wensleydale Come again.

Mousebender *(broad Northern accent)* I want to buy some cheese.

Wensleydale Oh, I thought you were complaining about the music.

Mousebender *(normal voice)* Heaven forbid. I am one who delights in all manifestations of the terpsichorean muse.

Wensleydale Sorry?

Mousebender I like a nice dance – you're forced to.

Quick cut to Viking.

Viking (MICHAEL) *(broad Northern accent)* Anyway.

Cut back to the shop.

Wensleydale Who said that?

Mousebender *(normal voice)* Now my good man, some cheese, please.

Wensleydale Yes certainly, sir. What would you like?

Mousebender Well, how about a little Red Leicester?

Wensleydale I'm afraid we're fresh out of Red Leicester, sir.

Mousebender Oh never mind. How are you on Tilsit?

Wensleydale Never at the end of the week, sir. Always get it fresh first thing on Monday.

Mousebender Tish, tish. No matter. Well, four ounces of Caerphilly, then, if you please, stout yeoman.

Wensleydale Ah, well, it's been on order for two weeks, sir, I was expecting it this morning.

Mousebender Yes, it's not my day is it. Er, Bel Paese?

Wensleydale Sorry.

Mousebender Red Windsor?

Wensleydale Normally sir, yes, but today the van broke down.

Mousebender Ah. Stilton?

Wensleydale Sorry.

Mousebender Gruyère, Emmental?

Wensleydale No.

Mousebender Any Norwegian Jarlsberger?

Wensleydale No.
Mousebender Liptauer?
Wensleydale No.
Mousebender Lancashire?
Wensleydale No.
Mousebender White Stilton?
Wensleydale No.
Mousebender Danish Blue?
Wensleydale No.
Mousebender Double Gloucester?
Wensleydale ... No.
Mousebender Cheshire?
Wensleydale No.
Mousebender Any Dorset Blue Vinney?
Wensleydale No.
Mousebender Brie, Rocquefort, Pont-l'Éveque, Port Salut, Savoyard, Saint-Paulin, Carre-de-L'Est, Boursin, Bresse-Bleue, Perle de Champagne, Camembert?
Mousebender Ah! We do have some Camembert, sir.
Mousebender You do. Excellent.
Wensleydale It's a bit runny, sir.
Mousebender Oh, I like it runny.
Wensleydale Well as a matter of fact it's *very* runny, sir.
Mousebender No matter. No matter. Hand over le fromage de la Belle France qui s'appelle Camembert, s'il vous plaît.
Wensleydale I think it's runnier than you like it, sir.
Mousebender *(smiling grimly)* I don't care how excrementally runny it is. Hand it over with all speed.
Wensleydale Yes, sir. *(bends below the counter and reappears)* Oh ...
Mousebender What?
Wensleydale The cat's eaten it.
Mousebender Has he?
Wensleydale She, sir.
Mousebender Gouda?
Wensleydale No.
Mousebender Edam?
Wensleydale No.
Mousebender Caithness?
Wensleydale No.

Mousebender Smoked Austrian?
Wensleydale No.
Mousebender Sage Derby?
Wensleydale No, sir.
Mousebender You do have some cheese, do you?
Wensleydale Certainly, sir. It's a cheese shop, sir. We've got . . .
Mousebender No, no, no, don't tell me. I'm keen to guess.
Wensleydale Fair enough.
Mousebender Wensleydale?
Wensleydale Yes, sir?
Mousebender Splendid. Well, I'll have some of that then, please.
Wensleydale Oh, I'm sorry sir, I thought you were referring to me, Mr Wensleydale.
Mousebender Gorgonzola?
Wensleydale No.
Mousebender Parmesan?
Wensleydale No.
Mousebender Mozzarella?
Wensleydale No.
Mousebender Pippo Crème?
Wensleydale No.
Mousebender Any Danish Fimboe?
Wensleydale No.
Mousebender Czechoslovakian Sheep's Milk Cheese?
Wensleydale No.
Mousebender Venezuelan Beaver Cheese?
Wensleydale Not today sir, no.
Mousebender Well let's keep it simple, how about Cheddar?
Wensleydale Well I'm afraid we don't get much call for it around these parts.
Mousebender No call for it? It's the single most popular cheese in the world!
Wensleydale Not round these parts, sir.
Mousebender And pray what is the most popular cheese round these parts?
Wensleydale Ilchester, sir.
Mousebender I see.
Wensleydale Yes, sir. It's quite staggeringly popular in the manor, squire.
Mousebender Is it?
Wensleydale Yes sir, it's our number-one seller.
Mousebender Is it?

Wensleydale Yes, sir.

Mousebender Ilchester eh?

Wensleydale Right.

Mousebender OK, I'm game. Have you got any, he asked expecting the answer no?

Wensleydale I'll have a look sir . . . nnnnnnoooooooo.

Mousebender It's not much of a cheese shop really, is it?

Wensleydale Finest in the district, sir.

Mousebender And what leads you to that conclusion?

Wensleydale Well, it's so clean.

Mousebender Well, it's certainly uncontaminated by cheese.

Wensleydale You haven't asked me about Limberger, sir.

Mousebender Is it worth it?

Wensleydale Could be.

Mousebender OK, have you . . . *will you shut that bloody dancing up! (the music stops)*

Wensleydale *(to dancers)* Told you so.

Mousebender Have you got any Limberger?

Wensleydale No.

Mousebender No, that figures. It was pretty predictable really. It was an act of pure optimism to pose the question in the first place. Tell me something, do you have any cheese at all?

Wensleydale Yes, sir.

Mousebender Now I'm going to ask you that question once more, and if you say 'no' I'm going to shoot you through the head. Now, do you have any cheese at all?

Wensleydale No.

Mousebender *(shoots him)* What a senseless waste of human life.

Mousebender puts a cowboy hat on his head. Cut to stock shot of man on horse riding into the sunset. Music swells dramatically.

    CAPTION: 'ROGUE CHEDDAR (1967)'

    CAPTION: 'FIN'

    Ordinary simple Philip Jenkinson at a desk set as seen in Monty Python's Flying Circus. Philip Jenkinson sits simpering and pouting like a cross between Truman Capote and a pederast vole.

Philip Jenkinson (ERIC) Horace Walpole's 'Rogue Cheddar', *(sniff)* one of the first of the Cheese Westerns to be later followed by 'Gunfight at Gruyere Corral', 'Ilchester 73', and 'The Cheese Who Shot Liberty Valence'. While I'm on the subject of Westerns, I want to take a closer look at one of my favourite film directors, Sam Peckinpah, the expatriate from Fresno, California.

SUPERIMPOSED CAPTION: 'GET ON WITH IT'

Philip Jenkinson In his earliest films, 'Major Dundee', *(sniff)*

SUPERIMPOSED CAPTION: 'AND STOP SNIFFING'

Philip Jenkinson 'The Wild Bunch' and 'Straw Dogs' he showed his predilection for the utterly truthful and very sexually arousing portrayal of violence *(sniff)* in its starkest form. *(sniff)*

SUPERIMPOSED CAPTION: 'WILL YOU STOP SNIFFING'

Philip Jenkinson In his latest film Peckinpah has moved into the calmer and more lyrical waters of Julian Slade's 'Salad Days'.

Lyrical scene of boys in white flannels and girls in pretty dresses frolicking on a lawn to the accompaniment of a piano played by one of the boys.

SUPERIMPOSED CAPTION: 'SALAD DAYS (1971) DIRECTOR SAM PECKINPAH'

The boys and girls cease frolicking and singing. Lionel enters holding a tennis racket.

Lionel (MICHAEL) Hello everybody.

All Hello, Lionel.

Lionel I say what a simply super day.

All Gosh yes.

Woman It's so, you know, sunny.

Lionel Yes isn't it? I say anyone for tennis?

Julian (GRAHAM) Oh super!

Charles (ERIC) What fun.

Julian I say, Lionel, catch.

He throws the tennis ball to Lionel. It hits Lionel on the head. Lionel claps one hand to his forehead. He roars in pain as blood seeps through his fingers.

Lionel Oh gosh.

He tosses his racket out of frame and we hear a hideous scream. The camera pans to pick up a pretty girl in summer frock with the handle of the racket embedded in her stomach. Blood is pouring out down her dress.

Girl Oh crikey.

Spitting blood out of her mouth she collapses onto the floor clutching at Charles's arm. The arm comes off. Buckets of blood burst out of the shoulder drenching the girl and anyone else in the area. He staggers backwards against the piano. The piano lid drops, severing the pianist's hands. The pianist screams. He stands, blood spurting from his hands over piano music. The piano collapses in slow motion, shot from several angles simultaneously as per 'Zabriskie Point'. Intercut terrified faces of girls screaming in slow motion. The piano eventually crushes them to death; an enormous pool of blood immediately swells up from beneath piano where the girls are. We see Julian stagger across the frame with the piano keyboard through his stomach. As he turns the end of the keyboard knocks off the head of a terrified girl who is sitting on the grass nearby. A volcanic quantity of blood geysers upwards. Pull out and upward from this scene as the music starts again. Cut back to Philip Jenkinson.

Philip Jenkinson Pretty strong meat there from *(sniff)* Sam Peckinpah.

There is the sound of a burst of machine-gun fire and holes appear in Philip Jenkinson's shirt. Blood spurting from each hole in slow motion. Intercut shots from different angles.

CAPTION: 'TEE HEE'

Roll credits over Jenkinson's dying agonies. Fade out.

Voice Over (JOHN) and ROLLER CAPTION: 'THE BBC WOULD LIKE TO APOLOGIZE TO EVERYONE IN THE WORLD FOR THE LAST ITEM. IT WAS DISGUSTING AND BAD AND THOROUGHLY DISOBEDIENT AND PLEASE DON'T BOTHER TO PHONE UP BECAUSE WE *KNOW* IT WAS VERY TASTELESS, BUT THEY DIDN'T REALLY MEAN IT AND THEY DO ALL COME FROM BROKEN HOMES AND HAVE VERY UNHAPPY PERSONAL LIVES, ESPECIALLY ERIC. ANYWAY, THEY'RE REALLY VERY NICE PEOPLE UNDERNEATH AND VERY WARM IN THE TRADITIONAL SHOW BUSINESS WAY AND PLEASE DON'T WRITE IN EITHER BECAUSE THE BBC IS GOING THROUGH AN UNHAPPY PHASE AT THE MOMENT – WHAT WITH ITS FATHER DYING AND THE MORTGAGE AND BBC 2 GOING OUT WITH MEN.'

Voice Over (ERIC) and ROLLER CAPTION: 'THE BBC WOULD LIKE TO DENY THE LAST APOLOGY. IT IS VERY HAPPY AT HOME AND BBC 2 IS BOUND TO GO THROUGH THIS PHASE, SO FROM ALL OF US HERE GOOD NIGHT, SLEEP WELL, AND HAVE AN ABSOLUTELY SUPER DAY TOMORROW, KISS, KISS.'

Cut to Richard Baker sitting at the traditional news desk.

Richard Baker We've just heard that an explosion in the kitchens of the House of Lords has resulted in the breakage of seventeen storage jars. Police ruled out foul play. *(pause)* Lemon curry?

Fade out. Fade up on film of seashore, waves breaking on beach.

SUPERIMPOSED CAPTION: 'INTERLUDE'

The film goes on for quite a long time. Eventually the announcer, dressed in medieval Spanish soldier's costume, walks into shot.

Announcer (JOHN) *(to camera)* Um, I'm sorry about the . . . the, er, pause, only I'm afraid the show is a couple of minutes short this week. You know, sometimes the shows aren't really quite as er, long as they ought to be. *(pause; he looks round at the sea)* Beautiful, isn't it. *(he walks out of shot; long pause; he walks back)* Look there's not really a great deal of point in your, sort of hanging on at your end, because I'm afraid there aren't any more jokes or anything.

He walks out of shot. We stay with the film for quite a long time before we finally fade out.

Thirty-four The Cycling Tour

The green lush Devon countryside. Theme music. The camera is tracking along a hedgerow beside a road. We see a head whizzing along, sometimes just above the hedgerow and sometimes bobbing down out of sight, occasionally for long periods.

SUPERIMPOSED CAPTION: 'THE CYCLING TOUR'

Mr Pither, the cyclist, bobs up and down a few more times, then disappears from sight. There is a crash and clang of a bicycle in collision, mixed with the scream of a frightened hen, and stifled shout of alarm. We are still in long shot and see nothing. The music stops abruptly on the crash.

Pither (MICHAEL) *(voice over)* August 18th. Fell off near Bovey Tracey. The pump caught in my trouser leg.

Cut to interior of a transport cafe. A rather surly proprietor with fag in mouth is operating an espresso coffee machine. Pither, a fussy, bespectacled little man, is leaning over the counter talking chattily.

Pither My pump caught in my trouser leg, and my sandwiches were badly crushed.

Proprietor (ERIC) 35p please.

He goes back to working the machine.

Pither These sandwiches, however, were an excellent substitute.

An enormous lorry driver comes up to the counter.

Driver (JOHN) Give us ten woods, Barney.

Pither Hello! *(the lorry driver looks at him without interest)* It's funny, isn't it how one can go through life, as I have, disliking bananas and being indifferent to cheese, but still be able to eat, and enjoy, a banana and cheese sandwich like this. *(the driver goes off with his cigarettes)*

Proprietor 35p please.

Pither Ah! Oh, I have only a fifty. Do you have change?

Proprietor *(with heavy sarcasm)* Well I'll have to look, but I may have to go to the bank.

Pither I'm most awfully sorry.

Proprietor *(handing him change)* 15p.

Pither Oh, what a stroke of luck. Well, all the very best. *(Pither proffers his hand, the proprietor ignores it)* And thank you again for the excellent banana and cheese delicacy.

He exits busily. The proprietor looks after him. Cut to hedgerows. Theme music. Pither's head bobbing up and down. At the same point in the music it disappears and there is a crash mingled with the grunting of a pig.

Pither *(voice over)* August 23rd. Fell off near Budleigh Salterton.

A brief shot of an unidentifiable animated Gilliam monster looking over the top of a hedge. Cut to a woman gardening. Behind her we see Pither's head peering over the hedge.

Pither ... and the pump got caught in my trouser leg ... *(she carries on digging trying to ignore him)* ... and that's how they were damaged *(no reaction)* ... the eggs ... you remember ... the hard-boiled eggs I was telling you about ... they were in a tupperware container, reputedly self-sealing, which fell open upon contact with a tarmacadam surface of the road ... *(she goes on digging)* the B489 ... the Dawlish Road .. *(again no reaction)* That shouldn't happen to a self-sealing container, now should it? What do you keep your hard-boiled eggs in?

The lady gardener goes back into house. Pither waits for a few moments.

Pither *(shouting)* I think in future I will lash them to the handlebars with adhesive tape ... this should obviate a recurrence of the same problem ... well I can't stand around here chatting all day ... I'm on a cycling tour of North Cornwall. Must be off.

Cut to hedgerows again. Pither's head bowling along. Theme music. He dips out of sight. Crash and a cow moos.

Pither *(voice over)* August 26th. Fell off near Ottery St Mary. The pump caught in my trouser leg. Decided to wear short trousers from now on.

Another brief shot of the animated monster peeking over a hedgerow. Cut to another hedgerow. Pither's head bowling along. Short burst of theme music. Crash.

Pither Fell off near Tiverton. Perhaps a shorter pump is the answer.

Another monster peeps briefly. Cut to a tiny village high street, deserted save for an old lady. Pither cycles into shot, he is in shorts, but still has bicycle clips on. He approaches the old lady.

Pither Excuse me, madam, I wonder if you could tell me of a good bicycle shop in this village where I could either find a means of adapting my present pump, or failing that, of purchasing a replacement?

Old Lady (ERIC) There's *only* one shop here.

She points with a shaking finger. Camera pans very slightly to one side to reveal a shop with a huge four-foot-high sign: 'Bicycle Pump Centre – Specialists In Shorter Bicycle Pumps'. Another sign: 'Short Pumps Available Here'. Another sign: 'We Shorten Pumps While-U-Wait'. The camera shows the shop only for a couple of seconds and pans back to the old lady and Pither.

Pither What a stroke of luck. Now perhaps cycling will become less precarious.

Cut to interior of a doctor's surgery. There is a knock on the door.

Doctor (ERIC) Yes? *(a nurse puts her head round the door)*

Nurse A Mr Pither to see you, doctor. His bicycle pump got caught in his sock.

Doctor Oh, thank you nurse, show him in please.
Nurse This way, please.
The nurse exits, Pither enters in shorts and sweater.
Pither Oh, a very good morning to you too, doctor.
Doctor Ah, I understand that you had an accident.
Pither That's right, my pump got...
Doctor Caught in your sock.
Pither Absolutely. Yes. My fruit cake was damaged on one side.
Doctor Well...
Pither It's got grit all over it.
Doctor Well now, are you in pain?
Pither Oh, heavens no.
Doctor Ah well, where are you hurt?
Pither Oh, fortunately, I escaped without injury.
Doctor Well, what is the trouble?
Pither Please could you tell me the way to Iddesleigh?
Doctor I'm a doctor, you know.
Pither Oh yes, absolutely. Normally I would have asked a policeman or minister of the Church, but finding no one available, I thought it better to consult a man with some professional qualifications, rather than rely on the possibly confused testimony of a passer-by.
Doctor Oh all right. *(he scribbles something on a piece of paper and hands it to Pither)* Take this to a chemist.
Pither Thank you.
Cut to exterior of a chemist's shop. A chemist comes out holding the paper and points up the street. Pither thanks him and mounts his bike. Cut to hedgerows again. Pither's head. The theme music reaches the point where Pither normally falls off, his head disappears and the music cuts off. There is no crash. Suddenly Pither's head reappears further on and the music starts up again.
Pither *(voice over)* September 2nd. Did not fall off outside Iddesleigh.
Cut to a small market town. A line of cars. Pither's head just above roofs of cars. Theme music. He suddenly disappears, the music stops and there is a crash.
Pither Fell off in Tavistock.
Cut to a discreet corner of a Watney's pub. Soft music. A middle-aged businessman and a sexy secretary who obviously want to be alone are sitting huddled over a table. At the next table is Pither, with a half-pint in front of him.
Pither My foot caught in my trouser leg and that's how the bottle broke.
Girl (CAROL) Tell her today, you could ring her.

Man (JOHN) I can't, I can't.
Pither I said you'd never guess.
Man Sixteen years we've been together. I can't just ring her up.
Girl Well, if you can't do it now, you never will.
Pither *(tapping the man on the leg)* Do you like Tizer?
Man *(to Pither)* What? No. No.
Girl Do you want me or not, James? It's your decision.
Pither I suppose it is still available in this area, is it?
Girl Do you want me or not, James?
Man What?
Pither Tizer.
Girl Yes or no.
Pither Is it still available in this area?
Man *(to Pither)* I don't know.
Girl I see, in that case it's goodbye for ever, James.
Man No! I mean yes!
Pither Oh it is, is it?
Man *(to Pither)* No.
Girl Oh! You never could make up your mind.
Man I can ... I have ...
Girl *(taking off her ring)* Goodbye James.
  She runs out sobbing.
Man No wait, Lucille!
Pither Does your lovely little daughter like Tizer? Eh?
Man Lucille!
Pither Wouldn't mind buying her a bottle of Tizer ... if it's still available in this area, that is.
Man *(turning on Pither)* Would you like me to show you the door?
Pither Oh, that's extremely kind of you, but I saw it on the way in.
Man You stupid, interfering little rat!
  The man picks Pither up by the scruff of the neck and the seat of his pants. He carries him bodily towards the door.
Pither I had just fallen off my bicycle, this is most kind of you, and my lemon curd tartlet had ...
Man Damn your lemon curd tartlet!
  Pither is thrown out. He picks himself up and sees the girl outside sobbing.
Pither Just had a chat with your dad.
  The girl bursts into further tears. Whistling cheerfully Pither gets on his bicycle and, happier than he has been for a long time, he cycles off

down the road and round a corner. Sounds of car-tyre screech and crash of Pither going straight into a car. Cut to interior of car speeding along highway. The driver is an earnest young man. Pither is sitting in the back seat with his bicycle. The driver, Mr Gulliver, talks with a professional precision.

Pither My rubber instep caught on the rear mudguard stanchion and . . .

Gulliver (TERRY J) Really? And what happened to the corned beef rolls?

Pither The corned beef rolls squashed out of all . . . here, how did you know about the corned beef rolls?

Gulliver I noticed them – or what remained of them – in the road. I noticed also that the lemon curd tart had sustained some superficial damage.

Pither That's right. The curd had become . . .

Gulliver Detached from the pastry base.

Pither *(with some surprise)* Absolutely right, yes.

Gulliver Otherwise the contents of the sandwich box were relatively unharmed, although I detected small particles of bitumen in the chocolate kup kakes.

Pither But they were wrapped in foil!

Gulliver Not the hard chocolate top, I'm afraid.

Pither Oh, that's the bit I like.

Gulliver The sausage roll, the crisps and the ginger biscuit were unscathed.

Pither How do you know so much about cycling?

Gulliver Well, I'm making a special study of accidents involving food.

Pither Really?

Gulliver Yes, do you know that in our laboratories, we have developed a cheese sandwich that can withstand an impact of up to 4,000 pounds per square inch?

Pither Good heavens!

Gulliver Amazing, isn't it? We've also developed a tomato which can eject itself when an accident is imminent.

Pither Even if it's in an egg and tomato roll?

Gulliver Anywhere. Even if it's in your stomach, if it senses an accident it will come up your throat and out of the window. Do you know what this means?

Pither Safer food?

Gulliver Exactly. No longer will food be squashed, crushed and damaged by the ignorance and stupidity of the driver. *(becoming slightly messianic)* Whole picnics will be built to withstand the most enormous forces! Snacks will be safer than ever! A simple pot of salad dressing, treated in our laboratories, has been subjected to the impact of a 4,000 pound steam hammer every day for the last sixteen years and has it broken?

Pither Er... well...

Gulliver Yes, of course it has... but there are other ideas – safety straps for sardines for example.

A tomato leaps up out of the glove compartment and hovers, then it ejects itself out of the car window.

Pither Here, that tomato has just ejected itself!

Gulliver Really? *(embracing Pither excitedly)* It works! It works! *(the car crashes)*

Fade out. Fade up on country road. Pither is cycling along with Gulliver on the back of the bicycle. Gulliver has his head bandaged and his arm in a sling. Occasional strains of Clodagh Rogers's hit 'Jack in a Box' float towards us as Gulliver moves rhythmically.

Pither *(voice over)* What a strange turn this cycling tour has taken. Mr Gulliver appears to have lost his memory and far from being interested in safer food is now convinced that he is Clodagh Rogers, the young girl singer. I am taking him for medical attention.

Cut to Pither and Gulliver cycling into a hospital. A sign says 'North Cornwall District Hospital'. Cut to nurse receptionist at a counter with a glass window which lifts up and down. Pither appears.

Pither Is this the casualty department?

Nurse (GRAHAM) Yes, that's right.

A noise of splintering wood and a crash out of vision. Pither and the nurse look up. A bench has collapsed in the middle and three patients sitting on it have slid into a heap in the middle. A nurse is on her way to assist. Cut back to Pither and nurse.

Nurse And what can I do for you?

The window comes down on her fingers. She winces sharply in pain. She pushes it up again.

Pither I am at present on a cycling tour of the North Cornwall area taking in Bude and...

Nurse Could I have your name please?

Pither Ah, my name is Pither.

Nurse What?

Pither P-I-T-H-E-R... as in Brotherhood, except with PI instead of the BRO and no Hood.

Nurse I see...

Pither I have just visited Taunton...

A terrific crash. Cut to a trolley on its side, and a bandaged patient under a mound of hospital instruments and a nurse standing looking down.

Nurse Sh!

Pither ... I was cycling north towards...

Nurse Yes, where were you injured?

Pither Just where the A237 Ilfracombe road meets the ...

Nurse On your *body* ...

Pither Ah no ... it's not I who was injured, it's my friend.

The nurse scowls, crumples up the paper, and throws it away. The piece of paper hits a smallish cabinet of glass which topples forward and smashes.

Nurse Tut ... name?

Pither Pither.

Nurse No, no, no, no. Your friend's name.

Pither Oh, Clodagh Rogers ...

Nurse Clodagh Rogers!?

Pither Well only since about 4.30 ...

Nurse Yes. I think you'd better talk to Dr Wu ... Doctor!

Cut to a doctor unloading a crate balanced on top of a medicine cupboard. He whips round knocking off the crate.

Doctor (JOHN) What? Damn!

Cut to patient in a wheelchair being pushed. The wheelchair completely collapses and the nurse is left holding the handles. Quick cut to the nurse as window comes down on her fingers again.

Nurse Aaaaaagh!

The doctor comes across to Pither, limping slightly, in some pain.

Pither I am on a cycling tour of North Cornwall, taking in ...

Nurse He *thinks* he's had an accident.

Pither I have a friend who, as a result of his injuries thinks he is Clodagh Rogers.

Doctor He what?

Pither Well, what happened was ...

A nurse carrying a tray walks past the doctor, making for the entrance doors. As she reaches them they swing open to admit Gulliver, with his head bandaged and his arm in a sling. He collides with the nurse; she drops her tray. He grabs Pither and they exit rapidly, stepping on the doctor's foot in the process. The doctor yells, grabs his foot, and as he does so the reception window slams down, trapping his hand. He howls in pain. Cut to a camp fire at midnight in a forest clearing. By the light of the fire, Pither is writing up his diary.

Pither *(voice over)* September 4th. Well I never. We are now in the Alpes Maritimes region of Southern France. Clodagh seems more intent on reaching Moscow than on rehearsing her new BBC 2 series with Buddy Rich and the Younger Generation ... *(Gulliver enters the scene; his head is still bandaged)* Oh hello!

Gulliver We cannot stay here. We must leave immediately. There is a ship in Marseille.

Pither I did enjoy your song for Europe, Clodagh.
Gulliver I have seen an agent in the town. My life is in danger.
Pither Danger, Clodagh?
Gulliver Stalin has always hated me.
Pither No one hates you, Clodagh.
Gulliver I will not let myself fall into the hands of these scum.
Pither I think you should go and have a little lie down, my dear. There is a busy day tomorrow of concerts and promotional tours.
Gulliver I? One of the founders of the greatest nation of the earth? I! Whom Lenin has called his greatest friend.
From the darkness we hear French voices.
M. Brun (JOHN) Taisez-vous. Taisez-vous.
Pither Oh dear.
Gulliver I! Who have worked all my life that my people should live.
A pair of middle-class French people in pyjamas appear.
M. Brun Taisez-vous. Qu'est-ce que le bruit? C'est impossible!
Pither Er... my name is Pither.
M. Brun Oh... you are English?
Pither Er yes, that's right. I'm on a cycling tour of North Cornwall, taking in Bude...
Gulliver I will not be defeated! I will return to my country to fight against this new tyranny!
Pither This is Clodagh Rogers, the Irish-born girl singer.
Mme Brun (ERIC) Mais oui – c'est Clodagh Rogers – 'Jack in a box'! *(sings)* I'm just a Jack in the box, I know whenever love knocks... *(calls)* Genevieve! Gerard! C'est Clodagh Rogers la fameuse chanteuse Anglaise.
Two teenagers in pyjamas and carrying autograph books appear and rush towards Gulliver.
Gulliver I will never surrender! I will never surrender!...
Genevieve (GRAHAM) Excusez-moi Madame Clodagh. Ecrivez-vous votre nom dans mon livre des hommes célèbres, s'il vous plaît. Là, au-dessous de le Denis Compton. *(Gulliver signs and hands the book back)* Maman! Ce n'est pas la belle Clodagh.
Mme Brun Quoi?
Genevieve C'est Trotsky le révolutionnaire.
M. Brun Trotsky!
Mme Brun Mais Trotsky ne chante pas.
M. Brun Il chante un peu.
Mme Brun Mais pas professionnellement. Qu'il pense de Lenin.
M. Brun Ah! Lenin!! Quel chanteur! 'If I ruled the world!'

A brief film clip of Lenin, apparently singing the next line of the song.

Gulliver Lenin! My friend! I come!

He dashes off into the forest possessed.

Pither Oh excuse her, she's not been very well recently, pressure of work, laryngitis, you know...

He gets on his bike and pedals off hurriedly after Gulliver into the forest.

M. Brun *(still reminiscing)* Et aussi Monsieur Kerensky avec le 'Little White Bull', eh?

Mme Brun Formidable.

Cut to a few quick shots of Gulliver dashing through the trees and then of Pither making much slower progress due to his bike. Cut to a shot of a French couple snogging in car.

Gulliver Lenin! I come! Lenin!

Frenchman Je t'aime.

French Girl *(seeing Gulliver)* Maurice! Regardez! C'est la chanteuse anglaise Clodagh Rogers.

Frenchman Ah mais oui. *(sings)* Jacques dans la boîte. *(he switches on car radio and the song is heard throughout the forest)*

Cut to a Russian street. Pither cycles along with Gulliver looking like Trotsky on the back.

Pither *(voice over)* After several days I succeeded in tracking down my friend Mr Gulliver on the outskirts of Smolensk.

Cut to a military man. He has a large map of Europe and Russia and a stick with which he raps at the places.

Military Man (ERIC) Smolensk, 200 miles east of Minsk. 200 north of Kursk. 1500 miles west of Omsk.

Cut back to Pither and Gulliver.

Pither Thank you.

They have stopped by a signpost which says 'Smolensk town centre ½, Tavistock 1612 miles'.

Pither *(voice over)* Anyway, as we were so far from home and as Mr Gulliver, still believing himself to be Trotsky, was very tired from haranguing the masses all the way from Monte Carlo.

Cut to the military man who thumps the map again.

Military Man Monte Carlo. 100 miles south of Turin, 100 miles east of Pisa, 500 miles west of Bilbao.

Cut back to Pither.

Pither Thank you. I decided to check...

Pither *(voice over)* I decided to check...

Pither No, sorry you go on.

Pither *(voice over)* I decided to check him into a hotel while I visited the British Embassy to ask for help in returning to Cornwall.
They leave the bicycle on the kerb and enter a door with the sign 'YMACA' over it.
Pither *(voice over)* And so we registered at the Smolensk Young Men's Anti-Christian Association.
Cut to the military man.
Military Man YMACA. Corner of Anti-Semitic Street and Pogrom Square.
Pither *(by now standing at the reception desk with Gulliver)* Go away. *(to departing desk clerk)* No, not you. A single room for my friend please.
Desk Clerk (TERRY G) Yes, sir. Bugged or unbugged?
Gulliver *(as Trotsky)* I think I'd be happier with a bugged one.
Desk Clerk Right, one bugged with bath.
Pither Well, just have a nice lie down, and I'll go down to the Embassy.
He goes. Gulliver signs hotel register.
Desk Clerk *(looking at the book)* Trotsky! My lack of God, it's Trotsky!
A couple of people race in excitedly.
Gulliver Comrades. Socialism is not a . . .
Mix through to the British Consulate. Pither cycles up, parks his bike and goes in. Imperial music. Mix through to smoky interior. A picture of the queen is dimly visible on the back wall. A Chinaman approaches. He is dressed in traditional Mandarin's robe and cap.
Pither Excuse me. Is this the British Consulate?
Chinaman (GRAHAM) Yes, yes . . . si si . . . that is correctment. Yes . . . Piccadilly Circus, miniskirt and Joe Lyons.
Pither I wish to see the consul, please.
Chinaman Yes, yes, speakee speakee . . . me Blitish consul.
Pither Oh! *(he examines his diary)* You are Rear Admiral Sir Dudley Compton?
Chinaman No. He died. He have heart attack and fell out of window on to exploding bomb, and was killed in a shooting accident. I . . . I his how you say . . . succ . . . sussor.
Pither Oh, successor.
Chinaman I'm his successor, Mr Atkinson.
Pither Oh.
Chinaman Would you like drinkee? Or game bingo?
Pither Well . . . A drink would be very nice.
The Chinaman claps his hands and another runs in and bows obsequiously.
Chinaman Mr Livingstone. Go and get sake.
Livingstone (JOHN) Yes, boss. *(goes)*

Chinaman Oh how is Tonblidge Wells? How I long to see again walls of famous Shakespeare-style theatre in Stlatford-on-Avon.

Pither Oh well I'm a West Country man myself, Mr Atkinson.

Chinaman Oh Texas – Arizona – Kit Carson Super Scout.

Pither No. No. West of England . . . Cornwall.

Chinaman *(with difficulty)* Coron . . . worll . . .

Pither Cornwall.

Chinaman Coronworl . . . oh yes know Coronworl very well. Went to school there, mother and father live there, ah yes. Go many weekend parties and polo playing in bildge club. Belong many clubs in Coronworl.

Livingstone reappears with drink and plate of pastries. He puts them down.

Chinaman Ah, Mr Livingstone thank you, sake and bakewells tart. *(hands a glass of sake to Pither)* Well, chaps, buttocks up!

Pither Rather. *(they drink)*

Chinaman Now then er . . . er . . .

Pither Ah, Pither.

Chinaman Ah Mr Pither. We British here in Smolensk very interested in cliket.

Pither Oh, cricket?

Chinaman No, no . . . you not speak English velly wells. Not clicket – clicket . . . clicketty click . . . clicket . . . housey housey . . . er, bingo.

Pither Bingo . . .

Chinaman Oh bingo . . . bingo . . . bingo.

Livingstone Bingo! Bingo!

Several Mao-suited Chinese people rush in waving the Red Book and shouting 'bingo'. The Chinaman remonstrates with Livingstone and eventually stops them.

Chinaman Hsai! Solly. Our boys got velly excited. *(the Maoists exit)*

Livingstone Bingo.

Chinaman *(to Livingstone)* Shut face! *(to Pither)* Mr Pither, perhaps you could put in a good word for so we could join a very smart bingo club in Coronworl.

Pither Well, it's not really my line . . .

Chinaman We all sit velly quiet at back, not say anything except shout 'Housey! Housey!'.

Livingstone Housey! Housey!

Maoists *(rushing back in)* Housey! Housey!

Cut to stock film of large Chinese crowds.

Chinese Hordes Housey! Housey! Housey housey!

Cut back to Consulate. The Chinaman is shouting out of window.

Chinaman Hi skwwati niyhi, keo t'sin feh t'sdung, hihi watai bingo cards! *(comes back into the room)*

Livingstone Nihi watai bingo cards?

Chinaman Nihi watai!

Livingstone Ah so . . .

Chinaman Now then, Mr Pither, tell me which better – Hackney Star Bingo or St Albans Top Rank Suite?

Pither Well I was hoping that you could help me and my friend to get back to England as . . . you see we're on a cycling tour of North Cornwall . . .

All Bingo, bingo, bingo . . .

The Chinaman ushers Pither out. Brief film clip of rioting Chinese.

Chinese Hordes Bingo! Bingo! Bingo! Bingo!

Cut to the hotel lobby.

Pither Is Mr Trotsky in his room, please?

Desk Clerk No. He has gone to Moscow.

Cut to the military man.

Military Man Moscow. 1500 miles south of . . .

Cut back to lobby.

Desk Clerk Shut up.

Pither Moscow!

He is surrounded by three secret policemen dressed in identical suits, dark glasses and pork pie hats.

Grip (ERIC) Come with us, please.

Pither Oh, who are you?

Bag (JOHN) Well we're not secret police anyway.

Wallet (GRAHAM) That's for sure.

Grip If anything we are ordinary Soviet citizens with no particular interest in politics.

Bag None at all. Come with us.

Pither Oh where are you taking me?

The secret police all move away to confer.

Wallet What do we tell him?

Grip Don't tell him any secrets.

Bag Agreed.

Grip Tell him anything except we are taking him to Moscow where Trotsky is reunited with the Central Committee.

They return to Pither.

Wallet We're taking you to a clambake.

Pither Oh a clambake! I've never been to one of those.

Grip Right, let's go.
Bag Who's giving the orders round here?
Grip I am. I'm senior to you.
Bag No you're not. You're a greengrocer, I'm an insurance salesman.
Grip Greengrocers are senior to insurance salesmen.
Bag No they're not!
Wallet Cool it. I'm an ice-cream salesman and I'am senior to both of you.
Bag You're an ice-cream salesman? I thought you were a veterinarian.
Wallet I got promoted. Let's go.
Bag Taxi!

> *A girl enters dressed as a New York cabbie.*

Taxi (CAROL) Yes.
Bag Drive us to Moscow.
Taxi I have no cab.
Wallet Why not?
Taxi I'm in the secret police. *(they all snap into the salute)*

> *Cut to shot of train wheels in the night. The siren sounds. Superimposed names zoom into camera, as in a musical: Petrograd, Ottograd, Lewgrad, Lesliegrad, Etceteragrad, Dukhovskoknabilebskohatsk, Moscva. Cut to the stage of a big Russian hall. A banner across the top of the stage reads 'Russian 42nd International Clambake'. At the back of the stage sits Pither with his bicycle. At one side of the stage, at an impressive table on a dais, are some very important Russian persons including generals. One of the generals addresses the audience.*

General (JOHN) . . . Dostoievye useye tovarich trotsky borodina . . . *(etc.)*
> SUBTITLE: 'THIS IS THE MAN WHO BROUGHT OUR BELOVED TROTSKY BACK TO US'

General Belutanks dretsky mihai ovna isky Mr Reg Pither.
> SUBTITLE: 'FIRST MAY I PRESENT MR PITHER FROM THE WEST OF ENGLAND'

> *Pandemonium lasting for about ten seconds.*

General Shi muska di scensand dravenka oblomov Engleska Solzhenitzhin.
> SUBTITLE: 'FORGIVE ME IF I CONTINUE IN ENGLISH IN ORDER TO SAVE TIME'

General And now, Comrades, the greatest moment of a great day, the moment when I ask you to welcome the return of one of Russia's greatest heroes, creator of the Red Army, Lenin's greatest friend, Lev Davidovich Trotsky!

> *Gulliver appears looking as much like Trotsky as possible. He wears a uniform and has a beard and glasses. Pandemonium breaks out. He eventually quietens them by raising his hands for silence.*

Gulliver Comrades. Bolsheviks. Friends of the Revolution. I have returned. *(renewed cheering)* The bloodstained shadow of Stalinist repression is past. I bring you the new light of Permanent Revolution. *(his movements are becoming a little camp and slinky)* Comrades, I may once have been ousted from power, I may have been expelled from the party in 1927, I may have been deported in 1926, but *(sings)* I'm just an old-fashioned girl with an old-fashioned mind. *(a certain amount of confusion is spreading among the audience and particularly the generals on the podium)* Comrades, I don't want to destroy in order to build, I don't want a state founded on hate and division. *(sings again)* I want an old-fashioned house with an old-fashioned fence, and an old-fashioned millionaire.

From now on Gulliver continues exactly as Eartha Kitt. He has acquired a fur stole which he manipulates slinkily. The confusion is complete on the stage.

Pither *(voice over)* Our friend Mr Gulliver was clearly undergoing another change of personality.

A senior general appears beside Pither with two guards.

General *(to Pither)* So! You have duped us. You shall pay for this. Guards, seize him.

The guards seize the startled Pither and drag him away. The senior general strides back across the stage avoiding Gulliver, towards the general who addressed the audience.

General Shall I seize him too?

Senior General (GRAHAM) No, I think we'll have to keep him, he's going down well.

General He's more fun than he used to be.

Senior General He's loosened up a lot. This is an old Lenin number.

Cut to Pither sitting in a cell.

Pither *(voice over)* April 26th. Thrown into Russian cell. Severely damaged my Mars bar. Shall I ever see Bude Bus Station again? *(two Russian guards throw the cell door open)* Oh excuse me . . . *(they grab him and march him out of the cell)*

Cut to exterior of a door leading out into the prison yard. The door is thrown open and Pither is marched over and stood against a blank wall. There are lots of small holes in the wall.

Pither *(voice over)* What a pleasant exercise yard. How friendly they were all being.

Officer (JOHN) Cigarettes?

Pither Oh, no thank you I don't smoke.

Pither facing a line of uniformed men with guns, obviously a firing squad.

Pither *(voice over)* After a few moments I perceived a line of gentlemen with rifles. They were looking in my direction... *(cut to Pither against the wall looking behind him)* I looked around but could not see the target.

Officer Blindfold?

Pither *(very cheerful)* No thank you, no.

Officer (stepping clear) Slowotny! *(the firing squad snaps to attention)* Grydenka... *(they raise their rifles)* Verschnitzen.

Drum roll. The firing squad takes aim. A messenger runs frantically up.

Messenger (GRAHAM) Nyet! Nyet! Nyet! *(he hands the officer a paper)*

Officer A telegram? *(examines it)* From the Kremlin! The Central Committee! *(reads)* It says... 'Carry on with the execution'. Verschnitzen... *(the squad raise their rifles)*

Pither *(voice over)* Now I was really for it.

Cut to shot of the officer with his hand raised. The same as before, only without Pither in shot. Drum rolls again. He brings his sword down. Volley of shots from the firing squad. The officer is looking in Pither's direction. Long pause.

Officer *(to soldiers)* How could you miss?

Soldier He moved.

Officer Shut up! Go and practise. *(to Pither)* I'm so sorry. Do you mind waiting in your cell?

Pither is flung back into his cell by the guards, and the door slammed.

Pither *(voice over)* What a stroke of luck. My Crunchie was totally intact. I settled down to a quick intermeal snack...

But he is bundled out again. Pause. Shots. He is bundled in. The officer appears at door.

Officer Next time, definitely! *(to aide)* Now then, how many have been injured? Oh God...

Pither *(voice over)* As I lay down to the sound of the Russian gentlemen practising their shooting, I realized I was in a bit of a pickle. My heart sank as I realized that I should never see the Okehampton by-pass again...

Mix to Pither's sleeping face, waking up, shaking himself in disbelief at finding himself in a beautiful garden, with the sun shining and the birds singing. He is in a deckchair, and his mother, having poured him a jug of iced fruit juice, is gently nudging Pither to wake him.

Mother (ERIC) Come on, dear, wake up, dear.

Pither Mother!

Mother Come on, dear.

Pither So, it was all a dream.

Mother No dear, *this* is the dream, you're still in the cell.

Mix to Pither waking up in the cell. The officer enters carrying a rifle.

Officer OK, we're going to have another try. I think we've got it now. My boys have been looking down the wrong bit, you see.

Pither Oh no, look, you've got to look down the bit there.

Officer I thought you had to look down that bit.

Pither No, no, you've got to look down that bit, or you won't hit anything.

Officer All right, we'll give it a whirl. Guards, seize him. *(they take him out)*

Officer *(as he leaves)* Listen. You've got to look down this bit.

As they leave, we can see on the wall of the cell a poster, saying: 'Saturday Night at the Moscow Praesidium, starring Eartha Kitt, with Burgess and Maclean. "A Song a Dance and a Piece of Treachery". Marshal Bulganin and "Charlie", Peter Cook, Dudley Moore, Leningrad has never laughed so much.'

Mix through to stock film of the Kremlin. Dubbed over laughter and applause. A cheerful band sing. Mix through to a stage where someone dressed as Marshal Bulganin, is standing with a little real ventriloquist's dummy. He gets up, takes his bow and walks off as the curtain swings down. Lots of applause and atmosphere. Terrible Russian compère comes on smiling and applauding.

Compère (ERIC) Osledi. Osledi.

He tells a quick joke in Russian and roars with laughter. Laughter from the audience. He holds up his hands and then becomes very sincere, saying obviously deeply moving, wonderful things about the next guest, whom he finally introduces.

Compère Eartha Kitt!

Gulliver comes on-stage in the full Eartha Kitt rig – white fur stole, slit skirt and jewellery. He mimes to the voice of Edward Heath.

Heath's Voice Trade Union leaders – I would say this – we've done our part. Now, on behalf of the community, we have a right to expect you, the Trade Union leaders, to do yours. *(etc.)*

Unrest in the audience as they recognize him. They start shouting 'sing "Old-Fashioned Girl"' and throwing vegetables. Slow motion shot of a tomato hitting Gulliver. He is seen to be holding a turnip.

Gulliver That turnip's certainly not safe. *(looking round and seeing where he is)* Oh no! Mr Pither! Mr Pither!

He runs off-stage, pursued by the guards. Cut to the stage-door of the hall. A sign on the door says 'Next week Clodagh Rogers'. Gulliver runs out, and then through the streets, hotly pursued by soldiers and secret service men, firing after him.

Gulliver *(calling)* Mr Pither! Mr Pither!

He is seen running through a dockyard. Finally he stops by a high stone wall.

Gulliver Mr Pither!

Pither's Voice Here!

> *Gulliver looks round and then rapidly climbs up and over the wall. He drops down to find Pither standing on the other side.*

Pither Gulliver.

Gulliver Pither! What a stroke of luck.

Pither Well yes and no.

> *He indicates with his head. Cut to show that both of them are standing in front of a firing squad. The officer is there as before. The squad runs towards them with fixed bayonets.*
>
> CAPTION: 'SCENE MISSING'
>
> *Cut to a Cornish country lane. A road sign says 'Tavistock 12 miles'. Pither stands beneath with Gulliver and his bicycle.*

Pither Phew, what an amazing escape. Well goodbye, Reginald.

Gulliver Goodbye, Mr Pither, and good luck with the tour!

> *They shake hands. Gulliver strides off. Pither mounts his bike and rides off into the sunset. Music swells. Roll credits. Cut to a field with hedgerow behind. The first animated monster peeks over the hedge.*

First Monster Hey, I think he's finally gone!

> *Second monster appears.*

Second Monster Ooh yes!

> *They hop over the fence into the field.*

First Monster Ready, Maurice?

Second Monster Right-ho, Kevin. Let's go.

First Monster All right, maestro, hit it!

> *We hear Clodagh Rogers singing 'Jack in a Box'. The two monsters jump up and down enthusiastically if not gracefully. Fade out.*

Thirty-five

Fade up on two pilots in the cockpit of an aeroplane. A stewardess is there too. After a moment or two the first pilot makes an announcement.

First Pilot (MICHAEL) This is Captain MacPherson welcoming you aboard East Scottish Airways. You'll have had your tea. Our destination is Glasgow. There is no need to panic.

The door of the cockpit opens and Mr Badger comes in.

Badger (ERIC) There's a bomb on board this plane, and I'll tell you where it is for a thousand pounds.

Second Pilot (JOHN) I don't believe you.

Badger If you don't tell me where the bomb is . . . if I don't give you the money . . . Unless you give me the bomb . . .

Stewardess (CAROL) The money.

Badger The money, thank you, pretty lady . . . the bomb will explode killing everybody.

Second Pilot Including you.

Badger I'll tell you where it is for a pound.

Second Pilot Here's a pound.

Badger I don't want Scottish money. They've got the numbers. It can be traced.

Second Pilot One English pound. Now where's the bomb?

Badger I can't remember.

Second Pilot You've forgotten.

Badger Ay, you'd better have your pound back. Oh . . . *(rubs it)* fingerprints.

First Pilot Now where's the bomb?

Badger Ah, wait a tic, wait a tic. *(closes eyes and thinks)* Er, my first is in Glasgow but not in Spain, my second is in steamer but not in train, my whole is in the luggage compartment on the plane . . . *(opens eyes)* I'll tell you where the bomb is for a pound.

Second Pilot It's in the luggage compartment.

Badger Right. Here's your pound.

Enter a man with headphones.

Headphones (GRAHAM) This character giving you any trouble?

First Pilot He's ruined this sketch.

Second Pilot Absolutely.

Headphones Let's go on to the next one.

Badger Wait a tic, wait a tic. No. I won't ruin your sketch for a pound.

Second Pilot No, no.

Badger 75p.

Headphones Next item. *(they start to leave)*

The nude organist is seated at his organ in the open air, with a lovely scarlet dressing-gown draped round his shoulders. It says on it 'Noël Coward' which is crossed out and 'Nude Organist' written underneath. He is holding forth to a journalist with a notepad who is nodding and interviewing him. Someone else holds a small tape recorder. Make-up ladies are adding the finishing touches. They bring him a mirror while he talks. Someone is taking photos of him, perhaps with flashbulbs.

Nude Man (TERRY J) Well I see my role in it as, er, how can I put it best – the nude man – as sort of symbolizing the two separate strands of existence, the essential nudity of man . . .

They realize that they are on camera. They remove the man's robe and clear the set. He grins at the camera and plays his chords.

Cut to the announcer. He is sitting at his desk in the middle of a field but he is talking earnestly to a trendy girl reporter.

Announcer (JOHN) It's an interesting question. Personally I rather adhere to the Bergsonian idea of laughter as a social sanction against inflexible behaviour but . . . excuse me a moment . . . And now . . .

It's Man (MICHAEL) It's . . .

Animated titles.

Voice Over (ERIC) and CAPTION: 'AND NOW THE TEN SECONDS OF SEX'

Black screen and the sound of a ticking clock for ten seconds.

Voice Over and CAPTION: 'ALL RIGHT, YOU CAN STOP NOW'

Cut to a little palm court set. A man seated.

Man in Tails (GRAHAM) Well, we'll be continuing with 'Monty Python's Flying Circus' in just a moment. Yes, yes, we're going back to the show, in just one moment *(consults his watch)* fr . . . o . . . m nnnnnnnnnnnn . . . now.

Cut to a building site. The camera pans over it.

Voice Over (MICHAEL) This new housing development in Bristol is one of the most interesting in the country. It's using a variety of new techniques: shock-proof curtain-walling, a central high voltage, self-generated electricity source, and extruded acrylic fibreglass fitments. It's also the first major housing project in Britain to be built entirely by characters from nineteenth-century English literature.

By this time the pan has come to rest on a section of the site where various nineteenth-century literary figures are at work round a cement mixer: two ladies in crinolines, Bob Cratchett on his father's back, Heathcliff and Catherine throwing bricks to each other with smouldering passion, Nelson, Mr Beadle as foreman. Cut to the interior of a half-finished concrete shell. A little girl is working on top of a ladder.

Voice Over Here Little Nell, from Dickens's 'Old Curiosity Shop' fits new nylon syphons into the asbestos-lined ceilings . . . *(shot of complicated electrical wiring in some impressive electrical installation)* But it's the electrical system which has attracted the most attention. *(cut to Arthur Huntingdon studying a plan; he has a builder's safety helmet on)* Arthur Huntingdon, who Helen Graham married as a young girl, and whose shameless conduct eventually drove her back to her brother Lawrence, in Anne Brontë's 'The Tenant of Wildfell Hall' describes why it's unique.

Huntingdon (ERIC) Because sir, it is self-generating. Because we have harnessed here in this box the very forces of life itself. The very forces that will send Helen running back to beg forgiveness!

Cut to a close up of big pre-fabricated concrete slabs being hoisted into the air by a crane and start to pull out, as the commentator speaks, to reveal a crowd of nineteenth-century farmhands working on them.

Voice Over The on-site building techniques involve the construction of twelve-foot walling blocks by a crowd of farmhands from 'Tess of the D'Urbervilles' supervised by the genial landlady, Mrs Jupp, from Samuel Butler's 'Way of All Flesh'.

Pan to reveal Mrs Jupp with a clipboard. Cut to voice over narrator in vision with a stick-mike, in front of an impressive piece of motorway interchange building. Behind him and working on the site are six angels, three devils, and Adam and Eve.

Narrator In contrast to the site in Bristol, it's progress here on Britain's first eighteen-level motorway interchange being built by characters from Milton's 'Paradise Lost' . . .

He turns and we zoom past him into the angels etc.

Narrator *(voice over)* What went wrong here?

Cut to a foreman in a donkey jacket and helmet.

Foreman (TERRY J) Well, no one really got on. Satan didn't get on with Eve . . . er . . . Archangel Gabriel didn't get on with Satan . . . nobody got on with the Serpent, so now they have to work a rota: forces of good from ten till three, forces of evil three to six.

The camera tracks through a high-rise development area.

Voice Over But even more modern building techniques are being used on an expanding new town site near Peterborough; here the Amazing Mystico and Janet can put up a block of flats by hypnosis in under a minute.

Mystico (Terry J) removes his cloak, gloves and top hat and hands them to Janet, who curtsies. He then makes several passes. Cut to stock film of flats falling down reversed so that they leap up. Cut back to Mystico and Janet. She hands him back his things as they make their way to their car, a little Austin 30.

Voice Over The local Council here have over fifty hypnosis-induced twenty-five storey blocks, put up by El Mystico and Janet. I asked Mr Ken Verybigliar the advantages of hypnosis compared to other building methods.

Cut to a man in a drab suit.

SUPERIMPOSED CAPTION: 'MR K. V. B. LIAR'

Mr Verybigliar (MICHAEL) Well there is a considerable financial advantage in using the services of El Mystico. A block, like Mystico Point here, *(indicating a high-rise block behind him)* would normally cost in the region of one-and-a-half million pounds. This was put up for five pounds and thirty bob for Janet.

Voice Over But the obvious question is are they safe?

Cut to an architect's office. The architect at his desk. Behind him on the wall are framed photos of various collapsed buildings. He is a well-dressed authoritative person.

SUPERIMPOSED CAPTION: 'MR CLEMENT ONAN, ARCHITECT TO THE COUNCIL'

Architect (GRAHAM) Of course they're safe. There's absolutely no doubt about that. They are as strong, solid and as safe as any other building method in this country . . . provided of course people *believe* in them.

Cut to a council flat. On the wall there is a picture of Mystico.

Tenant (ERIC) Yes, we received a note from the Council saying that if we ceased to believe in this building it would fall down.

Voice Over You don't mind living in a figment of another man's imagination?

Tenant No, it's much better than where we used to live.

Voice Over Where did you used to live?

Tenant We had an eighteen-roomed villa overlooking Nice.

Voice Over Really, that sounds much better.

Tenant Oh yes – yes you're right.

Cut to stock shot of block falling down in slow motion. Cut back to tenant and wife inside. Camera shaking and on the tilt.

Tenant No, no, no, of course not.

Cut to stock film again. The building rights itself. Cut back to interior again. Camera slightly on tilt. They are holding bits of crockery etc.

Tenant Phew, that was close.

Cut to tracking shot from back of camera car again. This time El Mystico striding through the towering blocks, his cloak swirling behind him.

Voice Over But the construction of these vast new housing developments, providing homes for many thousands of people, is not the only project to which he has applied his many talents. He also has an Infallible Pools Method, a School of Spanish Dancing and a Car Hire Service. *(cut to Mystico at wheel of his little Austin 30, his amazing* *eyes riveted on the road ahead; Janet occasionally tactfully guides the steering wheel)* What is the driving force behind a man of such restless energies, and boundless vision? Here as with so many great men of history, the answer lies in a woman ... *(the camera pans over on to Janet and starts to zoom in on her as she watches the road ahead; cut to a nineteenth-century engraving of Shakespeare's Antony and Cleopatra)* As Antony has his Cleopatra ... *(cut to picture of Napoleon and Josephine)* as Napoleon has his Josephine ... *(cut to Janet lying on a bed in a négligée in a rather seedy hotel)* So Mystico has his Janet.

Mystico leaps from top of the wardrobe on to the bed with a lusty yell. Cut to montage of black and white photos of Janet in various stage poses: three poses against black drapes; one against a building; one posed outside a terrace house with notice reading School of Spanish Dancing – Dentures Repaired'.

Voice Over Yes. Janet ... a quiet, shy girl. An honours graduate from Harvard University, American junior sprint record holder, ex-world skating champion, Nobel Prize winner, architect, novelist and surgeon. The girl who helped crack the Oppenheimer spy ring in 1947. She gave vital evidence to the Senate Narcotics Commission in 1958. She also helped to convict the woman at the chemist's in 1961, and a year later *(cut to Janet shaking hands with a police commissioner)* she gave police information which led to the arrest of her postman. In October of that same year *(cut to photo of Janet with a judge and a policeman standing on either side of her smiling at the camera)* she secured the conviction of her gardener for bigamy and three months later personally led the police swoop *(cut to Janet in a street with gaggles of policemen clustering round her grinning at the camera and two people obviously naked with blankets thrown over them)* on the couple next door. In 1967 she became suspicious of the man at the garage *(cut to a photo of a petrol attendant filling a car)* and it was her dogged perseverance and relentless enquiries *(another rather fuzzy photo of the man at the garage peering through the window of cash kiosk)* that two years later finally secured his conviction for not having a licence for his car radio. *(final photo of five police, Janet and the man from the garage in handcuffs all posing for the camera)* He was hanged at Leeds a year later *(cut to Janet posing outside a prison)* despite the abolition of capital punishment and the public outcry. Also in Leeds that year, a local butcher was hanged *(cut to a blurred family snap of a butcher in an apron with a knife)* for defaulting on mortgage repayments, and a Mr Jarvis *(photo)* was electrocuted for shouting in the corridor.

Cut to Superintendent Harry 'Boot-in' Swalk.

SUPERIMPOSED CAPTION: 'SUPERINTENDENT HARRY "BOOT-IN" SWALK'

Swalk (TERRY J) We admit that there have been outbreaks of hanging recently, but the police are trying to keep the situation under control. *(his personal two-way radio is making rather a noise)* You must remember the courts are very busy at the moment and the odd death sentence is bound to slip through. *(claps his hand over the radio to little avail)* Electrocutions are another big worry. But we hope that guillotining has been eradicated from the urban areas, and garrotting is confined almost entirely to Luton. So if you have a friend in prison or under sentence of death, be sure to let us know at this address.

Voice Over (ERIC) and CAPTION: 'THE POLICE FORCE, "SUNNYVIEW", YEOVIL, SOMERSET'

Cut to a mortuary. Various trolleys lie about with corpses covered by sheets. Two workmen are sitting at a low makeshift table with cups of tea and a transistor radio, shelling eggs and dropping them in a pickling jar.

Radio Voice (JOHN) . . . and Premier Chou En Lai, who called it 'a major breakthrough'. Twelve men were accidentally hanged at Whitby Assizes this afternoon whilst considering their verdict. This is one of the worst miscarriages of justice in Britain since Tuesday. *(music)*

PJ Voice (ERIC) Well it's thirteen minutes to the hour of nine-nine-nine, here on wonderful Radio One-One-One! So if you're still lying in your big big bed, now is the time to get up out of it! We've got another thirteen hours of tip-top sounds here on Wonderful Radio One! *(brief funny noises)* Sorry about that . . . So unless you have brain cells, or have completed the process of evolution, there's a wonderful day ahead!

Battersby (TERRY J) *(switching the radio off)* It must be on Radio Four. *(he gets another radio out from underneath the table)* Radio Two. *(he gets another radio out)* . . . Three . . . *(he opens the top of the third radio and gets out a fourth; he switches it on)*

Radio Voice (GRAHAM) It's 9 o'clock and time for 'Mortuary Hour'. An hour of talks, tunes and downright tomfoolery for all those who work in mortuaries, introduced as usual by Shirley Bassey. *(sinister chords)*

Shirley Well, we're going to kick straight off this week with our Mortuary Quiz, so have your pens and pencils ready.

A door at the back of the mortuary opens and Mr Wang, an official of the Department of Stiffs, enters. He wears an undertaker's suit and top hat plus a long blond wig.

Wang (JOHN) Turn that radio off and look lively!

Battersby Oh, it's 'Mortuary Quiz', Mr Wang . . .

Wang Don't argue, Battersby.

We hear voices off. Officials at the door spring to attention. Enter a mayor with a chain round his neck, and an elderly peer of the realm who is standing on a small platform, pushed by an attendant.

Mayor (GRAHAM) . . . This is our mortuary in here, Your Grace . . .

Peer (MICHAEL) I say, I say, I . . . er . . . I . . . er . . . I . . . er . . . I . . . I can't think of anything to say about it.

Mayor Well, we're very proud of it here, sir. It's one of the most up to date in the country.

Peer I see... yes... yes... now... um... what... what... ah... ah... what is it?... is it a power station?

Mayor No, Your Grace, it's a mortuary.

Peer I see... I see... good... good... good, good, good...

Mayor But it has one of the most advanced thermostat control systems in the country, and it has computer-controlled storage facilities.

Peer I see, I see... I... er... er... er... I... er... I'm a good little doggie.

Mayor I'm sorry, Your Grace?

Peer I'm a good little dog.

Attendant (CAROL) Oh dear...

Mayor Perhaps we should postpone the visit?

Attendant No, no, no – you see it's just that his brain is so tiny that the slightest movement can dislodge it. *(starts to slap the duke's head from side to side gently but firmly)* Your Grace... Oh dear... it's rather like one of those games you play where you have to get the ball into the hole... That's it!

Peer Ah! Now then, excellent, excellent, excellent, excellent. Now then... ah... what happens when the steel is poured into the ingots?

Mayor *(ushering everyone out)* Perhaps we should go and have a look at the new showers?

Peer Yes... yes... yes... yes... yes rather jolly good... jolly good... jolly good... jolly good... no fear...

They leave. Battersby turns the radio on again.

Radio Voice Well the answers were as follows: 1) the left hand, 2) no, 3) normal, 4) yes it has, in 1963 when a bird got caught in the mechanism. How did you get on?

Two men behind him push in a trolley with sheet-covered corpses on it.

Wang Turn that thing off!

Battersby Oh! It's 'Mortuary Dance Time', Mr Wang!

Wang Never mind that, Battersby, this is the big one. I've just had Whitby Police on the phone with twelve hangees...

Battersby Oh yes, I just heard about that on the radios...

Wang No, these are twelve different ones... so shtoom.

Battersby and friend gather round the body. Wang joins them. They start to work away busily and efficiently on the corpse. We suddenly become aware that Badger is standing with them around the body.

Badger I'll not interrupt this sketch for a pound.

Wang What?

Badger For one pound I'll leave this sketch totally uninterrupted.

Wang What?

Badger Fifty pence . . . I'm prepared to negotiate a forty-pence deal. *(an eye peers out from under the sheet on the corpse they are working on)* For 35p I won't interrupt any of the next three items.

The corpse is now sitting up waiting to see what happens. Another corpse sits up as they continue arguing. The sheet is pushed back on another trolley revealing a boy and girl on the same stretcher. They light cigarettes.

Wang No, no, it's no good . . .

Badger 25p.

Wang No.

Badger 10p and a kiss.

ANIMATION: *with Gilliam's hands in shot.*

Terry Gilliam *(voice over)* You see, it's very simple – I just take these cut-out figures and by putting them together . . . oh, you mean we're on? . . . *(Gilliam's head appears briefly)* Sorry.

The animated sketch starts. Then cut to Trafalgar Square. The Olympic symbol is superimposed briefly.

SUPERIMPOSED CAPTION: 'FINAL OF THE HIDE-AND-SEEK SECOND LEG'

Zoom in on commentator and the two finalists, forty-year-old men limbering up in shorts and singlets.

Commentator (ERIC) Hello, good afternoon and welcome to the second leg of the Olympic final of the men's Hide-and-Seek here in the heart of Britain's London. We'll be starting in just a couple of moments from now, and there you can see the two competitors Francisco Huron the Paraguayan, who in this leg is the seeker *(we see Francisco Huron darting about, looking behind things)* and there's the man he'll be looking for . . . *(we see Don Roberts (Graham) practising hiding)* our own Don Roberts from Hinckley in Leicestershire who, his trainer tells me, is at the height of his self-secreting form. And now in the first leg, which ended on Wednesday, Don succeeded in finding the Paraguayan in the new world record time of 11 years, 2 months, 26 days, 9 hours, 3 minutes, 27.4 seconds, in a sweetshop in Kilmarnock. And now they're under starter's orders.

We see Don Roberts and Francisco Huron standing side by side, poised, looking nervous.

Starter *(voice over)* On your marks . . . get set . . .

The starter fires his pistol. Francisco Huron immediately puts his hands over eyes and starts counting.

Francisco (TERRY J) Uno, dos, tres, quattro, cinque, seis, siete, ocho, nueve, diez . . .

Meanwhile Don Roberts hails a cab. He gets in and it drives off.

Francisco . . . trientay dos, trientay tres, trientay quattro . . .

SUPERIMPOSED CAPTION: '32, 33, 34'

Commentator Well Don's off to a really great start there. Remember the Paraguayan has got 11 years, 2 months, 26 days, 9 hours . . . *(cut to taxi on the way to London airport)* 3 minutes, 27.4 seconds to beat.

Cut back to Francisco still counting.

SUPERIMPOSED CAPTION: '998, 999, 1000'

Francisco Neuvecian no nuevetay ocho, nuevecientas nuevente ye nueve, mil. *(Francisco takes his hands from his eyes and shouts)* Coming!

He starts looking around the immediate locality suspiciously. We see a plane landing. There is a sign saying 'Benvenuto a Sardinia'. Cut to Don on a bicycle. Then running up a hill. Then going into castle. Running along corridors and eventually pausing, looking around agitatedly, and then hiding behind a pillar. Occasionally he looks out nervously. Then cut to Francisco looking in shops in the Tottenham Court Road. Cut to studio 'Sportsview' desk with a Frank Bough man at it.

Frank Bough (MICHAEL) Well, we'll be taking you back there as soon as there are any developments.

CAPTION: 'SIX YEARS LATER'

Cut back to desk. Frank Bough looks older.

Frank Bough We've just heard that something is happening in the Hide-and-Seek final, so let's go straight over there.

Cut to film of Francisco Huron. He is wandering around looking for Don Roberts in a beach setting. The commentator is some way from him. He speaks quietly into a microphone.

Commentator Hello again, and welcome to Madagascar, where Francisco Huron is seeking Don Roberts. And I've just been told that he has been told that he has been unofficially described as 'cold'. Ah, wait a minute. *(in the distance Francisco Huron consults with an official; the commentator moves out of shot briefly, then returns)* I've just been told that Huron has requested a plane ticket for Budapest! So he's definitely getting warmer. So we'll be back again in just a few years.

Cut to Frank Bough looking older. He is covered with cobwebs.

Frank Bough Really beginning to hot up now.

CAPTION: 'FIVE YEARS, TWO MONTHS AND TWENTY-SIX DAYS LATER'

Cut to a Portuguese-looking setting. Francisco Huron looking round desperately and glancing at his watch.

Commentator So here we are on the very last day of this fantastic final. Huron now has less than twelve hours left to find British ace Don Roberts. Early this morning he finished combing the outskirts of Lisbon and now he seems to have staked everything on one final desperate seek here in the Tagus valley. But Roberts is over fifteen hundred miles away, and it's beginning to look all over, bar the shouting. The sands of time are running out for this delving dago, this señor of seek, perspicacious Paraguayan. He's still desperately cold and it's beginning to look like another gold for Britain.

The camera shows Huron creeping up on a dustbin. He pauses, snatches off the lid and looks inside. He turns away disappointed, then does double take and looks back into the bin. He pulls out a sardine tin with the word 'Sardines' very obvious. Shot of Huron's reaction as he suddenly gets a tremendous idea. He snaps his fingers and hails a taxi and gets in. Cut to plane landing. Same sign as before 'Benvenuto a Sardinia'. Francisco cycles past. Cut to him discarding the bike and running up the hill straight into the castle. He runs along corridors into the right room, up to the pillar and finds Don Roberts skulking behind. They both look very tense as they await the official result, then react in fury and frustration when it is announced by a blazered official.

Official (MICHAEL) The official result of the World Hide-and-Seek, Mr Don Roberts from Hinckley, Leicestershire, 11 years, 2 months, 26 days, 9 hours, 3 minutes, 27 seconds. Mr Francisco Huron, Paraguay, 11 years, 2 months, 26 days, 9 hours, 3 minutes, 27 seconds. The result – a tie.

Voice Over (JOHN) A tie! Well what a fantastic result. Well the replay will start tomorrow at 7.30 a.m.

As they stand there the camera pans off them to a window and then zooms through the window to reveal a beach where there is a Redcoat.

Redcoat (MICHAEL) Well hello again ... nice to be back ... glad to see the series has been doing well. Well now, sorry about Mon-trerx.

At this point two men run past in the background carrying a donkey. A third runs behind carrying a sign saying 'Donkey Rides' and winking and pointing at the donkey, they run out of picture.

Redcoat That was a little item entitled Hide-and-Seek – very anarchic, very effective, not quite my cup of tea, but very nice for the younger people. Well, the next item the boys have put together takes place in a sitting room. Sorry it's just a sitting room, but the bank account's a bit low after the appallingly expensive production of 'Clochmerle'...

He is hit by Mr Robinson with a chicken. Robinson walks away and we follow him as he passes Badger in the foreground.

Badger This is a totally free interruption and no money has exchanged hands whatever.

The camera doesn't pause at all on Badger and we continue panning with Robinson until he reaches the knight in armour. He hands the chicken to the knight. He walks away from knight and into the distance. Mix through to a modern sitting room. Mrs Robinson is eating alone at the table looking at the clock.

Mr Robinson (JOHN) Sorry about that, darling... *(he sits)*

She serves him some vegetables. He unfolds his napkin.

Mrs Robinson (CAROL) Gravy?

Mr Robinson Yes please, dear.

They sit and eat in silence. Suddenly the doorbell rings.

Mrs Robinson Oh dear, that'll be the Cheap-Laughs from next door.

Various different doorbell sounds and chimes. Mr Robinson goes to the front door, and opens it. Standing outside are Mr and Mrs Cheap-Laugh. He is wearing a big floppy comedian's suit and a big bow tie and fright wig. She is a Mrs Equator sort of lady, with an enormous hairstyle, and dressed in very bad taste.

Mr Robinson Come in.

Mr Cheap-Laugh (TERRY J) No! Just breathing heavily!

He and his wife roar with laughter. As he comes in he slips and falls on the mat. His wife puts a custard pie in his face. More roars of laughter.

Mrs Cheap-Laugh (GRAHAM) Oh we just dropped in.

Mr Robinson Would you like to come through . . .

We mix through to the exterior of a house at night. Shrieks of laughter, crashes of crockery. The two men with the donkey run past in road, the third man behind pointing to the sign.

SUPERIMPOSED CAPTION: 'ONE EVENING WITH THE CHEAP-LAUGHS LATER'

The light comes on in hall. Cut to them in the hall at the front door.

Mr Cheap-Laugh Well goodnight and give us a kiss. *(kisses Mrs Robinson)*

Mrs Cheap-Laugh Oh thank you very much for a very nice evening.

Mr Cheap-Laugh After you, dear.

He trips her up and she falls out into the darkness. We hear her shriek with laughter. Mr Cheap-Laugh drops his trousers, makes lavatory chain pulling sign and noise and hurls himself out after wife and disappears into the darkness. More laughter. The host shuts the door. They heave a sigh of relief and go back into the sitting room. The crockery on the table is all smashed in a heap on the floor with the table cloth. The standard lamp is broken in half. There are large splodges of food and wine splashes on the walls. Some glasses and a moustache are drawn on the Tretchikoff picture of the Chinese girl. Mrs Robinson flops down on the sofa. There is a farting cushion. She removes it, irritated.

Mrs Robinson Oh honestly dear, why do we always have to buy everything just because the Cheap-Laughs have one?

He goes over to the wall cupboard for drinks. A bucket of whitewash is balanced on the half-open door. He opens the cupboard and the bucket of whitewash falls on him. Cut briefly to Mr Badger.

Badger This is not an interruption at all.

Cut back to Mr Robinson. He pours himself a drink, without reacting to the whitewash.

Mr Robinson It's just neighbourliness dear, that's all . . .

Mrs Robinson I think we should try and lead our own lives from now on.

She opens a sewing box and a boxing glove on a spring comes out and hits her on the chin.

Mr Robinson Can't you be serious for one moment?

He sits on the pouffe. The sixteen-ton weight falls on him. Cut to the exterior of the house. The lights go off downstairs and upstairs. The two men run past carrying a pantomime goose.

SUPERIMPOSED CAPTION: 'LATER THAT NIGHT'

Cut to a darkened bedroom. Mr and Mrs Robinson are in a double bed, talking.

Mr Robinson I'm sorry I was cross earlier.

Mrs Robinson Oh that's all right, dear. It's just that I get so sick of always having to be like the Cheap-Laughs.

Mr Robinson Well yes, from now on we'll be like ourselves.

Mrs Robinson Oh Roger...

Mr Robinson Oh Beatrice.

The bed springs up and folds into the back wall of the bedroom. On the underneath of the bed is a presenter on a chair. The underneath of the bed also consists of a flat as for current-affairs-type programme, with 'Probe' written above narrator.

Presenter (ERIC) Many people in this country are becoming increasingly worried about bull-fighting. They say it's not only cruel, vicious and immoral, but also blatantly unfair. The bull is heavy, violent, abusive and aggressive with four legs and great sharp teeth, whereas the bull-fighter is only a small, greasy Spaniard. Given this basic inequality what can be done to make bull-fighting safer? We asked Brigadier Arthur Farquar-Smith, Chairman of the British Well-Basically Club.

Cut to a brigadier.

Brigadier (JOHN) Well, basically it's quite apparent that these little dago chappies have got it all wrong. They prance round the bull like a lot of bally night club dancers looking like the Younger Generation or a less smooth version of the Lionel Blair Troupe, *(getting rather camp)* with much of the staccato rhythms of the Irving Davies Dancers at the height of their success. In recent years Pan's People have often recaptured a lyricism... *(a huge hammer strikes him on the head; he becomes butch again)* and what we must do now is to use devices like radar to locate the bull and SAM missiles fired from underground silos, to knock the bull over. Then I would send in Scottish boys with air cover to provide a diversion for the bull, whilst the navy came in round the back and finished him off. That to me would be bull-fighting and not this pansy kind of lyrical, *(getting camp)* evocative movement which George Balanchine and Martha Graham in the States and our very own Sadler's Wells... *(the hammer strikes him on the head again)* Troops could also be used in an auxiliary role in international chess, where... *(the lights go off)* What?... oh ...

Badger *(voice over)* I'll put the lights on again for a pound.

Cut to an animated sketch, and then to a strange moonlike landscape. Eerie science-fiction music plays in the background.

Voice Over (JOHN) This is the planet Algon, fifth world in the system of Aldebaran, the Red Giant in the constellation of Sagittarius. Here an ordinary cup of drinking chocolate costs four million pounds, an immersion heater for the hot-water tank costs over six billion pounds and a pair of split-crotch panties would be almost unobtainable. *(cut to a budget-day-type graphic, with a picture of the product and the price alongside)* A simple rear window de-misting device for an 1100 costs eight thousand million billion pounds and a new element for an electric kettle like this *(picture of electric kettle)* would cost as much as the entire gross national product of the United States of America from 1770 to the year 2000, *(graphic of American GNP)* and even then they wouldn't be able to afford the small fixing ring which attaches it to the kettle. *(graphic of an electric kettle showing all the separate pieces detached from each other, arrow points to the fixing ring)*

Cut to James M'Burke sitting at a desk. 'Algon I' motifs everywhere. Another expert stands by a model of the planet, and there is a panel of experts at a long desk who are all obviously dummies. Everyone has one of those single earphones.

M'Burke (MICHAEL) Well, our computers have been working all day to analyse the dramatic information that's come in from this first ever intergalactic probe, Algon . . . I . . . *(suddenly very excited as he hears something over his earphone)* . . . and we're just getting an interesting development now, which is that attachments for rotary mowers – that is mowers that have a central circular blade – are . . . relatively inexpensive! Still in the region of nine to ten million pounds, but it does seem to indicate that Algon might be a very good planet for those with larger gardens . . . or perhaps even an orchard that's been left for two years, needs some heavy work, some weeding . . . *(very indistinct pictures start to come through on the screen behind him)* But we're now getting some live pictures through from Algon! Harry – Perhaps you could talk us through them.

Cut into pictures from Algon.

SUPERIMPOSED CAPTION: 'LIVE FROM ALGON'

Very fuzzy pictures of the Algon landscape. Panning and tracking shots hand held.

Harry (TERRY J) *(voice over)* Very little evidence of shopping facilities here . . . there don't seem to be any large supermarkets. There may be some on-the-corner grocery stores behind those rocks, but it's difficult to tell from this angle. It does seem to suggest that most of the shopping here is by direct mail.

SUPERIMPOSED TELEPRINTER CAPTION: 'DIGESTIVE BISCUITS £8,000,000 PER PACKET'

Cut to James M'Burke.

M'Burke Of course the big question that everyone's asking here is, what about those split-crotch panties? Are they going to be unobtainable throughout the Universe or merely on Algon itself? Professor?

Cut to a professor sitting beside a contour model of an area of Algon. It has a little model of the probe marking where it has landed.

SUPERIMPOSED CAPTION: 'PROFESSOR HERMAN KHAN, DIRECTOR OF THE INSTITUTE OF SPLIT-CROTCH PANTIES'

Professor (ERIC) We must remember that Algon is over 75,000 miles wide. The probes come down to this area here and we're really only getting signals from a radius of only thirty or forty miles around the probe. Split-crotch panties, or indeed any items of what we scientists call, 'Sexy Underwear' or 'Erotic Lingerie' may be much more plentiful on other parts of the planet.

Camera pans to include M'Burke.

M'Burke Professor, you were responsible for finding Scanty-Panties and Golden Goddess High-Lift Bras on planets which were never thought able to sustain life, and now that man has discovered a new galaxy do you think we're going to see underwear become even naughtier?

Professor Oh naughtier and naughtier.

SUPERIMPOSED TELEPRINTER CAPTION: 'NO BANANAS ON ALGON'

M'Burke Well so much for that... But of course, the probe itself has excited a great deal of interest... for it contains uranium-based dual transmission cells entirely re-charged by solar radiation, which can take off a bra and panties in less than fifteen seconds. It is, of course, the first piece of space hardware to be specially designed to undress ladies, and so there are bound to be some teething troubles... such as how to cope with the combination of elastic-sided boots and tights.

He produces the bottom half of a tailor's dummy wearing boots and tights with panties over the tights halfway down. On the screen behind, more dim indecipherable TV pictures from Algon.

M'Burke But I think we're getting some pictures now from Algon itself, and it looks as though... yes! The satellite has found a bird! The probe has struck crumpet and she looks pretty good too! Professor?

Professor Ja – she's a real honey!

All we see on the screen is a blurred female figure.

M'Burke Well the pictures are a bit sporadic... I think probably... the solar radiation during the long journey to Algon... *(the screen goes blank)* Hoy! Look! Oh dear, I'm sorry we've lost contact. We'll try and re-establish contact with Algon...

Cut to presenter's-type chair. Mr Badger appears at side of screen.

Badger Hello... The BBC have offered me the sum of forty pence to read the credits of this show. *(sits)* Personally I thought they should have held out for the full seventy-five, but the BBC have explained to me about their financial difficulties and... er... I decided to accept the reduced offer ... so ... the show was conceived, written and performed by ... the usual lot ... *(the signature tune is heard)* Also appearing were Carol Cleveland, Marie Anderson, Mrs Idle, Make-up – Madelaine Gaffney, Costume – Hazel Pethig, Animations by Terry Gilliam, Visual Effects Designer – Bernard Wilkie, Graphics – Bob Blagden, Film Cameraman – Alan Featherstone, Film Editor – Ray Millichope, Sound – Richard Chubb, Lighting – Bill Bailey, Designer – Bob Berk, Produced by Ian MacNaughton for 92p and a bottle of Bell's whisky ... it was a BBC colour production. That's just it. I'd like to say if there are any BBC producers looking in who need people to read the credits for them, I would personally ...

The camera pulls out to reveal the sixteen-ton weight poised above him. As the picture fades the weight falls on him.

Thirty-six

Outside a shop. A sign reads 'Tudor Job Agency – Jobs a Speciality'. A man enters the shop. Inside it is decorated in Tudor style. The assistant is in Tudor dress.

Assistant (TERRY J) Morning, sir, can I help you?

Customer (GRAHAM) Yes, yes ... I wondered if you have any part-time vacancies on your books.

Assistant Part-time, I'll have a look, sir. *(he gets out a book and looks through it)* Let me look now. We've got, ah yes, Sir Walter Raleigh is equipping another expedition to Virginia; he needs traders and sailors. Vittlers needed at the Court of Philip of Spain, oh, yes, and they want master joiners and craftsmen for the building of the Globe Theatre.

Customer I see. Have you anything a bit more modern, you know, like a job on the buses, or digging the underground?

Assistant Oh no, we only have Tudor jobs.

Customer That can't be very profitable, can it?

Assistant Well, you'd be surprised, actually sir. The Tudor economy's booming, ever since Sir Humphrey Gilbert opened up the Northwest Passage to Cathay, and the Cabots' expansion in Canada, there's been a tremendous surge in exports, and trade with the Holy Roman Empire is going ... no, quite right, it's no good at all.

Customer What?

Assistant It's a dead loss. We haven't put anyone in a job since 1625.

Customer I see.

Assistant That's all?

Customer What?

Assistant That's all you say?

Customer Yes.

Assistant No, no, we were the tops then. Drake got all his sailors here. Elizabeth, we supplied the archbishops for her coronation. Shakespeare started off from here as a temp. Then came James the First and the bottom fell out of the Tudor jobs. 1603 – 800 vacancies filled, 1604 – 40, 1605 – none, 1606 – none. The rest of the Stuart period nothing. Hanoverians nothing. Victorians nothing. Saxe-Coburgs nothing. Windsors ... what did you want?

Customer Dirty books, please.

Assistant Right. *(produces selection of mags from under counter)* Sorry about the Tudor bit, but you can't be too careful, you know. Have a look through these.

Customer Have you got anything a bit ... er ...

Assistant A bit stronger?

Customer Yes.

Assistant Hold on ... a ... My Lord of Warwick!

Second Assistant (ERIC) *(off)* 'allo!

Assistant Raise high the drawbridge. Gloucester's troops approach.

Second Assistant *(off)* Right.

Assistant Can't be too careful you know, sir.

> *The wall of the Tudor shop slides back to reveal the interior of a Soho dirty bookshop in the back room – a bare room with a counter and magazines in racks on the walls at eye-level. Three drably dressed men are thumbing through books. One of them is a vicar, one of them is gathering a huge pile. Behind the counter is a Soho toughie in Tudor gear showing books to Mr Nid – a tweedy, rather academic, respectable-looking man of senior years. The customer goes through, and the wall slides back.*

Second Assistant There's a 'Bridget – Queen of the Whip'.

Nid (JOHN) Yes ...

Second Assistant Or 'Naughty Nora' ... or there's this one: 'Doug, Bob and Gordon Visit the *Ark Royal*'. Or there's 'Sister Teresa – The Spanking Nun'.

Nid Mmmm ... I see ... you don't have anything specially about Devon and Cornwall?

Second Assistant No. I'm afraid not, sir.

Nid The one I was really after was Arthur Hotchkiss's 'Devonshire Country Churches'.

Second Assistant Well how about this, sir: 'Bum Biters'.

Nid No ... not really ... I don't suppose you have any general surveys of English Church architecture?

Second Assistant No, it's not really our line, sir.

Nid No, I see. Well, never mind I'll just take the 'Lord Lieutenant in Nylons' then, and these two copies of 'Piggie Parade'. Thank you.

Second Assistant Right, sir.

First Assistant *(voice over)* My Lord of Warwick.

Second Assistant 'allo?

First Assistant *(voice over)* Raise high the drawbridge. Gloucester's troops approach!

Second Assistant Right.

> *He presses a button below counter and the wall slides back. The man with the big pile of books comes up to counter.*

Man (TERRY G) Just these, then.

> *Enter Gaskell in Tudor gear. The wall closes up behind him.*

Gaskell (MICHAEL) All right. This is a raid. My name is Superintendent Gaskell and this is Sergeant Maddox.

Second Assistant Ah! Sir Philip Sidney. 'tis good to see thee on these shores again.

Gaskell Shut up.

Second Assistant Your suit is fair and goodly cut. Was't from Antwerp?

Gaskell Shut up. It's a disguise. Right! Confiscate the smutty books, Maddox.

Second Assistant Sir Philip! Prithee nay!

Gaskell Listen, mate! Don't come that Philip Sidney bit with me. I'm not a bloody Tudor at all. I'm Gaskell of the Vice Squad and this is Sergeant Maddox.

They all look at him blankly. He looks to Maddox for support and realizes he isn't there.

Gaskell Maddox! Where's he gone?

Second Assistant Sir Philip, prithee rest awhile.

Gaskell Look. This is the last time. I'm warning you, I'm not Sir Philip Bleeding Sidney. I am Superintendent Harold Gaskell and this is a raid.

Everybody resumes their book-buying and ignores him. At the counter the assistant is still totting up the huge pile of books.

Second Assistant That'll be 540 quid sir.

Man Oh, I'll just have this one then. *(takes top one)*

Gaskell Maddox! *(addressing everyone in shop; they ignore him)* Look, this is a raid. *(no reaction)* Honestly, I promise you. *(people start to leave through the rear door of the shop; Gaskell blocks it)* Where are you going?

Customer I'm going home.

Gaskell Right. *(looks for his notebook but it's not in his Tudor clothing)* I'll remember you. Don't you worry. I'll remember you . . .

Customer Pray good, Sir Philip, that you . . .

Gaskell Don't you start! Maddox! *(the customer leaves; other customers start to leave)* Listen, I can prove to you I'm a policeman. I can give the names of all the men down in 'F' division at Acton: Inspector Arthur Perry, Superintendent Charles Frodwell, my best friend, police dogs, Butch, Wolf, Panther, Maudling. How would I know those names if I was Sir Philip Sidney? *(the vicar comes up to counter)* Look, vicar, you know me. The Gargoyle Club – I got you off the charge. *(the vicar leaves guiltily)*

Second Assistant Farewell, good Sir Philip.

He goes out carrying a pile of magazines. Then the vicar goes, followed by the Tudor man.

Gaskell Hey, stop! *(the door slams; Gaskell turns and looks round the empty shop; pause)* Maddox!

He rushes up to the sliding wall and beats on it. Then he turns and makes for the little back door and goes through.

Gaskell You'll never get away with this, you porn merchant. Blimey!

He stops and gapes. We cut to his eye-line to see he is standing in a beautiful, green, Tudor garden. In the distance a Tudor house. A girl is sitting on a stone bench, sobbing. Gaskell walks towards her, bewildered.

Gaskell Maddox!

The girl looks up at him with beseeching eyes. She is young and beautiful.

Girl Oh good sir, how glad I am to see thee come. Forgive me weeping, but my love has gone.

Gaskell Er, listen. My name is Gaskell... Superintendent Gaskell of Vice Squad. Myself and Sergeant Maddox are on a raid. We are not Tudor people. We are the police.

An Elizabethan gentleman appears through the trees.

Father (TERRY J) Frances, what idleness is this? Why, good Sir Philip Sidney. *(he bows extravagantly to Gaskell)* What hast thee here?

Girl *(turning to Gaskell with bated breath)* You are Sir Philip Sidney?

Gaskell ... Possibly... but I may be Superintendent Gaskell of the Vice Squad.

Father Ah good, Sir Philip, thy sharp-tongued wit has not deserted thee. Come. Let us eat and drink. Stay with us awhile.

Gaskell All right, sir. I think I will.

They walk off together arm in arm into the idyllic country garden. The girl looks after them with hope in her eyes. Bring up Elizabethan music.

SUPERIMPOSED CAPTION: 'THE LIFE OF SIR PHILIP SIDNEY'

Mix through to a Tudor dining room. At the table a group of Tudor gentry are sitting listening to Gaskell. Evidence of a banquet, and two minstrels in attendance. Gaskell has obviously just finished a story. Applause and laughter.

Gaskell ... then did we bust the Harry Tony mob, who did seek to import Scandinavian filth via Germany. For six years they cleaned up a packet – the day I got whiff of them through a squealer and within one week did a mop-up right good. They're now languishing doing five years bird in Parkhurst.

Applause. They are all very impressed. Cut to exterior. A messenger on a horse rides full pelt straight towards the camera. It is dusk. He stops outside the Elizabethan house, leaps off and dashes into the house. Cut to interior again. They are still all laughing from his last story. The messenger bursts into room.

Messenger (TERRY G) Sir Philip. The Spaniards have landed in the Netherlands. My Lord Walsingham needs you there forthwith.

Gaskell Let's go.

Cut to exterior. Gaskell is seated on the back of the messenger's horse and they gallop off. The dinner crowd are standing waving on the doorstep.

Dinner Crowd Good luck, Sir Philip!

Cut to a British Standard fluttering in the breeze against the blue sky. Fanfare. Two Elizabethan gentlemen, and four men dressed as Elizabethan soldiers are standing on a cliff top. Gaskell strides up to them, and takes up position on topmost point of the knoll.

Gaskell Where are the Spaniards?

Elizabethan Gent (ERIC) Down below Sir Philip, their first boats are landing even now.

Shot of a sailing-galley seen from above.

Gaskell Right, you stay here, I'll go and get them.

Elizabethan Gent Sir Philip! Not alone!

Cut to the beach. Suspense music. Gaskell strides up to the camera, until he is towering over it. The music reaches crescendo.

Gaskell 'allo allo! What's going on here?

Cut to beached rowing boat piled high with bundles of dirty magazines. Two Spaniards are unloading it.

Spaniard (TERRY J) Ees nothing, Señor, ees just some literature.

Gaskell I know what literature is, you dago dustbin. I also know what porn is. *(pulls out a loose magazine and brandishes it)* What's this then eh?

Spaniard It is one of Lope De Vega's latest play, Señor.

Gaskell 'Toledo Tit Parade'? What sort of play's that?

Spaniard It's very visual, Señor.

Gaskell Right. I'm taking this lot in the name of Her Gracious Majesty Queen Elizabeth.

Spaniard Oh, but Señor.

Gaskell Don't give me any trouble. Just pile up these baskets of filth and come with me.

The second Spaniard leaps out of the boat with a drawn sword and they both engage Gaskell in a fight. Then we start to draw away from them, leaving them tiny dots in the distance fighting. Fight music over all this and voice over.

Voice Over (TERRY J) The battle raged long and hard, but as night fell Sidney overcame the Spaniards. 6,000 copies of 'Tits and Bums' and 4,000 copies of 'Shower Sheila' were seized that day. The tide of Spanish porn was stemmed. Sir Philip Sidney returned to London in triumph.

Cut to stock film of Elizabethan London street during celebrations.

SUPERIMPOSED CAPTION: 'LONDON 1583'

Cut to side on close-up of Gaskell riding hard through woodland.

Voice Over Covered in glory, Sir Philip rode home to Penshurst to see his beloved wife... but all was not well.

Gaskell reins up outside another Tudor house and strides in. Cut to interior of an Elizabethan room – panelled walls, log fire, latticed windows, etc. Sir Philip's wife is sitting reading. Gaskell enters.

Gaskell Good evening all, my love. I have returned safe from the Low Countries. *(she hurriedly hides the book she is reading under some knitting and starts whistling)* What art thou reading, fair one?

Wife (CAROL) Oh, 'tis nothing, husband.

Gaskell I can see 'tis *something*.

Wife 'tis one of Shakespeare's latest works.

Gaskell picks up the book and reads the title.

Gaskell Oh... 'Gay Boys in Bondage' What, is't – tragedy? Comedy?

Wife 'tis a... er... 'tis a story of man's great love for his... fellow man.

Gaskell How fortunate we are indeed to have such a poet on these shores.

Wife Indeed. How was the war, my lord?

Gaskell The Spaniards were defeated thrice. Six dozen chests of hardcore captured.

Wife *(trying to look innocent)* Hast brought home any spoils of war?

Gaskell Yes, good my wife, this fair coat trimmed with ermine.

Wife *(without enthusiasm)* Oh, lovely, nowt else?

Gaskell No, no fair lady. The rest was too smutty.

He settles himself down in front of his lady's feet and the fire.

Gaskell Now, my good wife. Whilst I rest, read to me a while from Shakespeare's 'Gay Boys in Bondage'.

The wife looks a trifle taken aback but reluctantly opens the book and starts to read with a resigned air.

Wife Yes... my lord... 'Gay Boys in Bondage'... Ken, 25, is a mounted policeman with a difference... and what a difference. Even Roger is surprised and he's... *(she looks slightly sick with guilt)* he's used to real men...

Gaskell 'tis like 'Hamlet'... what a genius!

Wife 'But who's going to do the cooking tonight? Roddy's got a mouthful...'

Enter Maddox – a modern-day plain-clothed policeman.

Maddox (GRAHAM) All right, this is a raid.

The wife screams, Gaskell leaps to his feet.

Wife Oh! We are disgraced!

Gaskell There you are, Maddox!

Maddox Cut the chat... and get in the van.

Gaskell Maddox! You recognize me...

Maddox Indeed I do, Sir Philip Sidney, and sad I am to see you caught up in this morass of filth. *(he picks up the book)* Ooh – that's a long one.
Wife Oh oh . . . the glorious name of Sidney is besmirched . . . all is lost . . . oh alas the day.
Gaskell Shut up! I know this man – this is my old mate Sergeant Maddox . . .
Maddox You'll do time for this.
Gaskell Oh Maddox – it's me – Gaskell . . . 'F' division down at Acton . . . Inspector Arthur Frodwell.
Maddox Come on Sidney. *(he bundles them both out)* And you, miss.
Gaskell I'm not Sir Philip bleedin' Sidney . . . and where were you? We could have mopped up that Tudor shop . . .
They are bundled out. Maddox pauses only to pick a book from the bookcase near the door.
Maddox Ooh! That's a good one!
Cut to outside a modern theatre stage-door. Gaskell, still protesting, and Mrs Sidney are bundled out and into a police van. As it drives off, it reveals on the side of the theatre a poster saying: 'The Aldwych Theatre. The Royal Shakespeare Company Presents "Gay Boys In Bondage" By William Shakespeare'.
An animated excerpt from this little-known Shakespearian masterpiece leads us to a table outside a restaurant. A young couple are sitting blissfully at it.
She (CAROL) It's nice here, darling, isn't it.
He (JOHN) It's beautiful, it's Paris all over again.
Enter a vicar, dressed normally but has bald wig with fright hair at sides. He carries a suitcase.
Vicar (MICHAEL) Excuse me, do you mind if I join you?
He Er, no . . . no . . . no . . . not at all.
Vicar Are you *sure* you don't mind?
He Yes, yes, absolutely.
Vicar You're sure I won't be disturbing you?
He No, no.
Vicar You're absolutely sure I won't be disturbing you?
She No, no really.
Vicar Good. Because I don't want to disturb you. Specially as you're being so kind about me not disturbing you.
He Oh, no, no, we don't mind, do we, darling?
She Oh no, darling.
Vicar Good, so I can go ahead and join you then? Can I?
Both Yes . . . yes . . .
Vicar Won't be disturbing?

Both No. No.

Vicar Good, good. You're very kind. *(he sits down)* A lot of people are far less understanding than you are. A lot of people take offence even when I talk to them. *(he makes strange gestures with his hands)* Let alone when I specifically tell them about my being disturbing.

He Well, it's not *particularly* disturbing.

Vicar No, absolutely, absolutely, that's what I always say. *(he produces plates from his case and smashes them on the table)* But you'd be amazed at the number of people who really don't want me – I mean, even doing this *(he produces a rubber crab suspended from a ping-pong bat and a rubber baby doll and bobs them up and down, making loud silly noises as he does so)* gets people looking at me in the most extraordinary way. *(he breaks more plates and squirts shaving foam over his head; he and she get up to leave)*

He We must be getting on.

Vicar I knew I'd disturb you . . . I knew I'd disturb you . . . *(miserably)* It always happens . . . whenever I've found someone I really think I'm going to be able to get on with . . .

He No, the only thing is, you see, we're going to be a little bit late.

She *(sitting down and comforting vicar)* Let's stay.

He Well, just a little bit . . . I mean, we will be late if we don't . . . *(he sits down reluctantly)*

Vicar Oh, thank you. You're very kind.

More silly behaviour from the vicar. He and she look embarrassed. Dissolve to them sitting at home smashing plates, making silly noises and covering themselves with shaving foam.

She *(voice over)* As it turned out our chance meeting with Reverend Arthur Belling was to change our whole way of life, and every Sunday *(film of them running into a church)* we'd hurry along to St Loony up the Cream Bun and Jam.

Hold shot of the church. Sound of a congregation standing. We hear the silly noises. Cut to nude organist (Terry J). He plays a fanfare.

Announcer (JOHN) And now . . .

It's Man (MICHAEL) It's . . .

Animated titles.

Straight into animated sketch, ending with:

Voice Over (JOHN) and CAPTION: 'THE FREE REPETITION OF DOUBTFUL WORDS – SKIT, SPOOF, JAPE OR VIGNETTE, BY A VERY UNDER-RATED WRITER'

A post office counter window, with 'Telegram Enquiries' over the top. We see this through an ornate vignette. The clerk is behind the counter. Enter Mr Peepee. They speak very stiltedly.

Peepee (ERIC) I've come for some free repetition of doubtful words on an inland telegram.

Clerk (TERRY J) Have you got the telegram in question?

Peepee I have the very thing here.

Clerk Well, slip it to me my good chap and let me eye the contents.

Peepee At once Mr Telegram Enquiry Man.

Clerk Thank you Mr Customer Man. *(reads)* Aha. 'Parling I glove you. Clease clome at bronce, your troving swife, Pat.' Which was the word you wanted checking?

Peepee Pat.

Clerk Pat?

Peepee My wife's name is not Pat at all.

Clerk No?

Peepee It's Bat. With a B.

Clerk And therefore I will take a quick look in the book.

Peepee Ripping.

    CAPTION: 'ONE QUICK LOOK IN THE BOOK LATER'

Clerk You're quite right, old cock. There *has* been a mistake.

Peepee I thought as much. What really does it say?

Clerk It say 'Go away you silly little bleeder. I am having another man. Love Bat'. Quite some error.

Peepee Yes. She wouldn't call herself Pat, it's silly.

Clerk Daft, I call it.

Peepee Well it has been a pleasure working with you.

Clerk For me also it has been a pleasure. And that concludes our little skit.

    String quartet music starts to play, as at the beginning, only this time we widen to reveal a string quartet sitting in the set, playing. The clerk and Peepee adopt slightly frozen position. Mix to:

Voice Over and CAPTION: 'THE FREE REPETITION OF DOUBTFUL WORDS THING, BY A JUSTLY UNDER-RATED WRITER – THE END'

    Animation link to a late-night religious-type discussion. A chairman and three guests are slumped motionless in their seats.

Roger Last (JOHN) Good evening. Tonight on 'Is There' we examine the question, 'Is there a life after death?'. And here to discuss it are three dead people . . . The late Sir Brian Hardacre, former curator of the Imperial War Museum . . . *(superimposed captions identify them)* the late Professor Thynne, until recently an academic, critic, and broadcaster . . . and putting the view of the Church of England, the very late Prebendary Reverend Ross. Gentlemen, is there a life after death or not? Sir Brian? *(silence)* Professor? . . . Prebendary? . . . Well there we have it, three say no. On 'Is There' next week we'll be discussing the question 'Is there enough of it about', and until then, goodnight.

SUPERIMPOSED CREDITS:
'IS THERE'
INTRODUCED BY ROGER LAST
RESEARCH: J. LOSEY
L. ANDERSON
S. KUBRICK
P. P. PASOLINI
O. WELLES
THE LATE B. FORBES
PRODUCED BY: GILLIAN (AGED 3½)

Under these credits, we see the stiffs being carried off by people.

Cut to a doctor's surgery. The doctor has in front of him a plaque which says 'Dr E .H. Thripshaw'. Enter Burrows.

Burrows (MICHAEL) Good doctor morning! Nice year for the time of day!

Thripshaw (JOHN) Come in.

Burrows Can I down sit?

Thripshaw Certainly. *(Burrows sits)* Well, then?

Burrows Well, now, not going to bush the doctor about the beat too long. I'm going to come to point the straight immediately.

Thripshaw Good, good.

Burrows My particular prob, or buglem bear, I've had ages. For years, I've had it for donkeys.

Thripshaw What?

Burrows I'm up to here with it, I'm sick to death. I can't take you any longer so I've come to see it.

Thripshaw Ah, now this is your problem with words.

Burrows This is my problem with words. Oh, that seems to have cleared it. 'Oh I come from Alabama with my banjo on my knee'. Yes, that seems to be all right. Thank you very much.

Thripshaw I see. But recently you have been having this problem with your word order.

Burrows Well, absolutely, and what makes it worse, sometimes at the end of a sentence I'll come out with the wrong fusebox.

Thripshaw Fusebox?

Burrows And the thing about saying the wrong word is a) I don't notice it, and b) sometimes orange water given bucket of plaster.

Thripshaw Yes, tell me more about your problem.

Burrows Well, as I say, you'd just be talking and out'll pudenda the wrong word and ashtray's your uncle. So I'm really strawberry about it.

Thripshaw Upset?

Burrows It's so embarrassing when my wife and I go to an orgy.

Thripshaw A party?

Burrows No, an orgy. We live in Esher.

Thripshaw Quite.

Burrows That's what I said. It's such a bloody whack the diddle fa di la, fo di la, lo do di ... do di do, fum fum.

Thripshaw Mr Burrows, this is no common problem. You are suffering from a disease so rare that it hasn't got a name. Not yet. But it will have. Oh yes. This is the opportunity I've been waiting for. The chance of a lifetime! *(zoom in to close up on him as lighting changes to dramatic spotlight)* I'll show them at the Royal College of Surgeons! I'll make them sit up and take notice! Thripshaw's disease! Discovered by E. Henry Thripshaw MD! I'll be invited on 'Call My Bluff' and on merchandizing the E. Henry Thripshaw t-shirt ... I'll turn it into a game ... I'll sell the film rights.

Cut to front of a booklet, entitled 'A Dissertation on Thripshaw's Disease Presented to the Royal College of Surgeons by Dr E. Henry Thripshaw'. Captions zoom forward over it:

HARLEY STREET

FLEET STREET

BROADWAY

HOLLYWOOD

A page of the book turns to reveal the title 'David O. Seltzer Presents'. The page turns again to reveal 'Rip Clint in:'. The page turns again to reveal a title in stone lettering à la Ben-Hur, with searchlights behind à la 20th Century Fox: 'Dr E. Henry Thripshaw's Disease'.

Cut to stock film of marauding knights.

SUPERIMPOSED CAPTION: 'SYRIA 1203'

The knights sack a village, looting, pillaging, burning and murdering.

Cut to a studio set with interviewer and Thripshaw.

Interviewer *(speaking with frequent pauses, as of one reading from a slow autocue)* That clip ... comes from the new David O. Seltzer ... film. The author ... of that film clip ... is with me ... now. Doctor E. Henry ... Thripshaw.

Thripshaw Well, I feel that they have missed the whole point of my disease.

Interviewer This is ... always the problem ... with directors of film ... clips.

Thripshaw Yes, well you see, they've dragged in all this irrelevant mush ...

Interviewer What ... are you doing ... now?

Thripshaw Well at the moment I am working on a new disease, which I hope to turn into a musical, but, primarily we are working on a re-make of my first disease and this time we're hoping to do it properly.

Interviewer Well ... let's just ... take a ... look at this new film ... clip.

Film clip exactly as before. Cut to Thripshaw at a desk evidently in a castle. A knight in armour rushes up to him.

Thripshaw Well now, what seems to be the matter?

Cut to a corner of the set where a man emerges from a barrel.

Man (MICHAEL) The next sketch starts after some silly noises.

Black screen and a collection of really silly noises. Then fade up on a country church. Cut to interior, a vestry. A sign reads 'No Papists'. The door opens and the vicar enters as if from the end of a service. He takes off his cassock and is hanging it up. At one side of the set is a sculpture on a plinth. It is the vicar's head, but with an enormously long nose. Mr Kirkham has followed the vicar in. He is an earnest, quiet, self-effacing soul, with a tortured conscience.

Vicar (MICHAEL) Come in.

Kirkham (GRAHAM) I wondered if I could have a word with you for a moment.

Vicar By all means . . . by all means, sir. Do sit down. *(they look round for a chair)* Ah, sit on the desk here.

Kirkham Thank you.

Vicar Now then, a glass of sherry?

Kirkham No . . . no thank you . . .

Vicar *(getting a bottle from the cupboard)* Are you sure? I'm going to have some.

Kirkham Well, if you're having some, yes then, perhaps, vicar.

Vicar *(slightly taken aback)* Oh . . . well there's only just enough for me.

Kirkham Well in that case I won't, don't worry.

Vicar You see, if I split what's left, there'd be hardly any left for me at all.

Kirkham Well; I'm not a great sherry drinker.

Vicar Good! So, I can have it all . . . now then what's the problem?

Kirkham Well, just recently I've begun to worry about . . .

The vicar has been looking through his desk. He produces a bottle of sherry in triumph.

Vicar Ah! I've found another bottle! You can have some now if you want to.

Kirkham Well . . . yes, perhaps a little . . .

Vicar Oh you don't have to. I can drink the whole bottle.

Kirkham Well in that case, no . . .

Vicar Good! That's another bottle for me. Do go on.

The vicar opens the bottle and pours himself a glass. As soon as he has drunk it he replenishes it again.

Kirkham I've begun to worry recently that . . .

There is a knock on the door.

Vicar Come in!

A smooth man, Mr Husband, enters carrying a smart little briefcase.

Vicar Ah, Mr Husband... this is Mr Kirkham, one of my parishioners, this is Mr Husband of the British Sherry Corporation...

Kirkham Look, look, perhaps I'd better come back later...

Vicar No, no... no do stay here. Have a sherry... you won't be long will you, Husband?

Husband (ERIC) Oh no, vicar... it's just a question of signing a few forms.

The vicar pours Husband a sherry.

Vicar There we are... there we are, Mr Husband. Now, how about you, Mr Kirkham?

Kirkham Well only if there's enough.

Vicar Oh well, there's not much now.

Kirkham Oh, in that case... no... I won't bother.

Vicar *(pouring himself one)* Good. Right... now, then, what is the problem, Husband?

Husband Well, vicar, I've made enquiries with our shippers and the most sherry they can ship in any one load is 12,000 gallons.

Vicar And how many glasses is that?

Husband That's roughly 540,000 glasses, vicar.

Vicar That's excellent, Husband, excellent.

Husband Yes... it means you can still keep your main sherry supply on the roof, but you can have an emergency supply underneath the vestry of 5,000 gallons.

Vicar Yes... and I could have dry sherry on the roof and Amontillado in the underground tank!

Husband Absolutely.

The vicar signs a form that Husband hands to him.

Vicar Excellent work, Husband, excellent work.

Husband Not at all, vicar, you're one of our best customers... you and the United States. Well goodbye. *(he leaves)*

Vicar Terrific. Now then, Mr Kirkham *(pouring himself another sherry)* I am so sorry... do go on.

Kirkham Well, it's just that recently I've begun to worry about...

Vicar Well, look...

Kirkham I sometimes ask myself – does the Bible intend...

A group of Spanish singers in full national costume and guitars bursts into the vestry, noisily singing a song praising Amontillado. A man in an extravagant Spanish costume rushes in. His hat has a sign on it saying: 'Sherry, the drink of champions'. Two girls come in bearing maracas and Carmen Miranda style hats. Mr Kirkham looks fed up. The Spaniards finish their song, noisily.

Man (TERRY J) What did you want?

Vicar Dirty books, please.

As they carry out their transactions, noisily, we cut to the credits, rolled over a shot of the dirty postcards section of the Tudor dirty bookshop. The credits read:

'MONTY PYTHON'S FLYING CIRCUS *(with 'censored' notice over it)*
WAS CONCEIVED, WRITTEN AND CENSORED BY
MICHAEL 'BULKY' PALIN
TERRY JONES 'KING OF THE LASH'
JOHN CLEESE 'A SMILE, A SONG AND A REFILL'
TERRY GILLIAM 'AN AMERICAN IN PLASTER'
GRAHAM 'A DOZEN WHOLESALE' CHAPMAN
ERIC IDLE (ACTUAL SIZE – BATTERIES EXTRA)
ALSO APPEARING
CAROL CLEVELAND ('FOUR REVEALING POSES' HARD PUBLICATIONS PRICE 40P)
AND, IN A VARIETY OF INTERESTING POSITIONS, THE FRED TOMLINSON SINGERS UNDER THEIR LEADER 'BUTCH' TOMLINSON
ROSALIND ('AFORE YE GO') BAILEY NOW AVAILABLE FROM BBC ENTERPRISES
BODY MAKE-UP MADELAINE GAFFNEY AND THE BBC NAUGHTY LADIES' CLUB
UNUSUAL COSTUMES AND LEATHERWEAR HAZEL PETHIG AND THE NAUGHTY LADS OF 'Q' DIVISION
ROSTRUM CAMERA MOUNTED BY PETER WILLIS (MASSAGE IN YOUR OWN HOME OR HOTEL ROOM)
ANIMATIONS AND EROTIC CARTOONS TERRY GILLIAM AND MISS HEBBERN 043-7962
GRAPHIC DETAILS BOB BLAGDEN 'DENMARK HAS NEVER LAUGHED SO MUCH'
RED LIGHTING BILL BAILEY
HEAVY BREATHING AND SOUND RICHARD CHUBB
FILM CAMERAMAN AND 'RIK' ALAN FEATHERSTONE 'MEN IT CAN BE DONE'
BLUE FILM EDITOR RAY MILLICHOPE 'WHAT YOUR RIGHT ARM'S FOR'
DESIGNED BY BOB 'BIG, BLACK, BUTCH AND BEAUTIFUL' BERK
PRODUCED BY IAN MACNAUGHTON WHO IS ASSISTING POLICE WITH THEIR ENQUIRIES
UNE ÉMISSION NOCTURNALE PAR TÉLÉVISIONE FRANÇAISE ET BBC TV
COPYRIGHT BBC TV £5 IN A PLAIN WRAPPER'

Fade out. Fade up on the BBC world symbol.

Voice Over (MICHAEL) E. Henry Thripshaw t-shirts are now available from BBC Enterprises. The price hasn't finally been decided, and the address to write to . . . they haven't yet quite worked out.

Thirty-seven

A floodlit boxing ring. Sports programme music.
SUPERIMPOSED CAPTION: 'BOXING TONIGHT'

Voice Over (MICHAEL) 'Boxing Tonight' comes from the Empire Pool, Wembley and features the main heavyweight bout between Jack Bodell, British and Empire Heavyweight Champion. *(cheers; shot of Bodell (Nosher Powell) in his corner with two seconds)* And Sir Kenneth Clark... *(shot of Clark's corner; he is in a dressing-gown with 'Sir Kenneth Clark' on the back; both take off their dressing-gowns as referee calls them together; Sir Kenneth is wearing a tweed suit underneath)* It's the first time these two have met so there should be some real action tonight...

The bell goes. Crowd noise. Sir Kenneth wanders around as in 'Civilization'.

Sir Kenneth (GRAHAM) This then is the height of the English Renaissance, the triumph of Classical over Gothic... the ...

Bodell swings a left and knocks Sir Kenneth down.

Voice Over He's down! Sir Kenneth Clark is down in eight seconds. But he's up again. He's up at six...

Sir Kenneth The almost ordered façades of Palladio's villas reflects the...

Bodell knocks him down again.

Voice Over And he's down again, and I don't think he's going to get up this time. *(referee counts Sir Kenneth Clark out and holds up Bodell's hand)* No, so Jack Bodell has defeated Sir Kenneth Clark in the very first round here tonight and so this big Lincolnshire heavyweight becomes the new Oxford Professor of Fine Art.

Zoom in to the ring. The announcer appears in DJ and takes a mike lowered on a wire.

Announcer (JOHN) Thank you, thank you, thank you, ladies and gentlemen. And now...

Cut to a corner of the ring. The nude organist at his organ, plays a chord, turns and grins. Cut to the opposite corner; the 'It's' man on his stool.

It's Man (MICHAEL) It's...

Animated titles.

Slow pan across idyllic countryside. We see a traditional eighteenth-century coach and horses travelling along the valley floor. Suddenly a highwayman, Dennis Moore, spurs his horse forward and rides up to the coach brandishing pistols.

Moore (JOHN) Stand and deliver! Drop that gun! *(the coach comes to a halt; the drivers hold up their hands but the postilion reaches for a gun; Moore shoots him)* Let that be a warning to you all. You move at your peril for I have two pistols here. I know one of them isn't loaded any more, but the other one is, so that's one of you dead for sure, or just about for sure anyway, it certainly wouldn't be worth your while risking it because I'm a very good shot, I practise every day, well, not absolutely *every* day, but most days in the week... I expect I must practise four or five times a week, at least... at least four or five, only some weekends... like last weekend there wasn't much time so that moved the average down a bit... but I should say it's definitely a solid four days' practice every week... at least. I mean, I reckon I could hit that tree over there... the one behind that hillock, not the big hillock, the little hillock on the left. *(heads are coming out of the coach and peering)* You can see the three trees, the third from the left and back a bit – that one – I reckon I could hit that four times out of five... on a good day. Say with this wind... say, say, seven times out of ten...

Squire (TERRY J) What, that tree there?

Moore Which one?

Squire The big beech with the sort of bare branch coming out of the top left.

Moore No, no, no, not that one.

Girl (CAROL) No, no, he means the one over there. Look, you see that one there.

Squire Yes.

Girl Well now, go two along to the right.

Coachman (GRAHAM) Just near that little bush.

Girl Well, it's the one just behind it.

Squire Ah! The elm.

Moore No, that's not an elm. An elm's got sort of great clumps of leaves like that. That's either a beech or a... er... hornbeam.

Parson (ERIC) A hornbeam?

Moore Oh, no not a hornbeam. What's the tree that has a leaf with sort of regular veins coming out and the veins go all the way out to the...

Girl Serrated?

Moore ... to the serrated edges.

Parson A willow!

Moore That's right.

Parson That's nothing like a willow.

Moore Well it doesn't matter anyway! I could hit it seven times out of ten, that's the point.

Parson Never a willow.

Moore Shut up! This is a hold-up, not a botany lesson. Right, now my fine friends, no false moves please. I want you to hand over all the lupins you've got.

Squire Lupins?

Moore Yes, lupins. Come on, come on.

Parson What do you mean, lupins?

Moore Don't try and play for time.

Parson I'm not, you mean the flower lupin?

Moore Yes, that's right.

Squire Well, we haven't got any lupins.

Girl Honestly.

Moore Look, my fine friends, I happen to know that this is the Lupin Express.

Squire You must be out of your tiny mind.

Moore Get out of the coach. Come on, get out! *(they do so indicating that Moore is a loony; he dismounts and enters the coach; he immediately comes out with an enormous armful of lupins)* Just as I thought. Not clever enough, my fine friends. Come on, Concorde. *(he jumps on horse and rides away)*

Squire Well, so much for the lupins.

Montage of Dennis Moore, galloping through the sun-dappled glades, a little village, more glades and forest and arriving at a little peasant-type woodcutter's hut where two terribly poor peasants greet him and receive the lupins with a neutral reaction. During this the following song is heard.

Song Dennis Moore, Dennis Moore,
Galloping through the sward.
Dennis Moore, Dennis Moore,
And his horse Concorde.
He steals from the rich and
Gives to the poor.
Mr Moore, Mr Moore, Mr Moore.

Moore Here we are, I'll be back.

Moore wheels round and rides off.

SUPERIMPOSED CAPTION: 'THE END'

Pull back to reveal 'The End' is on TV in the house of Mrs Trepidatious. Another old ratbag enters and sits opposite Mrs Trepidatious.

Mrs O (ERIC) Morning, Mrs Trepidatious.

Mrs Trepidatious (GRAHAM) Oh, I don't know what's good about it, my right arm's hanging off something awful.

Mrs O Oh, you want to have that seen to.

Mrs Trepidatious What, by that Dr Morrison? He's killed more patients than I've had severe boils.

Mrs O What do the stars say?

Mrs Trepidatious Well, Petula Clark says burst them early, but David Frost...

Mrs O No, the stars in the paper, you cloth-eared heap of anteater's catarrh, the zodiacal signs, the horoscopic fates, the astrological portents, the omens, the genethliac prognostications, the mantalogical harbingers, the Vaticinal utterances, the fratidical premonitory uttering of the mantalogical omens – what do the bleeding stars in the paper predict, forecast, prophesy, foretell, prognosticate...

A big sheet is lowered with the words on.

Voice Over (MICHAEL) And this is where you at home can join in.

Mrs O ... forebode, bode, augur, spell, foretoken, *(the audience joins in)* presage, portend, foreshow, foreshadow, forerun, herald, point to, betoken, indicate!

Mrs Trepidatious I don't know.

The sheet is raised again.

Mrs O What are you?

Mrs Trepidatious I'm Nesbitt.

Mrs O There's not a zodiacal sign called Nesbitt...

Mrs Trepidatious All right, Derry and Toms.

Mrs O *(surveying paper)* Aquarius, Scorpio, Virgo, Derry and Toms. April 29th to March 22nd. Even dates only.

Mrs Trepidatious Well what does it presage?

Mrs O You have green, scaly skin, and a soft yellow underbelly with a series of fin-like ridges running down your spine and tail. Although lizard-like in shape, you can grow anything up to thirty feet in length with huge teeth that can bite off great rocks and trees. You inhabit arid sub-tropical zones and wear spectacles.

Mrs Trepidatious It's very good about the spectacles.

Mrs O It's amazing.

Mrs Trepidatious Mm... what's yours, Irene?

Mrs O Basil.

Mrs Trepidatious I'm sorry, what's yours, Basil?

Mrs O No. That's my star sign, Basil...

Mrs Trepidatious There isn't a...

Mrs O Yes there is... Aquarius, Sagittarius, Derry and Toms, Basil. June 21st to June 22nd.

Mrs Trepidatious Well, what does it say?

Mrs O You have green, scaly skin and a series of yellow underbellies running down your spine and tail...

Mrs Trepidatious That's Exactly the same!

Mrs O Try number one... what's Aquarius?

Mrs Trepidatious It's a zodiacal sign.

Mrs O I know that, what does it say in the paper Mrs Flan-and-pickle?

Mrs Trepidatious All right... Oh! It says, 'a wonderful day ahead'. You will be surrounded by family and friends. Roger Moore will drop in for lunch, bringing Tony Curtis with him. In the afternoon a substantial cash sum will come your way. In the evening Petula Clark will visit your home accompanied by Mike Sammes singers. She will sing for you in your own living room. Before you go to bed, Peter Wyngarde will come and declare his undying love for you.

Mrs O Urghh! What's Scorpio?

Mrs Trepidatious Oh, that's very good. 'You will have lunch with a schoolfriend of Duane Eddy's, who will insist on whistling some of Duane's greatest instrumental hits. In the afternoon you will die, you will be buried...'

A doctor is lowered on a wire.

Doctor (TERRY J) Good morning.

Mrs O Oh, morning, doctor.

Doctor How's the old arm this morning, Mrs Ikon?

Mrs Trepidatious Oh, it's still hanging off at the shoulder.

Doctor Good, well let's have a look at it, shall we? *(he tries unsuccessfully to open his bag)* Oh damn, damn, damn, damn... damn this wretched bag... oh the wretched, damn, bloody, little bag. It's the one thing I hate about being a doctor – it's this wretched bloody little bag!

He smashes a chair over it and finally produces a revolver and shoots the lock off. It opens and is stuffed full of pound notes, some of which spill out. He feels inside... eventually pulls out a stethoscope.

Doctor What's that doing here? *(he throws it away)*

Cut to another doctor walking along a street. The stethoscope flies out of window and lands on him.

Second Doctor (GRAHAM) *(brushing it off)* Eurgggh!

Cut back to the first doctor still rummaging in black bag. Eventually he produces a pair of black kid gloves and a black handkerchief. He folds it and puts it on and points the gun at Mrs Trepidatious.

Doctor Hand over the money. *(she goes to a sideboard, opens the bottom drawer and gets out a money box which she gives to him)* Come on, all of it! *(she looks scared; he jabs the gun at her; she goes over to a painting of a wall-safe on the wall and pushes it aside to reveal an identical wall-safe underneath. She opens it and a hand comes out holding a money box; she takes and gives it to the doctor)* Yes, that seems to be OK. Right! I'll just test your reflexes! *(he opens his mac like a flasher; they scream and jump)* Right, now then, everything seems to be OK, I'll see you next week. Keep collecting the pensions, and try not to spend too much on food. *(he starts to go up)*

Mrs Trepidatious Thank you, doctor. *(he disappears)*

Cut to a hospital ward. A man in bed, a chair with his clothes on it at the foot of the bed. A doctor enters and goes right for the jacket and starts to feel in the pockets.

Doctor (MICHAEL) Morning, Mr Henson . . . How are we today?

Henson (TERRY G) Not too bad, doctor.

Doctor OK, take it easy . . . *(he empties his wallet and puts it back)* Expecting any postal orders this week?

Henson No.

Doctor Righto.

A nurse comes and gets the loose change. The doctor goes to the next bed, where there is a man entirely in traction.

Doctor Ah, Mr Rodgers, have you got your unemployment benefit please? Right. Well can you write me a cheque then . . . please?

The patient writes him a cheque. He goes to the foot of the bed. There is a graph with a money symbol on it. He marks it down further.

Doctor Thank you very much. Soon have you down to nothing. Ah, Mr Millichope. *(he smiles and leaves, passing a man with a saline drip full of coins; chink of money)*

A Gilliam animation suitably connected with the foregoing concept leads us to a TV debate set-up. Stern music starts as the lights come on.

SUPERIMPOSED CAPTIONS:

'THE GREAT DEBATE'

'NUMBER 31'

'TV4 OR NOT TV4?'

Kennedy (ERIC) Hello. Should there be another television channel, or should there not? On tonight's programme the Minister for Broadcasting, The Right Honourable Mr Ian Throat MP.

Throat (TERRY J) Good evening.

Kennedy The Chairman of the Amalgamated Money TV, Sir Abe Sappenheim.

Sappenheim (GRAHAM) Good evening.

Kennedy The Shadow Spokesman for Television, Lord Kinwoodie.

Kinwoodie (JOHN) Hello.

Kennedy And a television critic, Mr Patrick Loone.

Loone (MICHAEL) Hello.

Kennedy Gentlemen – should there be a fourth television channel or not? Ian?

Throat Yes.

Kennedy Francis.

Kinwoodie No.

Kennedy Sir Abe?

Sappenheim Yes.

Kennedy Patrick.

Loone No.

SUPERIMPOSED CAPTION: 'YES 2 NO 2'

Kennedy Well there you have it. Two say will, two say won't. We'll be back again next week, and next week's 'Great Debate' will be about Government Interference in Broadcasting and will be cancelled mysteriously.

The lights fade down. Music.

SUPERIMPOSED ROLLER CAPTION:

'THE GREAT DEBATE

INTRODUCED BY LUDOVIC LUDOVIC

WITH SIR ABE SAPPENHEIM

IAN THROAT MP

LORD KINWOODIE

MR PATRICK LOONE'

Behind this the panel members are seen gesticulating strangely in silhouette. Fade out.

Fade up on a picture of Queen Victoria.

Voice Over (MICHAEL) Just starting on BBC 1 now, 'Victoria Regina' the inspiring tale of the simple crofter's daughter who worked her way up to become Queen of England and Empress of the Greatest Empire television has ever seen. On BBC 2 now Episode 3 of 'George I' the new 116 part serial about the famous English King who hasn't been done yet. On ITV now the *(sound of a punch)* Ugh!

Music starts. Picture of Royal crest.

SUPERIMPOSED CAPTION: 'GEORGE I'

The word 'Charles' below the crest has been crossed out and 'George I' written above it.

CAPTION: 'EPISODE 3 – THE GATHERING STORM'

This looks very dog-eared and thumb-printed.

Cut to studio set of an eighteenth-century ballroom. Some dancing is going on. A fop is talking to two ladies in the usual phony mouthing manner. They laugh meaninglessly.

Grantley (MICHAEL) Ah! 'tis my lord of Buckingham. Pray welcome, Your Grace.

Buckingham (TERRY J) Thank you, Grantley.

Grantley Ladies, may I introduce to you the man who prophesied that a German monarch would soon embroil this country in continental affairs.

First Lady (CAROL) Oh, how so, my lord?

Buckingham Madam, you will recall that prior to his accession our gracious sovereign George had become involved in the long standing Northern War, through his claims to Bremen and Verdun. These duchies would provide an outlet to the sea of the utmost value to Hanover. The Treaty of Westphalia has assigned them to Sweden.

Grantley In 1648.

Buckingham Exactly.

Grantley Meanwhile Frederick William of Denmark, taking advantage of the absence of Charles XII, seized them; 1712.

Second Lady Oh yes!

First Lady It all falls into place. More wine?

Grantley Oh, thank you.

Buckingham However, just prior to his accession, George had made an alliance with Frederick William of Prussia, on the grounds of party feeling.

Grantley While Frederick William had married George's only daughter.

First Lady I remember the wedding.

Buckingham But chiefly through concern at the concerted action against Charles XII . . .

There is a crash as Moore swings through the window on a rope. Everyone gasps and screams. He lands spectacularly.

Moore Stand and deliver.

All Dennis Moore!

Moore The same. And now my lords, my ladies . . . your lupins, please.

General bewilderment and consternation.

Buckingham Our what?

Moore Oh, come come, don't play games with me my Lord of Buckingham.

Buckingham What can you mean?

Moore *(putting pistol to his head)* Your life or your lupins, my lord.

Buckingham and the rest of the gathering now produce lupins which they have secreted about their several persons. They offer them to Moore.

Moore In a bunch, in a bunch. *(they arrange them in a bunch)* Thank you my friends, and now a good evening to you all.

He grabs the rope, is hauled into air and disappears out of the window. There is a bump, a whinny and the sound of galloping hooves. The guests rush to the window to watch him disappear.

Grantley He seeks them here . . . he seeks them there . . . he seeks those lupins everywhere. The murdering blackguard! He's taken all our lupins.

First Lady *(producing one from her garter)* Not quite.

Gasps of delight.

Buckingham Oh you tricked him!

Man We still have one! *(they all cheer)*

Cut to a similar montage as before of Moore galloping through forest, clearings and tiny villages. Song as follows.

Song Dennis Moore, Dennis Moore,
Riding through the night.
Soon every lupin in the land
Will be in his mighty hand
He steals them from the rich
And gives them to the poor
Mr Moore, Mr Moore, Mr Moore.

Towards the end of this he arrives at the same peasant's cottage as before, dismounts and runs to the cottage door. He pauses. From inside the cottage we hear quiet moaning. Cut to inside the cottage. In this rude hut, lit by a single candle, the female peasant lies apparently dying on a bunk. Lupins are everywhere, in the fire, on the bed, a large pile of them forms a pillow. The female peasant is moaning and the male peasant is kneeling beside her offering her a lupin. Moore enters slowly.

Male Peasant (MICHAEL) *(dressed largely in a lupin suit)* Try and eat some, my dear. It'll give you strength. *(Dennis Moore reverently approaches the bed; the male peasant looks round and sees him)* Oh Mr Moore, Mr Moore, she's going fast.

Moore Don't worry, I've . . . I've brought you something.

Male Peasant Medicine at last?

Moore No.

Male Peasant Food?

Moore No.

Male Peasant Some blankets perhaps . . . clothes . . . wood for the fire . . .

Moore No. Lupins!

Male Peasant *(exploding)* Oh Christ!

Moore *(astonished)* I thought you liked them.

Male Peasant I'm sick to bloody death of them.

Female Peasant (TERRY J) So am I.

Male Peasant She's bloody dying and all you bring us is lupins. All we've eaten mate for the last four bleeding weeks is lupin soup, roast lupin, steamed lupin, braised lupin in lupin sauce, lupin in the basket with sautéed lupins, lupin meringue pie, lupin sorbet . . . we sit on lupins, we sleep in lupins, we feed the cat on lupins, we bum lupins, we even *wear* the bloody things!

Moore Looks very smart.

Male Peasant Oh shut up! We're sick to death with the stench of them. *(sound of a miaow and then a bump)* Look. The cat's just choked itself to death on them. *(we see a dead cat with lupins coming out of its mouth)* I don't care if I never see another lupin till the day I die! Why don't you go out and steal something *useful*!

Moore Like what?

Male Peasant Like gold and silver and clothes and wood and jewels and . . .

Moore Hang on, I'll get a piece of paper.

Cut to a montage of shots of Moore riding away from the hut over which we hear the song.

Song Dennis Moore, Dennis Moore,
Dum dum dum the night.
Dennis Moore, Dennis Moore,
Dum de dum dum plight.
He steals dum dum dum
And dum dum dum dee
Dennis dum, Dennis dee, dum dum dum.

Cut back to the ballroom to find the same people discussing British history.

Buckingham This, coupled with the presence of Peter and his Prussians at Mecklenburg and Charles and his Swedes in Pomerania, made George and Stanhope eager to come to terms with France.

Grantley Meanwhile, a breach had now opened with . . .

Moore swings in as before.

Grantley Oh no, not again.

Buckingham Come on.

Moore Stand and deliver again! Your money, your jewellery, your . . . hang on. *(he takes out a list)* Your clothes, your snuff, your ornaments, your glasswear, your pussy cats . . .

Buckingham *(aside to the first lady)* Don't say anything about the lupins . . .

Moore Your watches, your lace, your spittoons . . .

Cut to a montage pretty much as before but with Moore riding through the glades dragging behind him a really enormous bag marked with 'swag' in very olde English lettering. This bag is about twenty feet long and bumps along the ground behind the horse with the appropriate sound effects to make it sound full of valuable jewels, gold, silver, etc. Song as follows.

Song Dennis Moore, Dennis Moore,
Riding through the woods.
Dennis Moore, Dennis Moore
With a bag of things.
He gives to the poor and he takes from the rich
Dennis Moore, Dennis Moore, Dennis Moore.

As he arrives at the poor peasant's cottage they run out. They all open the bag together to the peasants' enormous and unmeasurable joy.

Moore Here we are.

SUPERIMPOSED CAPTION: 'THE END'

Cut to stock film of people queuing at an exhibition hall.

Voice Over (ERIC) Well it may be the end of that, but it's certainly far from the end of – well in fact it's the beginning – well not quite the beginning – well certainly nearer the beginning than the end – well yes damn it, it is to all intents and purposes the beginning of this year's Ideal Loon Exhibition, sponsored by the 'Daily Express'. *(cut to interior of hall, people pouring through the doors; above their heads it says 'Ideal Loon Exhibition')* Numbskulls and boobies from all over the country have been arriving to go through their strange paces before a large paying crowd. This is the fifteenth Ideal Loon Exhibition and we took a good look round after it was opened by its patron ... *(quick flash of Edward Heath opening something)* There's Kevin Bruce the digger duffer from Down Under, who's ranked fourteenth in the world's silly positions league ... *(Kevin is in a roped-off exhibition area; with a number in front of him; people are walking past looking at him with programmes; he is dressed in Australian bush gear and he is leaning his forehead against a goldfish bowl on a four-foot-six plinth)* This kind of incoherent behaviour is really beginning to catch on Down Under. There's Norman Kirby from New Zealand, whose speciality is standing behind a screen with a lady with no clothes on ... *(again in an exhibition stand with a number in front; there is a screen which is higher than their heads, but it is cut off at knee height so you can see two pairs of legs, one female, totally bare, one male wearing some enormous boots, no socks)* In real life, Norman is a gynaecologist, but this is his lunch hour. And from France there's a superb exhibition of rather silly behaviour by the Friends of the Free French Osteopaths. *(on the stand five men dressed in Breton berets, striped French shirts, silly moustaches, with baguettes; in unison they make the silly sign, counting the while 'un, deux, trois)* They do this over four hundred times a day. Nobody knows why. But for sheer pointless behaviour you've got to admire Brian Broomers, the battling British boy who for two weeks has been suspended over a tin of condemned veal. *(quite a crowd watch this; again a roped-off exhibit, Brian (Graham) is suspended from the ceiling by two car tyres; he lies there smoking a pipe; underneath him there is a small opened tin, with 'veal' on the side)* Always popular with the crowd, is the Scotsman with Nae Trews exhibit, and this year's no exception. *(a very large man (John) dressed as a Scotsman in front of a sign saying 'Scotsman with Nae Trews Exhibit, Sponsored by Natural Gas'; an enormously long line of middle-aged Pepperpots stand waiting in a queue; each in turn lifts up a corner of Scotsman's kilt, has a tiny peek and walks off)* Sponsored by Natural Gas and Glasgow City Council, this exhibit is entirely supported by voluntary contributions. But for a truly magnificent waste of time you've got to go no further than the exhibit from Italy – Italian priests in custard, discussing vital matters of the day. *(four Italian priests standing up to their chests in a large vat of custard; in front of them it says 'Italian Priests in custard'; they are animatedly discussing vital matters; hung behind them is a sign saying 'Italy, Land of Custard')* These lads from a seminary near Cremona, have been practising for well over a year. As always one of the great attractions of this fourteen-day exhibition is the display of counter-marching given by the Massed Pipes and Toilet Requisites of the Colwyn Bay Massed Pipes and Toilet Requisites Club. *(a dozen people in blazers, flannels and white pumps are vigorously counter-marching, whilst Souza's Star Spangled Banner blares out; they are holding various items of plumbing, lengths of piping, a toilet, a bidet, a bath, back scrubbers, loofahs, shower attachments, hand basins, etc.)* An interesting point about these boys is they all have one thing in common. Hip injuries. Not far away the crowds are flocking to see a member of the famous Royal Canadian Mounted Geese. *(cut to pantomime goose on horseback)* But the climax of the whole event is the judging.

Cut to a sort of Miss World cat-walk. A judge (Eric) appears (holding number 41). A band plays 'A pretty girl is like a melody'.

PA Announcement (JOHN) Mr Justice Burke. *(the judge walks down, turns slightly at the edge of the stage, puts a knee forward and makes a cheesecake smile)* Well that's the last, and let's just see those last six once again. *(the judge on the stage is joined by five others in full judicial robes, with wigs, each holding a number)* And the winner is – number 41, Mr Justice Burke.

The winner reacts by bursting into tears. The others look rather sad. Cut to a still picture of Mr Justice Burke in bed having breakfast the next morning. He is still wearing his robes and wig but he has a sceptre and a terrible tiara crown on. This picture is in black and white and is large on the front page of a newspaper. The headline is 'Justice seen to be done'. A sub-heading says 'British Justice Triumphs'. This newspaper page takes us off into a couple of minutes of animation.

Cut to close up of a man's face.

McGough (ERIC) Yet fear, not like an aged florin, can so disseminate men's eyes, that fortune, straining at a kissing touch may stop her ceaseless search to sport amidst the rampant thrust of time, and bring the thing undone to pass by that with which the cock may chance an arm.

Cut to a wider shot to show that he is in an off-licence. Mr Bones is behind the counter.

Mr Bones (JOHN) Well that's all very well, sir, *but* this is an off-licence.

McGough Oh. Just a bottle of sherry then, please.

Mr Bones Certainly... Amontillado?

McGough Yes, I think Amontillado, finely grown... well chosen from the casque of Pluto's hills, cell'd deep within the vinous soil of Spain, wrench'd thence from fiery regions of the sun...

Mr Bones Yes, yes sir. Just one bottle?

McGough Just one bottle. Just one jot. Just one tittle. That's the lot.

Mr Bones There we are, sir. That'll be a pound, please.

McGough A pound a pound and all around abound
 A pound found found
 Lost lost the cost till was't embossed...

Mr Bones Excuse me, sir.

McGough Yes, good victualler, nature's trencherman, mine honest tapster...

Mr Bones I was just wondering. Are you a poet?

McGough No, no, I'm a solicitor... well versed within the written law of man, can to those who need...

Mr Bones Oh *shut* up.

McGough I'm sorry. I'm afraid I've caught poetry.

Mr Bones Oh really? Well, don't worry, sir – I used to suffer from short stories.

McGough Really? When?

Mr Bones Oh, once upon a time... there lived in Wiltshire a young chap called Dennis Moore. Now Dennis was a highwayman by profession... *(we ripple through to Dennis Moore riding along with a big bag of swag)*... and for several months he had been stealing from the rich to give to the poor. One day...

Mix through to a shot of Dennis Moore arriving with another bag of goodies. The peasants who greet him are by now very smartly dressed and the cottage has been refurbished.

Moore Here we are again, Mr Jenkins. *(Dennis leaves the bag and wheels his horse around)* There we are... I'll be back. *(he rides off again purposefully)*

Cut back to the ballroom. The walls are bare and the people are down to their undergarments. They sit around the table gnawing pieces of bread and dipping them in a watery soup. The central bowl of soup contains a lupin.

Buckingham Meanwhile Frederick William busily engaged in defending against the three great powers the province of Silesia...

Grantley ... which he had seized in the War of the Austrian succession against his word.

First Lady Yes, I remember.

Man ... was now dependent on Pitt's subsidies.

Moore swings in through the window. They all respond to him with listless moans of disappointment.

Moore My lords, my ladies, on your feet, please. *(he is ignored and therefore says commandingly)* I must ask you to do exactly as I say or I shall be forced to shoot you right between the eyes. *(they stand up hurriedly)* Well not right between the eyes, I mean when I say between the eyes, obviously I don't have to be that accurate, I mean, if I hit you in that sort of area, like that, obviously, that's all right for me, I mean, I don't have to try and sort of hit a point bisecting a line drawn between your pupils or anything like that. I mean, from *my* point of view, it's perfectly satisfactory...

First Lady What do you *want*? Why are you here?

Moore Why are *any* of us here? I mean, when you get down to it, it's all so *meaningless,* isn't it, I mean what do any of us want...

Buckingham No, no, what do you want *now*?

Moore Oh I see, oh just the usual things, a little place of my own, the right girl...

Grantley No, no, no! What do you want from *us*?

Moore Oh sorry. Um, your gold, your silver, your jewellery.

Buckingham You've taken it all.

First Lady This is all we've got left.

Moore That's nice. I'll have them. Come on. *(he takes all the spoons)*

Buckingham You'd better take the bloody lupin too.

Moore Thank you very much, I've gone through that stage. *(he grabs the rope and swings out again)*

   Short montage of Dennis riding accompanied by the song.
   Dennis Moore, Dennis Moore
   Et cetera, et cetera...

   He leaps off his horse and runs to the door of the hut, throws the door open and enters. The little hut is now stuffed with all possible signs of wealth and all imaginable treasures.

Male Peasant What you got for us today then.

Moore Well I've managed to find you four very nice silver spoons Mr Jenkins.

Male Peasant *(snatching them rudely)* Who do you think you are giving us poor this rubbish?

Female Peasant Bloody silver. Won't have it in the house. *(throws it away)* And those candlesticks you got us last week were only sixteen carat.

Male Peasant Yes, why don't you go out and steal something nice like some Venetian silver.

Female Peasant Or a Velásquez for the outside loo.

Moore Oh all right. *(turns purposefully)*
   Usual montage of Dennis Moore riding plus song.

Song Dennis Moore, Dennis Moore
   Riding through the land
   Dennis Moore, Dennis Moore
   Without a merry band
   He steals from the poor and gives to the rich
   Stupid bitch.
   Dennis Moore reins to sudden halt and rides over to camera.

Moore What did you sing?

Singers *(speaking)* We sang... he steals from the poor and gives to the rich.

Moore Wait a tic... blimey, this redistribution of wealth is trickier than I thought.

Women's Institute applause. A church-hall type stage, as if for a TV version of 'Down Your Way'. A vast sign across the backcloth reads 'Prejudice'. Russell Braddon enters. He wears a suit and has a clipboard.

Braddon (MICHAEL) Good evening and welcome to another edition of 'Prejudice' – the show that gives you a chance to have a go at Wops, Krauts, Nigs, Eyeries, Gippos, Bubbles, Froggies, Chinks, Yidds, Jocks, Polacks, Paddies and Dagoes. *(applause; he goes to desk at side of stage)*

SUPERIMPOSED CAPTION: 'ALL FACTS VERIFIED BY THE RHODESIAN POLICE'

Braddon Tonight's show comes live from the tiny village of Rabid in Buckinghamshire, and our first question tonight is from a Mrs Elizabeth Scrint who says she is going on a Mediterranean cruise next week and can't find anything wrong with the Syrians. Well, Mrs Scrint, apart from being totally unprincipled left-wing troublemakers, the Syrians are also born skivers, they're dirty, smelly and untrustworthy, and, of course, they're friends of the awful gippos. *(applause)* There you are, Mrs Scrint, I hope that answers some of your problems – have a nice trip. *(more applause)* Well now, the result of last week's competition when we asked you to find a derogatory term for the Belgians. Well, the response was enormous and we took quite a long time sorting out the winners. There were some very clever entries. Mrs Hatred of Leicester said 'let's not call them anything, let's just ignore them' . . . *(applause starts vigorously, but he holds his hands up for silence)* . . . and a Mr St John of Huntingdon said he couldn't think of anything more derogatory than Belgians. *(cheers and applause; a girl in showgirl costume comes on and holds up placards through next bit)* But in the end we settled on three choices: number three . . . the Sprouts *(placard: 'The Sprouts')*, sent in by Mrs Vicious of Hastings . . . very nice; number two . . . the Phlegms *(placard)* . . . from Mrs Childmolester of Worthing; but the winner was undoubtedly from Mrs No-Supper-For-You from Norwood in Lancashire . . . Miserable Fat Belgian Bastards. *(placard; roars of applause)* Very good – thank you, Carol. *(Carol exits)* But as you know on this programme we're not just prejudiced against race or colour, we're also prejudiced against – yes, you've guessed, stinking homosexuals! *(applause)* So before the streets start emptying in Chelsea tonight, let's go straight over to our popular prejudiced panel game and invite you once again to – Shoot The Poof! And could our first contestant sign in please.

Cut to blackboard and entrance as they used to have in 'What's My Line'. A contestant comes from behind screen and starts to write his name.

Voice Over (JOHN) Our first contestant is a hairdresser from . . .

A shot rings out and the contestant falls to the floor. Applause.

Cut to a camp highwayman in a pink mask who blows smoke from a gun and puts it back in the holster.

Highwayman (MICHAEL) I never did like that kind of person . . . !

A shot rings out. He dies. Cut to Dennis Moore on a horse blowing smoke from gun and putting it in his holster. He gallops off. We see him swooping down, after a couple of riding shots, on another stagecoach.

Moore Halt! Halt! *(the stagecoach comes to a halt and the occupants get out rapidly, their hands held high)* Gentlemen, ladies, bring out your valuables please. Come along sir, come along. Come along, madam, come along. Oh, is that all you've got . . . well, he's got much more than you . . . so you'd better have some of his . . . *(transfers money from one passenger to another, dropping some)* . . . sorry . . . pick them up in a moment . . . there's about oh, what, nine down there . . . so you must have about . . . oh, he's still got lots . . . oh you've got what? . . . you've got more than he started with . . . so if I give you some of those *(transferring more coins)* . . . well now, look . . . have you got a bit of jewellery? If I give you that one and you have some of his coins *(the credits start, superimposed)* . . . is that another box? Were you trying to hide it? Well, that's nice! Right! Now. I've got a tiara . . . you've got one . . . you've got one of the boxes . . . you've got one . . . anyone else got a tiara? Take your hat off! *(passenger does so to reveal a tiara)* . . . Oh, honestly, it's absolutely pointless trying to do this if you're going to cheat. It really is *awful* of you . . . *(fade out)*

CAPTION: 'ERRATUM, JACK BODELL WAS BORN IN SWADLINCOTE IN DERBYSHIRE'

Cut to the inside of a bus. A judge is sitting there in full robes, looking rather unhappy. He is obviously one of the competitors from earlier. His friend tries to cheer him up.

Friend (TERRY J) *I* thought you should have won. *I* mean, judicially you swept the board . . . all right, he has posture, but where was he in the summing up?

Behind these two another judge is sitting with his mother, crying.

Mother (ERIC) Oh shut up Melford, there's always next year.

Another judge further back petulantly rips up his number card. We cut to the outside back of this bus. The destination board says 'The End'. As the bus drives away we hold on a board sticking out from a building which reads 'Hospital. . . sorry no cheques'.

Thirty-eight

CAPTION: 'A PARTY POLITICAL BROADCAST ON BEHALF OF THE CONSERVATIVE AND UNIONIST PARTY'

Voice Over (ERIC) There now follows a Party Political Broadcast on behalf of the Conservative and Unionist Party.

Cut to a politician sitting on a chair. He is in fact in a rehearsal room, but we don't see this for the first six lines.

Politician (JOHN) Good evening. Figures talk. We have already fulfilled over three of our election pledges before the end of our second year of good Conservative rule. And, what is more *(gets up and starts to do dancing movements as he speaks)* we hope ... that *in* the *aut*-tumn we shall *int*-ro-*duce leg*-is-*lat*-tion *in* the *House* to *bene-fit* all *those* in *low*-er in-come *groups*. And *fur*-ther-*more* we *hope* ...

Enter a choreographer.

Choreographer (ERIC) No, no, no, no ... look, luv, it's *and* ... *(does the movements)* one and two and three and four, and five and six and seven and down.

Politician *(trying the last bit)* ... five and six and seven and down ... it's so much harder with the words.

Choreographer Well, don't think of them. Just count four in your head.

Politician And ... *one* and *fur*-ther *two* and *three* and ... no, I can't really ...

Choreographer Yes, well come on and do it with me, come on. And ...

Both *Fur*-ther-*more* we *hope* that *we* can *stop* the *ris*-ing *un*-em-*ploy*-ment. *(they finish up with finger on chin, as in a thirties musical)*

Choreographer And point 'unemployment' with your finger.

Politician I see. I can do it when you're here.

Choreographer I won't be far away. All right, Neville love, we're going from 'unemployment' through 'pensions' into 'good government is strong government' and the walk down, all right? And ... cue, love.

Politician And *fur*-ther-*more* we *hope* that *we* can *stop* the *ris*-ing *un*-em-*ploy*-ment at a *stroke* or e-ven *quick*-er.

Enter a line of six male dancers, doing high kicks and a dance routine.

Dancers And *so* when *you* get a *chance* to *vote*,
Kind-ly *vote* Con-ser-va-tive.
(the politician joins in)
Rising prices, unemployment,
Both stem from the wages spiral
Curb inflation, save the nation,
Join us now and save the economy.
They give an awful wave and cheesecake smile at the end, and hold it.

Choreographer That's where you'll get the bunting and the ticker tape, Chris. Right, big smiles, everybody, remember you're cabinet ministers. And relax. *(only now do they stop smiling and waving)* Lovely, it's trans at eight, so nobody be late.

The camera crabs away. Through an open door it passes we see two Labour MPs, one on points, the other walking around with his hands on his hips. They are in leotards and dancers' leg warmers.

Labour MPs We in the *Lab-*our *Par-*ty have *al-*ways *made* our po-*si-*tion quite clear . . . we have *al-*ways *been* op-*posed* to . . .

The camera continues to crab away. It comes to a door which says Star on it. We zoom into this and mix through to:

ANIMATION: *Wilson and Heath dance to "The Dance of the Sugar Plum Fairy'.*

Cut to the nude organist; he plays a chord.

Cut to the announcer at his desk.

Announcer (JOHN) And now . . .

It's Man (MICHAEL) It's . . .

Animated titles.

Cut to studio: a silhouette of a man sitting on high stool with book.

SUPERIMPOSED CAPTION: 'A BOOK AT BEDTIME'

Voice Over (ERIC) 'Book at Bedtime'. Tonight Jeremy Toogood reads 'Redgauntlet' by Sir Walter Scott.

The lights come up.

Jeremy (MICHAEL) Hello. *(he follows the words closely with a finger and reads with great difficulty)* The sunsoot . . . the siunsiett . . . the sunset! . . . the sunset . . . waas . . . was was . . . the sunset was . . . deeing . . . d . . . ying dying . . . o . . . over . . . the . . . hile . . . hiel . . . heels . . . halls . . . hills! of . . . slow . . . Sol . . . way . . . Firth . . . The . . . love piper . . . the *lone* piper . . . the lone piper . . . on . . . the . . . batt . . . ly . . . ments . . . *(smiles nervously)* . . . of Edingrund . . . dydburing . . . Edingbir . . . Edinburgh! Castle . . . was . . . siluted . . . sil . . . sillhou . . .

Another man enters, takes the book from his hands rather testily and stands by the chair. He smiles apologetically at the camera and reads.

Second Reader (JOHN) The sunset was dying over the hills of Solway Firth. The lone piper on the battlements of Edinburgh Castle was silhouetted against the crim . . . crim . . . crimisy . . . crimson! against the crimson strays . . . stree . . .

One more reader enters and reads over his shoulder.

Third Reader (ERIC) Streaked!

Second Reader Streaked?

Third Reader Crimson-streaked sky . . . in the shadows of . . . crrignu . . .

He can't make out the next word. The second reader also tries to puzzle it out and eventually Jeremy pulls the book down towards him and they all try to puzzle it out. A lot of head shaking. A technician enters wearing headphones.

Technician (GRAHAM) Cairngorm! In the shadows of Cairngorm!

Third Reader In the shadows of Cairngorm, the l . . . layered . . .

A second technician and a make-up girl enter.

Second Technician Laird! The Laird of Monteu . . . Montreaux . . .

Make-up Girl Montrose.

All The Laird of Montrose!

Second Technician Gal-lopped . . .

Jeremy Galloped!

Everybody joins in helping with words. We mix through to Edinburgh Castle at dusk. The lone piper is silhouetted against the crimson-streaked sky.

Jeremy *(voice over)* The lone piper on the battlements of Edinburgh Castle . . .

There are a few bars of bagpipe music. Suddenly there is a scream and he disappears. Cut to interior of stone-walled guardroom inside Edinburgh Castle. Ten kilted Scottish guardsmen with bagpipes in a line. A sergeant major at the door taps one on the shoulder.

RSM (TERRY J) Next!

The next goes outside. We hear pipes start, the sergeant smiles. Cut to castle battlements. The piper plays and then jumps off. We hear the scream as before. Another piper emerges and goes through the same routine.

Voice Over (MICHAEL) *(Scottish accent)* Here on top of Edinburgh Castle, in conditions of extreme secrecy, men are being trained for the British Army's first Kamikaze Regiment, the Queen's Own McKamikaze Highlanders. *(there is a scream and a piper jumps off; another one emerges and starts to play)* So successful has been the training of the Kamikaze Regiment that the numbers have dwindled from 30,000 to just over a dozen in three weeks. What makes these young Scotsmen so keen to kill themselves?

Close-ups of soldiers.

Scots Soldier (MICHAEL) The money's good!

Second Soldier (ERIC) And the water skiing! *(he falls down with a scream)*

Cut to interior of the guardroom in Edinburgh Castle. As before, but with only six men left plus the sergeant major. Bagpipes and a scream. The sergeant major dispatches another man. A captain enters. Bagpipes again.

RSM Ten-shun.

Captain (JOHN) All right, sergeant major. At ease. Now, how many chaps have you got left?

RSM Six, sir.

Captain Six? *(there is a scream)*

RSM Five, sir. *(to another highlander carrying bagpipes)* Good luck, Johnson. *(Johnson leaves)*

Captain Jolly good show, sergeant major. *(we hear bagpipes starting up outside)* Well, I've come to tell you that we've got a job for your five lads.

There is a scream.

RSM Four, sir.

Captain For your four lads.

RSM *(whispering to another man)* Good luck, Taggart.

Taggart Thank you, sarge. *(he goes)*

Captain *(looking rather uncertainly at the man leaving)* Now this mission's going to be dangerous, *(bagpipes start)* and it's going to be tough, and we're going to need every lad of yours to pull his weight. *(the usual scream in the background)* Now, which ... er ... which four are they?

RSM These three here, sir. OK. Off you go, Smith.

Smith *(with manic eagerness)* Right!! *(he charges out through door before captain can stop him)*

Captain *(with mounting concern)* ... er ... sergeant major!

RSM Yes, sir? *(bagpipes start outside)*

Captain You don't think it might be a good idea ... er ... to stop the training programme for a little bit?

RSM They got to be trained, sir. It's a dangerous job.

Captain Yes ... I know ... but ... er ... *(the usual scream)*

RSM All right MacPherson, you're next, off you go.

Captain You see what is worrying me, sergeant major, is ...

MacPherson I'll make it a gud'un, sir! *(he dashes off)*

RSM Good luck, MacPherson.

Captain Er ... MacPherson ... *(the bagpipes start up)* only this mission really is very dangerous. We're going to need both the chaps that you've got left. *(scream)*

RSM Both of who, sir?

Captain Sergeant major, what's this man's name?

RSM This one sir? This one is MacDonald, sir.

Captain No, no, no, no. *(the captain stops MacDonald (Graham) who is straining quite hard to get away)* Hang on to MacDonald, sergeant major, hang on to him.

RSM I don't know whether I can, sir ... *(MacDonald's eyes are staring in a strange way)* he's in a state of Itsubishi Kyoko McSayonara.

Captain What's that?

They are both struggling to restrain MacDonald.

RSM It's the fifth state that a Scotsman can achieve, sir. He's got to finish himself off by lunchtime or he thinks he's let down the Emperor, sir.

Captain Well, can't we get him out of it?

RSM Oh, I dunno how to, sir. Our Kamikaze instructor, Mr Yashimoto, was so good he never left Tokyo airport.

Captain Well, there must be someone else who can advise us?

Exterior of smart London health-salon-type frontage. A big sign reads 'Kamikaze Advice Centre'. A bowler-hatted man enters. A receptionist sits behind a posh desk.

Man (MICHAEL) *(very businesslike)* Good morning, Kamikaze, please.

Receptionist *(indicating door)* Yes, would you go through, please?

Man Thank you.

The man walks over to the door, opens it, walks through and disappears from sight. There is nothing but sky and clouds through the door.

Scream.

Cut back to castle guardroom.

Captain Right, sergeant major – there's no time to lose.

The sergeant is sitting on MacDonald. He strikes him on head.

RSM Beg pardon, sir?

Captain No time to lose.

RSM No what, sir?

Captain No *time* ... no time to lose.

RSM Oh, I see, sir. *(making gestures)* No time ... to ... lose!!

Captain Yes, that's right, yes.

RSM Yes, no time to lose, sir!

Captain Right.

RSM Isn't that funny, sir ... I've never come across that phrase before – 'no time to lose'. Forty-two years I've been in the regular army and I've never heard that phrase.

Captain Well, it's in perfectly common parlance.

RSM In what, sir?

Captain Oh never mind ... right ... no time to lose.

RSM Eventually, yes, sir.

Captain What?

RSM Like you say, sir. We'll be able to make time, eventually without to lose, sir, no.

Captain Look, I don't think you've quite got the hang of this phrase, sergeant major.

The same frontage of smart London salon as before. Only this time the big sign reads 'No Time To Lose Advice Centre'. The same bowler-hatted man goes in. The same interior, same desk. A consultant sits behind it, and motions for the man to sit down.

Consultant (ERIC) Morning, no time to lose... *(he picks up a card which reads 'no time to lose'; he keeps flashing it every so often)* Now then, how were you thinking of using the phrase?

He pulls down a blind behind him on the right which also reads 'no time to lose' in large letters. He lets it go and it rolls up again fast.

Man (MICHAEL) Well, I was thinking of using it... er... like... well... good morning dear, what is in no time to lose?

Consultant Er yes... well... you've not quite got the hang of that, have you.

He gets out a two-foot-square cube with 'no time to lose' in the same lettering as it always is, and puts it on the desk. He points to this in a manic way with a forefinger. He has the words 'no time to lose' on the back of his hand.

Consultant *(sings)* No time to lose, no time to lose, no time to lose, no time to lose. *(to stop the manic fit he reaches inside desk, pours a drink from a bottle on which is written 'no time to lose')* Now, you want to use this phrase in everyday conversation, is that right?

Man Yes, that's right.

Consultant Yes... good...

He stands up, makes a strange noise, and flings the back of his jacket up over his head revealing 'no time to lose' written on the inside of the back lining of his jacket, upside down so that it is the right way up when it is revealed.

Man You see my wife and I have never had a great deal to say to each other... *(tragic, heart-rending music creeps in under the dialogue)* In the old days we used to find things to say, like 'pass the sugar'... or, 'that's *my* flannel', but in the last ten or fifteen years there just hasn't seemed to be anything to say, and anyway I saw your phrase advertised in the paper and I thought, that's the kind of thing I'd like to say to her...

The consultant pushes down a handle and a large screen comes up in front of him. On it is written 'no time to lose'. He bursts through the paper.

Consultant Yes, well, what we normally suggest for a beginner such as yourself, is that you put your alarm clock back ten minutes in the morning, so you can wake up, look at the clock and use the phrase immediately. *(he holds up the card briefly)* Shall we try it?

Man Yes.

Consultant All right – I'll be the alarm clock. When I go off, look at me and use the phrase, OK? *(ticks then imitates ringing)*

Man No! *Time* to lose!

Consultant No... No time to lose.

Man No time to *lose*?

Consultant No time to lose.

Man No *time* to lose.

Consultant No – to *lose*... like Toulouse in France. No time Toulouse.

Man No time *too* lose...

Consultant No time Toulouse.

Man No time Toulouse...

Consultant No! – no time to *lose*!

Man No-no time to *lose*!

> ANIMATION: *Toulouse-Lautrec in a Wild West gunfight.*

Voice Over No-time Toulouse. The story of the wild and lawless days of the post-impressionists.

> *Cut back to the guardroom at Edinburgh Castle. MacDonald is edging towards the window.*

Captain Anyway, no time to lose, sergeant major.

RSM Look out, sir! MacDonald!

> *They both rush to window and grab MacDonald's legs as he disappears through it.*

RSM We'll have to hurry, sir. *(they haul him back into the room to reveal he is carrying a saw with which he starts trying to saw off his head)* No, put that down MacDonald. *(he snatches the saw and throws it away)* He's reached the sixth plane already, sir.

Captain Right, here are the plans sergeant major, good luck.

RSM Thank you, sir. *(he salutes)*

> *MacDonald is by now trying to strangle himself with his bare hands.*

Captain And good luck to you, MacDonald.

> *MacDonald breaks off from strangling himself, to offer a snappy salute.*

MacDonald Thank you, sir.

> *He immediately snaps back into trying to strangle himself.*

RSM Right you are, MacDonald. No time to lose.

Captain Very good, sergeant major.

> *Quick cut to the consultant in the office.*

Consultant Yes, excellent...

> *Cut back to the gates of Edinburgh Castle. Dawn. Music. As the voice starts the gates open and a lorry emerges.*

Voice Over (MICHAEL) So it was that on a cold January morning, RSM Urdoch and Sapper MacDonald, one of the most highly trained Kamikaze experts the Scottish Highlands have ever witnessed, left on a mission which was to... oh I can't go on with this drivel.

By this time we have cut to a close-up of the cab to show RSM Urdoch at the wheel, with MacDonald beside him. MacDonald has a revolver and is apparently having an unsuccessful game of Russian roulette.

RSM All right, MacDonald, no time to lose.

Suddenly MacDonald hurls himself out of the lorry.

MacDonald Aaaaaaugh!

The RSM slams the brakes on. Skidding noises. Cut to shot of the lorry skidding to a halt. The RSM leaps out, picks up MacDonald who is lying on the floor hitting himself, and loads him into the back of the lorry. He gets back into the lorry and they start off again. They haven't gone more than a few yards before we see MacDonald leap out of the back of the lorry, race round to the front and throw himself down in front of the lorry. The lorry runs right over him. He picks himself up after it has gone, races up to the front and tries it again ... and again ... and again ... and again ... and again ...

Cut to the captain, standing in front of a huge map. He points with a stick.

Captain Well, that's the mission – now here's the method. RSM Urdoch will lull the enemy into a false sense of security by giving them large quantities of money, a good home, and a steady job. Then, when they're upstairs with the wife, Sapper MacDonald will hurl himself at the secret documents, destroying them and himself. Well, that's the plan, the time is now 1942 hours. I want you to get to bed, have a good night's rest and be up on parade early in the morning. Thank you for listening and thank you for a lovely supper.

Pull out to reveal that he is in a very small sitting room, alone apart from his wife who sits knitting by the fire not listening to a word he's saying.

Cut to the 'Book at Bedtime' set. Seven or eight technicians, a make-up girl, etc. still crowding round Toogood as he tries to read.

Toogood And ... and ... sue ... so ... the ... the ... intriptid ...

Make-up Girl Intrepid.

All Intrepid.

Toogood Intrepid RSM Urdoch and super ...

Technician Sapper.

Toogood Sapper MacDonald ... mead ...

Several Made!

Toogood Made their why ...

Several Way!

Toogood Way toarro ...

Make-up Girl Towards ...

Toogood Towards the Rusty ... Ritzy ...

All Russian!

Toogood Russian bolder...

All Border!

Map with an animated line showing the route.

Toogood's Voice ... and so RSM Urdoch and Sapper MacDonald made their way towards the Russian bolder...

All Border!! ... Border.

> ANIMATION: *the line becomes part of an animated skit on the famous film '2001'.*
>
> *Cut to stock film of penguins.*
>
> SUPERIMPOSED CAPTIONS:
>
> 'FRONTIERS OF MEDICINE PART 2'
>
> 'THE GATHERING STORM'
>
> *Cut to presenter at desk.*

Presenter (JOHN) Penguins, yes, penguins. What relevance do penguins have to the furtherance of medical science? Well, strangely enough quite a lot, a major breakthrough, maybe. It was from such an unlikely beginning as an unwanted fungus accidentally growing on a sterile plate that Sir Alexander Fleming gave the world penicillin. James Watt watched an ordinary household kettle boiling and conceived the potentiality of steam power. Would Albert Einstein ever have hit upon the theory of relativity if he hadn't been clever? All these tremendous leaps forward have been taken in the dark. Would Rutherford ever have split the atom if he hadn't tried? Could Marconi have invented the radio if he hadn't by pure chance spent years working at the problem? Are these amazing breakthroughs ever achieved except by years and years of unremitting study? Of course not. What I said earlier about accidental discoveries must have been wrong. Nevertheless scientists believe that these penguins, these comic flightless web-footed little bastards may finally unwittingly help man to fathom the uncharted depths of the human mind. Professor Rosewall of the Laver Institute.

> *A scientist with tennis courts in the background. He wears a white coat.*
>
> SUPERIMPOSED CAPTION: 'PROF. KEN ROSEWALL'

Scientist (GRAHAM) *(Australian accent)* Hello. Here at the Institute Professor Charles Pasarell, Dr Peaches Bartkowicz and myself have been working on the theory originally postulated by the late Dr Kramer that the penguin is intrinsically more intelligent than the human being.

> *He moves over to a large diagram which is being held by two tennis players in full tennis kit but wearing the brown coats of ordinary laboratory technicians. The diagram shows a penguin and a man in correct proportional size with their comparative brain capacities marked out clearly showing the man's to be much larger than the penguin's.*

Scientist The first thing that Dr Kramer came up with was that the penguin has a much smaller brain than the man. This postulate formed the fundamental basis of all his thinking and remained with him until his death.

Flash cut of elderly man in tennis shirt and green eye shade getting an arrow in the head. Cut back to the scientist now with diagram behind him. It shows a man and a six-foot penguin.

Scientist Now we've taken this theory one stage further. If we increase the size of the penguin until it is the same height as the man and then compare the relative brain size, we now find that the penguin's brain is still smaller. But, and this is the point, it is larger than it *was*.

Very quick cut of tennis crowd going 'oh' and applauding. Dr Peaches Bartkowicz standing by tennis net.

SUPERIMPOSED CAPTION: 'DR PEACHES BARTKOWICZ'

Peaches (MICHAEL) For a penguin to have the same size of brain as a man the penguin would have to be over sixty-six feet high.

She moves to the left and comes upon a cut-out of the lower visible part of a sixty-six feet high penguin. She looks up at it. Cut back to the scientist.

Scientist This theory has become known as the waste of time theory and was abandoned in 1956. *(slight edit with jump visible)* Hello again. Standard IQ tests gave the following results. The penguins scored badly when compared with primitive human sub-groups like the bushmen of the Kalahari but better than BBC programme planners. *(he refers to graph decorated with little racquets which shows bushmen with 23, penguins with 13 and BBC planners with 8)* The BBC programme planners surprisingly high total here can be explained away as being within the ordinary limits of statistical error. One particularly dim programme planner can cock the whole thing up.

CAPTION: 'YOU CAN SAY THAT AGAIN'

Cut to a tennis player in a changing room taking off his gym shoes. In the background two other players discuss shots.

SUPERIMPOSED CAPTION: 'DR LEWIS HOAD'

Hoad (ERIC) These IQ tests were thought to contain an unfair cultural bias against the penguin. For example, it didn't take into account the penguins' extremely poor educational system. To devise a fairer system of test, a team of our researchers spent eighteen months in Antarctica living like penguins, and subsequently dying like penguins – only quicker – proving that the penguin is a clever little sod in his own environment.

Cut to the scientist.

Scientist Therefore we devised tests to be given to the penguins in the fourth set ... I do beg your pardon, in their own environment.

Voice Net!

Scientist Shh!

Cut to a professor and team surrounding penguins standing in a pool.

Professor (TERRY J) What is the next number in this sequence – 2, 4, 6 . . .

A penguin squawks.

Professor Did he say eight? . . . *(sighs)* What is . . .

Cut back to the scientist.

Scientist The environmental barrier had been removed but we'd hit another: the language barrier. The penguins could not speak English and were therefore unable to give the answers. This problem was removed in the next series of experiments by asking the same questions to the penguins and to a random group of non-English-speaking humans in the same conditions.

Cut to the professor and his team now surrounding a group of foreigners who are standing in a pool looking bewildered.

Professor What is the next number? 2, 4, 6 . . . *(long pause)*

Swedish Person (ERIC) . . . Hello?

Cut back to the scientist.

Scientist The results of these tests were most illuminating. The penguins' scores were consistently equal to those of the non-English-speaking group.

Cut to the foreigners having fish thrown at them, which they try to catch in their mouths, and a penguin with a menu at a candlelit table with a woman in evening dress and a waiter trying to take an order.

Cut to Dr Hoad taking a shower.

Hoad These enquiries led to certain changes at the BBC . . .

Cut to the boardroom of BBC. Penguins sit at a table with signs saying 'Programme Controller', 'Head of Planning', 'Director General'. Noise of penguins squawking. Cut to the penguin pool. Hoad's voice over.

Hoad . . . while attendances at zoos boomed.

The camera pans across to a sign reading 'The programme planners are to be fed at 3 o'clock'.

Voice Over (MICHAEL) Soon these feathery little hustlers were infiltrating important positions everywhere.

Mr Gilliam's animation shows penguins infiltrating important positions everywhere.

Cut to RSM Urdoch having his lorry checked by a penguin border guard.

SUPERIMPOSED CAPTION: 'MEANWHILE AT A CHECKPOINT ON THE RUSSO-POLISH BORDER'

The lorry drives off past sign saying 'Russian bolder' with 'bolder' crossed out and 'border' written in.

Cut to Red Square.

SUPERIMPOSED CAPTION: 'THE KREMLIT'

The 't' is crossed out and 'n' written in. Cut to two Russian majors in a conference room.

First Major (ERIC) Svientitzi hobonwy kratow svegurninurdy.

SUPERIMPOSED SUBTITLES: 'THESE ARE THE VERY IMPORTANT SECRET DOCUMENTS I WAS TELLING YOU ABOUT'

Second Major (JOHN) We must study them in conditions of absolute secrecy.

Superimposed subtitle in Russian.

First Major *(speaks in Russian)*

SUPERIMPOSED SUBTITLE: 'WHAT?'

Second Major *(looking up)* Look out!

SUPERIMPOSED SUBTITLE: 'REGARDEZ LA!'

They cower as MacDonald crashes through the skylight and lands on the table where he lies rigid with his knees drawn up. He ticks ominously.

Second Major He hasn't gone off.

SUPERIMPOSED CAPTION: 'ZE HADE NICHT GESHPLODEN'

First Major *(speaks in Russian)*

SUBTITLE: 'QUICK! RING THE UNEXPLODED SCOTSMAN SQUAD'

Second Major Yes my General!

Superimposed subtitle in Chinese.

Cut to a phone ringing on the branch of a tree. Pull back to show a Scotsman lying on his back with his knees drawn up in the middle of a field. Two Russian bomb experts are crawling towards him cautiously.

SUPERIMPOSED CAPTION: 'UNEXPLODED SCOTSMAN DISPOSAL SQUAD'

They get to work on him. Tense close-ups. They sweat. Finally they remove his head. One of them runs hurriedly and places it in a bucket labelled 'Vodka'.

SUPERIMPOSED CAPTION: 'WHISKY'

The sound of drunken gurglings comes from the bucket. Pull back to show that this is on a screen at the back of a panel game set. Fade it out as camera in studio pans down to the presenter.

Presenter (ERIC) And welcome to 'Spot the Loony', where once again we invite you to come with us all over the world to meet all kinds of people in all kinds of places, and ask you to . . . Spot the Loony! *(crescendo of music)*

SUPERIMPOSED CAPTION: 'ALL ANSWERS VERIFIED BY ENCYCLOPAEDIA BRITANNICA'

Presenter Our panel this evening . . . Gurt Svensson, the Swedish mammal abuser and part-time radiator.

Cut to Svensson. He is standing on his head on the desk with his legs crossed in a yoga position. He wears a loincloth and high-heeled shoes. He talks through a megaphone which is strapped to his head.

Svensson (TERRY J) Good evening.

Cut back to the presenter.

Presenter Dame Elsie Occluded, historian, wit, bon viveur, and rear half of the Johnson brothers...

Cut to another section of the panel's desk. Dame Elsie. Her bottom half is encased in the side of a block of concrete which is also on top of the desk. Dame Elsie is thus parallel to the ground. She has fairy wings on her back, a striped t-shirt, flying gloves, goggles and a green wig.

Dame Elsie (MICHAEL) Good evening.

Cut back to the presenter.

Presenter And Miles Yellowbird, up high in banana tree, the golfer and inventor of Catholicism.

Cut to final section of the desk. A man dressed as a rabbit, with a megaphone strapped to one eye.

Miles (TERRY G) Good evening.

Presenter And we'll be inviting them to... Spot the Loony. *(a phone rings on the desk; he picks it up)* Yes? Quite right... A viewer from Preston there who's pointed out correctly that the entire panel are loonies. Five points to Preston there, and on to our first piece of film. It's about mountaineering and remember you have to... Spot the Loony!

Cut to a shot of a mountain. Very impressive stirring music.

Voice Over (MICHAEL) The legendary south face of Ben Medhui, dark... forbidding...

In the middle distance are two bushes a few yards apart. At this point a loony dressed in a long Roman toga, with tam o'shanter, holding a cricket bat, runs from one bush to the other. Loud buzz. The film freezes. Pull out from screen to reveal the freeze frame of the film with the loony in the middle bush on the screen immediately behind the presenter. The presenter is on the phone.

Presenter Yes, well done, Mrs Nesbitt of York, spotted the loony in 1.8 seconds. *(cut to stock film of Women's Institute applauding)* On to our second round, and it's photo time. We're going to invite you to look at photographs of Tony Jacklin, Anthony Barber, Edgar Allan Poe, Katie Boyle, Reginald Maudling, and a loony. All you have to do is... Spot the Loony! *(cut to a photo of Anthony Barber; the buzzer goes immediately)* No... I must ask you please not to ring in until you've seen all the photos.

Back to the photo sequence and music. Each photo is on the screen for only two seconds, and in between each there is a click as of a slide projector changing or even the sound of the shutter of a camera. The photos show in sequence: Anthony Barber, Katie Boyle, Edgar Allan Poe, a loony head and shoulders (he has ping-pong ball eyes, several teeth blacked out, a fright wig and his chest is bare but across it is written 'A Loony'), Reginald Maudling, Tony Jacklin. A buzzer sounds.

Presenter Yes, you're right. The answer was, of course, number two! *(cut to stock film of Women's Institute applauding)* I'm afraid there's been an error in our computer. The correct answer should of course have been number four, and not Katie Boyle. Katie Boyle is not a loony, she is a television personality. *(fanfare as for historical pageant; a historical-looking shield comes up on screen)* And now it's time for 'Spot the Loony, historical adaptation'. *(historical music)* And this time it's the thrilling medieval romance: 'Ivanoe' . . . a stirring story of love and war, violence and chivalry, set amidst the pageantry and splendour of thirteenth-century England. All you have to do is, Spot the Loony.

CAPTION: 'IVANOE'

Cut to a butcher's shop. A loony stands in the middle (this is Michael's loony from 'Silly Election' with enormous trousers and arms inside them and green fright wig). Another loony in a long vest down to his knees with a little frilly tutu starting at the knees and bare feet is dancing with a side of beef also wearing a tutu. Another loony in oilskins with waders and sou'wester and fairy wings is flying across the top of picture. Another man dressed as a bee is standing on the counter. Another loony is dressed as a carrot leaning against the counter going: 'pretty boy, pretty boy'. A cacophony of noise. We see this sight for approximately five seconds. Fantastic loud buzzes.

Presenter Yes, well done, Mrs L of Leicester, Mrs B of Buxton and Mrs G of Gatwick, the loony was of course the writer, Sir Walter Scott.

Cut to Sir Walter Scott in his study.

SUPERIMPOSED CAPTION: 'SIR WALTER SCOTT 1771–1832'

Scott (GRAHAM) *(looking through his papers indignantly)* I didn't write that! Sounds more like Dickens . . .

Cut to Dickens at work in his study. He looks up.

SUPERIMPOSED CAPTION: 'CHARLES DICKENS 1812–1870'

Dickens (TERRY J) You bastard!

Cut to a documentary producer standing in forested hillside.

Producer (JOHN) Was Sir Walter Scott a loony, or was he the greatest flowering of the early nineteenth-century romantic tradition? The most underestimated novelist of the nineteenth century *(another introducer of documentaries comes into shot and walks up to the first)* . . .or merely a disillusioned and embittered man . . .

Second Producer (MICHAEL) Excuse me . . . *(pointing at the microphone)* can I borrow that, please.

Producer Thank you. *(he immediately starts on his own documentary)* These trees behind me now were planted over forty years ago as part of a policy by the then Crown Woods, who became the Forestry Commission in 1924. *(he starts to walk towards the forest)* The Forestry Commission systematically replanted this entire area . . .

The first producer follows behind.

First Producer Excuse me.

Second Producer Sh! That's forty thousand acres of virgin forest. By 1980 this will have risen to two hundred thousand acres of soft woods. In commercial terms, a coniferous cornucopia ... an evergreen El Dorado ... *(the first producer runs and makes a feeble grab for the mike)* ... a tree-lined treasure trove ... No ... a fat fir-coned future for the financiers ... but what of the cost ...

First Producer It's mine!

Second Producer *(to first producer)* Go away ... in human terms? Who are the casualties?

The first producer makes a lunge and grabs the mike. He stops and the camera stops with him.

First Producer For this was Sir Walter Scott's country. Many of his finest romances, such as 'Guy Mannering' and 'Redgauntlet' ...

Second Producer Give that back!

First Producer No. *(they grapple a bit. The first producer just manages to keep hold of it as he goes down onto the ground)* Scott showed himself to be not only a fine ...

The second producer manages to grab the mike and runs off leaving the first producer on the ground. The camera follows the second producer

Second Producer *(running)* The spruces and flowers of this forest will be used to create a whole new industry here in ...

The first producer brings him down with a diving rugger tackle and grabs the mike.

First Producer ... also a writer of humour and ...

They are both fighting and rolling around on the ground.

Second Producer Britain's timber resources are being used up at a rate of ...

The first producer hits him, and grabs the mike.

First Producer One man who knew Scott was Angus Tinker.

A sunlit university quad with classical pillars. Gentle classical music. Tinker is standing next to one of the pillars. He is a tweed-suited academic.

CAPTION: 'ANGUS TINKER'

Tinker (GRAHAM) Much of Scott's greatest work, and I'm thinking here particularly of 'Heart of Midlothian' and 'Old Mortality' for example, was concerned with ... *(at this point a hand appears from behind the pillar and starts to go slowly but surely for the mike)* preserving the life and conditions of a ... *(the mike is grabbed away from him)*

Voice (TERRY J) Forestry- research here has shown that the wholly synthetic soft timber fibre can be created ... *(Tinker looks behind the pillar to discover a forestry expert in tweeds crouched)* ... leaving the harder trees, the oaks, the beeches and the larches ... *(Tinker chases him out into the quad)* and the pines, and even some of the deciduous hardwoods.

CAPTION: 'A FORESTRY EXPERT'

Forestry Expert This new soft-timber fibre would totally replace the plywoods, hardboards and chipboards at present dominating the . . .

A Morris Minor speeds up round the quad and passes straight in front of the expert and the first producer's hand comes out and grabs the mike. Cut to interior of the Morris Minor as it speeds out of quad and out into country. The first producer keeps glancing nervously over shoulder.

First Producer In the Waverley novels . . . Scott was constantly concerned to protect a way of life . . .

He ducks as we hear the sound of a bullet ricochet from the car. Cut to shot through the back window. The second producer is chasing in a huge open American 1930s gangster car driven by a chauffeur in a Thirties kit. He is shooting.

First Producer . . . safeguarding nationalist traditions and aspiration, within the necessary limitations of the gothic novel . . .

More bullets. The American car draws level. The second producer leans over trying to grab the mike. Still attempting to say their lines, both of them scramble for the microphone as the cars race along. Eventually the cars disappear round a corner and we hear a crash.

Cut to Toogood, surrounded by people, holding the book very close to his face and peering closely at the print. MacDonald lies on the floor in front of them.

Toogood Then . . . theen . . . the . . . the end! The End. *(looks up)*

Cut to film (no sound) of Edward Heath. The 'Spot The Loony buzzer goes. Roll credits. Cut to BBC world symbol.

Voice Over (ERIC) Next week on 'Book at Bedtime', Jeremy Toogood will be reading Anna Sewell's Black Bu . . . Bue . . . Bueton . . . Black Bottom . . . *(fade out)*

Fade BBC world symbol back up.

Continuity Voice (ERIC) Tomorrow night comedy returns to BBC TV with a new series of half-hour situation comedies for you to spot the winners. Ronnie Thompson stars in 'Dad's Doctor' . . . *(cut to a doctor (Terry J) with no trousers)*

SUPERIMPOSED CAPTION: 'DAD'S DOCTOR'

Continuity Voice . . . the daffy exploits of the RAMC training school. He's in charge of a group of mad medicos, and when they run wild it's titty jokes galore. *(medical students run past him waving bras)* Newcomer Veronica Papp plays the girl with the large breasts. *(a young lady runs past wearing only briefs)* Week two sees the return of the wacky exploits of the oddest couple you've ever seen — yes, 'Dad's Pooves' . . .

A kitchen set. A man (Terry G) in sexy female underwear. Another man (Terry J) dressed as a judge, runs in with flowers.

SUPERIMPOSED CAPTION: 'DAD'S POOVES'

Continuity Voice ... the kooky oddball laugh-a-minute fun-a-plenty world of unnatural sexual practices. *(the first man spanks the judge with a string of sausages)* Week three brings a change of pace with a new comedy schedule. With Reg Cuttleworth, Trevor Quantas, and Cindy Rommel as Bob, in 'On the Dad's Liver Bachelors at Large', *(caption of this title and several loony still photos of the cast)* keeping the buses running from typical bedsit land in pre-war Liverpool. That's followed by 'The Ratings Game' – the loony life of a BBC programme planner with the accent on repeats. *(Michael's loony again)*

SUPERIMPOSED CAPTION: 'THE RATINGS GAME'

Continuity Voice Edie Phillips-Bong plays Kevin Vole, the programme planner with a problem and his comic attempts to pass the time. Week six sees the return of 'Up The Palace' ... *(stock film of the investiture of the Prince of Wales)*

SUPERIMPOSED CAPTION: 'UP THE PALACE'

Continuity Voice ... the zany exploits of a wacky Queen, and that's followed by 'Limestone, Dear Limestone' ... *(long shot of a cliff with two people high up on it)*

SUPERIMPOSED CAPTION: 'LIMESTONE DEAR LIMESTONE'

Continuity Voice ... the wacky days of the late Pleistocene era when much of Britain's rock strata was being formed. All this and less on 'Comedy Ahoy'. But now, BBC Television is closing down for the night. Don't forget to switch off your sets. Goodnight.

We see the little dot as of a TV set being switched off.

Thirty-nine Grandstand

Begin with Thames Television logo and fanfare. Cut to David Hamilton in their presentation studios.

David Hamilton Good evening. We've got an action-packed evening for you tonight on Thames, but right now here's a rotten old BBC programme.

Cut to the nude man (Terry J) at the organ.

Announcer (JOHN) And now...

It's Man (MICHAEL) It's...

Cut to a photo of Piccadilly Circus.

SUPERIMPOSED CAPTIONS:

'THE BRITISH SHOWBIZ AWARDS'

'PRESENTED BY HRH THE DUMMY PRINCESS MARGARET'

We mix through to the dummy Princess Margaret at a desk, as for awards ceremony. At the desk also, on either side of her, two men in dinner jackets and a pantomime goose. Bill Cotton is nowhere to be seen. High up above them, there is a screen. Enter Dickie Attenborough.

Dickie (ERIC) Ladies and gentlemen, Mr Chairman, friends of the society, your dummy Royal Highness. Once again, the year has come full circle, and for me there can be no greater privilege, and honour, than to that to which it is my lot to have befallen this evening. There can be no finer honour than to welcome into our midst tonight a guest who has not only done only more than not anyone for our Society, but nonetheless has only done more. He started in the film industry in 1924, he started again in 1946, and finally in 1963. He has been dead for four years, but he has not let that prevent him from coming here this evening. *(he gets out an onion and holds it to his eyes; tears pour out)* Ladies and gentlemen, no welcome could be more heartfelt than that which I have no doubt you will all want to join with me in giving this great showbiz stiff. Ladies and gentlemen, to read the nominations for the Light Entertainment Award, the remains of the late Sir Alan Waddle.

There is awful continuity music. Terrific applause. Attenborough weeps profusely. A man in a brown coat comes in carrying a white five-foot plinth. He puts it down. Behind him comes another man carrying a bronze funeral urn. It has a black tie on. Cut to stock film of the audience standing in rapturous applause. The urn is put on top of the plinth and a microphone placed in front of it. Slight pause. Cut to Dickie weeping profusely. The urn clears its throat.

The Urn *(silly voice)* The nominations are Mr Edward Heath, for the new suit sketch, *(zoom quickly in to film on the screen of the lady of Brussels throwing ink all over Mr Heath; cut back to the hall for applause)* Mr Richard Baker for Lemon Curry.

Cut to Richard Baker.

Richard Baker Lemon Curry?

Cut back to the urn.

The Urn And the Third Parachute Brigade Amateur Dramatic Society for the Oscar Wilde skit.

Zoom in to overlay showing some stock film of hansom cabs galloping past.

SUPERIMPOSED CAPTION: 'LONDON 1895'

SUPERIMPOSED CAPTION: 'THE RESIDENCE OF MR OSCAR WILDE'

Suitable classy music starts. Mix through to Wilde's drawing room. A crowd of suitably dressed folk are engaged in typically brilliant conversation, laughing affectedly and drinking champagne.

Prince of Wales (TERRY J) My congratulations, Wilde. Your latest play is a great success. The whole of London's talking about you.

Oscar (GRAHAM) There is only one thing in the world worse than being talked about, and that is *not* being talked about.

There follows fifteen seconds of restrained and sycophantic laughter.

Prince Very very witty ... very very witty.

Whistler (JOHN) There is only one thing in the world worse than being witty, and that is not being witty.

Fifteen more seconds of the same.

Oscar I wish *I* had said that.

Whistler You will, Oscar, you will. *(more laughter)*

Oscar Your Majesty, have you met James McNeill Whistler.

Prince Yes, we've played squash together.

Oscar There is only one thing worse than playing squash together, and that is playing it by yourself. *(silence)* I wish I hadn't said that.

Whistler You did, Oscar, you did. *(a little laughter)*

Prince I've got to get back up the palace.

Oscar Your Majesty is like a big jam doughnut with, cream on the top.

Prince I beg your pardon?

Oscar Um ... It was one of Whistler's.

Whistler I never said that.

Oscar You did, James, you did.

The Prince of Wales stares expectantly at Whistler.

Whistler ... Well, Your Highness, what I meant was that, like a doughnut, um, your arrival gives us pleasure ... and your departure only makes us hungry for more. *(laughter)* Your Highness, you are also like a stream of bat's piss.

Prince What?

Whistler It was one of Wilde's. One of Wilde's.

Oscar It sodding was not! It was Shaw!

Shaw (MICHAEL) I . . . I merely meant, Your Majesty, that you shine out like a shaft of gold when all around is dark.

Prince *(accepting the compliment)* Oh.

Oscar *(to Whistler)* Right. *(to Prince)* Your Majesty is like a dose of clap. Before you arrive is pleasure, and after is a pain in the dong.

Prince What?

Whistler and Oscar One of Shaw's, one of Shaw's.

Shaw You bastards. Um . . . what I meant, Your Majesty, what I meant . . .

Oscar We've got him, Jim.

Whistler Come on, Shaw-y.

Oscar Come on, Shaw-y.

Shaw I merely meant . . .

Oscar Come on, Shaw-y.

Whistler Let's have a bit of wit, then, man.

Shaw *(blows a raspberry)*

The Prince shakes Shaw's hand. Laughter all round. We then link to animation for a few minutes, then back to Dickie Attenborough at the awards ceremony. He now has bunches of onions slung round his neck.

Dickie Ladies and gentlemen, seldom can it have been a greater pleasure and privilege than it is for me now to announce that the next award gave me the great pleasure and privilege of asking a man without whose ceaseless energy and tireless skill the British Film Industry would be today. I refer of course to my friend and colleague, Mr David Niven. *(vast applause, a bit of emotion from Dickie)* Sadly, David Niven cannot be with us tonight, but he has sent his fridge. *(applause; 'Around the world in eighty days' music; the fridge is pushed down by a man in a brown coat)* This is the fridge in which David keeps most of his milk, butter and eggs. What a typically selfless gesture, that he should send this fridge, of all of his fridges, to be with us tonight.

Another cut of the audience applauding. The fridge has a black tie on. They adjust the mike for it.

Fridge *(the same silly voice)* The nominations for the Best Foreign Film Director are: Monsieur Richard Attenborough, Ricardo de Attenbergie, Rik Attenborough, Ri Char Dat En Bollo, and Pier Paolo Pasolini.

Dickie Before we hear the joint winner, let's see the one that came sixth. Let us see Pier Paolo Pasolini's latest film.

Close-up of grass on cricket pitch. In the background we hear the buzzing of insects. A cricket ball rolls into shot and a hand reaches down and picks it up. Pull out to reveal he is a bowler, behind him a couple of fielders. He is shot from low down.

CAPTION: 'PASOLINI'S THE THIRD TEST MATCH'

Close-up on the bowler as he turns to look at his field. Cut to a skeleton on the boundary in tattered remnants of cricket gear. Noise of flies buzzing becomes louder. Sounds of mocking laughter. Cut to the bowler in close-up turning into the direction of the laughter. Shot of the batsman at his crease, but behind him the wicket keeper and first slip are monks in brown cowls. They are laughing at him. Cut back to the bowler's horrified eyes, he looks again. Cut to same shot of the batsman only now the wicket keeper and first slip are cricketers again. Wind, buzzing. Cut back to the bowler, who starts to rub the ball on his trousers. Music comes in. Close-up bowler's face starting to sweat. Close-up ball rubbing on trousers. Close-up face sweating. Cut to a girl in the pavilion licking her lips. Cut back to ball rubbing. Cut to his sweating face. Cut to girl. Cut back to bowler as he starts his run. Close-up of bowler running. He runs over a couple making love in the nude. Mounting music. Cut back to the bowler, as he releases ball. Cut to the ball smashing into stumps. The music reaches crescendo. Silence. In slow motion the bowler turns, arms outstretched to the umpire. The umpire turns into a cardinal who produces a cross and holds it up like a dismissal sign.

Cut to a vociferous group of cricketers in a TV studio. They are all in pads and white flannels. They are on staggered rostra as in 'Talk-back'. Facing them is Pier Paolo Pasolini.

First Cricketer (GRAHAM) There's lots of people making love, but no mention of Geoff Boycott's average.

Pasolini (JOHN) *(Italian accent)* Who is-a Geoff Boycott?

SUPERIMPOSED CAPTION: 'PIER PAOLO PASOLINI'

Second Cricketer (MICHAEL) And in t'film, we get Fred Titmus...

Pasolini Si, Titmus, si, si...

SUPERIMPOSED CAPTION: 'YORKSHIRE'

Second Cricketer ... the symbol of man's regeneration through radical Marxism... fair enough... but we never once get a chance to see him turn his off-breaks on that Brisbane sticky.

Third Cricketer (ERIC) Aye, and what were all that dancing through Ray Illingworth's innings? Forty-seven not out and the bird comes up and feeds him some grapes!

General cricketorial condemnation. We pull back to show that it is on a television set in an ordinary sitting room. Two Pepperpots are watching the television. They are both called Mrs Zambesi.

First Zambesi (GRAHAM) What's on the other side?

The second Mrs Zambesi switches channels to reveal Dickie Attenborough still at it.

Dickie Nobody could be prouder than...

Second Zambesi (TERRY J) Ugh! *(she switches the set off)*

First Zambesi Um, shall we go down and give blood?

Second Zambesi Oh, I don't want a great bat flapping round my neck.

First Zambesi They don't do it like that! They take it from your arm!
Second Zambesi I can't give it. I caught swamp fever in the Tropics.
First Zambesi You've never even been to the Tropics. You've never been south of Sidcup.
Second Zambesi You can catch it off lampposts.
First Zambesi Catch what?
Second Zambesi I don't know, I'm all confused.
First Zambesi You ought to go and see a psychiatrist. You're a loony. You might even need a new brain.
Second Zambesi Oh, I couldn't afford a whole new brain.
First Zambesi Well, you could get one of those Curry's brains.
Second Zambesi How much are they?
First Zambesi *(picking up a catalogue)* I don't know. I'll have a look in the catalogue. Here we are. Battery lights, dynamo lights, rear lights, brains – here we are ...
Second Zambesi I'm still confused.
First Zambesi Oh, there's a nice one here, thirteen-and-six, it's one of Curry's own brains.
Second Zambesi That one looks nice, what's that?
First Zambesi That's a mudguard!
Second Zambesi It's only eight bob.
First Zambesi Oh, I think it's worth the extra five bob for the brain. I'll give them a ring. *(she goes to the phone and dials one number)* Hello, Curry's? I'd like to try one of your thirteen-and-sixpenny brains please. Yes ... yes ... yes, ye ... um ... *(looks at her shoe)* five-and-a-half ... yes ... thank you. *(replaces phone)* They're sending someone round *(there is a knock at the door)*
Second Zambesi Oh, that was quick. Come in.
Man.(JOHN) Hello Mr and Mrs and Mrs Zambesi?
First Zambesi Yes, that's right. Are you the man from Curry's?
Man No, I've just come to say that he's on his way. Would you sign this please.
He hands a bare leg severed from the knee downwards round the door. She signs it.
Man Thank you very much. Thank you. Sorry to bother you.
First Zambesi Thank you.
The man goes. A knock at the door and he reappears.
Man Um, he's just coming now. Here he is.
The door opens and a pair of hands fling in a dummy salesman carrying a briefcase. He flops down on to the floor. The door shuts. The two Pepperpots go over and look at him for some time.
First Zambesi Hello ... hello ...

Second Zambesi *(picking up the dummy)* That's not a proper salesman. I'm not buying one from him, he doesn't give you confidence.

First Zambesi He doesn't give me any confidence at all – he's obviously a dummy. I'll ring Curry's. *(she just picks up the phone without dialling this time)* Hello, Curry's – that salesman you sent round is obviously a dummy . . . Oh, thank you very much. *(she puts the phone down)* They're sending round a real one. *(a knock on the door)*

Second Zambesi Come in.

The salesman enters.

Salesman (MICHAEL) Good morning – Mr and Mrs and Mrs Zambesi.

Second Zambesi Yes, that's right.

First Zambesi Yes, that's right . . . *(out of the side of the mouth in a man's voice)* Yes that's right.

Salesman *(to dummy)* All right, Rutherford, I'll take over.

He opens a box and produces a two foot square silver cube with various gadgets and wires on it.

Second Zambesi Oh, that's nice.

Salesman Yes, we sell a lot of these. Right, shall we try a fitting.

Second Zambesi Oh, do I have to have an operation?

Salesman No, madam, you just strap it on.

He starts to put it on her head.

Second Zambesi Doesn't it go inside my head?

Salesman Not the roadster, madam, no. You're thinking of the brainette major.

Second Zambesi How much is that?

Salesman Forty-four-and-six.

Second Zambesi Oh no, it's not worth it.

Salesman Not with the Curry's surgery we use, no, madam. Now then. The best bet is the Bertrand Russell super silver. That's a real beauty – 250 quid plus hospital treatment.

First Zambesi Ooh, that's a lot.

Salesman It's colour. Right. *(he straps the brain to her head and begins to twiddle a few knobs; lights flash on occasionally as he does this)* One, two, three, testing, testing.

Second Zambesi Mince pie for me, please.

First Zambesi What did she say that for?

Salesman Quiet please. It's not adjusted yet. *(he makes more adjustments)*

Second Zambesi Oh, I am enjoying this rickshaw ride. I've been a Tory all my life, my life, my life. Good morning Mr Presley. How well you look, you look very well . . . our cruising speed is 610 per hour . . . well . . . well, well, well, hello hello dear . . .

Salesman Right, one, two, three ... *(the salesman adjusts a switch)*
Second Zambesi ... eight, seven, *(he adjusts another switch)* four.
First Zambesi Oh, she never knew that before.
Salesman Quiet please. Mrs Zambesi, who wrote the theory of relativity?
First Zambesi I know! I know.
Salesman Quiet, please! *(he adjusts a tuning control)*
Second Zambesi Einstone ... Einstone ... Einsteen ... Einston ... Einstin ... Einstan ... Einstein.
Salesman Good.
Second Zambesi Noel Einstein.
Salesman Right. That'll be 13/6d please.
First Zambesi *(paying him with invisible money)* That's marvellous.
Salesman She can take it off at night, unless she wants to read, of course. And don't ask her too many questions because it will get hot. If you do have any trouble here is my card. *(he reaches in his case and hands her the dismembered part of an arm)* Give us a ring and either myself, or Mr Rutherford *(he picks the dummy up and drags it towards the door)* will come and see you. Goodbye.
First Zambesi Thank you very much.
As soon as the door is shut, the man's head pops round.
Man He's gone now.
He withdraws head and shuts the door.
First Zambesi *(tentatively)* Shall we go down and give blood?
Second Zambesi *(with slightly glazed eyes)* Yes, please Mr Roosevelt, but try and keep the noise to a minimum.
First Zambesi I'll go and get your coat for you.
Second Zambesi I'm quite warm in this stick of celery, thank you, Senator Muskie.
The Pepperpots appear out of their gate and walk down the street. We follow them closely.
Second Zambesi *(to neighbour)* Stapling machine, Mr Clarke.
First Zambesi *(explaining)* New brain.
Second Zambesi Stapling machine, Mrs Worral.
Cut to a Pepperpot with identical brain strapped to head.
Mrs Worral Stapling machine, Mrs Zambesi.
They walk on passing a bus stop at which a penguin is standing reading a paper. One or two unexploded Scotsmen lie on the ground at various places.
First Zambesi Are you sure that's working all right?
Second Zambesi Yes, thank you dear. It's marvellous. I think if we can win one or two of the early primaries, we could split the urban Republican vote wide open.

First Zambesi Um . . . here we are then.
> *They go into a door marked 'Blood Donors'.*

Second Zambesi Well being President of the United States is something that I shall have to think about.
> *They walk through and out of shot. A hospital lobby. A line of people are being ushered through. A sign says 'Blood Donors' with an arrow in the direction they're all going. Mr Samson is in a white coat.*

Samson (JOHN) Blood donors that way, please.

Donor Oh thank you very much *(joins the line).*

Samson Thank you. *(Grimshaw comes up to him and whispers in his ear; Samson looks at him, slightly surprised)* What? *(Grimshaw whispers again)* No. No, I'm sorry but no. *(Grimshaw whispers again)* No, you may not give urine instead of blood. *(Grimshaw whispers again)* No, well, I don't care if you want to. *(Grimshaw whispers again)* No. There is no such thing as a urine bank.

Grimshaw (ERIC) Please.

Samson No. We have no call for it. We've quite enough of it without volunteers coming in here donating it.

Grimshaw Just a specimen.

Samson No, we don't want a specimen. We either want your blood or nothing.

Grimshaw I'll give you some blood if you'll give me . . .

Samson What?

Grimshaw A thing to do some urine in.

Samson No, no, just go away please.

Grimshaw Anyway, I don't want to give you any blood.

Samson Fine, well you don't have to, you see, just go away.

Grimshaw Can I give you some spit?

Samson No.

Grimshaw Sweat?

Samson No.

Grimshaw Earwax?

Samson No, look, this is a blood bank – all we want is blood.

Grimshaw All right, I'll give you some blood.
> *He holds out a jar full of blood.*

Samson Where did you get that?

Grimshaw Today. It's today's.

Samson What group is it?

Grimshaw What groups are there?

Samson There's A . . .

Grimshaw It's A.

Samson *(sniffing the blood)* Wait a moment. It's mine. This blood is mine! What are you doing with it?

Grimshaw I found it.

Samson You *found* it? You stole it out of my body, didn't you?

Grimshaw No.

Samson No wonder I'm feeling off-colour. *(he starts to drink the blood; Grimshaw grabs the bottle)* Give that back.

Grimshaw It's mine.

Samson It is not yours. You stole it.

Grimshaw Never.

Samson Give it back to me.

Grimshaw All right. But only if I can give urine.

Samson ... Get in the queue.

Cut to John Rickman type person with hat which he raises. There are white rails behind him which might be a racecourse.

Rickman (MICHAEL) Good afternoon and welcome to Wife-Swapping from Redcar. And the big news this morning is that the British boy Boris Rogers has succeeded in swapping his nine-stone Welsh-born wife for a Ford Popular and a complete set of Dickens. Well now, I can see they're ready at the start and so let's go now over for the start of the 3.30.

Cut to high shot of a street with about ten houses on each side.

Rickman And first let's catch up with the latest news of the betting.

SUPERIMPOSED CAPTIONS:

'NO. 12 BETTY PARKINSON 7/4 ON FAV

NO. 27 MRS E. COLYER 9/4

NO. 14 MRS CASEY 4/1

5/1 BAR'

Voice Over (ERIC) Number 12 Betty Parkinson 7 to 4 on favourite, number 27 Mrs Colyer 9 to 4, 5 to 1 bar those.

Rickman And here's the starter Mrs Alec Marsh, *(she climbs onto a rostrum and fires a gun)* and they're off.

One of the doors opens and a lady rushes across the street into another house. Other doors start opening up and down the street, with ladies criss-crossing out of each others' houses. About twenty seconds of this high activity.

Rickman And Mrs Rogers is the first to show, there she goes into Mr Johnson's, and Mrs Johnson across to Mr Colyer, followed closely by Mrs Casey on the inside. Mrs Parkinson, number 12, going well there into Mr Webster's from the Co-op, Mrs Colyer's making ground fast after a poor start, she's out of Mr Casey's into Mr Parkinson's, she's a couple of lengths ahead of Mrs Johnson who's still not out of Mr Casey's. Mrs Penguin and Mrs Colyer – these two now at the head of the field from Mrs Brown, Mrs Atkins, Mrs Parkinson, Mrs Warner and Mrs Rudd – all still at Mr Philips's. Mrs Penguin making the running now, challenged strongly by Mrs Casey, Mrs Casey coming very fast on the inside, it's going to be Mrs Casey coining from behind. Now she's making a break on the outside, Mrs Penguin running... and at the line, it's Mrs Casey who's got it by a short head from Mrs Penguin in second place, Mrs Parkinson in third, Mrs Rudd, Mrs Colyer, Mrs Warner and there's Mrs Griffiths who's remained unswapped.

One lady is left in the middle of the road. Cut back to Rickman at the course railing.

Rickman Well, a very exciting race there, and I have with me now the man who owned and trained the winner, Mrs Casey — Mr Casey. Well done, Jack.

Mr Casey (TERRY J) Thank you, John.

Rickman Well, were you at all surprised about this, Jack?

Mr Casey No, not really, no she's been going very well in training, and at Doncaster last week, and I fancy her very strongly for the Cheltenham weekend.

Rickman Well, thank you very much indeed, Jack. We must leave you now because it's time for the team event.

Peter West type figure in a white DJ sitting at a ballroom side table. He has one or two ballroom dancers beside him.

SUPERIMPOSED TITLES: 'COME WIFE-SWAPPING — NORTH WEST V THE SOUTH EAST'

Peter (ERIC) Hello, and a very warm welcome from the Tower ballroom suite at Reading, where there's very little in it, they're neck and neck, crop and grummit, real rack and saddle, brick and bucket, horse and tooth, cap and thigh, arse over tip, they're absolutely birds of a feather, there's not a new pin in it, you couldn't get a melon between them. Well, now, everything rests on the formation event and here come North West with the Mambo.

Cut to lines of ballroom dancers being led out. Four gentlemen and four ladies in each team, sixteen altogether.

Peter Maestro, take it away, please.

The dancers form up in two lines opposite each other, as though they are about to dance. The ladies are in nasty tulle, the gents in tails, with numbers on their backs. At the back of the hall a large banner says 'Mecca Wife-Swapping'. Mambo music starts its intro. After four bars the two teams start grabbing each other and wrestling on the ground. A vast orgy breaks out as they roll all over the floor. Cut quickly to Frank Bough in the 'Sportsview' studio.

Frank Bough (MICHAEL) And now it's time for Rugby league, and highlights of this afternoon's game between Keighley and Hull Kingston Rovers.

Cut to a field where mud-caked rugby league players in hooped shirts are getting ready for a scrum.

SUPERIMPOSED CAPTION: 'KEIGHLEY 2 HULL K.R. 23'

Eddie Waring (ERIC) *(voice over)* Well, good afternoon and as you can see, Hull Kingston Rovers are well in the lead, it's a scrum down on the twenty-five, Keighley's Tom Colyer with the put in, Mrs Colyer to be put.

The scrum has formed up, the scrum half has a dummy woman, small and light but real looking, tucked under his arm, while he steadies the scrum. He puts her into the scrum, and after a lot of kicking she is eventually heeled out.

Eddie Waring And there goes his wife into the scrum. And Hull have got the heel against the head. Doing nicely with this scrum, some very good packing here. Warrington's picked her up, is he going to let her go, Wrigley's with him, grand lad is this.

Mrs Colyer is picked up by the scrum half who makes a run with her. Handing off a strong tackle and dodging with her, he side steps and slips Mrs Colyer to a back who makes a run through and touches her down between the posts. They leave the lady dumped down between the posts and rush to congratulate and hug each other.

Eddie Waring Well, that was right on the whistle, Rovers walkin' it there, winnin' easily by twenty-six points to two.

Cut to Frank Bough again in the 'Sportsview' set.

Frank Bough Just a reminder that on 'Match of the Day' tonight you can see highlights of two of this afternoon's big games. Mrs Robinson v Manchester United and Southampton v Mr Rogers, a rather unusual game that. And here's a late result ... Coventry nil, Mr Johnson's Una three – Coventry going down at home, there. Just a little reminder that the next sport you can see on BBC 1 will be 9.20 on Wednesday night, when 'Wife Swapping with Coleman' comes live from my place. Till then, goodnight.

Credits roll over four screens of naughty activity to the 'Grandstand' signature tune.

GRANDSTAND
A BBC INSIDE BROADCAST
CONCEIVED WRITTEN AND PERFORMED BY
MICHAEL PALIN AND MRS CLEESE
ERIC IDLE AND MRS PALIN
JOHN CLEESE AND MRS JONES
TERRY GILLIAM AND TERRY JONES AND MRS IDLE
GRAHAM CHAPMAN AND MR SHERLOCK
ALSO APPEARING CAROL CLEVELAND AND MRS AND MRS ZAMBESI
CARON GARDENER AND MR A.
MAKE-UP BY MISS GAFFNEY AND MR LAST
COSTUMES HAZEL PETHIG AND MR CLARKE

GRAPHICS BY BOB BLAGDEN AND 'NAUGHTY' ROSY
ANIMATIONS BY TERRY GILLIAM AND RABBI COLQUHOUN
FILM CAMERAMAN ALAN FEATHERSTONE AND MISS WESTON
FILM EDITOR MR RAY MILLICHOPE AND HIS ORCHESTRA
SOUND RICHARD CHUBB AND MRS LIGHTING
LIGHTING BILL BAILEY AND MR SOUND
CHOREOGRAPHY BY JEAN CLARKE AND AN UNNAMED MAN IN ESHER
DESIGNED BY CHRIS THOMPSON AND MRS ARMSTRONG-JONES
PRODUCED BY IAN MACNAUGHTON AND DICKIE
A BBC TV AND MRS THAMES PRODUCTION

Pull out from screen to see that this is on the screen in the awards set and Dickie is working a stirrup pump which pumps tears out from the side of his head via rather obvious tubes.

Dickie There they go, the credits of the year. Credits that you and the Society voted as the credits that brought the most credit to the Society. Sadly, the man who designed them cannot be with us tonight, as he is at home asleep, but we are going to wake him up and tell him the good news.

We see a darkened bedroom. The light is suddenly switched on. A man sits up. He has no clothes on.

Dickie Are you there in Bristol, Arthur Briggs . . . ?

Briggs looks terrified. We see that another man (John) is in bed with him.

Briggs (MICHAEL) Oh, my God! *(pulls a sheet over the other man)*

Cut back to Dickie.

Dickie And now for the moment you've all been waiting for . . .

CAPTION: THE END

Dickie No, not that moment. Although that moment is coming, *in* a moment. The moment I'm talking about is the moment when we present the award for the cast with the most awards award, and this year is no exception. Ladies and gentlemen will you join me and welcome please, the winners of this year's Mountbatten trophy, Showbusiness's highest accolade, the cast of the Dirty Vicar sketch.

Very patriotic music. The cast of the Dirty Vicar sketch come on. They curtsy to Princess Margaret. Attenborough embraces them all.

Dickie Well now, let us see the performances which brought them this award. Let us see the Dirty Vicar sketch.

Cut to two ladies taking tea in an Edwardian drawing room.

First Lady (CAROL) Have you seen Lady Windermere's new carriage, dear?

Second Lady (CARON GARDENER) Absolutely enchanting!

First Lady Isn't it!

Chivers the butler enters.

Chivers (GRAHAM) The new vicar to see you, m'lady.

First Lady Send him in, Chivers.

Chivers Certainly, m'lady. *(he goes)*

> *Enter a Swiss mountaineer (Terry G) in Tyrolean hat, lederhosen, haversack, icepick, etc. Followed by two men in evening dress. They look round and exit.*

First Lady Now, how is your tea, dear? A little more water perhaps?

Second Lady Thank you. It is delightful as it is.

Chivers The Reverend Ronald Simms, the Dirty Vicar of St Michael's . . . ooh!

> *Chivers is obviously goosed from behind by the Dirty Vicar.*

Vicar (TERRY J) Cor, what a lovely bit of stuff. I'd like to get my fingers around those knockers.

> *He pounces upon the second lady, throws her skirt over her head and pushes her over the back of the sofa.*

First Lady How do you find the vicarage?

> *The vicar stands up from behind the sofa, his shirt open and his hair awry; he reaches over and puts his hand down the first lady's front.*

Vicar I like tits!

First Lady Oh Vicar! Vicar!

> *The vicar suddenly pulls back and looks around him as if in the horror of dawning realization.*

Vicar Oh my goodness. I do beg your pardon. How dreadful! The first day in my new parish, I completely . . . so sorry!

First Lady *(readjusting her dress)* Yes. Never mind, never mind. Chivers – send Mary in with a new gown, will you?

> *The second lady struggles to her feet from behind the couch, completely dishevelled. Her own gown completely ripped open.*

Chivers Certainly, m'lady.

Vicar *(to the second lady)* I do beg your pardon . . . I must sit down.

First Lady As I was saying, how do you find the new vicarage?

> *They take their seats on the couch.*

Vicar Oh yes, certainly, yes indeed, I find the grounds delightful, and the servants most attentive and particularly the little serving maid with the great big knockers . . .

> *He throws himself on the hostess across the tea table, knocking it over and they disappear over the back of the hostess's chair. Grunts etc. Enter Dickie applauding. Also, we hear audience applause.*

Dickie Well, there we are, another year has been too soon alas ended and I think none more than myself can be happier at this time than I . . . am.

> *The cast of the sketch stand in a line at the back, looking awkward and smiling. Fade out.*

Forty The golden age of ballooning

Animation of balloons ascending.
CAPTION: 'THE GOLDEN AGE OF BALLOONING'
CAPTION: 'THE BEGINNINGS'
Cut to a suburban bathroom. A plumber with a bag of tools open beside him is doing an elaborate repair on the toilet. He is in rather an awkward position.

Plumber (MICHAEL) *(working away)* The Golden Age of Ballooning can be said to begin in 1783 . . . when the Montgolfier brothers made their first ascent in a fire balloon. On the eve of that . . . *(struggling with the work)* come on . . . come on . . . momentous ascent, the brothers took one last look at their craft, as it stood on the field of Annencay.

Pleasant elegant eighteenth-century music. Mix to a French small country-house interior. At the window Joseph and Jacques Montgolfier are looking out at their balloon. In the background a plumber is working away at a bit of eighteenth-century French piping.

Jacques (ERIC) This is a great moment for us, Joseph.

Joseph (TERRY J) It is a great moment for France.

Jacques Ah, oui!

Joseph First ascent in a hot-air balloon, by the Montgolfier brothers – 1783 . . . I can see us now . . . just after Montesquieu and just before Mozart.

Jacques I think I'll go and wash . . .

Joseph Good luck.

Jacques Oh . . . it's quite easy, really . . . I just slap a little water on my face, then . . .

Joseph No . . . good luck for tomorrow.

Jacques Oh I see, yes. You too. Yours has been the work.

Joseph Let us hope for a safe ascent . . . and don't use my flannel.

Jacques You know, when you showed me the plans in Paris, I could not believe that we should be the first men who would fly.

Joseph Yes . . . it's wonderful.

Jacques I am so excited I could hardly wash.

Joseph Yes . . . I too have had some difficulty washing these past few days.

Jacques Still, what is washing when we are on the verge of a great scientific breakthrough?

Joseph Jacques . . .

Jacques Yes, Joseph . . .

Joseph I have not been washing very thoroughly for many years now.

Jacques What do you mean? You must have been washing your face?

Joseph Oh yes, my face, I wash my face . . . but my legs . . . my stomach . . . my chest, they're filthy.

Jacques Well, I don't wash my stomach every day.

Joseph *(with increasing self-remorse)* Ah, but you wash far more than me . . . you are the cleaner of the Montgolfier brothers.

Jacques This is nothing, Joseph . . .

A very formal butler enters.

Butler (GRAHAM) Monsieur Montgolfier . . . A Mr Parfitt to see you, sir.

A head appears round the door and corrects the butler, in a very stage whisper.

Mr Bartlett No, no . . . no . . . Bartlett! *(the head disappears again)*

Butler A Mr Barklit, to see you, sir.

Mr Bartlett No! Bartlett with a 't'. *(the head disappears again)*

Butler *(with difficulty)* Barr . . . at . . . elett . . . to see you, sir.

Mr Bartlett Bartlett *(he disappears again)*

Butler Barkit . . .

Mr Bartlett Bartlett!

Butler Barlit . . . Bartlett . . . A Mr Bartlett to see you, sir.

Joseph I don't want to see anyone, O'Toole . . . tell him to go away.

Butler Thank you, sir. *(he exits)*

Jacques Well, it's getting late. I must go and have a wash.

Joseph What will you be washing?

Jacques Oh . . . just my face and neck . . . perhaps my feet . . . and possibly . . . but no . . . no . . . lock up the plans, Joseph . . . tomorrow they will make us the toast of France. 'The first ascent by the Montgolfier brothers in a balloon'. Just after Ballcock and just before Bang . . . what a position!

Some men have now entered the room, chosen a spot and are briskly but quietly setting up a screen and a projector. The projector is turned on and a film comes up on the screen together with triumphant music, applause and commentary. We zoom in to the screen. It shows an animation of two naked men boxing in a large tub of water.

Voice Over (GRAHAM) So, on June 7th, 1783, the Montgolfier brothers had a really good wash . . . starting on his face and arms, Joseph Michael Montgolfier went on to scrub his torso, his legs and his naughty bits, before rinsing his whole body. That June night, he and his brother between them washed seventeen square feet of body area. They used a kilo and a half of carbolic soap and nearly fourteen gallons of nice hot water. It was indeed an impressive sight.

Music crescendo.

CAPTION: 'THE END'

Picture of a balloon.

SUPERIMPOSED CAPTION: 'THE GOLDEN AGE OF BALLOONING'.
This is over the BBC 2 logo.

Voice Over (GRAHAM) Next week on 'The Golden Age of Ballooning', we examine the work of Glaisher and Coxwell, the English balloonists who ascended to a height of seven miles in 1862 without washing. There is also a book called 'The Golden Age of Ballooning' published by the BBC to coincide with the series. It's in an attractive hand-tooled binding, is priced £5 and failure to buy it will make you liable to a £50 fine or three months' imprisonment. There's also a record of someone reading the book of 'The Golden Age of Ballooning', a crochet-work bedspread with the words 'The Golden Age of Ballooning' on it, available from the BBC, price £18 (or five months' imprisonment) and there are matching toilet-seat covers and courtesy mats with illustrations of many of the balloons mentioned. Also available is a life-size model frog which croaks the words 'The Golden Age of Ballooning' and an attractive bakelite case for storing motorway construction plans in, made in the shape of a balloon. And now, another chance to see a repeat of this morning's re-run of last night's second showing of episode two of the award-winning series 'The Golden Age of Ballooning'.

ANIMATION: *balloons ascending as before.*
CAPTION: 'THE GOLDEN AGE OF BALLOONING'
CAPTION: 'EPISODE TWO: THE MONTGOLFIER BROTHERS IN LOVE'
CAPTION: 'NOT WITH EACH OTHER, OBVIOUSLY'

Joseph Montgolfier's workshop. We see plans and drawing boards, and at one end of the room, Joseph's fiancée, Antoinette, in a pretty dress. She is hanging suspended in a harness horizontally, attached to a gas bag. In other words she is floating like the bottom half of an airship. Joseph is making calculations excitedly. Occasionally he goes over to her, takes a measurement and goes back to his desk to write it down.

Antoinette (CAROL) Oh Joseph, all you think about is balloons... all you talk about is balloons. Your beautiful house is full of bits and pieces of balloons... your books are all about balloons... every time you sing a song, it is in some way obliquely connected with balloons... everything you eat has to have 'balloon' incorporated in the title... your dogs are all called 'balloonno'... you tie balloons to your ankles in the evenings.

Joseph I don't do that!

Antoinette Well, no, you don't do that, but you do duck down and shout 'Hey! Balloons!' when there are none about. Your whole life is becoming obsessively balloonic, you know. Why do I have to hang from this bloody gas bag all day? Don't I mean anything to you?

Joseph *(busy measuring)* Oh ma chérie, you mean more to me than any heavier than air dirigible could ever...

Antoinette Oh there you go again!

Joseph Don't waggle!

Jacques enters.

Jacques I've run your bath for you, Joseph. *(he sees Antoinette)* Oh . . . I'm so sorry, I didn't realize.

Joseph It's all right, we've done the difficult bit.

Jacques Well, don't forget we have our special guest coming this evening.

Joseph Oh?

Jacques Don't tell me you have forgotten already. The man who is giving us thousands of francs for our experiments.

Joseph What man?

Jacques Louis XIV!

Joseph Isn't he dead?

Jacques Evidently not . . .

Joseph All right, I'll be round.

Jacques Oh, and Joseph . . .

Joseph Yes, Jacques?

Jacques You will . . . wash . . . won't you?

Joseph Yes, of course!

    CAPTION: 'LATER THAT EVENING'

Fade up on the Montgolfiers' sitting room. Jacques sits there rather nervously. The plumber is working away. The door opens and the butler appears.

Butler His Royal Majesty, Louis XIV of France.

Mr Bartlett's head pops in and whispers loudly to butler.

Mr Bartlett And Mr Bartlett.

The butler pushes him aside. Fanfare. Enter Louis XIV and two tough-looking advisers. He is resplendent in state robes.

Jacques Your Majesty. It's a great privilege. Welcome to our humble abode.

Louis (MICHAEL) *(in very broad Glaswegian accent)* It's er . . . very nice to be here.

Jacques *(calling)* O'Toole.

Butler Sir?

Jacques Claret for His Majesty please.

Butler There's a Mr Bartlett outside again, sir.

Jacques Not now, I can't see him, we have the King of France here.

Butler Yes, sir.

He exits. Jacques and the king stand in rather embarrassed silence. Jacques eventually speaks.

Jacques Your Majesty. You had a pleasant journey, I trust?

Louis Yes . . . yes, oh definitely . . . yes . . . yes. Oh aye, aye.

Silence.

Jacques You have come from Paris?

Louis Where?

Jacques From Paris... you have travelled from Paris?

Louis Oh yes, we've come from Paris... yes... yes, yes, we've just come from... er... Paris... yes.

The butler comes back in.

Butler Sir?

Jacques Yes, O'Toole?

Butler Which one is the claret, sir?

Jacques The claret is in the decanter.

Butler The wooden thing?

Jacques No no... the glass thing... the glass decanter with the round glass stopper.

Butler Oh yes, behind the door.

Jacques No no... on the sideboard.

Butler The sideboard?

Jacques The sideboard... yes. Look... you go into the salle à manger... the *dining room,* right? – and the sideboard is on your left, by the wall, beside the master's portrait.

Butler Ah! Above the mirror, sir?

Jacques No! No! The mirror is on the other side. It's *opposite* the mirror.

Butler But that's the *table,* sir.

Jacques No... you don't go as *far* as the table. You go into the room, right?... on your right is the door to the orangery, straight ahead of you is the door to the library, and to your left is the sideboard.

Butler Ah, yes, I see, sir...

Jacque And the claret is on top of the sideboard, to the left.

Butler On the left.

Jacques Yes...

Butler As one looks at it, sir?

Jacques Yes.

Butler I see, sir, thank you. *(he turns to go)*

Jacques O'Toole.

Butler Yes, sir.

Jacques Will you please tell Monsieur Joseph our guest is here.

Butler Yes, sir.

He leaves. There is another embarrassed silence.

Jacques I'm sorry about that, Your Majesty.

Butler *(re-entering)* Apparently, sir, there is a plan to build a canal between the two Egyptian towns of . . .

Jacques Not now, O'Toole!

The butler exits. More silence.

Louis Well . . . er . . . Mr Montgolfier . . . let's not beat around the bush . . . my . . . dukes and I are very busy men. What we'd like to do is see the plans of your proposed balloon . . . if that's at all possible.

Jacques Certainly, Your Majesty . . . I have them here ready prepared.

Louis Oh, great . . . hen . . . what we would like to do . . . is er . . . to take them back wi'us for the Royal Archives of er . . .

First Duke *(also Glaswegian)* France.

Louis France, aye.

Jacques Well, it is indeed a great honour Your Majesty, that I cannot refuse.

Louis Right! OK! Let's get 'em.

He and his two dukes are suddenly galvanized into action. They are about to grab the plans when Joseph enters, clad only in a towel and rather silly bath hat.

Joseph Just a moment!

Jacques Joseph!

Joseph *(indicating the king)* This man is not Louis XIV.

Jacque Joseph! Are you out of your mind!

Joseph I've been looking it up in my bath. Louis XIV died in 1717. It's now 1783! Answer me that!

Louis Did I say Louis XIV? Oh, sorry, I meant Louis XV . . . Louis XV.

Joseph He died in 1774!

Louis, getting rather hot and angry, comes over to Joseph belligerently.

Louis All right, Louis *XVI*! . . . listen to me, smartarse, when you're King of France, . . . you've got better things to do than go around all day remembering your bloody number.

Putting his face very close to Joseph's. He butts him sharply and viciously on the bridge of the nose with his forehead, in the time-honoured Glaswegian way.

Joseph Aaaaaarh!

He reels away, clutching his nose in agony. Louis approaches Jacques, equally belligerently.

Louis Right! You want to argue about numbers?

Jacques Er . . . no, no.

Louis Right, well . . . let's get hold of the plans for the Royal Archives. We've got to get back to . . . er . . .

First Duke Paris.

Louis Paris by tonight so get a move on.

Joseph Aaaargh! Ow! Ooooohh!

The butler reappears.

Butler I got as far as the sideboard, sir . . .

Louis and his dukes grab the plans and push past the butler and across to an open window. There is a bit of a scuffle at the window as they are clambering out at the same time as two men in black with a projector and screen are clambering in.

Joseph Stop them . . . oh! Ah . . . oooooohh!

Butler *(to Jacques)* No news on the canal I'm afraid, sir, but apparently in India they're thinking of building a railway between the towns of Lahore . . .

Joseph Stop . . . ow! Stop them, O'Toole for . . . oh! shit! God's sake . . . stop them, they've got the plans! *(he rushes to the window)*

By now the men in black have set up the screen. On the screen comes film of Louis and his men racing through the gardens away from the Montgolfier's house.

Voice Over (MICHAEL) Will Louis XVI get away with the Montgolfiers' precious plans? Is sixteen years of work to be stolen by this suspect sovereign? Is France really in the grip of a Glaswegian monarch? Watch next week's episode of 'The Golden Age of Ballooning' . . . Now!

Cut to animation/titles as before. Music.

CAPTION: 'THE GOLDEN AGE OF BALLOONING'

CAPTION: 'EPISODE THREE: THE GREAT DAY FOR FRANCE'

Cut to a TV discussion in progress. An urgent, impressive current affairs show called 'Decision'. Two opulent-looking men and a presenter.

SUPERIMPOSED CAPTION: 'SIR CHARLES DIVIDENDS'

Sir Dividends (GRAHAM) . . . But now that the Government has collapsed and shown itself incapable of providing any sort of unifying force, I feel we do need the stability and the breathing space that a military presence would provide.

Presenter (MICHAEL) Lord Interest?

SUPERIMPOSED CAPTION: 'LORD INTEREST'

Lord Interest (ERIC) Oh yes . . . I agree that the army should take over, but I think it should not interfere with the programme of street executions, which I feel have been the shot in the arm that the British economy so desperately needed.

As they drone on, the presenter turns away from them to talk softly into the camera.

Presenter The Montgolfier brothers' plans did indeed turn up . . . six months later, and a long way from Paris, at the court of King George III of England.

Cut to a throne room. George III is being read to by an adviser.
CAPTION: 'THE COURT OF GEORGE III, 1781'

Reader (ERIC) ... Titty was very worried. Where could Mary be? He looked everywhere. Under the stones and behind the bushes ... and Mr Squirrel helped him by looking up in the trees, and Mr Badger helped him by looking under the ground ...

There is a knock on the door. George III looks up quickly. The reader with obviously well-practised skill, shuts the book, slips it beneath another book which he opens and carries on reading.

Reader ... and so, Your Majesty, we the Commons do herein crave and beseech that ...

George III (GRAHAM) Enter!

Lord North enters and bows briefly.

Lord North (TERRY J) Your Majesty ... Louis XVIII is here!

George III Who is Louis XVIII?

Lord North The King of France, Your Majesty! This is a great moment to have, sir.

George III There is no Louis XVIII.

We hear a Scottish voice outside the door. Lord North ducks his head out for a moment, then reappears.

Lord North He craves Your Majesty's pardon. He has had a long journey here and miscounted ... He is Louis XVII.

George III Louis XVI is dead already?

A trace of worry crosses North's face. He goes outside the door again for a moment. Sounds of a slight argument between himself and the Glaswegians. Suddenly there is a yell of pain and Lord North reels in holding the bridge of his nose.

Lord North Aaaaaaaaaaaaghh! Oh my God! Oh ... ah ... oh Christ!

Louis strides in with the two dukes. They all wear tam o'shanters.

Louis *(to the reader)* Your Majesty, I am Louis XVI ... Oh Christ ... *(to George III)* Your Majesty ... I am Louis XVI as you so rightly say, and I don't want to muck about. I have a wee proposition which could make the name of George IV the most respected in Europe ...

George III George *III*.

Louis George III! Sorry. Where can we talk?

Lord North Oh! God! ... did you see that? ... Oh! ... aaaargh! Oh dear!

(he is in great pain still and clutching his nose)

George III We shall have a state banquet at St James' Palace!

Louis No, look, I can't hang about. It's take it or leave ... we got to get back to ... er ...

First Duke Paris.

Louis Paris, by tonight ...

George III Must you leave us, Louis?

Louis I'd rather just sell the plans and nip off, Georgie boy.

George III All right... we will buy the plans... if you will undertake to disengage your troops in America.

Louis Do what?

George III And, I shall give you £10,000 for the plans...

Louis Ten thousand *pounds*! Right, well, we'll disengage the, um, you know... like you said – we'll disengage 'em... tell you what, hen, I'll put a duke on to it... OK? Right!

Lord North *(still clutching his nose)* That's the worst thing you can do to anybody.

Louis You asked for it, sonny.

Lord North You could have broken my bloody nose!

George III North! Please!

Lord North You saw it! It was right on the bone.

George III North! Will you send for the Duke of Portland... we have a financial matter to discuss.

Lord North Well, it really hurt.

Louis No, look, I think it's better if you give the money to us. We're going back. We've got a bag.

George III No, no... don't worry, Louis. We shall talk to your Monsieur Necker.

Louis Ah! Well, actually, we'd rather you didn't... we've been having a wee bit of trouble with him... you know what I mean?

George III Monsieur Necker? The man who introduced so many valuable reforms and who proved so popular despite his opposition to Mirabeau's policy of issuing 'assignats'?

    SUPERIMPOSED CAPTION: 'THIS SPEECH HAS BEEN VERIFIED BY ENCYCLOPAEDIA BRITANNICA'

Louis Er... aye, yeah... the trouble is he's been drinking a bit recently... you know, fourteen lagers wi' his breakfast... that sort of thing.

George III Well... very well, Louis...

The door flies open and there is Joseph Montgolfier, still clad only in towel and silly bath hat.

Joseph Just a moment!

Louis Oh, Christ!

George III What are you doing?

Joseph I am Joseph Montgolfier, the inventor of the fire balloon. The man before you is an impostor!

George III Ooh! I am not... honestly!

Joseph No, not you, Your Majesty. *(he points at Louis)* This man – this Louis, the so-called King of France man. Which number did you give this time – Louis the 23rd?

Louis I got it right!

Joseph I bet you took a few guesses.

Louis Listen, you spotty sassenach pillock . . .

Dr Hamer (TERRY G) *(not a doctor but a period butler)* Your Majesty! The Ronettes are here.

Bartlett And Mr Bartlett.

Three black ladies wearing modern showbiz costumes come in and sing 'George III' song. Two men come in and set up a screen as before.

The Ronettes *(singing)* George III . . . etc. . . . etc. . . .

George III Oh dear, I'm not supposed to go mad till 1800!

Louis, arguing violently with the butler, butts him. Music comes up and the sound fades on this strange scene. George III falls to the floor and waggles his legs around in the air. Zoom in as the men in black take cover off the caption.

CAPTION: 'MEANWHILE, IN FRANCE . . .'

Cut to drawing room in the Montgolfiers' house. Jacques is at a table working on some drawings. Behind him Antoinette paces the room nervously. She is still wearing her harness, but it is no longer attached to the gas balloon. In a corner of the room a plumber is still mending the elaborate plumbing.

Antoinette Joseph has been gone for six months now . . . we have heard nothing!

Jacques He can look after himself.

Antoinette But he had only on a towel, you know.

Jacques takes off his false ears and walks over to Antoinette.

Jacques Antoinette . . . from now on there is only one Montgolfier brother.

Antoinette But Louis XIV has the plans . . . you must wait until Joseph returns.

Jacques *(casually loosening her harness)* The plans are here, chérie. *(he indicates the desk where he has been working)* Let me put my tongue in your mouth.

Antoinette What do you mean?

Jacques We're supposed to be French, aren't we?

Antoinette No, I mean what are the plans which Joseph after is chasing?

Jacques Please, let me put it in a little way.

Antoinette Oh, Jacques, ze *plans*!

Jacques I take it out if you don't like it.

He chases her a bit with his tongue out. Antoinette is about to react rather violently one way or the other, when her dramatic moment is cut short by the entrance of O'Toole the butler.

Butler Are you sure the claret was on the left of the sideboard, sir?

Jacques Yes, O'Toole, it's always been there.

Butler Well I'll look for one more month, sir. *(he turns and goes out; Jacques eyes Antoinette lasciviously and is about to try and make contact in the French way when the butler returns)* By the way sir, Mr Bartlett has gone, sir. He said he couldn't wait any longer.

Jacques Thank you, O'Toole . . .

Butler Not at all, sir . . . I've enjoyed being in it . . .

Jacques *(impatiently)* Right!

Butler Thank you, sir . . . mam'selle.

> *He exits. Tremendous applause. He reappears, takes a bow and leaves again. Jacques and Antoinette look nonplussed. He reappears. Terrific applause. He gestures for them to quieten down. Eventually there is silence.*

Butler By the way, sir, Mr Bartlett has gone, sir. *(tremendous applause)* He said he couldn't wait any longer, sir.

> *Incredible volume of laughter here brings the house down. The rest of the scene is pandemonium with laughter developing into prolonged applause.*

Jacques Thank you, O'Toole.

Butler Not at all, sir . . . I've enjoyed being in it.

Jacques Right!

Butler Thank you, sir . . . mam'selle.

Audience More! More! More! etc. . . . etc. . . . etc. . . .

> *Crescendo of applause. Over shouts of more! More! Superimposed Python credits. The butler is showered with flowers. Fans come on and congratulate him. A BBC security man restrains them. Other members of the cast appear and shake hands, and stand in a row behind, applauding. A dear old middle-aged lady comes in and stands beside him, weeping proudly.*

Voice Over (MICHAEL) George III was arranged and composed by Neil Innes. He is available from the BBC price £4 or eight months' imprisonment.

> *The credits end. Cut to BBC world symbol.*

Voice Over (GRAHAM) That was episode three of 'The Golden Age of Ballooning'. May I remind you that there's still time to get your 'Golden Age of Ballooning' suppositories direct from the BBC, price £4.50, or £19 for a set of six. Well, in a moment the BBC will be closing down for the night, but first, here is a Party Political Broadcast on behalf of the Norwegian Party.

> *A very straight Norwegian in light blue suit and tie appears. He speaks earnestly in Norwegian. Ad-libbed, on the lines of the following.*

Norwegian (ERIC) Ik tvika nasai . . .

SUBTITLE: 'GOOD EVENING'

Norwegian ... Stivianka sobjiord ki niyanska ik takka Norge weginda zokiy yniet...

SUBTITLE: 'YOU MAY THINK IT STRANGE THAT WE SHOULD BE ASKING YOU TO VOTE NORWEGIAN AT THE NEXT ELECTION'

Norwegian ... Ik vietta nogiunda sti jibiora...

SUBTITLE: 'BUT CONSIDER THE ADVANTAGES'

Norwegian In Norge we hatta svinska offikiose buinni a gogik in Europa.

SUBTITLE: 'IN NORWAY, WE HAVE ONE OF THE HIGHEST PER CAPITA INCOME RATES IN EUROPE'

Norwegian Sti glikka in Norge tijik dinstianna gikloosi stijioska kary.

SUBTITLE: 'WE HAVE AN INDUSTRIAL RE-INVESTMENT RATE OF 14%

Norwegian E in Norge we hatta siddinkarvo dikinik chaila osto tykka hennakska.

SUBTITLE: 'AND GIRLS WITH MASSIVE KNOCKERS!'

Norwegian Gikkiaski ungurden kola bijiusti stonosse.

SUBTITLE: 'HONESTLY, THEY'LL DO ANYTHING FOR YOU'

Norwegian Hijiasgo biunderten ki yikilpa stivvora niski ofidae.

SUBTITLE: 'THEY'LL GO THROUGH THE CARD'

Norwegian E stavaskija, E stonioska.

SUBTITLE: 'YOU NAME IT, THEY KNOW IT'

Norwegian Stingik oloshoyert okka in Trondheim khi oyplitz

SUBTITLE: 'THERE'S ONE IN TRONDHEIM WHO CAN PUT HER...'

Blackout.

CAPTION; 'PARTY POLITICAL BROADCAST ON BEHALF OF THE NORWEGIAN PARTY'

Voice Over (GRAHAM) Highlights of that broadcast will be discussed later by Lord George-Brown, ex-Foreign Secretary, Mr Sven Olafson, the ex-Norwegian Minster of Finance, Sir Charles Ollendorff, ex-Chairman of the Norwegian Trades Council, Mr Hamish McLavell, the Mayor of Wick, the nearest large town to Norway, Mrs Betty Norday, whose name sounds remarkably like Norway, Mr Brian Waynor, whose name is an anagram of Norway, Mr and Mrs Ford, whose name sounds like Fiord, of which there are a lot in Norway, Ron and Christine Boslo...

Balloons ascending. The montage as before with music.

CAPTION: 'THE GOLDEN AGE OF BALLOONING'

CAPTION: 'EPISODE SIX: FERDINAND VON ZEPPELIN – PIONEER OF THE AIRSHIP'

Cut to photo of family group.

Voice Over (MICHAEL) Ferdinand von Zeppelin was born in Constance in 1838, the brother of Barry Zeppelin, the least talented of the fourteen Zeppelin brothers.

Black and white film of Barry (Terry J) blowing up balloons of increasing size. They all sink to the ground. The last one blows back and inflates him (specially made balloon); he rises into the air. Cut to stock film of a zeppelin.

Voice Over Meanwhile for Ferdinand von Zeppelin, the year 1908 was a year of triumph.

Cut to interior of a zeppelin. A party. Expensively dressed guests. Champagne. A palm court orchestra playing. Some guests looking out of the windows in wonderment.

Von Bulow (MICHAEL) *(approaching Zeppelin)* Herr Zeppelin – it's wonderful! It's put ballooning right back on the map.

Zeppelin goes instantly berserk with anger.

Zeppelin (GRAHAM) It's not a *balloon*! D'you hear? ... It's not a balloon ... It's an *airship* ... an airship ... d'you hear?

He hits him very hard on the top of the head with the underside of his fist.

Von Bulow Well, it's very nice anyway.

Tirpitz (TERRY J) *(to Zeppelin)* Tell me, what is the principle of these balloons?

Zeppelin It's not a balloon! You stupid little thick-headed Saxon git! It's not a balloon! Balloons is for kiddy-winkies. If you want to play with balloons, get outside.

Drags Tirpitz over to the door, opens it and flings him out into the clouds.

Tirpitz Aaaaaaaaaghhh!

Cut to an old German couple in a cottage. The man is reading from a big book, the lady is knitting. The man is in underpants. There are a pair of lederhosen drying in front of the fire.

Helmut (MICHAEL) *(reading)* Yorkshire ... pudding. A type of thick pancake, eaten with large ...

Roof splitting noise. A thump and the house shakes. They both look up. Cut back to the airship. The party is still going on.

Hollweg (ERIC) I hear you are to name the balloon after Bismarck?

Zeppelin *(flying into hysterical rage)* Bismarck? Of course I'm not calling it after Bismarck. It's a zeppelin. It's nothing to do with bloody Bismarck!

Hollweg Surely he gave you some money for it?

Zeppelin Get outside!

He opens the door and flings Hollweg out. Cut back to the old couple in the cottage.

Helmut Za ... bag ... lione ... a sort of cream mouse ... mousse of Italian origin ...

Roof splintering noise. A thump and the house shakes. Cut back to the airship. A little cluster of people round the door. The party is still going on but there is a little tension in the atmosphere.

Von Bulow Ferdinand . . . that was a Minister of State you just threw out of the balloon.

Zeppelin It's not a balloon! It's an airship!

Von Bulow All right, I'm sorry.

Zeppelin All right – go and have a look! *(he throws the protesting Von Bulow out)* And you!

Animation of several men being thrown from airship.

Helmut Zu . . . cchin . . . ni . . . Italian . . . ma . . . rrows . . . *(splintering crash, thump, the house shakes)* Zingara . . . A garnish of finely chopped . . . or shredded lean ham . . . *(splintering crash, thump, the house shakes)* . . . tongue . . . *(another splintering crash, thump, the house shakes)* . . . mushrooms and truffles. *(same again)* . . . Zakuski. A Russian . . . hors d'oeuvre . . . *(a very loud splintering crash, thump and the house shudders; Mrs Helmut stops knitting and crosses the room to the door and into the next room, where the sounds are coming from)* with tiny pieces of sliced . . .

Mrs Helmut (TERRY J) *(looking in the other room)* Oh, look! It's the Chancellor!

Helmut's hand immediately goes to his tie. He half makes to rise.

Helmut What? Prince Von Bulow? Here?

Mrs Helmut Ja!

Helmut Coming here?

Mrs Helmut No – he *is* here.

Helmut *(jumping to his feet)* Oh, I must go and put my old uniform on.

Mrs Helmut He won't notice, Helmut. He's dead.

Helmut Dead? Here?

Mrs Helmut Ja. In our sitting room.

Helmut *This* is our sitting room, dear.

Mrs Helmut Well, you know what I mean.

Helmut *(wagging his finger at her)* The *drawing* room!

Mrs Helmut Yes . . . but it's a *kind* of sitting room.

Helmut *(doubtfully)* Well . . .

Mrs Helmut Look!

She opens the door wider to reveal heap of about ten bodies in the other room. There is dust rising from them and a big hole in the ceiling. Helmut goes to the door.

Helmut Which one is Von Bulow?

They walk round the pile. Mrs Helmut looks at a few bodies and then points.

Mrs Helmut Here . . . look!

Helmut Oh, ja . . . and Admiral Tirpitz!

They are both momentarily overawed.

Mrs Helmut Ja.

Helmut And Von Muller... and Herr Reichner... and Hollweg and Von Graunberg...

Mrs Helmut That isn't Graunberg – *that's* Graunberg... das ist Moltke...
She lifts the body's head up by the hair as it's facing down.

Mr Helmut He's a lot older than I thought.

Mrs Helmut He's a clever man, ja.

Helmut ... and Zimmermann... and Kimpte...

Mrs Helmut What shall we do, Helmut?

Helmut We must ring the Government.

Mrs Helmut This *is* the Government, Helmut.

Helmut Oh dear.

Mrs Helmut It is a great honour to have so many members of the Government dead in our sitting room.

Helmut *Drawing* room.

Mrs Helmut Ja, well...

Helmut There are no members of the Government dead in our sitting room.

Mrs Helmut Ja, you know what I mean.

Helmut Perhaps I should make a little speech or something?

Mrs Helmut Not a speech, Helmut no...

Helmut Shall we make them a cup of tea?

Mrs Helmut It would be a waste of tea.

Helmut But we must do something – so many important people in our drawing room – we must do *something*.
They think for a little while.

Mrs Helmut We could sort them out.

Helmut And make a little list.

Mrs Helmut Ja, ja. We could put the ministers for internal affairs over against the wall, and those for foreign here by the clock.

Helmut And we can sort them out alphabetically?

Mrs Helmut Nein, nein – just put the cleanest by the door.

Helmut Ja.
They start to hump the corpses around. Helmut starts to hump Von Bulow towards the clock.

Mrs Helmut No, no! That's Von Bulow! He must go over here.

Helmut That is my reading chair.

Mrs Helmut He is the Reich Chancellor of Germany, Helmut.
Helmut starts to take him towards the reading chair.

Helmut All right . . . but I think he would have been better up against the clock, you know.

Mrs Helmut No, he would not look nice under the clock.

Helmut I did not say *under* the clock. I said *against* the clock.

Mrs Helmut Well then we could not see the clock!

Helmut We could put the Minister for Colonies under the clock. He's small.

Mrs Helmut No. Colonies are *internal* affairs. He must go against the wall. *(Helmut lifts up the head of another corpse)* Education!

Helmut starts to drag him over to the wall.

Helmut Soon we shall be able to make a list.

Mrs Helmut Ja, ja, wait a minute! . . . Who's that by the cat litter?

Helmut I don't know. I've never seen him before.

Mrs Helmut He is not a member of the Government. Get him out of here. Put him in the drawing room.

Helmut He's *in* the drawing room, my dear.

Mrs Helmut Ja, well you know what I mean.

Helmut Put him in the sitting room.

Mrs Helmut Ja, ja, the sitting room, it's all the same.

Helmut You can put him in the sitting room if he's in the drawing room.

Cut to stock film of the zeppelin.

Voice Over (MICHAEL) Count Ferdinand Von Zeppelin's behaviour on that flight in 1900 had incredible, far-reaching consequences, for one of the falling Ministers . . . *(cut to an old Edwardian photo of a German minister)* the talented Herr Von Maintlitz, architect of the new German expansionist farm policy, fell on top of an old lady *(old Edwardian photo of an elderly lady)* in Nimwegen, killing her outright. Her daughter, Alice *(old Edwardian photo of attractive young girl in the nude)* suffered severe cerebral damage from the talented minister's *(picture of Maintlitz again)* heavy briefcase *(Edwardian photo of a briefcase)* but was nursed back to life *(another Edwardian erotic postcard)* by an English doctor, Henderson. *(a Muybridge photo of a nude man)* Eventually, they married *(Edwardian nude couple)* and their eldest son, George Henderson . . . *(1930s nude man)* was the father of Mike Henderson . . . *(health and efficiency nudist camp group photo; a figure at the back is arrowed)* producer and director of 'The Golden Age of Ballooning'.

ANIMATION: *balloons as before.*

SUPERIMPOSED CAPTION: 'GOLDEN AGE OF BALLOONING'

Pointed surgical instruments fly on in formation and puncture the balloons.

SUPERIMPOSED CAPTION: 'THE GOLDEN YEARS OF COLONIC IRRIGATION'

Cut to black.

Voice Over (GRAHAM) Mr and Mrs Rita Trondheim; Reginald Bo-sankway, who would be next to Norway in a rhyming dictionary, if it included proper names, and if he pronounced his name like that.

Cut to a Victorian couple in the countryside.

SUPERIMPOSED CAPTION: 'THE MILL ON THE FLOSS'
SUPERIMPOSED CAPTION: 'PART I: BALLOONING'

The couple rise slowly in the air. Fade out.

Forty-one Michael Ellis

Animated titles.
CAPTION: 'THE END'
Roll credits.
Establishing shot of large Harrods-type store. Outside limousines and taxis are disgorging very rich customers. Small doormen in enormously large coats opening doors of cars. A man with his nose bandaged comes out of the store. One large car pulls softly up to the kerb, and as small doorman (Michael) opens its door, an enormously opulent lady (Terry J) in furs gets out. The doorman holds the door open. She knees him in the groin and walks on into the store. Chris Quinn (Eric) arrives on a bicycle. He parks the bicycle against the kerb (the doorman flings it into the road) and goes into the outer hall of the store. He passes a couple leaving who also have noses bandaged. A gaggle of customers, mostly Pepperpots, rush out. A very eager Pepperpot lady shopper, going the other way, rushes between the two and bangs into a set of glass doors which have closed behind the gaggle. She cries out with pain clutching her nose and is escorted away by a large, coated attendant. Chris Quinn looks up at the list on the wall. It reads:

> BASEMENT: DANGEROUS GASES, VIRUSES, CONTAGIOUS DISEASES, RESTAURANT AND TOILET FIXINGS.
>
> GROUND FLOOR: MENSWEAR, BOYSWEAR, EFFEMINATE GOODS HALL, ILL HEALTH FOODS.
>
> MEZZANINE: TABLEWARE, KITCHEN GOODS, SOFT FURNISHINGS, HARD FURNISHINGS, ROCK-HARD FURNISHINGS.
>
> FIRST FLOOR: COMPLAINTS.
>
> SECOND FLOOR: COSMETICS, JEWELLERY, ELECTRICAL, SATIRE.
>
> THIRD FLOOR: NASAL INJURIES HALL, OTHER THINGS.
>
> FOURTH FLOOR: GRANITE HALL – ROCKS, SHALES, ALLUVIAL DEPOSITS, FELSPAR, CARPATHIANS, ANDES, URALS, MINING REQUISITES, ATOM-SPLITTING SERVICE.
>
> FIFTH FLOOR: COMPLAINTS.
>
> SIXTH FLOOR: COMPLAINTS.
>
> SEVENTH FLOOR: COMPLAINTS.
>
> EIGHTH FLOOR: ROOF GARDEN.
>
> NINTH FLOOR: TELEVISION AERIALS.
>
> TENTH FLOOR: FRESH AIR, CLOUDS, OCCASIONAL PERIODS OF SUNSHINE.

Quinn, knowing that there are doors, goes forward more cautiously and enters. The banging of noses on glass doors is a constant background theme. Cut to the gift department. A large lady is standing by counter holding a large cylinder, with a rose attachment.

Lady (CAROL) Yes this looks the sort of thing. May I just try it?
Assistant (TERRY G) Certainly, madam.

> *The lady presses button and a sheet of flame shoots out across the hall.*

Lady Oh! Sorry! *So* sorry! *(she is happy though)* Yes that's fine.
Assistant Is that on account, madam?
Lady Yes.

> *Chris walks by, watching with interest but not much concern, passing a customer whose back is on fire but who has not noticed He approaches a counter with a sign saying 'Ant Counter'. He stands by the apparently empty counter for one moment, then rings a bell.*

Chris Hello? Hello?

> *A strange rubber-masked head appears from below the other side of he counter and gesticulates at him making a strange noise. This soon stops.*

First Assistant (GRAHAM) Oh, I'm terribly sorry . . . *(he takes off the mask to reveal a straightforward assistant)* I thought you were someone else.
Chris Oh I see, yes.
First Assistant I'm sorry sir, can I help you.
Chris Yes, yes, as a matter of fact you can, actually I was interested in the possibility . . . of purchasing one of your . . . can I ask who you thought I was?
First Assistant What?
Chris Who did you think I was . . . just then . . . when you thought I *was* somebody.
First Assistant Oh, it's no one you'd know, sir.
Chris Well I might know them.
First Assistant It's possible, obviously, but I think it's really unlikely.
Chris Well, I know quite a lot . . .
First Assistant I mean he's hardly likely to move in your circles, sir . . .
Chris Why, is he very *rich*?
First Assistant Oh, no, I didn't mean that, sir.
Chris Is he a lord or something?
First Assistant Oh, no, not at all.
Chris Well look, this is very easy to settle. What is his name?
First Assistant What?
Chris What is his name?
First Assistant Well . . . er . . .
Chris Yes?
First Assistant Michael Ellis.
Chris Who?

First Assistant Michael Ellis.

Chris I see

First Assistant Do you know him, sir?

Chris Er... Michael Ellis. Michael Ellis...

First Assistant You don't?

Chris Well, I don't remember the name.

First Assistant I think you would remember him, sir.

Chris Why do you say that?

First Assistant Well, would you remember a man six foot nine inches high, forty-ish, and he's got a long scar from here to here and absolutely no nose?

Chris ... oh, I think I do remember somebody like that...

First Assistant Well, that's not Michael Ellis.

Chris What?

First Assistant He's a small man about this high with a high-pitched voice.

Chris Right, I'm not going to buy an ant from you now.

First Assistant *(distressed)* Oh, no, please.

Chris No. You've not been properly trained. I demand another assistant.

First Assistant Oh, no, come on... please...

Chris No, I want *another assistant*.

First Assistant All right! I'll get another assistant. *(he disappears behind a curtain)*

Chris Thank you.

The same assistant reappears with a long Mandarin-style Chinese moustache.

First Assistant *(high-pitched voice)* Hello sir, can I help you, sir?

Chris No, I want a *different* assistant.

First Assistant I *am* sir, I'm Mr Abanazar, sir.

Chris Don't be silly.

First Assistant *(normal voice)* Oh no, please please please let me help you...

Chris No! I want another assistant.

First Assistant Oh, no, come on, please...

Chris If you don't give me another assistant...

First Assistant No, no, I'll be very good, sir, really. *(he becomes exaggeratedly polite)* Good morning, sir... how are you, sir... bit parky outside today... isn't it, sir...? A very nice suit you've got there, sir... you had a very close shave this morning, sir...

Chris Right I'm going!

First Assistant No, no, please... *(he takes off his moustache)* I'll get another assistant... *(he rings the bell on the counter)*

> *After a pause, very slowly indeed an identical mask to the first appears over the top of the counter right next to the first assistant, making the same noise very quietly. The first assistant sees him, starts and nudges him hard.*

Second Assistant (MICHAEL) Woooooo . . . ooooo . . .
First Assistant It's not him!
> *The second assistant makes a disappointed noise and disappears below.*

Chris *(pointing over the counter at the disappeared assistant)* I don't want him!
First Assistant Oh please, give him a chance!
Chris No!
Second Assistant *(appearing from below counter without a mask, looking immaculate)* Yes, sir, can I be of any assistance?
Chris Oh no, come on, don't try that!
Second Assistant I'm sorry, sir . . . try what?
Chris You know perfectly well what I mean.
Second Assistant I'm afraid I don't, sir.
Chris You were down behind there with a silly mask on going wooo-ooo . . .
Second Assistant I don't think I was, sir.
Chris All right, get the manager.
Second Assistant There seems to have been some sort of misunderstanding, sir.
Chris Manager!
First Assistant This *is* the manager, sir.
Chris What?
Second Assistant *(in a silly voice)* Yes, I'm the manager.
Chris Manager! *(he keeps calling)*
Second Assistant It's a smashing store this, I can't recommend it too highly, well-lit, rat-free. It's a joy to manage. Oh yes, the freshest haddock in London, second floor, third floor Ribena, ants here, television and flame throwers over there, behind them our dinner-wagon exhibition closes at six . . .
First Assistant *(nudging him)* Quick!
> *They both disappear under the counter. The real manager arrives and presents himself to Chris.*

Real Manager (TERRY J) Yes, sir? Can I help you, sir?
Chris *(noticing the 'manager' badge on his lapel)* Yes, I want to complain about the assistants on this counter.
Real Manager I'm sorry to hear that, sir, which ones?
Chris Well, they're hiding now.
Real Manager Sir?

Chris They're hiding, down there behind the counter.

Real Manager I see, sir. *(he goes round counter, looks, but obviously can't see them; Chris goes round to join in the search)* ... well ... there's nobody down here, sir.

Chris They must have crawled through here, and made their escape through 'Soft Toys'. *(he points)*

Real Manager Yes, of course.

Chris They were wearing masks and making silly noises and one of them pretended to be the manager. He spoke like this ... *(he does an impression)*

Real Manager Ah! I think I've got it, sir, I think I've got it! It's rag week.

Chris Rag week?

Real Manager Yes, you know, for charity, sir.

Chris Oh! I see. Some local college or university?

Real Manager No, no it's the *store's* rag week.

Chris The *store's* rag week?

Real Manager Yes. The senior staff don't join in much – it's for the trainees really ...

Chris It's not very good for business is it?

Real Manager Oh, it's for charity, sir. People are awfully good about it, you know. *(he rattles a collecting tin)*

Chris Yes, yes, of course. *(he puts a coin in)*

Real Manager Right, sir, I'll get you a senior assistant – ants, was it?

Chris Yes, please.

Real Manager *(calling)* Mr Snetterton? *(Mr Snetterton approaches immediately; he is clearly the first assistant with very bad short crew-cut wig on)* Could you look after this gentleman, Mr Snetterton?

Chris I don't want him!

First Assistant Oh *please*! Give me a chance!

Chris No!

Real Manager All right – Mr Hartford!

Hartford (MICHAEL) Yes – good morning, sir – can I help you?

Chris Yes, please. I'm interested in buying an ant.

Hartford Ah yes – and what price were you thinking of paying, sir?

Chris Oh, well, I hadn't actually got as far as that.

Hartford Well sir, they start about half a p. but they can go as high as three p. or even three and a half p. for a champion – inflation I'm afraid ...

Chris Well, I should think one about one and a half p., please.

Hartford Ah yes, well you should get a very serviceable little animal for that, sir. Quite frankly the half pence ones are a bit on the mangy side ... What length was sir thinking of?

Chris Oh... medium?

Hartford Medium. Medium. Here we are, sir. *(he tips some ants – which we can't see – out into a special ring on counter)* That one there is an Ayrshire, and that one there is a King George bitch I think... and that one killing the little flitbat is an Afghan.

Chris That's a nice one.

Hartford Let's see how you get on with him, eh? *(he puts it on Chris's hand)* Ah yes, he likes you. He's taken to you.

Chris What do you feed them on?

Hartford Blancmange.

Chris Blancmange?

Hartford I'm sorry. I don't know why I said that. No, you don't feed them at all.

Chris Well, what do they live on?

Hartford They don't. They die.

Chris They die?

Hartford Well of course they do, if you don't feed them.

Chris I don't understand.

Hartford You let them die, then you buy another one. It's much cheaper than feeding them and that way you have a constant variety of little companions.

Chris Oh, I see.

Hartford That's the advantage of owning an ant.

Chris Right, well I'll take this one. Oh dear, I've dropped it...

Hartford Never mind. Here's another one.

Chris Is there anything else I'll need?

Hartford Yes, sir – you'll need an ant house. *(he produces a birdcage)* This is the model we recommend, sir.

Chris Won't it get out of there?

Hartford Yes.

Chris Well what's the point of having the cage?

Hartford Well, none at all really. And then some pieces of cage furniture which will keep him entertained. *(he produces microscopic things)* Here's an ant-wheel, ant-swing, and a very nice one here, a little ladder – he can run up there and ring the bell at the top, that's a little trick he can learn.

Chris Will he live long enough?

Hartford Not really, no, but it's best to have one just in case, and here's a two-way radio he can play with... and of course you'll need the book. *(he produces an expensive-looking book, thoughtlessly slams it down where the ants were, then hurriedly brushes them away)*

Chris The book?

Hartford Yes, the book on ants.

Chris *(looking unsure)* Yes . . .

Hartford So, sir, that is, if I may say so, one hundred and eighty-four pounds one and a half p., sir.

Chris Will you take a cheque?

Hartford Yes, sir, if you don't mind leaving a blood-sample, and a piece of skin off the back of the scalp just here, sir . . . *(indicates a point behind his ear)* sorry . . . it's just for identification . . . you can't be too careful. *(he hands him a little knife and some cotton wool)*

Chris Oh, well I think I'll put it on account.

Hartford I should, sir . . . much less painful. Anyway, sir, you know what they say about an ant. A friend for life, eh? Well, a friend for its life anyway . . . *(Hartford loads the large cage, furniture, two-way radio and the book on ants into a huge box; with some difficulty he finds the ant; he picks it up carefully)* His name is Marcus. *(he drops him in the big box and pushes it across the counter; the box has on one side, in large letters 'live ant: handle with care'; it has breathing holes in it)* If the little chap should go to an early grave, sir, give us a ring and we'll stick a few in an envelope, all right?

Chris Thanks very much indeed.

Hartford Not at all, thank *you*, Mr Ellis.

Chris turns sharply. The first assistant comes quickly up to Hartford.

First Assistant Ssssshh!

Chris What did you say?

Hartford I said thank you, Mr Ellis . . .

First Assistant It's not him.

Hartford Oh!

Chris Why did you say I was Mr Ellis?

Hartford *(innocently)* Who?

First Assistant No, he didn't say that.

Chris Yes he did. I heard him say 'Thank you, Mr Ellis'.

First Assistant Oh, no, no – he said 'I'm jealous'.

Chris What?

First Assistant I'm jealous of your ant. Goodbye. Goodbye. *(waves pointedly)*

Chris *(leaving the counter)* I don't care who Michael Ellis is!

Chris passes a shop area labelled 'The Paisley Counter' where two customers are talking to mirrors in thick Irish accents. Chris moves on to lift. A little old lady passes, oblivious to the fact that her shopping trolley is smouldering. The lift comes and Chris is about to enter.

PA System Will Mr Michael Ellis please go straight to the manager's office... I'll repeat that... *(Chris wheels round and listens)* Will Mr Nigel Mellish please go straight to the manager's office.

Chris narrows his eyes suspiciously and gets into the lift cautiously. Cut to the kitchen in Chris Quinn's home. His mother is putting chopped meat into a line of at least half a dozen feeding bowls with various animal names on them. 'Baboon', 'Dromedary', 'Gorilla', 'Trout', and 'Pangolin'. There is a tiger in a cage in the middle of the kitchen, with a bowl marked 'Tiger' in front of him. A large cobra is hanging from the clothes drier and a wolf is in a cage below the sink. A monkey is on top of one of the cupboards. Chris enters with the box.

Mother (TERRY J) What have you got now?

Chris I bought an ant, mother.

Mother What d'you want one of them for! I'm not going to clean it out. You said you'd clean the tiger out, but do you? No. I suppose you've lost interest in it now. Now it'll be ant ant ant for a couple of days, then all of a sudden, 'oh, Mum, I've bought a sloth' or some other odd-toed ungulate like a tapir.

Chris It's really different this time, mum. I'm really going to look after this ant.

Mother That's what you said about the sperm whale... now your Papa's having to use it as a garage.

Chris Well, you didn't feed it properly.

Mother Where are we going to get forty-four tons of plankton from every morning? Your papa was dead vexed about that. They thought he was mad in the deli.

Chris Well at least he's got a free garage. *(growl from the tiger)*

Mother That's no good to him... his Hillman smells all fishy. *(we hear a roar)* Oh blimey, that's the tiger. He'll want his mandies.

Chris Are you giving that tiger drugs?

Mother 'course I'm giving it drugs!

Chris It's illegal.

Mother You try telling that to the tiger.

Chris I think it's dangerous.

Mother Listen... before he started fixing, he used to get through four Jehovah's witnesses a day. And he used to eat all of them, except the pamphlets.

Chris Well he's not dim.

A very loud roar and rattling of cage.

Mother All right!

She loads a syringe and starts to leave.

Chris Well, I'm going to watch one of the televisions... come on Marcus.

Forty-one 265

He puts Marcus in cage and is just about to take it through to the next room.

Mother Michael's been on the phone all day for you.

Chris Michael?

Mother You know, Michael... *Michael*. Michael *Ellis*. He's been on the phone all day... he came round twice.

Chris What did he look like?

Mother Oh, I didn't see him. The orange-rumped agouti answered the door. Only useful animal you ever bought, that.

Chris Where is he now?

Mother He's upstairs forging prescriptions for the sodding tiger!

Chris No, no, where is Michael Ellis now?

Mother Oh, I don't know... he said it wasn't important, anyway... all right, here I come.

She goes to the tiger. Chris looks confused, then shrugs and goes into the sitting room with Marcus. In the room there are about twenty old televisions on shelves. Chris selects one of the televisions, puts it on the table, switches it on and settles down to watch it with Marcus.

CAPTION (ON THE TV): 'UNIVERSITY OF THE AIR'

announcer (MICHAEL) *(on the TV)* Hello and welcome to the University of the Air. And first this afternoon, part seventeen in our series of lectures on animal communications. This afternoon we look at recent discoveries in the field of intraspecific signalling codes in the family formicidea.

Chris That's a stroke of luck, Marcus...

Cut to a restaurant. A waiter (Graham) stands at one side. Our hero (Terry J) enters, the waiter approaches him and they go through an elaborate signalling or greeting ceremony, stamping and so forth. The waiter does a strange series of movements.

CAPTION: 'MAY I TAKE YOUR COAT'

Hero stamps a lot and clasps the waiter's bottom.

CAPTION: 'I DON'T HAVE A COAT, I AM AN ANT'

Waiter routine.

CAPTION: 'AREN'T WE ALL?'

Hero routine.

CAPTION: 'WHERE'S BRUNO?'

Waiter routine.

CAPTION: 'HE GOT TRODDEN ON'

Hero routine.

CAPTION: 'WHAT'S THE SPECIAL TODAY?'

Waiter routine.

CAPTION: 'FILLET OF ANTEATER'

Hero routine.

CAPTION: 'THAT'LL LEARN IT'

Mother enters. She is rather torn and tattered and her face is bloodstained.

Mother Turn that bloody thing off!

Announcer We interrupt this programme to bring you the latest news of the extraordinary Michael Ellis saga. Apparently Michael Ellis... *(mother switches it off)*

Chris Hey! I was watching that...

Mother Bloody thing. It's upsetting the tiger. *(there is a roar and a crash of breaking crockery from the kitchen)* Oh Christ!

She dashes across to the door and goes into the kitchen; Chris quickly switches the TV on.

Announcer *(waits for noises to stop)* ... nd of the announcement. And now back to 'University of the Air', and our series for advanced medical students, 'Elements of Surgical Homeopathic Practice'. Part 68 – 'Ants'.

Chris Ah! We're in luck again, Marcus.

A surgeon appears on television. He makes a few ant gestures.

Surgeon (MICHAEL) Hello formicidophiles! Before the blood and guts that you're waiting to see, let's have a look at the anatomy of the little ant.

Cut to a drawing of an ant.

Ant Expert's Voice (TERRY J) The body of the ant is divided into three sections. *(arrow indicates)* The head, the thorax and the abdomen. They are enclosed in a hard armour-like covering called the exoskeleton, which provides some protection from other nasty little insects but unfortunately not from the dissector's scalpel. *(an animated hand with a knife slices bits off the ant)* See, nothing to it, he's not such a toughy. And his legs... they help him carry hundreds of times his own weight, but look at this... *(a hand pulls the legs off)* you're not so strong compared with me, four, five, six ... Ha!

Chris I didn't know ants had *six* legs, Marcus!

Ant Expert Well I can assure you they do, Mr Ellis.

Chris Hey! You've got two legs missing! And that's a false feeler Marcus. Blimey!

He leaps up, switches the TV off and hurls it into the corner onto a pile of used TVs, and hurries out. The tiger is quiet now. Mother, bloody and torn, is emptying a tin of 'Kit-E-Cobra' into a box marked 'Cobra'.

Chris I'm taking this ant back, mother – he's got two legs missing.

Mother Hey! Mrs McWong's been on the phone! The polar bear's been in her garden again.

Chris Well I'll get it on the way back from the store.

Mother Well mind you do – his droppings are enormous. *(Chris goes through the door, mother shouts after him)* Oh, and by the way, while you're out get us another couple of tellies would you, here's 180 quid. *(she tosses a wad out to him)*

Cut to the garden outside. There are TVs heaped in the garden path.

Chris catches the wad of notes and leaves through the garden gate as a TV van is unloading half a dozen TVs onto a trolley, prior to wheeling them into the house.

Cut back to the store. Inside the lift. Chris stands there with his ant in his hand. There are also two ladies in German national costume. The lift lady, who has a wall-eye, a wooden leg, a tooth-brace, a hearing aid, a built-up shoe, a neck-brace and a hook, is reciting.

Lift Woman (MICHAEL) Second floor . . . stationery, leather goods, nasal injuries, cricket bats, film stars, dolphinariums.

The lift stops with some difficulty. The German girls get out with their baggage. In gets a man in Greek national costume holding an oar.

Lift Woman Third floor . . . cosmetics, books, Irish massage, tribal head gear, ants . . . *(Chris starts to get out)* but not complaints about ants!

Chris Oh, where do I go to complain?

Lift Woman Straight on, then left, then right past the thing, then, up the little stairs, then right by where it's gone all soft, then down the wobbly bit, past the nail, past the brown stain on the wall to your right and it's the door marked exit straight ahead of you on the left.

Chris Thank you.

Lift Woman *(the doors shut but we can just hear her voice)* Fourth floor . . . kiddies' vasectomies . . .

The ant counter. It is obviously the same place with a roughly made sign 'Complaints'. Chris is standing there with the original assistant, who now has a plate in his lip and an enormous false chin about eight inches long and six inches across.

Chris I don't want you.

First Assistant *(speaking with difficulty)* Oh, something wrong with your little ant friend . . . ?

Chris No! I'm not going to tell you.

First Assistant Something missing in the leg department?

The manager appears.

Manager Can I help you, sir?

Chris looks down and sees that the manager is half in a sack.

Chris No! No! No! No!

Manager Oh, it's all right, sir, it's for the sack race later on.

Chris No, no, no, I want to speak to the General Manager, I want to complain.

Manager Oh, well you want the Toupee Hall in that case, sir.

Chris The what?

Manager The Toupee Hall, Mr Ellis. *(he hops off)*

Chris approaches a stocking counter where lady assistant is serving two heavies who are trying on nylons over their heads. Chris speaks to the assistant.

Chris *(embarrassed)* Excuse me – could you tell me the way to the Toupee Hall, please?

Assistant (MICHAEL) Sorry?

Chris The Toupee Hall.

Assistant The what?

Chris The Toupee Hall.

Assistant Oh, the *Toupee Hall!* *(loudly)* Gladys, where are toupees now?

Gladys (GRAHAM) Toupees? *(people start to look)*

Assistant This gentleman wants one.

Gladys *(even louder)* A toupee?

Chris Well, no, actually ...

Gladys I think they're in surgical appliances now.

Assistant That's right, yes, you go left at artificial limbs and hearing aids, right at dentures and it's on your left just by glass eyes. It doesn't say toupees to avoid embarrassing people, but you can smell 'em.

People by this time have formed a ring round to see who it is.

Chris Thank you.

As he moves off people peer at his head.

Woman *(to friend)* You can see the join.

Chris, in order to avoid this embarrassment, dives into the nearest department. A sign over the door reads 'Victorian poetry reading hall'.

Cut to a poetry reading. Wordsworth, Shelley, Keats and Tennyson are present. Chris stands quietly in the corner hoping not to be noticed.

Old Lady (GRAHAM) Good afternoon, ladies and gentlemen, it's so nice to see such a large turnout this afternoon. And I'd like to start off by welcoming our guest speakers for this afternoon, ... Mr Wadsworth ...

Wordsworth (TERRY J) Wordsworth!

Old Lady Sorry, Wordsworth ... Mr John Koots, and Percy Bysshe.

Shelley (TERRY G) Shelley!

Old Lady Just a little one, medium dry, *(a dwarf assistant pours her a sherry)* and Alfred Lorde.

Tennyson Tennyson.

Old Lady Tennis ball.

Tennyson Son, son.

Old Lady Sorry – Alfred Lord, who is evidently Lord Tennisball's son. And to start off I'm going to ask Mr Wadsworth to read his latest offering, a little pram entitled 'I wandered lonely as a crab' and it's all about ants.

Mumur of excited anticipation. Wordsworth rises rather gloomily.

Wordsworth I wandered lonely as a *cloud*
That floats on high over vales and hills
When all at once I saw a crowd
A host of golden worker ants.
Ripples of applause.

Old Lady Thank you, thank you, Mr Bradlaugh. Now, Mr Bysshe.

Shelley Shelley.

Old Lady Oh . . . *(the dwarf refills her glass)* . . . is going to read one of his latest psalms, entitled 'Ode to a crab'.

Shelley *(rising and taking his place quietly)* Well, it's not about crabs actually, it's called 'Ozymandias'. It's not an ode.
I met a traveller from an antique land
Who said 'Six vast and trunkless legs of stone
Stand in the desert
And on the pedestal these words appear
My name is Ozymandias, King of Ants
(oohs from his audience)
Look on my feelers, termites, and despair
I am the biggest ant you'll ever see
The ants of old weren't half as bold and big
And fierce as me'.
Enormous applause.

Old Lady Thank you Mr Amontillado. I'd like to ask one or two of you at the back not to soil the carpet, there is a restroom upstairs if you find the poems too exciting. *(she falls over)* Good afternoon, next, Mr Dennis Keat will recite his latest problem 'Ode to a glass of sherry'. *(she falls off the podium)*

Keats (ERIC) My heart aches and a drowsy numbness pains
My senses, as though an anteater I'd seen
(panic spreads and the audience half rise)
A nasty long-nosed brute
(screams from the audience)
With furry legs and sticky darting tongue
I seem to feel its cruel jaws
Crunch crunch there go my legs
Snap snap my thorax too
(various screaming women faint)
My head's in a twain, there goes my brain
Swallow, swallow, swallow, slurp
(he loses control)

Old Lady Mr Keats, Mr Keats, please leave immediately.

Keats It's true. Don't you see. It's true. It happens.

Old Lady *(she bustles him out)* Ladies and gentlemen, I do apologize for that last... well I hesitate to call it a pram... but I had no idea... and talking of filth... I *have* asked you once about the carpet... Now, I do appreciate that last poem was very frightening... but please! Now before we move on to tea and pramwiches, I would like to ask Arthur Lord Tenniscourt to give us his latest little plum entitled 'The Charge of the Ant Brigade'.

Tennyson Half an inch, half an inch...

Enter Queen Victoria with a fanfare, followed by Albert's coffin.

All The Queen, the Queen. *(they all bow and scrape)*

Queen Victoria (MICHAEL) My loyal subjects, we are here today on a matter of national import. My late husband and we are increasingly concerned by recent developments in literary style *(developing a German accent)* that have taken place here in Germany... er England. There seems to be an increasing tendency for ze ent... the ent... the ant... to become the dominant... was is der deutsches Entwicklungsbund...

Attendant Theme.

Queen Victoria Theme... of modern poetry here in Germany. We are not... amusiert? *(an attendant whispers)* Entertained. From now on, ants is verboten. Instead it's skylarks, daffodils, nightingales, light brigades and... was ist das schreckliche Gepong... es schmecke wie ein Scheisshaus... und so weiter. Well, we must away now or we shall be late for the races. God bless you alles.

Chris leaves. We cut to him outside a door with a sign saying 'Electric Kettles'.

Voice Psst! Electric kettles over here, sir.

A hand holding a sign saying 'Toupees' beckons him. He goes over to door and is ushered through. There are pictures of famous bald world figures with toupees on the walls.

Toupee Manager (TERRY J) Don't worry, sir, you're among friends now, sir. *(the manager has an appalling toupee; Chris sees it and tries not to stare; the manager introduces his assistants)* Mr Bradford, Mr Crawley. *(Bradford and Crawley come forward; each has a toupee worse than the others)* These are our fitters, sir. We've had a lot of experience in this field and we do pride ourselves we offer the best and most discreet service available. I don't know whether you'll believe this sir, but one of us is actually wearing a toupee at this moment...

Chris Well, you all are, aren't you?

They rush to a mirror.

Bradford (MICHAEL) Have you got one?

Crawley (GRAHAM) Yes, but I didn't know . . .
Toupee Manager I didn't realize that you two . . . I thought it was me.
Crawley Yes, I thought it was me.
Bradford So did I. *(to Crawley)* That is good.
Chris Actually, I only came in here to ask where the manager's office was.
Toupee Manager Just a minute – someone *told* you we all had toupees?
Chris No.
Crawley Oh yeah?
Bradford How did you know?
Chris Well . . . it's pretty obvious, isn't it?
Crawley What do you mean obvious! His is undetectable.
Chris Well, it's a different colour, for a start.
Bradford Is it?
Crawley 'course it isn't!
Chris And it doesn't fit in with the rest of his hair . . . it sort of sticks up in the middle.
Bradford It's better than yours.
Crawley Yes.
Chris I'm not wearing one. *(they all jeer)*
Toupee Manager Oh, I see, you haven't got one.
Crawley Why did you come in here then?
Chris They told me to find the manager's office here.
  They all jeer again.
Bradford Oh no, not again.
Crawley That's a bit lame, isn't it . . .
Chris It's the truth!
All Manager's office. *(they laugh mockingly)*
Bradford Yeah, look at it. Where did you get that, Mac Fisheries?
Toupee Manager Dreadful, isn't it?
Crawley Nylon?
Chris It's not, it's real look. *(he pulls it)*
All Oh yeah, anyone can do that.
  They all do the same. Bradford incautiously pulls his loose.
Crawley Come on, get if off.
Chris Get away.
Toupee Manager Look, do you want a proper one?
Chris No, I don't need one.
Bradford There's no need to be ashamed.
Crawley We've all owned up.

Chris I'm not wearing one.

> *They all look at each other for a moment, registering 'a hard case'.*

Toupee Manager Don't you see . . . this is something you've got to come to terms with.

Chris I am not wearing a toupee! They just told me to come in here to find the manager's office, to complain about my ant!

> *They look at each other.*

Crawley Pathetic, isn't it.

Bradford Complain about an ant?

Toupee Manager This is for your own good.

> *He grabs Chris's hair. A fight ensues in which all the assistants get their toupees dislodged. Chris is backed up against a door marked: 'Strictly no admittance'. He suddenly ducks out through this door. Cut to the other side of the door. Chris turns and double takes. It is the manager's office. There is a long line of people sitting waiting to complain. The manager looks up.*

Complaints Manager (MICHAEL) *(irritably)* All right. Take a seat.

> *Chris shuts the door and takes a seat at the end of a line of ten people waiting to complain: the German clothes prop man; the Icelandic honey week man; a Greek with a motor tyre; a man with a lawn mower with a cat sticking out of it; a man with a bandaged nose holding a dog with a bandaged nose; a lady with a bandaged nose; a lady with a bandaged nose and a pram with a small column of smoke rising from it; a rather butch lady with her head through a tennis racket; a man with a cigar in his mouth that has obviously exploded – his face is blackened and his collar awry; a man in a terrible suit with one arm twice as long as a normal sleeve and trousers that finish at mid-thigh. A uniformed shop attendant is sitting next to a rather well dressed lady in twin set and pearls, and her equally distinguished looking husband. The attendant is occasionally touching the lady's cheek and peering into her eyes. The lady and the husband stare straight ahead. Next to them is Colonel Ewing. At the desk is the lady with the flame thrower. Part of the manager's desk and the entire corner of the office are blackened and smoking.*

Lady (CAROL) You see! There ought to be a safety catch on it, I mean . . . ohhhh! *(a spurt of flame shoots out)* I mean, what if this fell into the wrong hands?

Complaints Manager Yes, madam. I'll speak to the makers personally, all right.

Lady Would you? It would put my mind at ease.

> *She leaves closing the door. We hear the flame thrower.*

Lady's Voice Sorry . . .

Complaints Manager Next?

> *The colonel gets up. As he does so Mr Zyndersky (the husband) indicates his wife and the attendant.*

Mr Zyndersky (TERRY G) He's still molesting her.

Complaints Manager Yes, yes, I'll see to you in a moment, sir. *(the colonel sits at the manager's desk)*

Colonel Ewing (GRAHAM) I've got a complaint to make.

Complaints Manager Do take a seat. I'm sorry it's on fire.

Colonel Ewing Oh, not at all. *(he sits on it)* I got used to this out east.

Complaints Manager Where were you out east?

Colonel Ewing Oh, Norway... Sweden... places like that... oh I'm awfully sorry, my suit seems to keep catching fire.

Complaints Manager Extinguisher?

Colonel Ewing Oh no, thank you, I think we'd better let it run its course. I was just thinking... Norway is not very east, is it? I should have said when I was out north. *(he slaps at the flames)*

Complaints Manager Are there many fires in Norway?

Colonel Ewing Good Lord yes. The place is a constant blaze. Wooden buildings, d'you know. I lost my wife in Norway.

Complaints Manager I am sorry to hear that.

Colonel Ewing Why, did you know her?

Complaints Manager No, I meant...

Colonel Ewing Oh I see. No, she wasn't a favourite of mine. We were out strolling across a fiord one day when one of the local matadors came out of his tree house and flung a lot of old scimitars and guillotines out that he'd got cluttering up his wine cellar and apparently rather a large proportion of them landed on my wife causing her to snuff it without much more ado.

Complaints Manager Yes, yes – well look...

Ding-dong of store PA. An announcer speaks.

Announcer Here is an important announcement about Michael Ellis. *(Chris look up at loudspeaker; everyone turns towards it)* It is now the end of 'Michael Ellis' week. From now on it is 'Chris Quinn' week. *(murmur of excitement)*

Chris What a rotten ending.

Cut to a polite, well dressed assistant at a counter with a big sign saying 'End of Show Department' behind him.

Assistant (TERRY J) Well it is one of our cheapest, sir.

Chris What else have you got?

Assistant Well, there's the long slow pull-out, sir, you know, the camera tracks back and back and mixes...

As he speak we pull out and mix through to the exterior of the store. Mix through to even wider zoom ending up in aerial view of London. It stops abruptly and we cut back to Chris.

Chris No, have you got anything more exciting?

Assistant How about a chase?

The manager and the toupee assistants suddenly appear at a door.

Manager There he is!

Exciting chase music. They pursue Chris out of the hall and into another part of the store. Then cut back to Chris at counter.

Chris Oh, no, no, no.

Assistant Walking into the sunset?

Chris What's that one?

Dramatic sunset shot on a beach. We can just see the back of Chris and the assistant as they walk together towards the setting sun. The assistant is gesturing and describing it.

Assistant You know ... two lone figures silhouetted against the dying rays of the setting sun. The music swells, you've got a lump in your throat and a tear in your eye ...

Cut back to the store.

Chris Oh no.

Assistant Oh, pity, I rather like that one ...

Chris They're all a bit off the point, you see.

Assistant Well there is one that ties up the whole Michael Ellis thing, but ...

Chris But what ... ?

Assistant Oh, no, nothing, nothing ...

Chris Look, who is this Michael Ellis?

Assistant How about a *happy* ending, sir?

A girl rushes up to Chris and flings her arms around him.

Girl (CAROL) Oh Chris! Thank God you're safe.

Assistant No, you wouldn't want that, would you.

This time we see the girl has disappeared.

Chris Why wouldn't I want that?

Assistant What about summing up from the panel? That's cheap. You know – the big match experts.

Panel in typical football panel set. Malcolm Allison, Brian Clough, and huge still of Jimmy Hill on set behind.

Malcolm Allison (MICHAEL) Yes. It was quite a good show. I think that the Michael Ellis character was a little overdone.

Brian Clough (ERIC) Well, I don't agree with that, Malcolm, quite frankly the only bit I liked was this bit with me in it now.

Cut back to the store.

Assistant No? Slow fade?

The picture begins to fade.

Chris Nnnn . . . no.

The picture comes up again.

Assistant Well, how about a sudden ending?

Blackout.

Forty-two Light entertainment war

A high street. Musical theme played on a banjo à la 'Steptoe and Son' opening. Cut to a tracking shot of two tramps (Terry J & Michael) walking jauntily along. They are very arch, over-the-top jolly fellows. They nod at the occasional passer-by and do mock bows to a city gent.
TITLE CAPTION: 'UP YOUR PAVEMENT'
CAPTION: 'BY THE REV. & MRS A. G. PHIPPS'
CAPTION: 'FROM AN IDEA BY LORD CARRINGTON'
They come to a litter bin, root in it, and one of them produces a newspaper. He hands it to the other, looks in again and brings out a pork pie. He looks in again, his eyes light up, and he produces a bottle of champagne. He passes it to his mate. He looks in again and finds two highly polished glasses. Meanwhile over all this and as they set off down the road again we hear:

Voice Over (MICHAEL) Taking life as it comes, sharing the good things and the bad things, finding laughter and fun wherever they go – it is with these two happy-go-lucky rogues that our story begins. *(by this time the tramps have walked out of shot; cut to a shot of a sports car up on the pavement with the legs of the two tramps sticking out from underneath; the music turns more urgent and transatlantic)* For it is they who were run over by Alex Diamond... *(appropriate music; a James Bond character (Graham) climbs out of the car and looks down at the dead tramps)* international crime fighter... *(shot of him rushing into a film première past photographers with flashing bulbs)* and playboy... *(cut to him on yacht)* fast-moving... tough-talking... *(still of him with Henry Kissinger; cut to him striding down a street)* and just one of the many hundreds of famous people who suffer from lumbago, the epidemic disease about which no one knows more than this man... *(we see him go into a doorway; cut to a low angle close-up of Dr Koning (John) donning gloves prior to the operation; the music changes to the Dr Kildare theme)* Dr Emile Koning... doctor... surgeon... proctologist... and selfless fighter against human suffering, whose doorbell... *(cut to a doorbell and pan down)* was the one above the hero of our story tonight... *(pan down to find the doorbell and name)* Rear-Admiral Humphrey De Vere! *(the door opens and the rear-admiral (Eric) comes striding out; naval music; he walks up the road)* Yes! This is the story of Rear-Admiral Humphrey De Vere... or rather, the story of his daughter... *(cut to a still of a young inspired and devoted nurse; the music instantly changes to the heroic)* For it was her courage, foresight and understanding that enabled us to probe beneath the sophisticated veneer of... *(mix to impressive college grounds)* the Royal Arsenal Women's College, Bagshot... *(zoom in across lawns towards the college building)* and learn the true history of this man... *(the camera suddenly veers off away from college and homes in on a*

solitary bush from which appears a seedy fellow (Michael) in a terrible lightweight suit of several years ago that has got all stained and creased around the crutch) Len Hanky! Chiropodist, voyeur, hen-teaser. The man of whom the chairman of Fiat once said . . .
Cut to a high-powered Italian businessman at a desk in a very modern casa-type Italian office.

Chairman (ERIC) Che cosa è lo stucciacatori di polli?

SUPERIMPOSED CAPTION: 'WHAT IS A HEN-TEASER?'

The phone rings. He answers it dynamically and we zoom in on his tense, alert, executive face.

Voice Over Yes! Tonight we examine the career of Gino Agnelli! The man who started from nothing to build up one of the greatest firms in Europe. *(mix through to stock film of a big car-producing plant)* And whose telescope was bought from the shop part-owned by a man who, at the age of eight, stole a penknife from the son of this man's brother's housekeeper's dental hygienist's uncle. *(as each of these things is mentioned we see a momentary flash of a still of each)* The Reverend Charlie 'Drooper' Hyper-Squawk Smith, *(at this point the freeze frame starts moving as the chaplain (Terry J) lifts himself out of the cockpit and jumps down beside his Spitfire)* the cleft-palated RAF chaplain, who single-handed shot down over five hundred German chaplains. *(smiling cheerfully he crosses off another emblem of a vicar in a German helmet on the side of the plane. Beside this is written '"Here we come Kraut" Luke 17, verse 3')* This is the story of the men who flew with him . . . it really is! *(a squadron leader, just off on a mission, runs past, and dashes into a Nissen hut)*

CAPTION: 'SOMEWHERE IN ENGLAND, 1944'

The squadron leader enters an RAF officers' mess and takes off his helmet.

Bovril (TERRY J) Morning, squadron leader.

Squadron Leader (ERIC) What-ho, Squiffy.

Bovril How was it?

Squadron Leader Top hole. Bally Jerry pranged his kite right in the how's your father. Hairy blighter, dicky-birdied, feathered back on his Sammy, took a waspy, flipped over on his Betty Harper's and caught his can in the Bertie.

Bovril Er, I'm afraid I don't quite follow you, squadron leader.

Squadron Leader It's perfectly ordinary banter, Squiffy. Bally Jerry . . . pranged his kite, right in the how's yer father . . . hairy blighter, dicky-birdied, feathered back on his Sammy, took a waspy, flipped over on his Betty Harper's and caught his can in the Bertie.

Bovril No, I'm just not understanding banter at all well today. Give us it slower.

Squadron Leader Banter's not the *same* if you say it slower, Squiffy.

Bovril Hold on, then. *(shouts)* Wingco!

Wingco (GRAHAM) Yes!

Bovril Bend an ear to the squadron leader's banter for a sec, would you?

Wingco Can do.

Bovril Jolly good.

Wingco Fire away.

Squadron Leader *(draws a deep breath and looks slightly uncertain, then starts even more deliberately than before)* Bally Jerry... pranged his kite... right in the how's yer father... hairy blighter... dicky-birdied... feathered back on his Sammy... took a waspy... flipped over on his Betty Harper's and caught his *can* in the *Bertie*...

Wingco ...No, don't understand that banter at all.

Squadron Leader Something up with my banter, chaps?

A siren goes. The door bursts open and an out-of-breath young pilot rushes in in his flying gear.

Pilot (MICHAEL) Bunch of monkeys on your ceiling, sir! Grab your egg and fours and let's get the bacon delivered.

General incomprehension. They look at each other.

Wingco Do you understand that?

Squadron Leader No, didn't get a word of it.

Wingco Sorry old man, we don't understand your banter.

Pilot You know... bally ten-penny ones dropping in the custard... *(searching for the words)* um... Charlie Choppers chucking a handful...

Wingco No, no... sorry.

Bovril Say it a bit slower, old chap.

Pilot Slower *banter*, sir?

Wingco Ra-ther!

Pilot Um... sausage squad up the blue end!

Squadron Leader No, still don't get it.

Pilot Um... cabbage crates coming over the briny?

Squadron Leader No.

Others No, no...

Stock film of a German bombing raid.

Voice Over But by then it was too late. The first cabbage crates hit London on July 7th. That was just the beginning...

Cut to a Whitehall war office conference room. A general is on the phone. Four other generals sit there.

General (GRAHAM) Five shillings a dozen? That's ordinary cabbages, is it? And what about the bombs? Good Lord, they *are* expensive!

A corporal rushes in.

Corporal (ERIC) Sir!

General Yes, what is it?

Corporal News from the Western Front, sir.

General Yes . . . ?

Corporal Big enemy attack at dawn, sir . . .

General Yes . . . ?

Corporal Well, the enemy were all wearing little silver halos, sir . . . and . . . they had fairy wands with big stars on the end . . . and . . .

General They what . . . ?

Corporal . . . and . . . they had spiders in matchboxes, sir.

General *(in disbelief)* Good God! How did our chaps react?

Corporal Well, they were jolly interested, sir. Some of them . . . I think it was the 4th Armoured Brigade, sir, they . . .

General Yes?

Corporal Well . . . they went and had a look at the spiders, sir.

General Oh my God! All right, thank you, Shirley.

A girl emerges from under the table. She is a blonde WAAF.

Corporal Sir!

General *(to a sergeant)* Get me the Prime Minister. *(the sergeant opens door, Churchill stands outside)* Not that quickly! *(the sergeant shuts the door)* Gentlemen, it's now quite apparent that the enemy are not only fighting this war on the cheap, but they're also not taking it seriously.

Ageing General (TERRY G) Bastards . . .

General First they drop cabbages instead of decent bombs . . .

Corporal The crates were probably quite expensive, sir.

General Quiet, critic! And now they're doing very silly things in one of the most vital areas of the war!

Ageing General What are we going to do, Shirley?

General Well, we've got to act fast before it saps morale. We going to show these Chinese . . .

Captain Germans, sir.

General These Germans . . . we're going to show them that no British soldier will descend to their level. Anyone found trivializing this war will face the supreme penalty that military law can provide. *(he holds a heroic pose; there is a pause during which we expect to cut; we don't; suddenly he breaks out of the pose into informality)* That was all right, I think?

Captain *(getting out drinks)* Seemed to go quite well.

Cut to a courtroom in the 1940s. A court martial is in progress. An elderly general presides, with two others beside him. There is a defence counsel, a prosecutor, a clerk of court, and two men guarding the prisoner.

Presiding General (TERRY J) Sapper Walters, you stand before this court accused of carrying on the war by other than warlike means – to wit, that you did on April 16th, 1942, dressed up as a bag of dainties, flick wet towels at the enemy during an important offensive ...

Walters (ERIC) Well, sir ...

Presiding General Shut up! Colonel Fawcett for the prosecution ...

Fawcett (MICHAEL) Sir, we all know ...

Presiding General Shut up!

Fawcett I'm sorry?

Presiding General Carry on.

Fawcett Sir, we all know the facts of the case; that Sapper Walters, being in possession of expensive military equipment, to wit one Lee Enfield .303 Rifle and 72 rounds of ammunition, valued at a hundred and forty pounds three shillings and sixpence, chose instead to use wet towels to take an enemy command post in the area of Basingstoke ...

Presiding General Basingstoke? Basingstoke in Hampshire?

Fawcett No, no, no, sir, no.

Presiding General I see, carry on.

Fawcett The result of his action was that the enemy ...

Presiding General Basingstoke *where*?

Fawcett Basingstoke Westphalia, sir.

Presiding General Oh I *see*. Carry on.

Fawcett The result of Sapper Walters's action was that the enemy received wet patches upon their trousers and in some cases small red strawberry marks upon their thighs ...

Presiding General I didn't know there *was* a Basingstoke in Westphalia.

Fawcett *(slightly irritated)* It's on the map, sir.

Presiding General What map?

Fawcett *(more irritably)* The map of Westphalia as used by the army, sir.

Presiding General Well, I've certainly never heard of Basingstoke in Westphalia.

Fawcett *(patiently)* It's a municipal borough sir, twenty-seven miles north north east of Southampton. Its chief manufactures ...

Presiding General What ... Southampton in Westphalia?

Fawcett Yes sir ... bricks ... clothing. Nearby are the remains of Basing House, burned down by Cromwell's cavalry in 1645 ...

Presiding General Who compiled this map?

Fawcett Cole Porter, sir.

Presiding General *(incredulously)* Cole Porter ... who wrote 'Kiss Me Kate'?

Fawcett No, alas not, sir ... this was the Cole Porter who wrote 'Anything Goes'. Sir I shall seek to prove that the man before this court ...

Presiding General That's the same one! *(he sings)* 'In olden days a glimpse of stocking...'

Fawcett I *beg* your pardon, sir?

Presiding General *(singing)* 'In olden days a glimpse of stocking, was looked on as something shocking, now heaven knows, anything goes...'

Fawcett No, this one's different, sir.

Presiding General How does it go?

Fawcett What, sir?

Presiding General How does *your* 'Anything Goes' go?

Walters Can I go home now?

Presiding General Shut up! *(to Fawcett)* Come on!

Fawcett Sir, really, this is rather...

Presiding General Come on, how does your 'Anything Goes' go?

Fawcett *(clearing his throat and going into an extraordinary tuneless and very loud song)*
Anything goes in.
Anything goes out!
Fish, bananas, old pyjamas,
Mutton! Beef! and Trout!
Anything goes in...

Presiding General No, that's not it... carry on.

Fawcett With respect sir, I shall seek to prove that the man before you in the dock, being in possession of the following: one pair of army boots, value three pounds seven and six, one pair of serge trousers, value two pounds three and six, one pair of gaiters value sixty-eight pounds ten shillings, one...

Presiding General Sixty-eight pounds ten shillings for a pair of *gaiters*?

Fawcett *(dismissively)* They were special gaiters, sir.

Presiding General Special gaiters?

Fawcett Yes sir, they were made in France. One beret costing fourteen shillings, one pair of...

Presiding General What was special about them?

Fawcett Oh... *(as if he can hardly be bothered to reply)* they were made of a special fabric, sir. The buckles were made of empire silver instead of brass. The total value of the uniform was there...

Presiding General Why was the accused wearing special gaiters?

Fawcett *(irritably)* They were a presentation pair, from the regiment. The total value of the uniform...

Presiding General Why did they present him with a special pair of gaiters?

Fawcett Sir, it seems to me totally irrelevant to the case whether the gaiters were presented to him or not, sir.

Presiding General I think the court will be able to judge that for themselves. I want to know *why* the regiment presented the accused with a special pair of gaiters.

Fawcett *(stifling his impatience)* He ... used to do things for them. The total value ...

Presiding General What things?

Fawcett *(exasperated)* He ... he used to oblige them, sir. The total value ...

Presiding General *Oblige* them?

Fawcett Yes sir. The total value of the uniform ...

Presiding General How did he *oblige* them?

Fawcett What, sir?

Presiding General How did he *oblige* them?

Fawcett *(more and more irritated)* He ... um ... he used to make them happy in little ways, sir. The total value of the uniform could therefore not have been less than ...

Presiding General Did he touch them at all?

Fawcett Sir! I submit that this is totally irrelevant.

Presiding General I want to know how he made them happy.

Fawcett *(losing his temper)* He used to ram things up their ...

Presiding General *(quickly)* All right! All right! No need to spell it out! What er ... what has the accused got to say?

Walters *(taken off guard)* What, me?

Presiding General Yes. What have you got to say?

Walters What can I say? I mean, how can I encapsulate in mere words my scorn for any military solution? The futility of modern warfare? And the hypocrisy by which contemporary government applies one standard to violence within the community and another to violence perpetrated by one community upon another?

Defence Counsel (TERRY G) I'm sorry, but my client has become pretentious. I will say in his defence he has suffered ...

Fawcett Sir! We haven't finished the prosecution!

Presiding Counsel Shut up! I'm in charge of this court. *(to the court)* Stand up! *(everyone stands up)* Sit down! *(everyone sits down)* Go moo! *(everyone goes moo; the presiding general turns to Fawcett)* See? Right, now, on with the pixie hats! *(everyone puts on pixie hats with large pointed ears)* And order in the skating vicar. *(a skating vicar enters and everyone bursts into song)*

Everyone Anything goes in. Anything goes out!
Fish, bananas, old pyjamas,
Mutton! Beef! and Trout!
Anything goes in. Anything goes out. *(etc.)*

Cut to the coast of Norway. Night. Tense music. Shots of big coastal guns, cliff-top fortifications.

SUPERIMPOSED CAPTIONS: 'DRAMA!' 'ACTION!'

Build up for about ten seconds. Cut to a cliff top looking out to sea. A grappling hook comes over and sticks in, then another, and another. Whispered voices, music, the tension rises as the rope is tightened. Then over the top comes a German, head blackened and camouflaged. Then others climb over; they are wearing haloes, pink tutus, jackboots, wands. They charge over. Stock film of guns blazing.

Voice Over (MICHAEL) Yes! Coming to this cinema soon! *(cut to stock film of a destroyer in the midst of a pitched sea-battle; victory-at-sea music)* The tender compassionate story of one man's love for another man in drag. *(cut to a sailor on a ship in rough sea; he calls to the captain who is in an evening gown)* THRILL! to the excitement of a night emission over Germany.

SUPERIMPOSED CAPTION: 'THRILL!'

Cut to stock shots of bombers on a night raid. Cut to interior of a bomber. Various shots of pilot and navigator. There is flak outside and explosions occasionally light up the cabin.

Voice Over When the pilot, Jennifer *(shot of the pilot)* has to choose between his secret love for Louis, *(shot of the navigator)* the hot bloodedly bi-sexual navigator and Andy, *(shot of the rear gunner)* the rear gunner, who, though quite assertive with girls, tends to take the submissive role in his relationships with men. *(cut to close-up of gritty pipe-smoking RAF top brass)* And sensational Mexican starlet, Rosetta Nixon, plays the head of Bomber Command, *(insert of WAAF)* whose passion for sea-birds ends in tragedy. *(cut to montage of war footage, explosions, guns firing, etc.)* With Ginger, as the half-man, half-woman, parrot whose unnatural instincts brought forbidden love to the aviary. And Roger as Pip, the half-parrot, half-man, half-woman, three-quarter badger, ex-bigamist negro preacher, for whom banjo-playing was very difficult, and he never mastered it although he took several courses and went to banjo college . . . er . . . and everything . . . don't miss it!

During this last lot are superimposed in quick succession the following captions:

'DRAMA'

'SUSPENSE'

'THRILLS'

'MARQUETRY'

'ADVENTURES'

'DON'T MISS IT'

'COMING TO YOUR CINEMA SOON'

Voice Over Coming to your cinema soon! *(cut to an Indian restaurant)* Only five minutes from this restaurant! But now!

Cut to the nude organist (Terry J) and 'It's' man.

It's Man (MICHAEL) It's ...

Opening titles.

At the end of the title cut to tramps exactly as at the beginning of the show.

Then cut to two twin-set-and-pearls ladies, Mrs Elizabeth III and Mrs Mock Tudor. They are in a sitting room with vulgar furnishings. By the TV, which they are watching, stands a small Arab boy (Terry G). He has electrodes fixed to him and wires stretching from a control box held by Mrs Elizabeth III. They are watching the tramps.

Mrs Mock Tudor (GRAHAM) Bloody repeats!

She presses the switch. The Arab boy flinches with pain and turns and switches off the TV set.

Mrs Elizabeth III (TERRY J) Yes, repeats or war films. It really makes you want to micturate.

Mrs Mock Tudor People on television treat the general public like idiots.

Mrs Elizabeth III Well we *are* idiots.

Mrs Mock Tudor Oh no we are *not*!

Mrs Elizabeth III Well *I* am.

Mrs Mock Tudor How do you know you're an idiot?

Mrs Elizabeth III Oh, I can show you!

Mrs Mock Tudor How?

Mrs Elizabeth III Look!

Cut to Mrs Elizabeth III coming out of the front door in a fairly well-to-do mock Tudor detached house in its own grounds. She runs headlong into a tree opposite the front door. Repeat a few times. Then she rushes into a field, digs a hole three feet deep and stands in it. Cut to her standing beside a letter box. She straps on a long false nose and bends down and pokes it through the letter box. She drinks a delicate cup of tea at a posh café and eats the whole cup. Cut to her nailing something to a lorry. The lorry starts off to reveal that she had been nailing herself to the lorry. She is dragged away. Cut to TV planners at a window, watching Mrs Elizabeth III doing silly things in a car park below them. She has a cream bun hanging down from a long stick which comes out of her hat. She walks along strangely.

Chief Executive (TERRY J) You see the public are idiots ... (*he has a conference tag on his lapel which reads 'Chief TV Planner'; he turns from the window to a conference table, piled with drinks*) Yes ... you might just as well show them the last five miles of the M2 ... they'd watch it, eh?

Cut back to Mrs Mock Tudor and Mrs Elizabeth III watching TV. There is film of the motorway on it, filmed from the bank beside a bridge.

Mrs Mock Tudor At last they done been put on something interesting.

Mrs Elizabeth III Oh, most interesting.
Cut back to the programme planners' conference.
First Planner (ERIC) *(reading figures)* ... and our figures show conclusively that the motorways are extremely popular. I mean, last time we showed a repeat of the Leicester bypass our ratings gave us 97,300,912, and ITV nought. So I do feel we ought to give B roads their own series.
Chief Executive I'm sorry ... we just can't give you a bigger budget.
Second Planner (MICHAEL) Budgie?
First Planner *(to the second planner)* No, he's left I think. *(to the chief executive)* Why not?
Chief Executive We're only one slice of the cake, you know.
Third Planner (GRAHAM) Wouldn't mind a slice of cake. Nice, chocolate cake ... delicious ...
Second Planner I had a budgie once you know, amusing little chap, used to stick his head in a bell ... what was his name, now ... Joey? ... Xerxes? ...
First Planner We could repeat them ...
Third Planner Re-heat them?
First Planner No, repeat them ...
Third Planner You don't *re-heat* cakes. Not chocolate cakes.
Chief Executive What, repeat the cakes?
Second Planner Mr Heath, that was the name of the budgie.
Chief Executive *(looking at his watch)* Good Lord, the bar's open! *(they all scramble madly to their feet)* Oh no it isn't, I was looking at the little hand that goes round very fast ...
All Damn. Blast.
They sit down again reluctantly. There is a short pause.
First Planner I've got it. We can retitle the repeats.
Second Planner What ... give them different names?
Chief Executive Wouldn't that mean retitling them?
Third Planner Brilliant!
Chief Executive Right – all we need is new titles. And they must be damned new!
Second Planner How about 'Dad's Navy'?
Chief Executive Mm, good, good.
First Planner 'Up Your Mother Next Door.'
Chief Executive Even better ...
Third Planner 'Doctor at Bee'!
All What?
There is a knock at the door.

First Planner Someone's knocking at the door.
Chief Executive Quite like it – bit long, though, I think.
Third Planner Far too long.
Second Planner 'I Married Lucy.'
Chief Executive Hasn't that been done?
Second Planner Oh, yes, a long time ago, though, they'd never remember it.
Third Planner 'Doctor at Three'!
Chief Executive What?
There is a knock at the door.
First Planner I think someone's knocking at the door.
Chief Executive That's even longer!
Second Planner 'I Married A Tree.'
Chief Executive 'And Mother Makes Tree.'
Third Planner 'Doctor At Cake'!
Continuous knocking on the door.
First Planner Look! I'm not absolutely certain, but, well I do *rather* get the impression that there is someone actually knocking at the door at this very moment.
Chief Executive That's ridiculous. Half the programme gone. Stop lengthening it!
Third Planner *(desperate)* 'I Married A Cake'?
Second Planner *(over excited)* 'I Married Three Rabbit Jelly Moulds!
Third Planner Prefer cake... specially chocky cake...
There is by now a constant hammering.
Voice *(yells from outside door)* Open the sodding door!
Chief Executive No, no. You can't say 'sodding' on the television.
All shake their heads. The door is broken in. Enter a neo-fascist-looking security man in a wheelchair with an oriental sword through his head.
Chief Executive You're supposed to *knock*.
Security Man (TERRY G) Sorry, sir, but there's trouble at studio five.
Second Planner You're in security, aren't you?
Security Man Yes, sir.
Second Planner *(triumphantly)* Well, you're not allowed to suggest programme titles. *(he smiles victoriously at others)*
Security Man Sir! It's the World War series in studio five – they're not taking it seriously any more.
First Planner You're not allowed to suggest programme titles!
Security Man *(switching on a TV set)* Look!
They rush to the monitor. One of them brushes the oriental sword which is through his head.

Security Man Ow! Mind me war wound!

All That's it! Very good title!

> *On the screen we see the court martial in progress as we saw it earlier in the show, with the whole court singing.*

Everyone Anything goes in. Anything goes out!
Fish, bananas, old pyjamas,
Mutton, beef and trout!
Anything goes in. Anything goes out! *(etc.)*

> ANIMATION: *'What a lovely day'.*
>
> *Exterior; a large, tasteful, Georgian rich person's house with extensive gardens beautifully tended, croquet hoops on the lawn – all in superb taste, nothing vulgar. The sun shines tastefully. The atmosphere is calm. Birds sing. Sound of lawnmowers and cricket in the distance. Laughter from the tennis court. Sound of gardener sharpening spades in the potting shed. Out of vision, a Red Indian struggles to free himself from the rope bonds that bind him. We hear 'Where does a dream begin' being played on a cracked record.*

CAPTION: '1942
~~EGYPT~~
~~ECUADOR~~
~~ETHIOPIA~~
ENGLAND'

> *The caption fades and we cut to an upper-class drawing room. Father, mother and daughter having tea. Four motionless servants stand behind them.*

Father (GRAHAM) I say...

Daughter (CAROL) Yes, daddy?

Father Croquet hoops look damn pretty this afternoon.

Daughter Frightfully damn pretty.

Mother (ERIC) They're coming along awfully well this year.

Father Yes, better than your Aunt Lavinia's croquet hoops.

Daughter Ugh! – dreadful tin things.

Mother I did tell her to stick to wood.

Father Yes, you can't beat wood... Gorn!

Mother What's gorn dear?

Father Nothing, nothing, I just like the word. It gives me confidence. Gorn... gorn. It's got a sort of woody quality about it. Gorn. Gorn. Much better than 'newspaper' or 'litterbin'.

Daughter Frightful words.

Mother Perfectly dreadful.

Father Ugh! Newspaper!... litterbin... dreadful tinny sort of words. Tin, tin, tin.

The daughter bursts into tears.

Mother Oh, dear, don't say 'tin' to Rebecca, you know how it upsets her.
Father *(to the daughter)* Sorry old horse.
Mother Sausage!
Father Sausage... there's a good woody sort of word, 'sausage'... gorn.
Daughter Antelope.
Father Where? On the lawn? *(he picks up a rifle)*
Daughter No, no, daddy... just the word.
Father Don't want an antelope nibbling the hoops.
Daughter No, antelope... sort of nice and woody type of thing.
Mother Don't think so, Becky old chap.
Father No, no 'antelope', 'antelope' – tinny sort of word *(the daughter bursts into tears)* Oh! Sorry old man...
Mother Really, Mansfield.
Father Well, she's got to come to terms with these things... seemly... prodding... vacuum... leap...
Daughter *(miserably)* Hate leap.
Mother Perfectly dreadful.
Daughter Sort of PVC-y sort of word, don't you know.
Mother Lower-middle.
Father Bound!
Mother Now you're talking.
Father Bound... Vole... Recidivist.
Mother Bit tinny. *(the daughter howls)* Oh! Sorry, Becky old beast. *(the daughter runs out crying)*
Father Oh dear, suppose she'll be gorn for a few days now.
Mother Caribou!
Father Splendid word.
Mother No dear... nibbling the hoops.
Father *(he fires a shot)* Caribou gorn.
Mother *(laughs politely)*
Father Intercourse.
Mother Later, dear.
Father No, no, the word, 'intercourse' – good and woody... inter... course... pert... pert thighs... botty, botty botty... *(the mother leaves the room)*... erogenous... zone... concubine... erogenous zone! Loose woman... erogenous zone... *(the mother returns and throws a bucket of water over him)* Oh thank you, dear... you know, it's a funny thing, dear... all the naughty words sound woody.
Mother Really, dear?... How about tit?

Father Oh dear, I hadn't thought about that. Tit. Tit. Oh, that's very tinny isn't it? *(the daughter returns)* Ugh! Tinny, tinny ... *(the daughter runs out crying)* Oh dear ... ocelot ... wasp ... yowling ... Oh dear, I'm bored ... I'd better go and have a bath, I suppose.

Mother Oh really, must you dear? You've had nine today.

Father All right, I'll sack one of the servants ... Simkins! ... nasty tinny sort of name. Simkins! *(he exits)*

A pilot from the RAF banter scene enters.

Pilot (MICHAEL) I say, mater, cabbage crates coming over the briny.

Mother *(frowns and shakes her head)* Sorry dear, don't understand.

Pilot Er ... cowcatchers creeping up on the conning towers ...

Mother No ... sorry ... old sport.

Pilot Caribou nibbling at the croquet hoops.

Mother Yes, Mansfield shot one in the antlers.

Pilot Oh, jolly good show. Is 'Becca about?

Mother No, she's gorn off.

Pilot What a super woody sort of phrase. 'Gorn orff'.

Mother Yes, she's gorn orff because Mansfield said tin to her.

Pilot Oh, what rotten luck ... oh well ... whole afternoon to kill ... better have a bath I suppose.

Mother Oh, Gervaise do sing me a song ...

Pilot Oh, OK.

Mother Something woody.

The pilot launches into a quite enormously loud rendering of 'She's going to marry Yum Yum'. The impact of this on the mother causes her to have a heart attack. She dies and the song ends.

Pilot For ... she's going to marry Yum Yum ... oh crikey. The old song finished her orff.

Father *(entering)* What's urp?

Pilot I'm afraid Mrs Vermin Jones appears to have passed orn.

Father Dead, is she?

Pilot 'fraid so.

Father What a blow for her.

Cut to the scene on a TV screen and pull out from the TV to Mrs Mock Tudor and Mrs Elizabeth III in their sitting room watching it.

Mrs Mock Tudor What I want to know Mrs Elizabeth III, is why they gives us crap like that, when there's bits of the Leicester bypass what have never been shown. Biskwit?

Mrs Elizabeth III *(takes biskwit from plate)* Oh, thank yew ...

> Mrs Mock Tudor switches her TV switch. The Arab boy winces in great pain and moves over to the set. He changes channels. Up comes a picture of the motorway again. Roller caption superimposed over the motorway. Appropriate 'Crossroads' type theme music

Voice Over (ERIC) *(reading the roller caption)* Appearing on the M2 were 4,281 Vauxhall Vivas, 2,117 Vauxhall Vivas de luxe, 153 Vauxhall Vivas with ...

> Mrs Elizabeth III throws the switch and the Arab boy winces with real pain and turns the knob of the television set which changes channels. On the TV set we see the same two ladies watching their set as before with the tramps on it. They continue watching until the two ladies on the set speak.

Mrs Mock Tudor *(on the TV set)* Bloody repeats.

Mrs Mock Tudor *(not on the TV set)* Bloody repeats.

> As before she switches switch. The Arab boy winces in pain and changes channels.

Mrs Elizabeth III *(on the TV set)* Yes, repeats or war films ... makes you want to ...

> She throws the switch. The Arab boy winces in pain and turns over. The White City as for show-jumping. Close-up of a mounted female rider waiting to start. Voice over of Dorian Williams.

Dorian (ERIC) Hello and welcome to Show-Jumping from White City ...

Mrs Mock Tudor Oh, moto-cross!

Dorian ... and it's Anneli Drummond-Hay on Mr Softee just about to go into jump-off against the clock. The slight pause is for the stewards who are repairing the Sound of Music. *(cut to shot of stewards who are organizing eight nuns, Von Trapp in Tyrolean gear, Julie Andrews, and the six Von Trapp children into a group forming a fence; cut back to Anneli)* ... Captain Phillips on 'Streuth' just caught one of the nuns at the very start of what would have been a fine clear round. It's a formidable obstacle this Sound of Music – eight nuns high but they're ready now, and singing. *(the group start singing 'The Hills are Alive'; the bell goes for the start of the round and the lady rider sets off towards the group)* And there's the bell. She's got 1.07 seconds to beat, but she needs a clear round to win. As she comes towards the Sound of Music and ...

> Cut away to the two ladies watching their TV. Shot from an angle so we can't see the screen.

Mrs Elizabeth III Quite exciting.

> Cut back to White City to see the lady rider has just cleared the obstacle. A cheer from the crowd. The music changes to 'Oklahoma'. Follow her round to see a similar group dressed as for 'Oklahoma'. Ten hayseeds and six wenches with a hay wagon. Most have primitive pitch forks and are sucking on straws.

Dorian ... beautifully taken, and now she needs to pick up speed for Oklahoma, but not too much. This is where Alan Jones knocked down poor Judd, but ... and ... she's taken it superbly!

Mrs Mock Tudor You notice how we never actually see the horses jump.

Cheer from TV. Cut back to White City. The horse is coming away from Oklahoma. Cut to run up to Black and White Minstrels.

Mrs Mock Tudor Wait for it ...

Cut back to White City.

Dorian And! She's taken it ... *(cheer; we actually see the lady jumper jump over the chorus of minstrels)* She's over the Minstrels. She just flicked Leslie Crowther with her tail, but the time's good, and now she turns before coming into the final jump ... this is a tough one ... It's Ben-Hur – forty-six chariots ... 6,000 spectators ... 400 slaves, lion-handlers, the Emperor Nero and the entire Coliseum. 198 feet high. 400 years across!

The lady jumper is now coming right towards the camera. Cut back to the ladies watching.

Mrs Mock Tudor I bet we don't see this one.

Cut back to horse actually jumping towards the camera. Cut to newsreader Peter Woods in a news studio.

Peter Woods We interrupt show jumping to bring you a news flash. The Second World War has now entered a sentimental stage. This morning on the Ardennes Front, the Germans started spooning at dawn, but the British Fifth Army responded by gazing deep in their eyes, and the Germans are now reported to have gone 'all coy'.

Music comes in underneath: 'When does a dream begin'. Mix to a young airman on an airfield gazing into a WAAF's eyes. Black and white, soft focus and scratched film to look like a not very good print of a Forties' film. Airman sings.

Airman (NEIL INNES) When does a dream begin?
Does it start with a goodnight kiss?
Is it conceived or simply achieved
When does a dream begin?
Is it born in a moment of bliss?
Or is it begun when two hearts are one
When does a dream exist?
The vision of you appears somehow
Impossible to resist
But I'm not imagining seeing you
For who could have dreamed of this?
When does a dream begin?
When reality is dismissed?
Or does it commence when we lose all pretence
When does a dream begin?

Mix sound to end of signature tune. Halfway through the song the credits roll, superimposed. They read:

MONTY PYTHON (SOCIAL CLASS 9)
WAS PERFORMED BY
GRAHAM CHAPMAN
TERRY GILLIAM
ERIC IDLE
TERRY JONES
MICHAEL PALIN (SOCIAL CLASS 2, ARSENAL 0)
CONCEIVED AND WRITTEN BY
GRAHAM CHAPMAN
JOHN CLEESE
TERRY GILLIAM
ERIC IDLE
NEIL INNES
TERRY JONES
MICHAEL PALIN (SOCIAL CLASS DERRY AND TOMS)
ALSO APPEARING
CAROL CLEVELAND
BOB R. RAYMOND
MARION MOULD (SOCIAL CLASS 47 ACTORS)
'WHEN DOES A DREAM BEGIN' BY NEIL INNES (SOCIAL CLASS 137 MUSICIANS)
VARIATIONS ON THE THEME BY BILL MCGUFFIE (SOCIAL CLASS 137A OTHER MUSICIANS)
MAKE-UP
MAGGIE WESTON (SOCIAL CLASS 5 TILL MIDNIGHT)
COSTUMES
ANDREW ROSE (SOCIAL CLASS 35 28 34)
FILM CAMERAMAN
STAN SPEEL (SOCIAL CLASS F8 AT 25TH SEC.)
SOUND RECORDIST
RON BLIGHT (SOCIAL CLASS UNRECORDABLE)
FILM EDITOR
BOB DEARBERG (SOCIAL CLASS LOWER 6TH) (MR POTTER'S)
SOUND
MIKE JONES (SOCIAL CLASS SLIGHTLY ABOVE THE QUEEN)
LIGHTING
JIMMY PURDIE (SOCIAL CLASS A BOTTLE OF BELL'S)
VISUAL EFFECTS
JOHN HORTON (SOCIAL CLASS ANT)
PRODUCTION ASSISTANT
BRIAN JONES (SOCIAL BUT NO CLASS)
DESIGNER
ROBERT BERK (NO SOCIAL CLASS AT ALL)
PRODUCED BY
IAN MACNAUGHTON (SOCIAL CLASS 238–470 SCOTSMAN)
BBC COLOUR (BY PERMISSION OF SIR K. JOSEPH)

Forty-three Hamlet

Tragic music in background.
CAPTION: 'HAMLET'
CAPTION: 'BY WILLIAM SHAKESPEARE'
CAPTION: 'ACT ONE'
Quick cut to a close shot of a big American car skidding round a corner. Music. Montage of close-ups of tyres, foot on accelerator shots, etc. with a deafening sound track. The car skids to a halt at the side of the kerb. Pull out to reveal it is in a smart Harley Street type location. The door opens and out gets a man in black leotard, with make-up and a small crown – Hamlet, in fact. He goes into a doorway, presses the doorbell and waits. Cut to modern psychiatrist's office. Hamlet is lying on the couch.

Hamlet (TERRY J) It's just that everywhere I go it's the same old thing. All anyone wants me to say is 'To be or not to be . . .'

Psychiatrist (GRAHAM) '. . . that is the question. Whether 'tis nobler in the mind to suffer the slings and arrows of outrageous . . .'

Hamlet *(quickly)* Yes, it's either that, or 'Oh that this too too solid flesh would melt . . .'

Psychiatrist *(taking over)* ' . . . would melt, thaw and resolve itself into a dew. Or that the everlasting had not fixed his canon 'gainst self slaughter . . .'

Hamlet Yes. All that sort of thing. And I'm just getting really fed up.

Psychiatrist *(picking up a skull)* Now do the bit about 'Alas poor Yorick . . .'

Hamlet No. I'm sick of it! I want to do something else. I want to *make* something of my life.

Psychiatrist No. I don't know that bit.

Hamlet I want to get away from all that. Be different.

Psychiatrist Well um . . . what do you want to be?

Hamlet A private dick!

Psychiatrist A private dick?

Hamlet Yes, a private dick!

Psychiatrist Why do you want to be a private dick?

Hamlet Ooh . . . why does anyone want to be a private dick? Fame, money, glamour, excitement, sex!

Psychiatrist Ah! It's the sex, is it?

Hamlet Well, that's one of the things, yes.

Psychiatrist Yes, what's the sex problem?

Hamlet Well, there's no problem.

Psychiatrist Now, come on, come on. You've got the girl on the bed and she's all ready for it.

Hamlet No, no, it's nothing to do with that.

Psychiatrist *(getting excited)* Now come on, come on, there she is, she's all ready for it. She's a real stunner, she's got great big tits, she's really well stacked and you've got her legs up against the mantelpiece.

Dr Natal (ERIC) All right, Mr Butler, I'll take over. *(a distinguished-looking man in a suit enters; the psychiatrist leaves)* Morning, Mr Hamlet. My name's Natal. Sorry to keep you waiting. Now what seems to be the problem.

Hamlet Well, I was telling the other psychiatrist . . .

Dr Natal He's . . . he's *not* a psychiatrist.

Hamlet Oh. He said he was a psychiatrist.

Dr Natal Well . . . yes . . . um, he's a *kind* of psychiatrist but he's . . . he's not a *proper* psychiatrist. He's not er . . . fully qualified . . . in, um, quite the sort of way we should want. Anyway the problem I believe is basically sexual is it?

The psychiatrist puts his head round door.

Psychiatrist I asked him that!

Dr Natal Get out! *(the psychiatrist goes; to Hamlet)* Now then, you've got the girl on the bed. You've been having a bit of a feel up during the evening. You've got your tongue down her throat. She's got both her legs up on the mantelpiece . . .

Enter a distinguished-looking psychiatrist in a white coat.

Third Psychiatrist (MICHAEL) *(quietly and authoritatively, indicating the door)* Dr Natal . . . out please!

Dr Natal I'm talking to a patient! Oh . . . *(he goes)*

Third Psychiatrist Out please! I'm terribly sorry, sir. We have a lot of problems here with bogus psychiatrists. One of the risks in psychiatry I'm afraid. Unfortunately they do tend to frighten the patient and they can cause real and permanent damage to the treatment. But I assure you that I am a completely bona fide psychiatrist. Here's my diploma in psychiatry from the University of Oxford. This here shows that I'm a member of the British Psychiatric Association, a very important body indeed. Here's a letter from another psychiatrist in which he mentions that I'm a psychiatrist. This is my psychiatric club tie, and as you can see the cufflinks match. I've got a copy of 'Psychiatry Today' in my bag, which I think is pretty convincing. And a letter here from my mother in which she asks how the psychiatry is going, and I think you'll realize that the one person you can't fool is your mother. So if you'd like to ask me any questions about psychiatry, I bet I can answer them.

Hamlet No, no, it's all right, really.

Third Psychiatrist OK, you've got this girl on your bed, you've had a few drinks, you've got her stretched out and her feet on the mantelpiece . . . *(the intercom buzzes)* Yes, what is it?

Intercom Voice There's a proper psychiatrist to see you, Dr Rufus Berg.

Third Psychiatrist Oh, oh my God! OK, thank you. *(he hurriedly changes into a police constable's uniform)* Right, thank you very much for answering the questions, sir. We'll try not to trouble you again, sir. *(exits hurriedly)*

A fourth psychiatrist rushes in.

Fourth Psychiatrist (TERRY G) Right you've got the girl down on the bed, you've got her legs up on the mantelpiece.

Two men in white coats bundle him out. Dr Natal enters.

Dr Natal Well, well done, Mr Hamlet. You've done extremely well in our disorientation tests.

Hamlet Oh? Oh!

Dr Natal You see, I'm sorry it might have confused you a little, but we do this to try to establish a very good doctor/patient relationship, you see ... we do it to sort of, as it were, to break down the barriers. All right?

Hamlet Yes fine.

Dr Natal Good! Well, you've got her legs up on the mantelpiece...

The two men come in and chase him out. Cut to a man at a consultant's desk in a smart West End surgery.

CAPTION: 'DR BRUCE, GENUINE CHAIRMAN OF THE PSYCHIATRIC ASSOCIATION'

Dr Bruce (TERRY J) On behalf of the Psychiatric Association, I should like to say that we are taking firm action to clamp down on the activities of bogus psychiatrists. In fact in many areas of modern psychiatry computers are now being increasingly used for the first basic diagnosis and this has gone a long way in eliminating the danger of unqualified impostors.

Cut to Hamlet in an office. A big, impressive-looking computer beside him.

Computer *(in tinny computer voice)* You've had your tongue down her throat and she's got her legs on the mantelpiece.

The door opens and a nurse appears.

Nurse (CAROL) Out!

The computer scuttles for the door, revealing that underneath it are six pairs of legs, in pin-striped trousers and expensive well-shaped shoes. Cut to the same computer in a field. The nurse picks up a bazooka. The computer rises into the air, the nurse fires at it and it explodes. 'Nationwide' type music and credits. Michael Charlton in a studio.

Charlton (ERIC) Good evening and welcome to 'Nationwide'. The programme where we do rather wet things nationally and also give you the chance to see some rather wet items in the Regions. Well, everyone is talking today about the Third World War which broke out this morning. But here on 'Nationwide' we're going to get away from that a bit and look instead at the latest theory that sitting down regularly in a comfortable chair can rest your legs. It sounds very nice doesn't it, but can it be done? Is it possible or practical for many of us in our jobs and with the sort of busy lives we lead to sit down in a comfortable chair just when we want? We sent our reporter John Dull to find out.

Cut to Dull sitting in a chair on Westminster Bridge.

Reporter (GRAHAM) Well, here I am on London's busy Westminster Bridge, seeing just how much time sitting down can take. Well, I arrived here by train at about 8.50, it's now 9.05, so I've been here approximately twelve minutes and if it's any encouragement, I must say that my legs *do* feel rested.

A policeman walks up to him.

Policeman (MICHAEL) Is this your chair?

Reporter Er... well no, it's a prop.

Policeman It's been stolen!

Reporter What?

Policeman This belongs to a Mrs Edgeworth of Pinner – she's standing over there.

Cut to worried middle-aged lady, standing on the other side of the road, peering across. She has an identical chair in one hand.

Reporter Ah well, it's nothing to do with me. It's just a prop which the BBC... aaargh!

The policeman pushes the reporter off and picks up the chair.

Policeman It's got her name on the bottom. *(he indicates: Mrs E. Edgeworth)*

Reporter Well er... perhaps you'd better give it back to her.

Policeman You don't believe I'm a policeman, do you?

Reporter Yes I do!

Policeman What am I wearing on my head?

Reporter A helmet.

Policeman *(correcting him)* A policeman's helmet!

Reporter Yes.

Policeman *(taking off his helmet and demonstrating)* You see that?

Reporter Yes.

Policeman That little number there?

Reporter Yes.

Policeman That is a Metropolitan Area Identification Code. No helmet is authentic without that number.

Reporter I see.

Policeman Kids' helmets, helmets you get in toy shops, helmets you buy at Christmas. None of them has that number. None of them is authentic... Hang on. *(he turns and crosses the busy road)*

Reporter Oh could I...

Policeman Hang on!

He goes across to Mrs Edgeworth, and tries to grab the other chair from her. Mrs Edgeworth resists. He clouts her and pulls the chair away. He brings it back across the road and sits down next to reporter.

Policeman Mind you I didn't join the police force just to wear the helmet you know. That just happens to be one of the little perks. There are plenty of jobs where I could have worn a helmet, but not such a *nice* helmet. *(Mrs Edgeworth is gesticulating; another policeman comes up and drags her away)* This helmet, I think, beats even some of the more elaborate helmets worn by the Tsar's private army, the so-called Axi red warriors. You know about them?

Reporter Well, no I don't.

Policeman Ah! Their helmets used to look like... you got any paper?

Reporter Well only these scripts.

The policeman gets up, looks up the street, and selects a businessman with a briefcase, who is hurrying away from him. The policeman runs up to him, grabs his arm, twists it up behind his back and wrenches the briefcase from his hand. He opens it, gets out some paper, then drops briefcase before the amazed owner, and ambles back to his chair, neatly grabbing a pen from a passer-by's inside pocket.

Policeman I'll have that!

Man I say!

The policeman sits down again and starts to draw, talking the while.

Policeman Now then. Their helmet was not unlike the bobby's helmet in basic shape. It had an emblem here, and three gold – and in those days it really was gold, that's part of the reason the Tsar was so unpopular – three gold bands surmounted by a golden eagle on the apex here. Pretty nice helmet, eh?

Reporter Yes.

Policeman I think the domed helmet wins every time over the flattened job, you know, even when they're three cornered... *(suddenly his eyes light on two office secretaries opening their packed lunch on a nearby seat)*... you want something to eat?

Reporter *(sensing what's going to happen, hurriedly)* Well no, er really...

Policeman *(approaching the girls and getting out his notebook)* Hang on. You can't park here you know.

Women *(bewildered)* We're not parked!

Policeman Not parked! What's that then?

Women That's our lunch.

Policeman Right. I'm taking that in for a forensic examination.

Women Why?

Policeman Because it might have been used as a murder weapon, that's why! *(the girls look at each other; the policeman grabs their lunch)* Yeah, not bad. Could be worse. *(to the reporter)* Beer?

Reporter *(desperately)* No, no, please ... honestly ... please ...

The policeman walks off. There is a crash of breaking glass. An alarm bell starts to ring. The reporter winces. The policeman walks into shot again, holding two bottles of beer. He sits down, opens the beers with his teeth and hands one to reporter who is very very embarrassed.

Policeman Now, the Chaldeans, who used to inhabit the area in between the Tigris and Euphrates rivers, their helmets were of the modular restrained kind of type ...

To lyrical music the camera pans across the road, and comes across a couple making love on the pavement. Pedestrians step over them.

Carol Oh Robert, tell me I'm beautiful.

Robert (TERRY J) Oh you are, you are!

Carol Oh Robert, do you mean that?

Robert Of course I do.

Carol You're not just saying that because I asked you to?

Robert Of course not.

Carol Oh Robert ... Robert, are you sure it doesn't put you off?

Robert What?

Carol My father wanting to come and live with us.

Robert No, of course I don't mind your father coming to live with us.

Carol He wouldn't just be *living* with us.

Robert What do you mean?

Carol Well, he finds it very difficult to get to sleep on his own, so I said he could sleep with us.

Robert He wants to put his bed in our room?

Carol No, no, of course not.

Robert Oh good ...

Carol Our bed is plenty big enough for three ...

Robert What?

Carol He'd just get into bed and go to sleep.

Robert No. I'm not having that!

Carol Oh Robert, I thought you loved me?

Robert Well I do, but . . .

Carol Well, he wouldn't look.

Robert He's bound to peek.

Carol No, no, he wouldn't honestly.

Robert No! No! No!!

Cut to the three of them in bed. Robert is in the middle. Father wears striped pyjamas, the others are nude. There is an uncomfortable silence.

Father (GRAHAM) You young couple just carry on. Take no notice of me . . . *(silence; they smile half-heartedly)* I don't want to feel as though I'm getting in the way.

Carol Oh no Dad, you're not.

Robert No, no.

Father Good.

Silence again.

Carol Well, I think I'll get to sleep.

Father Are you sure?

Carol Oh yes, I'm a bit tired after the wedding.

Father Bob, what about you?

Robert Oh yes, all right, yes.

Father Oh well, I seem to be O/C lights.

Carol *(to Robert)* Good night, darling.

Robert Good night.

Father Good night!

He switches the light off. It is pitch dark. There is a long pause, then a strange scraping noise like a pencil being sharpened. The scraping is followed by sawing and is eventually replaced by short sharp knocking sounds. This goes on for some time.

Carol's Voice Father. Father, what are you doing?

Father's Voice I'm making a boat.

Carol's Voice What?

Father's Voice It's a Cutty Sark. It's a model I've been making in the dark for some years now.

Carol's Voice Well, wouldn't it be better with the light on?

Father's Voice No, no, I'm making it in the dark, that's the point.

There is a click. The light goes on. He looks disappointed. In his hands is a completely shapeless mass of wood and nails.

Father Oh dear, not as accurate as I thought.

Robert It's not the Cutty Sark!

Father Well it hasn't got its sails on yet. Oh well I'll . . . I'll have a look at it in the dark room in the morning. Good night. *(grunts from the others who are already snuggling down; lights go off; silence)*

Animated opening titles.

Banging on the wall from next door.

Man (TERRY G) Shut up! Will you shut up in there!

Cut to a middle-aged man with small moustache and neat pyjamas banging on the wall with what appears to be an Indian club.

Man Shut up! *(it goes quiet next door)* That's better.

He walks to a side wall and hangs his club on a hook beneath big old-fashioned art-nouveau sign clearly labelled 'The Burlington Wallbanger. He goes across to bed and gets in. In the bed are a party of four Japanese businessmen in suits with lapel badges, two lady American tourists with rain hats on and cellophane over their hats and cameras, three other moustached English gentlemen in pyjamas, four Tour De France riders, three Swedish businessmen, and Winston Churchill. In the corner of the room are three Tour De France bicycles. All the people are watching TV. All in the bed are slightly tearstained and sad, and eating popcorn and crisps, utterly absorbed. On TV we hear a Hamlet sad speech.

Hamlet I am myself indifferent honest, but then I could accuse me of such things that it were better my mother had not borne me.

Cut to the TV set in the room. Close in on TV set to see Hamlet lying beside Ophelia, who is gazing at him intently. It is the same Hamlet we saw in the psychiatrist's scene. They are in one of those rather austere modern theatre sets.

Hamlet O fair Ophelia, nymph, in thy orisons, be all my sins remembered . . .

Ophelia (CONNIE) So anyway, you've got the girl on the bed and her legs are on the mantelpiece . . .

The nurse from the psychiatrist's office enters.

Nurse Out! *(bundles her off)*

ANIMATION: *ends with a poster 'Boxing Tonite! The Killer vs. The Champ. 15 Rounds'.*

Cut to a dressing room at Madison Square Gardens, table, chairs, towels, and the usual boxing paraphernalia. Noise of a crowd outside. The door opens and in comes Mr Gabriello, and two assistants carrying a boxer on a stretcher. Smoke, action, excitement come in with them.

Mr Gabriello (MICHAEL) That was a great fight, champ, a great fight, you hear! Oh boy, what a fight, champ, what a great fight! You nearly had him, champ, you nearly had him . . . where's his head?

Assistant I got it in here, Mr Gabriello.

He holds up a carrier bag. Gabriello goes over to it, looks inside and shouts into it.

Mr Gabriello You were great, champ, d'you hear, you were great!

Assistant *(looking in the bag)* He's got a nasty cut over his eye.

Mr Gabriello Yeah, I think it was a mistake him wearing spectacles. *(gives the bag to the assistant)* Oh well, get that sewn onto his body in time for the press pictures.

Assistant OK, Mr Gabriello.

Mr Gabriello *(to second assistant)* Wasn't he great my boy?

Second Assistant (ERIC) He was great, Mr Gabriello.

Mr Gabriello The way he kept on fighting after his head came off!

Second Assistant He was better when the head came off, Mr Gabriello. He was really dodging the guy.

Mr Gabriello Yeah, I reckon that if he could've lasted till the end of that first minute, he would've had the killer worried.

Second Assistant Sure, Mr Gabriello.

Mr Gabriello Oh he was great. Did you see his left arm?

Second Assistant No!

Mr Gabriello OK, well look around the hall after everyone's gone.

Second Assistant Do you realize Mr Gabriello, some of those guys out there paid over $2,000 for a ringside seat.

Mr Gabriello And where did the head land? Right at the back, that's justice . . . *(the door opens; a black cleaner comes in)* What d'you want?

The cleaner holds up a carrier bag.

Black Man (TERRY G) This your boy's head?

Mr Gabriello No, no, we've got his head. He ain't hurt that bad.

Second Assistant *(looking in the bag)* Hey, that's Gerry Marinello. He fought the killer last week.

Mr Gabriello OK, give it to me. I'm seeing his trainer tomorrow. I'll give it to him.

The cleaner is ushered out.

Second Assistant Hey, Mr Gabriello. The press is still outside. Are you ready for them?

Mr Gabriello How's the champ?

First Assistant *(working away with needle and thread)* Well, the head's on OK. But there's still a left arm missing.

Mr Gabriello OK, well keep the dressing gown kinda loose, OK. *(Gabriello goes to door and opens it)* OK boys, come on in!

The press surge in. The fighter is propped up.

First Reporter (TERRY J) Hey Mr Gabriello, Mr Gabriello. Did you expect your boy to last the full twenty-eight seconds?

Mr Gabriello This boy has never let me down. He's the pluckiest goddamn fighter I've ever trained.

Second Reporter (CAROL) Were you worried when his head started to come loose?

Mr Gabriello No, no, we were expecting that. I told them to expect it to and it did. He ain't stupid.

First Reporter Hey, can we have a word with the champ?

Mr Gabriello Yeah OK. But keep the questions simple.

First Reporter Hey champ! How're you feeling?

Mr Gabriello *(angrily)* I said keep the questions simple!

Second Reporter Mr Gabriello. People are saying the kid ought to be buried. His head's come off in the last six fights.

Mr Gabriello There's no question of burying the kid. He's just reaching the top.

Second Reporter Well, shouldn't he just stay in hospital?

Mr Gabriello No, he ain't going to no hospital. He's got the return fight next week.

Shot of the 'New York Times' headline 'Champ to be kept alive for big return'.

Cut to a hospital ward. Numerous doctors and nurses are listening to the radio.

Radio Voice (MICHAEL) And there's Frank Sinatra leaving the ring. Behind him is George Raft, another great boxing fan, Martin Bormann, acknowledging the applause, and with him of course is Gus Himmler, who did an awful lot for the sport in his country in the early 1940s. And here comes the champ now and he seems in good shape to meet the killer once again. Before an audience, some of them will have paid $920,000 million for the privilege of seeing this boy get beaten up. And there's the bell.

Patient *(having a heart attack on the bed in the corner)* Aaarghhh!

All Quiet!!

Radio Voice And a left and a right and a right jab that's taken the champ's shoulder off. And here's the killer again with a right and another left and a bash with a hammer and a terrific smack with a heavy thud right into the skull and there's a gaping hole right through the champ's body now. And now the killer's working on the cut eye with a series of beautifully placed punches and the head's coming loose. *(the doctors and nurses getting increasingly excited)* The champ must try and keep his head on. The killer's kicked him in the groin and he's bitten half his left buttock off and the referee's stepped in with a warning there. What a plucky fighter this champ is. He's fighting as well as I've ever seen him. Must be losing blood at a rate of a pint a second now. It's everywhere. Certainly those who paid one and a half million dollars for those ringside seats are really getting their money's worth. They're covered in it. And his head's off! *(everyone cheers)* His head that's come off in so many fights is off in the thirty-first second. It's rolled away down to the left . . . but what's happening? The killer's being talked to by the referee. There's the champ . . . plucky little body racing around the ring, trying to find his opponent. And the killer has been disqualified. *(pandemonium breaks out in the ward – some patients cheering, doctors thumping them in disagreement)* He's been disqualified . . . this great fighter who has killed more than twenty people in his boxing career has at last been defeated by this courageous headless little southpaw from New York. And there's a great roar here as the referee raises the arm of the new world heavyweight champion. What a pity the rest of his body wasn't here to see it. *(general disappointment; someone changes channels)*

Second Radio Voice (TERRY J) Well here in London it's 12.30 and time for the Robinsons. *(everyone perks up)* An everyday story of bla-di-bl-di-bla . . . *(sings 'Archers' theme tune)* da di da di da di da . . . and so on.

Mrs Non-Robinson *(on radio)* Morning Mrs Robinson.

Mrs Robinson *(on radio)* Morning Mrs Non-Robinson.

Mrs Non-Robinson Been shopping?

Mrs Robinson No, . . . I've been shopping.

During this exchange there have been six cuts to close-ups of radios of different shapes and sizes.

Mrs Non-Robinson What'd you buy?

Pull out to reveal a Pepperpot. Mrs Non-Gorilla sitting beside a radio on a park bench.

Mrs Robinson *(on radio)* A piston engine.

Mrs Non-Robinson What d'you buy that for?

Mrs Robinson It was a bargain.

Mrs Non-Gorilla (ERIC) Bloody rubbish. *(she turns the radio off)*

Quick cut to a hospital, doctor on a bed listening to the radio. It switches off.

Doctor (GRAHAM) I wanted to listen to that!

Cut back to Mrs Non-Gorilla. Another Pepperpot approaches.

Mrs Non-Gorilla Morning Mrs Gorilla.

Mrs Gorilla (MICHAEL) Morning Mrs Non-Gorilla.

Mrs Non-Gorilla Have you been shopping?

Mrs Gorilla No . . . been shopping.

Mrs Non-Gorilla Did you buy anything?

Mrs Gorilla A piston engine!

She reveals a six-cylinder car engine on a white tray, on a trolley.

Mrs Non-Gorilla What d'you buy that for?

Mrs Gorilla Oooh! It was a bargain.

Start to pan away from them, their voices become fainter . . .

Mrs Non-Gorilla Oooohhh!

Pan across a civic park, of which the only occupants are about ten Pepperpots, dressed identically, scattered around on benches. One Pepperpot is in a wheelchair. We come in to Mrs Non-Smoker, unwrapping a parcel and calling to the birds.

Mrs Non-Smoker (TERRY J) Come on little birdies . . . come on little birdies . . . tweet tweet . . . come and see what mummy's got for you . . .

She unwraps the parcel revealing a leg of lamb which she hurls at the gathered birds. A screech. She kills a pigeon. She reaches in another bag and produces two tins of pineapple chunks and throws them.

Mrs Non-Smoker Come on little birdies . . . tweety tweety . . . oooh look at this . . . tweet tweet . . . ooohhhnice one . . . come on little birdies . . .

She chortles with delight as she hurls a huge jar of mayonnaise which smashes messily. She then throws a large frozen turkey, a jar of onions, a bag of frozen peas, and a bottle of wine. We widen as Mrs Smoker, with an identical piston engine to the last Pepperpot, comes up to Mrs Non-Smoker. Quite a large area in front of Mrs Non-Smoker is littered with packaged foods and dead birds; a bird is pecking at a tin of pâté; a small pond in front of her has a swan upside down with its feet sticking in the air, a huge tin floating beside it.

Mrs Non-Smoker Oohh hello, Mrs Smoker.

Mrs Smoker (GRAHAM) Hello, Mrs Non-Smoker.

Mrs Non-Smoker What, you been shopping then?

Mrs Smoker Nope . . . I've been shopping!

Mrs Non-Smoker What d'you buy?

Mrs Smoker A piston engine!

Mrs Non-Smoker What d'you buy that for?

Mrs Smoker It was a bargain!

Mrs Non-Smoke How much d'you want for it?

Mrs Smoker Three quid!

Mrs Non-Smoker Done. *(she hands over the money)*

Mrs Smoker Right. Thank you.

Mrs Non-Smoker How d'you cook it?

Mrs Smoker You don't cook it.

Mrs Non-Smoker You can't eat that raw!

Mrs Smoker Ooooh . . . never thought of that. Oh, day and night, but this is wondrous strange . . .

Mrs Non-Smoker . . . and therefore is a stranger welcome it. There are more things in Heaven and Earth Horatio, than are dreamt of in your philosophy. But come, the time is out of joint. Oh cursed spite, that ever I was born to set it right. Let's go together.

They get up and go. Fade to black.

CAPTION: 'ACT TWO – A ROOM IN POLONIUS'S HOUSE'

Cut to a Frank Bough type presenter. Behind him are sports pictures.

Presenter (MICHAEL) Hello, and welcome to 'A Room in Polonius's House'. Well tonight is European Cup night. One result is already in from Munich. The European Cup, first round, second leg, Bayern Munchen 4,397, Wrexham 1. So Wrexham going through there on aggregate. Well, now it's time for racing, so let's go straight over to Epsom and Brian McNutty.

Cut to a dentist's surgery. A dentist is filling a patient. He talks to camera.

SUPERIMPOSED CAPTION: 'LIVE FROM EPSOM'

Dentist (TERRY J) Well over here at Epsom, there are chances a-plenty for those who want to make a good start in . . .

Patient Dentistry.

Dentist Dentistry. It's a well-off suburb, so most people have their own teeth and surgeries are opening at a rate of four or five a week

Cut to a housewife in a back garden standing in front of a washing line with really nasty stained washing on it: some man's trousers with very nasty stain on crotch and running down the leg, a badly torn sheet with melted chocolate biscuit stuck on it, a huge bra, with cups eighteen inches across, two pieces of streaky bacon and a fried egg pegged on the line, and more dirty washing.

CAPTION: 'LIVE FROM EPSOM'

Housewife (GRAHAM) Well, it's only forty-four minutes from the West End on the train and it's not too built up, so you can have a nice garden. And the people of Epsom are a very nice class of person. *Cut to a property developer in a main street.*

CAPTION: 'LIVE FROM EPSOM'

Property Dealer (MICHAEL) Well here in High Street Epsom, there are ample opportunities for all kinds of redevelopment. As you can see, *(he indicates old houses)* behind me now there are a high level of low density consumer units, still not fully maximizing site value. This could be radically improved by a carefully planned programme of demolition. And of course most of the occupants are . . . er . . . elderly folks, so they wouldn't put up much of a fight.

Cut to Epsom Racecourse, and a presenter, Brian MacThighbone, up against the paddock rail.

CAPTION: 'LIVE FROM EPSOM'

Brian (ERIC) Good afternoon. Well in fact there's still a few minutes to go before the main race on the card this afternoon – the Queen Victoria Handicap. So let's have a quick word with the winner of the last race, one of the season's top jockeys – Ronnie Mau-Mau. *(a jockey's cap comes into shot, which is all we ever see of him)* Good afternoon,

Ronnie.

First Jockey (MICHAEL) Good afternoon, Brian.

Brian *(pointing his stick-mike down)* A very fine ride there, Ronnie.

First Jockey Well, a fine horse, Brian. You know you can't go wrong.

Brian Do you fancy your chances for the Derby?

First Jockey *(vigorously nodding)* Oh very definitely, very definitely, indeed, certainly Brian.

Brian Well, let's just see if a colleague of yours agrees with that. Let's just have a quick word with Desmond Willet. Afternoon Des.

Another different silk hat comes into the bottom of frame. Again all we see is the jockey's cap.

Second Jockey (GRAHAM) *(Irish accent)* Afternoon, Brian. *(he shakes his head)* No chance, no chance at all.

First Jockey *(nodding vigorously)* No, no I think you're wrong there, Des, with the right kind of going, he's going to be in there at the finish, Des.

Second Jockey *(shaking vigorously)* No chance, there's no chance.

Brian Well in fact I can see last season's top jockey, Johnny Knowles. *(two caps move over)* Good afternoon, Johnny.

Pause. Not even a cap is seen.

Third Jockey *(faintly)* Hello, Brian.

Brian Er, could we have a box for Johnny please. *(a cap comes into sight)* Thank you.

Third Jockey Hello, Brian.

Brian That's better. Well there you are. Three very well-known faces from the racing world. Thanks very much for coming along this afternoon, lads.

All Not at all. *(vigorous nodding of caps)*

Brian And best wishes for the Derby.

All Ah, thank you Brian, thanks very much. *(they leave nodding)*

Brian Well in fact I hear they're ready for us now at the start of the main race this afternoon. So let's go right away and join Peter, at the start. *A view of the starting stalls, shot so we cannot see inside.*

CAPTION: '3.15 QUEEN VICTORIA HANDICAP'

Voice Over (ERIC) Well they're under starter's orders for this very valuable Queen Victoria Handicap. And they're off, *(the starting stall doors fly open; out come eight identically dressed Queen Victorias who go bustling off up the field)* and Queen Victoria got a clean jump off, followed by Queen Victoria, Queen Victoria and Queen Victoria. It's Queen Victoria from Queen Victoria and Queen Victoria. It's Queen Victoria making the early running on the inside. And at the back Queen Victoria already a couple of lengths behind the leaders. Queen Victoria now moved up to challenge Queen Victoria with Queen

Victoria losing ground. Queen Victoria tucked in neatly on the stand side with a clear view. Queen Victoria still the back marker as they approach the halfway mark, but making ground now, suddenly pass Queen Victoria with Queen Victoria, Queen Victoria and Queen Victoria still well placed as they approach the first fence. *(a low angle shot as the Queen Victorias appear over the fence and thunder towards the camera)* And at the first fence it's Queen Victoria just ahead of Queen Victoria and Queen Victoria falling away in third place. And Queen Victoria in the lead as they ...

Cut back to the presenter in the studio; he is completely dressed as Queen Victoria, apart from his face.

Presenter (MICHAEL) Well a very exciting race there at Epsom. And now over to the European Cup at Barcelona where the latest news is that Miguel Otana, the burly Real Madrid striker was sent off for breaking wind in the forty-third minute. He'd already been cautioned for pursing his lips earlier on in the game and now he's off! So let's see a playback of that ... Brian.

Cut to Brian, dressed the same way.

Brian (ERIC) Yes ... er ... well as you can see ... there's Otana now *(brief stock shot of football match)* ... he gets the ... er ... through ball from Gomez *(cut back to Brian)* and er ... he makes no attempt to play the ball. He quite deliberately lets off! And to my mind he was within the box and the referee had no option whatsoever but to send him off.

Cut to the presenter.

Presenter Jimmy?

We cut to the real Jimmy Hill dressed as Queen Victoria, veil, crown and all.

Jimmy Hill Good evening.

Presenter What do you make of that?

Jimmy Hill Well the referees really are clamping down these days. Only last week the Belgian captain was sent off for having a Sony radio cassette player. And Gonerelli, the huge Italian defender, was sent off in Turin for having his sitting and dining room knocked through to form an open living area.

Cut to the presenter.

Presenter Hamlet?

Cut to Hamlet.

Hamlet Good evening.

Cut quickly back to the presenter.

Presenter Well you've got the girl on the bed and her legs up on the mantelpiece ...

The nurse enters.

Nurse Out, out, come on, come on, out ... *(she hustles the presenter out of studio)*

Animated sketch.

CAPTION: 'ACT FIVE – A HAM IN THE CASTLE'

Mix to the theatre set we saw before. All the cast are dressed as Queen Victorias, except for Hamlet and Ophelia.

First Queen Victoria Let four captains bear Hamlet like a soldier to the stage. For he was likely had he been put on to have proved most royally...

SUPERIMPOSED CAPTION: 'THE END'

They come on and take bows. Superimposed Python credits in Shakespearian style and graphics.

MONTY PYTHON
BY WILLIAM SHAKESPEARE
DRAMATIS PERSONAE
HAMLET – TERRY JONES
A BACHELOR FRIEND OF HAMLET'S
GRAHAM CHAPMAN
QUITE A BUTCH FRIEND OF HAMLET'S BUT STILL A BACHELOR
TERRY GILLIAM
A FRIEND OF HAMLET'S WHO, THOUGH MARRIED, STILL SEES
HAMLET OCCASIONALLY
MICHAEL PALIN
A VERY CLOSE BACHELOR FRIEND OF HAMLET'S WHO, THOUGH
ABOVE SUSPICION, DOES WEAR RATHER LOUD SHIRTS
ERIC IDLE
ANOTHER PART OF THE DRAMATIS PERSONAE:
A FRIEND OF HAMLET'S WHO LOVES BACHELORS – CAROL
CLEVELAND
A JIMMY HILL NEAR LONDON – JIMMY HILL
A BACHELOR GENTLEMAN – BOB E. RAYMOND
AN OPHELIA – CONSTANCE BOOTH
A LOONY, BUT NOT A BACHELOR – SIR K. JOSEPH
ADDITIONAL BLANK VERSE
J. CLEESE (NO RELATION) (OF HAMLET'S, THAT IS)
PERSONAE NON DRAMATIS BUT TECHNICALIS
(SOME BACHELORS, SOME NOT)
A MAKER-UPPER
MAGGIE WESTON
A COSTUME DESIGNER AND BACHELOR
ANDREW ROSE
A CAMERAMAN OF LONDON
STAN SPEEL
A SOUND RECORDIST OF ILL REPUTE
JOHN BLIGHT
AN EDITOR OF FILM WHO IS PARTLY BACHELOR AND PARTLY
VEGETABLE WITH MINERAL CONNECTIONS
BOB DEARBERG

A STUDIO SOUND MAN
MIKE JONES
A LIGHTING SCOTSMAN
JIMMY PURDIE
A VISUAL EFFECTOR KEEN ON BACHELORS
JOHN HORTON
AN ASSISTANT PRODUCER FRIEND OF HAMLET S
BRIAN JONES
A DESIGNER WHO PREFERS MARRIED MEN BUT KNOWS QUITE A FEW BACHELORS
VALERIE WARRENDER
A PROFESSIONAL PRODUCER AND AMATEUR BACHELOR
IAN MACNAUGHTON
A BACHELOR BROADCASTING CORPORATION
BBC COLOUR.

Fade out. Fade up on a moor. An explosion has just taken place. Out of the smoke a ragged man walks towards the camera.

Man (MICHAEL) And then...

Forty-four Mr Neutron

Animated titles.
A street in Ruislip, morning. A scrap cart is going down the street.
Scrap Man (TERRY J) Let's bring 'em out! Any old iron! Any old iron!
A door opens and a housewife brings out a rather sophisticated-looking ground-to-air missile system, and dumps it on the cart.
Scrap Man Thank you.
Another door opens and a couple of rather respectable-looking old ladies bring out two bazookas and assorted shells and put them by the gate. There are further contributions of arms from householders. A GPO van comes up the street, passes the scrap cart and comes to rest up by the camera. There is a pillar box with a cover on it on the pavement, plus a rostrum with PA and bunting. A lord mayor is ushered out of the van by a post office official. The mayor and several ladies sit on the rostrum. Clearing his throat, the GPO official gets up, tests the microphone and starts to speak in a slightly strange voice.
GPO Official (MICHAEL) We are here today to witness the opening of a new *box* to replace the *box* which used to stand at the corner of Ulverston Road and Sandwood Crescent. Owing to the road-widening programme carried out by the Borough Council, the Ulverston Road *box* was removed, leaving the wall *box* in Esher Road as the only *box* for the Ulverston Road area. This new *box* will enable the people of the Ulverston Road area to post letters, post-cards and small packages without recourse to the Esher Road *box* or to the *box* outside the post office at Turner's Parade which many people used to use, but which has now been discontinued owing to the opening of this *box* and also the re-organization of *box* distribution throughout the whole area, which comes into force with the opening of new *boxes* at the Wyatt Road Post Office in July. *(a moment's pause)* Nous sommes ici ce matin pour faire témoin a l'ouverture de la nouvelle *boîte* pour remplacer la *boîte* qui autrefois était placée au coin d'Ulverston Road et Sandwood Crescent. Parce que du projet pour l'élargissement de la rue qui fait par le Borough Council, la *boîte* dans Ulverston Road est remplacée, et la *boîte* de mur dans Esher Road, est la seule *boîte* pour le région d'Ulverston Road. Cette *boîte* nouvelle rendra capables les hommes d'Ulverston Road de mettre dans la poste les lettres, les carte-postales, et des petits paquets sans avant besoin de la *boîte* de mur dans Esher Road, ou les *boîtes* de la Turner's Parade bureau de poste, qui beaucoup des hommes ont fait usage mais qui est maintenant discontinuée parce que l'ouverture de cette boîte ici, et le réorganisation régionale que commence avec l'ouverture des boîtes au bureau de poste en Wyatt Road le juillet. *(a moment's pause)* Wir kommen hier heute Morgen für die Einfang auf dem neue Kabinett für die Poste.

The first two sentences of the next voice over are laid over the end of the French speech.

Voice Over (MICHAEL) A perfectly ordinary morning in a perfectly ordinary English suburb. Life goes on as it has done for years.

Cut to a suburban railway station.

Voice Over But soon this quiet pattern of life was to change irrevocably. The commonplace routine of a typical Monday morning would never be the same again, for into this quiet little community came... Mr Neutron!

A train stops at the station. The train doors open and out steps Mr Neutron. He looks like an American footballer, with enormous shoulders, tapering to a thin waist. He has very regular features and piercing eyes and is most impressive. He stands at the door of the train for a moment. The words 'Mr Neutron' are written in bold diagonally across his chest. He carries a Sainsbury's shopping bag.

Voice Over Mr Neutron! The most dangerous and terrifying man in the world! The man with the strength of an army! The wisdom of all the scholars in history! The man who had the power to destroy the world. *(animation of planets in space)* Mr Neutron. No one knows what strange and distant planet he came from, or where he was going to!... Wherever he went, terror and destruction were sure to follow.

Cut to Neutron's garden. He has three little picnic chairs out and is having tea with Mr and Mrs Entrail, a middle-aged couple. The lady, a little overdressed, dominates. Mr Entrail sits there rather sourly.

Voice Over Mr Neutron! The man whose incredible power has made him the most feared man of all time... waits for his moment to destroy this little world utterly!

Mrs Entrail (MICHAEL) Then there's Stanley... he's our eldest... he's a biochemist in Sutton. He's married to Shirley...

Mr Neutron (GRAHAM) *(in a strange disembodied voice, grammatically correct but poor in intonation)* Shirley who used to be the hairdresser?

Mrs Entrail Yes, that's right, I think she's a lovely person. *(indicates her husband)* My husband doesn't... he thinks she's a bit flash.

Mr Entrail (TERRY J) I hate 'er! I hate 'er guts.

Mrs Entrail And they, of course, they come down most weekends, so you'll be able to meet them then.

Mr Neutron I'd... love... to. Hairdressing is very interesting.

Mrs Entrail And very important, too. If you don't care for your scalp, you get rabies. Then there's Kenneth, he's our youngest. Mind you, he's a bit of a problem... at least my husband thinks he is, anyway.

Mr Entrail Nasty little piece of work, he is, I hate him!

Mrs Entrail Mind you, the one we hear so much about nowadays is Karen. She married a Canadian – he's a dentist – they live in Alberta – two *lovely* children, Gary who's three, Leslie who's six. They look like the spitting image of Karen. D'you want to see a photo . . . ?

Mr Neutron Oh, yes please.

Mrs Entrail All right.

She goes to get a photograph.

Mr Entrail They're a couple of little bastards. I hate 'em. They've got eyes like little pigs, just like their mother. She's a disaster . . . a really horrible-looking person, she is. I thought that one would stay on the shelf, but along comes this stupid dentist git. He's a real creepy little bastard, he is. I hate 'im.

Mr Neutron This is a nice area.

Mr Entrail It's like a bloody graveyard. I hate it.

Mr Neutron It's handy for the shops and convenient for the West End.

Mr Entrail If you like going to the West End. I think it's a stinking dump.

Cut to a well-guarded American government building, with the letters 'FEAR' on a board outside.

Voice Over Meanwhile in Washington, at the headquarters of 'FEAR' – the Federal Egg Answering Room – in reality a front name for 'FEEBLE' – the Free World Extra-Earthly Bodies Location and Extermination Centre . . . all was not well.

A high-security operations room – maps, charts, monitor screens. A message comes chattering over the teleprinter. A teleprinter operator rips it out and takes it over to Captain Carpenter who sits at a control desk.

Captain Carpenter (ERIC) Good God! *(he grabs a red flashing phone)* Get me the Supreme Commander Land, Sea and Air Forces, immediately!

Cut to a large room, empty apart from a very large desk with a large American eagle emblem above it. We hear American military music. There is nothing on the desk, except for a very futuristic, dynamic-looking intercom. Behind the desk the supreme commander sits. After a moment, slowly and rather surreptitiously, he sniffs his left armpit inside his jacket. Then, with a quick look around to see that no one is watching, he smells the other armpit. He sits up again, then cups his hand in front of his face to smell his breath. He looks worried still. He reaches down slowly and takes his shoe off. He has just brought it up to his nose when the intercom buzzes loudly and a light flashes. The music stops. He jumps, and quickly takes his shoe off the desk. He presses a switch on the intercom.

Commander (MICHAEL) Hello?

Voice This is Captain Carpenter sir, from FEAR.

Commander You mean FEEBLE?

Voice Yes, sir . . .

Commander What is it?

Voice Mr Neutron is missing, sir!

Commander Mr Neutron! Oh my God! OK – Surround the entire city! Send in four waves of armed paratroopers with full ground-to-air missile support! Alert all air bases! Destroy all roads! We'll bomb the town flat if we have to!

Voice Sir! Sir! He's not in Washington, sir.

Commander OK! Hold everything! Hold everything! Hold it! Lay off! Lay off ... Where is he?

Voice We don't know, sir ... all we know is he checked out of his hotel and took a bus to the airport.

Commander All right! I want a full-scale Red Alert throughout the world! Surround everyone with everything we've got! Mobilize every fighting unit and every weapon we can lay our hands on! I want ... I want three full-scale global nuclear alerts with every army, navy and air force unit on eternal standby!

Voice Right, sir!

Commander And introduce conscription!

Voice Yes, sir!

Commander Right!

He slams the intercom button down and sits there. Silence again. His eyes look from side to side then slowly he goes back to smelling himself.

Voice Over So the world was in the grip of FEAR! A huge and terrifying crisis generated by one man! *(zoom into Neutron in his front garden, weeding; behind him the group of GPO people are sitting opening another box fifty yards further down from the first one; a line of six recently opened boxes stretches up the road)* ... easily the most dangerous man the world has ever seen, honestly. Though still biding his time, he could strike at any moment. Could he be stopped in time?

A lady stops and chats to him.

Mrs Smailes (ERIC) You've got a bit of work to do there, then.

Mr Neutron Yes, it is a problem.

Mrs Smailes Mrs Ottershaw never used to bother ... then of course she was very old ... she was 206! Well, must be going ... if you need any help I'll send Frank round. He could do with a bit of exercise, ha! ha! ha! ha! ... Fat old bastard ...

She walks off. Neutron goes back to his weeding. Cut back to the supreme commander's office. He is sniffing himself again, only this time he has his whole shirt front pulled up and he is trying to smell under his shirt. The intercom goes. He quickly tucks his shirt in and depresses the switch.

Commander Yes?

Voice Captain Carpenter here, sir. We've been on red alert now for three days, sir, and still no sign of Mr Neutron.

Commander Have we bombed anywhere? Have we shown 'em we got *teeth!*
Voice Oh yes, sir. We've bombed a lot of places flat, sir.
Commander Good. Good. We don't want anyone to think we're chicken.
Voice Oh no! They don't think that, sir. Everyone's really scared of us, sir.
Commander Of us?
Voice Yes, sir.
Commander *(pleased)* Of our *power!*
Voice Oh yes, sir! They're really scared when they see those big planes come over.
Commander Wow! I bet they are. I bet they are. I bet they're *really* scared.
Voice Oh they are, sir.
Commander Do we have any figures on how scared they are?
Voice No ... no figures, sir. But they sure were scared.
Commander Ah! But it's not working?
Voice No, sir.
Commander OK. We'll try another tactic. We'll try and out-smart this Neutron guy. Yes, there's one man who could nail him.
Voice One guy? That won't frighten anyone, sir.
Commander He's the most brilliant man I ever met. We were in the CIA together. He's retired now. He breeds rabbits up in the Yukon ...
Voice What's his name, sir?
Commander His name is Teddy Salad.
Voice Salad as in ... ?
Commander Lettuces, cucumber, radishes. Yeah, yeah, yeah.
Voice Where do I find him, sir?
Commander The Yukon. Oh, and Carpenter ...
Voice Yes, sir?
Commander Make sure you get a decent disguise.
> *Cut to the Yukon. Carpenter is trekking along. He is in ballet tights and heavy make-up with a big knapsack with 'Nothing to do with FEEBLE' on the back. He comes across a log cabin in the middle of nowhere. He presses the doorbell. A rather twee little chime. The door is opened by a huge lumberjack.*

Carpenter Oh, hello. My name's Carpenter. I'm from the US Government.
Lumberjack (GRAHAM) Are you from the army?
Carpenter Er ... no ... I'm ... er ... I'm ... I'm from the ballet. The US Government Ballet.
> *The lumberjack's eyes light up.*

Lumberjack The ballet! The ballet's coming here?
Carpenter Well maybe ...

Lumberjack Oh, that's great! We love the ballet. Last year some of us from Yellow River got a party to go see the ballet in Montreal.
Dimly we can see behind the lumberjack a bevy of beautiful boys of all nations.

Carpenter Look, I was wondering...

Lumberjack Oh, we had a *marvellous* time. It was Margot Fonteyn dancing 'Les Sylphides'... oh, it was so beautiful...

Carpenter Do you know...

Lumberjack Do you know how old she is?

Carpenter Who?

Lumberjack Margot Fonteyn.

Carpenter No.

Lumberjack She's 206!

Carpenter Look, I hear there's a US *ballet* organizer round these parts by the name of Teddy Salad.

Lumberjack You mean the special agent?

Carpenter Well...

Lumberjack He's an ex-CIA man. He's not a *ballet* dancer.
Laughter from the boys in the hut.

Carpenter Well, I just want to see him on some ballet business...

Lumberjack Well, you could try the store...

Carpenter Oh, thank you. *(he turns to go)*

Lumberjack Hey! Can you get us Lionel Blair's autograph?
Carpenter walks away.

Voice Over While precious time was being lost in Canada, the seconds were ticking away for the free world...
Jarring chord. Cut to Neutron's house. He is hanging flowery print wallpaper in his sitting room. Helping him is the quite enormously vast Frank Smailes who stands rather helplessly looking up at Neutron who is on a plank between two ladders.

Voice Over Already Neutron – who, you will remember, is infinitely the most dangerous man in the world, he *really* is – was gathering allies together.

Mr Neutron Try having an omelette for your evening meal... perhaps with yoghurt and grapefruit.

Mr Smailes (MICHAEL) Oh, I've tried that... I once got down to fifty-six stone. But I couldn't stay like that. I used to take potatoes wherever I went. I used to go to the cinema with three hundredweight of King Edwards, I'd eat 'em all before I got out of the toilet. I had to go on to bread.

Mr Neutron What about salad?

Mr Smailes Teddy Salad?

Mr Neutron No, no, no – salad – as in lettuces, radishes, cucumber...

Cut to Carpenter in a log cabin trading post with trestle tables. Six Eskimos are sitting in a group at one end of the other tables. An Italian chef in a long white apron and greasy shirt, is standing over Carpenter. Carpenter sits at one table with a huge fresh salad in front of him.

Italian (MICHAEL) YOU don't like it?

Carpenter No, I didn't want to *eat* a salad. I wanted to find out about a man called Salad.

Italian You're the first person to order a salad for two years. All the Eskimos eat here is fish, fish...

Eskimo (GRAHAM) *(very British accent)* We're not Eskimos.

Second Eskimo (TERRY J) Where's our fish. We've finished our fish.

Italian What fish you want today, uh?

First Eskimo Bream please.

Italian Bream! Where do I get a bream this time of year? You bloody choosy Eskimo pests.

First Eskimo We are *not* Eskimos!

Italian Why don't you like a nice plate of canelloni?

Eskimos Eurrrrghhhh!

First Eskimo That's not fish.

Italian *(as he turns to go in kitchen)* I've had my lot of the Arctic Circle. I wish I was back in Oldham...

Carpenter crosses to the Eskimos.

Carpenter *(speaking slowly and clearly as for foreigners)* Do any of you Eskimos... speak... English?

First Eskimo We're not Eskimos!

Third Eskimo I am.

Others Sh!

Italian *(off)* Haddock!

Eskimos Where?

Carpenter *(still speaking as if to foreigners)* Do any of... you... know... a man... called... Salad?

Eskimo What, Salad as in...

Carpenter Lettuce, cucumbers, tomatoes... yes.

First Eskimo Like you have on your plate?

Carpenter Yes. That's right.

First Eskimo No, I'm afraid not.

Second Eskimo Where's our fish?

First Eskimo What does this Teddy Salad do?

Carpenter He's a... er... hen-teaser.

Quick cut to the chairman of Fiat in his office.

Chairman (ERIC) Che cosa è la stucciacatori di polli?

SUPERIMPOSED CAPTION: 'WHAT IS A HEN-TEASER?'

Cut back to the cabin.

First Eskimo No, the only Teddy Salad we know is a CIA man.

Carpenter Oh, he might know.

Eskimos *(chanting)* Gunga gunga, where's our fish?

Carpenter Where will I find him?

Second Eskimo Oh, he lives up at Kipper Sound.

Carpenter Thanks a lot.

Eskimos Fishy fishy iyoooiyooo.

First Eskimo Are you in international spying, too?

Carpenter No . . . no . . . I'm with the . . . US Ballet . . . force . . . who are you with?

First Eskimo *(leans forward confidentially)* MI6. But not a word to the Eskimos.

Eskimos Fishy fishy igooo.

The Italian chef appears.

Italian Here's your bloody fish.

First Eskimo Thank you, Anouk.

Italian I'm not an Eskimo!

Cut to Arctic wastes – ice and snow and bitter blasting winds. Carpenter – his little tadger tiny as a tapir's tits – struggles on. He stops and peers ahead. He sees a trapper figure with a sledge pulled by four huskies. Carpenter hurries on and catches him up.

Carpenter Hey! Hey!

The man stops. On his sledge are supplies including two ladies in bikinis, deep-frozen and wrapped in cellophane bags.

Carpenter Hi! I'm Carpenter of the US Ballet.

Trapper (TERRY J) Hey, great to have you around. The last decent ballet we got around here was Ballet Rambert. On Thursday they did 'Petrouchka', then on Saturday they did 'Fille Mai Gardee'. I thought it was a bit slow . . .

Carpenter *(stopping him short)* It sure is nice to see you, Mr Salad.

Trapper I ain't Salad.

Carpenter What?

Trapper You want Teddy Salad?

Carpenter Yeah . . . *(the man looks around rather furtively, to see if anyone is watching, then takes Carpenter's arm and indicates the dog team)* I don't see anyone.

Trapper The one on the end, on the right. That's Salad.

Carpenter That's a dog!

Trapper *(confidentially)* No only *bits* of it.

Carpenter What do you mean?

Trapper Listen, Teddy Salad is the most brilliant agent the CIA ever had, right?

Carpenter Right.

Trapper That's how he made his name *(indicates the dog)* – disguise!
They look at the dog in silence for a moment.

Carpenter That's incredible!

Trapper He had to slim down to one and a half pounds to get into that costume. He cut eighteen inches off each arm and over three feet off each leg. The most brilliant surgeon in Europe stuck that tail on.

Carpenter What about the head?

Trapper All of the head was removed apart from the eyes and the brain in order to fit into the costume.

Carpenter That's incredible!

Trapper D'you want to talk to him?

Carpenter Yeah, sure.

Trapper *(looking around him again)* OK, let's move over to those trees over there ... anyone might be watching.
They pull over to a lone deciduous tree in the middle of the empty tundra wastes. They pull in. The man goes round to the dog and kneels down beside it.

Trapper *(softly)* Mr Salad? ... There's Mr Carpenter to see you.

Carpenter What does he say?

Trapper *(to Carpenter)* Do you have a bone? *(Carpenter feels rather helplessly in his pockets)* It's all part of the disguise *(he produces a bone, which he gives to the dog)* OK, Teddy ... here's the bone. *(the dog tucks into the bone)* All right, you've got his trust, now, you can talk to him.

Carpenter *(kneeling rather awkwardly down beside the dog, and speaking confidentially)* Sir ... sir ... Mr Salad ... sir, I've come direct from the Commander of Land, Sea and Air Forces ... There's a pretty dangerous situation, sir. Mr Neutron ... is missing. *(he looks significantly at the dog, but the dog doesn't react)* The General says you're the only one who'll know where to find him ... What's he say?

Trapper He wants to go walkies.

Carpenter Walkies?

Trapper Yeah, he's right into it today – d'you mind taking him for walkies?
He gives the dog to Carpenter on a lead. Carpenter hesitates and then walks off with the dog, bending down occasionally and explaining the situation.

Voice Over While Carpenter took the most brilliant agent the CIA ever had for walkies, events in the world's capitals were moving fast!

Cut to a picture of the outside of 10 Downing Street. Zoom in on the door. Music: 'Rule Britannia' type theme. Cut to interior – a few circular tables, dim lighting. The decor of a rather exclusive restaurant. Subdued murmur of upper-class people stuffing their faces. A gypsy violinist is going from table to table playing and singing. In the middle of all this there is the prime minister at a big leather-topped desk, covered with official papers, three telephones, an intercom, tape recorder, a photo of Eisenhower with a very small bunch of flowers in front of it in a sort of self-contained shrine, an in/out tray, blotter, etc. The intercom buzzes.

Voice The Secretary of State to see you, Prime Minister.

Prime Minister (ERIC) Very well, show him in.

The prime minister switches off. The secretary of state enters, wending his way through the tables. He sits at the desk. He is in a rather agitated condition.

Secretary of State (MICHAEL) Prime Minister.

Prime Minister Do take a seat.

He takes a seat from the next table; the lady sitting on it falls to the floor.

Secretary of State Prime Minister, we've just had the Supreme Commander US Forces on the phone. Apparently they want a full-scale Red Alert!

Prime Minister They *what*?

The gypsy violinist has come round to the desk. He is playing a sad, slow melody and smiling encouragingly at them. They glance at him. He flashes a white smile. The secretary of state drops his voice and huddles closer to the prime minister.

Secretary of State They want a full-scale Red Alert – every troop movement . . .

As the secretary leans forward so does the gypsy, causing the secretary to break off in mid-sentence.

Prime Minister It's all right – don't worry about Giuseppe . . . *(the secretary looks at the gypsy who smiles again toothily)* He's English really.

Secretary of State Well apparently the whole structure of world peace may be threatened unless we immediately . . .

Giuseppe (TERRY J) *(heavy accent, leaning forwards)* Your anniversary, signore?

Prime Minister No, no, Giuseppe – not now.

Giuseppe *(indicating the secretary of state)* You mean zis isn't ze lady?

Prime Minister No.

Giuseppe Oh, signora . . . my mistake! I play for you 'My Mistake'. *(before the prime minister can stop him he goes into a strident Italian song)* 'My mistake, I have made my mistake! What a dreadful mistake! Is this mistake that I make!' *(strums violently and starts on the second verse)* 'Oh my mistake...'

Prime Minister Giuseppe, do you mind playing over there.

Giuseppe *(flashing a winning smile)* Very well, signor. But I play only for you... and your beautiful companion.

He moves off mysteriously, singing the mistake song.

Secretary of State Well anyway, this Mr Neutron, is located somewhere in the London area. We must find and exterminate him. The Americans say if we don't, they will.

Prime Minister *(straining to hear over noise of singing)* What?

Secretary of State The Americans say if we won't *they* will!

Prime Minister That he doesn't know *what*?

Secretary of State They'll bomb the entire London area.

Prime Minister *(getting up)* We'd better get out of here!... *(he grabs the photo of Eisenhower)*

Secretary of State They won't bomb *here*.

Prime Minister Are you sure?

Secretary of State Sure.

Prime Minister *(sitting down with great relief)* Right. When are they going to start?

Secretary of State Well apparently they haven't got Neutron yet... but when they do...

The diners have by this time joined a conga led by the gypsy violinist playing 'My Mistake'. Awfully heartily they dance past the prime minister's desk.

Cut to Arctic wastes. The wind howls. The trapper is sitting beside a fire, picking his nose thoughtfully and tending a stewpan. The dog bounds back, Carpenter on the end of his lead, breathless from trying to keep up.

Trapper Well. Did he tell you anything?

Carpenter *(worn out by the walk)* No... we chased sticks... we chased a few reindeer...

Trapper *(patting the dog)* You been chasing reindeer, have you? You're a naughty boy... yes... ain't you a naughty boy...

Carpenter Look, we haven't got much time... He hasn't given me any information yet...

Trapper OK. Tell you what, let's eat. You give him one of your meatballs, he'll tell you anything... OK?

Carpenter OK.

Suddenly the dog woofs, gets up on back legs and starts pawing the trapper.

Trapper Wait a minute – he's trying to tell us something.

A strangled, strained American voice comes from within the dog. Slightly muffled perhaps.

Dog *(Michael's voice)* Carpenter ... er ... agh ... ah ... Carpenter ...

Carpenter *(kneeling down and peering into the dog's face)* Yes, Mr Salad? Can you hear me?

Dog Yes ... yes ... it's just it's so goddam painful in here ... what's the problem?

Carpenter It's Mr Neutron, sir ... he's gone missing. The Supreme Commander wants you to take charge.

Dog I ... oh God ... I ... I ... I ...

Carpenter Yes, Mr Salad?

Dog I gotta go walkies again.

Cut to the office of the supreme commander. He is now nude behind his desk. A kidney bowl full of water is on desk; he is dabbing at himself with a sponge. The intercom buzzes. He switches it on.

Voice Still no sign of Captain Carpenter, sir ... or Mr Neutron.

Commander OK. We'll *bomb* Neutron out. Get me Moscow! Peking! and Shanklin, Isle of Wight!

Cut to stock film of B52s on a bombing raid.

Voice Over (MICHAEL) And so the Great Powers and the people of Shanklin, Isle of Wight, drew their net in ever-tightening circles around the most dangerous threat to peace the world has ever faced. They bombed Cairo, Bangkok, Cape Town, Buenos Aires, Harrow, Hammersmith, Stepney, Wandsworth and Enfield ... But always it was the wrong place.

Cut to an area of smoking rubble. A van with the words 'US Air Force' on the side trundles through the rubble. It has a loudspeaker on the top of it.

Loudspeaker Sorry Enfield! ... We apologize for any inconvenience caused by our bombing ... sorry ...

Voice Over But what of Mr Neutron, the most fearfully dangerous man in the world! The man who could destroy entire galaxies with his wrist, the man who could tear fruit machines apart with his eyeballs ... He had not been idle!

Meantime we have mixed through to Neutron's suburban sitting room.

He is standing in the doorway gazing at something off camera. He holds an envelope which he has just opened and a letter.

Voice Over In fact he had fallen in love ... with the lady who 'does' for Mrs Entrail ...

The camera pans across to a slovenly char in paisley apron, furry slippers and head scarf. Throughout this scene we hear the sound of bombers and the distant muffled sound of explosions.

Mrs Scum (TERRY J) Oh 'ello Mr N, terrible about Enfield, innit? It's all gone. So's Staines... lovely shops they used to have in Staines... and Stanmore, where the AA offices used to be. I don't know where we'll pay our AA subscriptions to now. Do you know where we'll have to pay our AA subscriptions to now, Mr N?

Mr Neutron I didn't know you were a member of the AA Mrs S.C.U.M.

Mrs Scum Oh yes. Ever since the Corsair broke down in Leytonstone... they towed it all the way to Deauville FOC. *(Mr Neutron looks blank)* Free of Charge. Well my husband Ken, K.E.N., he said...

Mr Neutron Oh, forget about your husband, Mrs S.C.U.M. – or may I call you Mrs S?

Mrs Scum You can call me Linda, if you like.

Mr Neutron No, I'd rather call you Mrs S.

Mrs Scum Oh...

Mr Neutron *(as if trying to soften the blow)* And you can call me Mr N.

Mrs Scum Well... that's what I *was* calling you.

Mr Neutron Mrs S, there is something I have to tell you...

Mrs Scum Yes, Mr N?

Mr Neutron I have just won a Kellogg's Corn Flake Competition.

Mrs Scum Oh Mr N! That's wonderful!

Mr Neutron I got the ball in exactly the right place. The prize is £5,000 in cash, or as much ice cream as you can eat.

Her eyes go round as saucers and all thoughts of returning to her marital bed vanish under the impact of such imminent wealth.

Mrs Scum £5,000!

Mr Neutron I was thinking of taking the ice cream.

Mrs Scum *(alarmed)* Oh no!

Mr Neutron It's been so hot recently.

Mrs Scum You couldn't *eat* that much ice cream Mr N.

Mr Neutron Mrs S, I can eat enormous quantities of ice cream without being sick.

Mrs Scum Oh no! Take the £5,000! Please take the £5,000.

Mr Neutron I was thinking. If we got married...

Mrs Scum Oh yes! *(she sits very close to him)*

Mr Neutron We could use the £5,000 to buy a spoon...

Mrs Scum Oh! We could buy a lot more than that!

Mr Neutron And then fill up with ice cream.

Mrs Scum No! Forget about the ice cream. We need the money.

Mr Neutron We need nothing. For there is something I have not told you Mrs S.C.U.M.

Mrs Scum Oh please call me Mrs S.

Mr Neutron No I would rather go back to calling you Mrs S.C.U.M., Mrs S.C.U.M. I am the most powerful man in the universe. There is nothing I cannot do.

Mrs Scum Oh Mr N.

Mr Neutron I want you to be my helpmate. As Tarzan had his Jane, as Napoleon had his Josephine, as Frankie Laine had whoever he had, I want you to help me in my plan to dominate the world!

Mrs Scum Oh Mr N. That I should be so lucky!

Mr Neutron You're not Jewish are you?

Cut back to the Yukon. The trapper, Captain Carpenter and the dog are still sitting round the dying campfire over the remains of supper. They are all looking a little bit bored. The dog has obviously been telling long reminiscences.

Dog Another time when I was in Cairo, I was disguised as a water hydrant. The whole top part of my head had been removed and . . .

Carpenter Please, Mr Salad, . . . you *must* tell us where Neutron is.

Dog And I functioned! D'you hear? I really worked. I could put out a fire.

Carpenter Please, Mr Salad . . .

Dog Mind you, it hurt a bit . . .

Carpenter Please, Mr Salad – there isn't much time. Where will we find Neutron?

Dog OK. Give me another meatball and I'll tell you.

Carpenter grabs a meatball and throws it down for the dog. The dog wolfs it. Carpenter and Trapper exchange glances. Carpenter bends nearer the dog. The dog finishes the meatball with much slurping. Carpenter crouches beside him patiently.

Dog OK listen carefully . . . I won't repeat this. You understand?

Carpenter Yes yes – quick.

Dog I know where Neutron is right now. I know the exact address and the exact house and the exact road . . .

Carpenter OK where is he?

Dog He's not in America . . .

Carpenter No?

Dog He's not in . . . Asia!

Carpenter No?

Dog He's not in . . . Australia!

Carpenter No?

Dog He's in . . . Europe!

Carpenter Yeah?

Dog And you wanna know where in Europe?

Carpenter Yeah!

Dog OK. OK, I'll tell you. He's in England... In London... at Number 19....

A sudden explosion completely engulfs them. Cut to the supreme commander's office. He is still nude and has an enormous display of talcs and powders on his desk. He is talking to the intercom.

Commander OK. That's the Yukon – what's left?

Voice Only Ruislip, the Gobi Desert, and your office, sir.

Commander OK! Let's start with my office. *(a big explosion)*

Cut to the Gobi Desert. Sweltering heat. We come onto a group opening a GPO box. There is a line of boxes stretching into the distance as far as the eye can see. Arabic is being spoken by the GPO official.

GPO Official Ankwat i odr inkerat Gobi Desert Ulverston Road ...

SUBTITLE: 'THIS NEW BOX COMPLETES THE ENCIRCLEMENT OF THE GOBI DESERT'

GPO Official Ik anwar, hyaddin ... *(etc.)*

SUBTITLE: 'THE POST OFFICE IS NOW IN A POSITION TO ACHIEVE COMPLETE WORLD DOMINATION'

A terrific explosion. Cut to Neutron and Mrs Scum.

Mr Neutron I will take you away from all this Mrs S.C.U.M.

Mrs Scum Oh, Mr N ... I'd follow you anywhere.

Mr Neutron We will have two weeks in Benidorm.

Mrs Scum Oh yes ... yes.

Mr Neutron And I will make you the most beautiful woman in the world.

He stretches out his hands towards her. His piercing eyes narrow in concentration. There is a flash, a jump cut, and Mrs S stands before him as dumpy and unattractive as ever, but in a brand new C&A twin set and pearls, a nice new handbag, and a rather fussy hat.

Mrs Scum Oh ... it's beautiful ... oh, Mr N, you have made my heart sing ... *(quick cut to stock film of bomber then back to Mrs Scum)* Late in life's pageant it may be ... but you have made roses bloom anew for me ... *(quick flash of bomber then back to Mrs Scum)* Life's rich harvest is being ...

Mr Neutron Shut up, Mrs S. We must hurry ...

He takes her hand and pulls her away.

Mrs Scum I'd better leave a note for Ken ... he'll be expecting us ... *(explosion)*

ANIMATION: THE WORLD DESTROYED AND BURNING.

Voice Over Has Mr Neutron escaped in time? Is the world utterly destroyed? How can Mr Neutron and his child bride survive? Will his mighty powers be of any avail against the holocaust? Stay tuned to *this* channel!

Cut to a man in a grey suit in a studio.
Man (ERIC) Hello. Well in fact what happens is that they are saved by Mr Neutron's mighty powers just as the last bomb falls on Ruislip.
SUPERIMPOSED CAPTION: 'A MAN FROM THE "RADIO TIMES"'
Man However, the Earth has been blown off its axis, and in a most dramatic and dangerous and expensive sequence, it spins off into space. There are appallingly expensive scenes of devastation and horror and the final incredibly expensive climax is reached as thousands of ape monsters in very expensive costumes descend from the sky onto these, plug up a whole city which has to be specially built and fling them all into the sea very expensively. And we can see those very expensive scenes right now. *(the credits start on his TV set)* Just after the credits have gone through . . . incidentally, these are going to be the most expensive and lavish scenes ever filmed by the BBC in conjunction with Time-Life of course . . . these are some of the technical people who have been involved in filming these very expensive scenes, expensive sound, expensive visual effects there, expensive production assistant, expensive designer . . . cheap director. Well you can see those expensive scenes right now.

CAPTION: 'THE END'
Man *(voice over)* Oh come on you can give us another minute, Mr Cotton, please.
CAPTION: 'CONJURING TODAY'
Fade up on a conjurer with a fright wig and ping-pong eyes. He holds a bloodstained saw.
Conjurer (MICHAEL) Good evening, last week we learned how to saw a lady in half. This week we're going to learn how to saw a lady into three bits and dispose of the body . . .
Two policemen chase him off the set. They run past the man from the previous announcement who is on the phone. On his TV set we see the policemen pursuing the conjurer.
Man Look if you can put on rubbish like that, and 'Horse of the Year Show', you can afford us another minute, Mr Cotton, please, I mean look at this load of old . . . *(fades out)*
Fade up on the entrance to TV Centre. The man walks out.
Voice Over (ERIC) World Domination t-shirts are available from BBC, World Domination Department, Cardiff.
A man (Terry J) hits him on the head with an absolutely enormous hammer. He falls, stunned. Fade out.

Forty-five Party Political Broadcast

CAPTION: 'A PARTY POLITICAL BROADCAST ON BEHALF OF THE LIBERAL PARTY'

Voice Over (MICHAEL) There now follows a Party Political Broadcast on behalf of the Liberal Party...

Cut to a kitchen. Mr Garibaldi is eating a packet of 'Ano-Weet'. On the back of the packet in big letters it reads 'Free Inside – The Pope + Demonstration Record'. Kevin Garibaldi is stretched out the whole length of the sofa, eating a huge plate of baked beans. His father occasionally flaps the copy of the paper he is reading at him to clear the air. The paper is called 'The Scun' and has a pin-up on the front page with big headline 'What a Scorcher! Phew! Can Resist this Miss'; at the bottom of the page in small print 'China Declares War'. The banner across top reads 'In the Scun Today "Tits and Inflation"'. Ralph Garibaldi is sitting at the table eating. At one point he stretches across the table, and his arm sticks in the butter. He tries to clean it off and knocks the sugar over. There is a large photo of Ian Smith on the wall; built around it is a plaster shrine, with flowers in front of it. Mrs Garibaldi is ironing.

She irons some underclothes, then she irons a transistor radio. Dotted about the room are a flat telephone, a flat standard lamp, and a flat cat. Valerie Garibaldi is wearing a shiny red miniskirt. She has bright yellow 'beehive' hair so stiffly lacquered that it is quite a hazard to various ornaments on the mantelpiece. She is continuously making herself up in the mantelpiece mirror which is shaped like a lavatory. The other member of the family is a very fat old dog. As we see all this, the football commentary is droning throughout on the radio.

Radio Voice (ERIC) Pratt... back to Pratt... Pratt again... a long ball out to Pratt... and now Pratt is on the ball, a neat little flick back inside to Pratt, who takes it nicely and sends it through on the far side to Pratt, Pratt with it but passes instead to Pratt, Pratt again, oh and well intercepted by the swarthy little number nine, Concito Maracon. This twenty-one-year-old half back, remarkably stocky for 6' 3", square shouldered, balding giant, hair flowing in the wind, bright-eyed, pert, young for his age but oh so old in so many ways. For a thirty-nine-year-old you wouldn't expect such speed. Normally considered slow, he's incredibly fast as he wanders aimlessly around, sweeping up and taking the defence to the cleaners. Who would have thought, though many expected it, that this remarkable forty-five-year-old, 9' 4" *dwarf* of a man, who is still only seventeen in some parts of the world, would ever really be... Oh and there was a goal there apparently... and now it's Pratt... back to Pratt... Pratt again... a long ball to Pratt... *(crackle)*

By now mother has succeeded in flattening the radio with the iron. She folds it neatly and puts it on the pile.

Mr Garibaldi (TERRY J) I like this Ano-Weet, it really unclogs me.
Ralph Garibaldi knocks a bowl onto the floor. It smashes.
Mrs Garibaldi (ERIC) Oh, *do* be careful.
Ralph Garibaldi (MICHAEL) Sorry, Mum.
Kevin opens another can of beans and pours them on to his plate, throwing the tin on the floor. The radio drones on.
Mr Garibaldi I mean a lot of others say they unclog you, but I never had a single bowel movement with the 'Recto-Puffs'.
Ralph Garibaldi Now if we . . . *(he knocks the cereal box off table)* Oh, sorry, Mum . . . Now if we lived in Rhodesia there'd be someone to mop that up for you.
Valerie Garibaldi (GRAHAM) *(turning from the mirror in mid make-up)* Don't be so bleedin' stupid. If you lived in bleedin' Rhodesia, you'd be out at bleedin' fascist rallies every bleedin' day. You're a bleedin' racist, you bleedin' are.
Mr Garibaldi Language!
Valerie Garibaldi Well he gets on my sodding wick.
Mr Garibaldi That's better.
Mother is now ironing the telephone and the cat. She irons them flat and pins them on the line.
Mr Garibaldi No, the stuff I liked was that stuff they gave us before the war, what was it – Wilkinson's Number 8 Laxative Cereal. Phew. That one went through you like a bloody Ferrari . . .
The doorbell rings.
Mrs Garibaldi Now, who's that at this time of day . . . *(she goes out)*
Mr Garibaldi If it's the man to empty the Elsan, tell him it's in the hall.
Mrs Garibaldi Right, dear.
Mr Garibaldi And make sure that you hold it the right way up!
Ralph Garibaldi Dad . . . ?
A middle-aged man appears from the broom cupboard.
Strange Man Yeah?
Ralph Garibaldi No no, *my* Dad . . .
Strange Man Oh . . . *(he gets back into the cupboard again)*
Ralph Garibaldi Dad? Why is Rhodesia called Rhodesia? . . . *(he knocks the teapot on to the floor, it smashes)* Oh sorry, Dad.
Cut to the doorway in the hall. A man in a dark suit, very smart and well-dressed, is doing strange kung-fu antics.
Mrs Garibaldi No . . . no, really, thank you very much . . . no, thank you for calling, not today, thank you. Good morning.
She shuts the door on him. As she does so Mr Garibaldi shouts out to her.

Mr Garibaldi Who was that?

Mrs Garibaldi *(coming in again)* The Liberal Party candidate, darling... oh... what have you done *now*?

Ralph Garibaldi Sorry, mum. *(he is standing beside the sink which has just split in two)* I was just washing up...

Mrs Garibaldi Go and sit down!

Ralph Garibaldi Mum? Do *you* know why Rhodesia's called Rhodesia?

Mr Garibaldi Do you remember 'Go-Eazi'? They were hopeless... *(Kevin opens another can of beans; dad notices in disgust and flaps his paper again)* little black pellets... tasted foul and stuck inside you like flooring adhesive.

Valerie Garibaldi *(she has finally finished her startling make-up)* Right, I'm off.

Mrs Garibaldi When are you coming back tonight?

Valerie Garibaldi 3 a.m.

Mrs Garibaldi I think it's disgusting... you a Member of Parliament.

Mr Garibaldi I heard you in the hall last night, snogging away.

Valerie Garibaldi I wasn't *snogging*!

Mr Garibaldi Sounded like snogging to me. I could hear his great wet slobbering lips going at yer... and his hand going up yer...

Mrs Garibaldi Dad!

Strange Man *(coming out of the cupboard)* Yes.

Mrs Garibaldi No... not you.

Strange Man Oh! *(he goes back in again)*

Mrs Garibaldi Just mind your language...

Ralph knocks a leg off the table. It collapses entirely.

Ralph Garibaldi Oh, sorry, Mum.

Kevin Garibaldi (TERRY G) *(too fat and flatulent to get up)* I've run out of beans!

Valerie Garibaldi We was talking, we was not snogging.

Mr Garibaldi Talking about snogging, I'll bet...

The phone rings. Mrs Garibaldi answers it.

Valerie Garibaldi If you must know, we was talking about Council re-housing.

Mrs Garibaldi *(on the phone)* Would it mean going to live in Hollywood?

Kevin Garibaldi *(desperate but unable to move)* I run out of beans!

Mr Garibaldi Where to re-house his right hand, that's what he was interested in!

Mrs Garibaldi And has Faye Dunaway *definitely* said yes?

Valerie Garibaldi He is the Chairman of the Housing sub-committee.

The bell rings.

Mr Garibaldi Snogging sub-committee, more like...

Mrs Garibaldi Ralph, do answer that door will you!

Kevin Garibaldi Beans!!

Mrs Garibaldi Shut up!!

Ralph Garibaldi Yes, Mum.

Mr Garibaldi *(shouting to Ralph)* If it's the man from the Probbo-Rib, tell him it's in the bed.

Ralph gets up. As he goes he knocks the leg off the old-fashioned gas cooker. It falls to one side bringing down shelves next to it, plates, crockery and a section of the wall, revealing the hallway the other side.

Ralph Garibaldi Sorry, mum.

Kevin Garibaldi *(roaring)* Beans! Beans!

Mrs Garibaldi Shut up!

A man in a Tarzan outfit, except with a postman's hat and a little mailbag, swings in on a liana shouting a jungle yell.

Postman Postma-a-a-n!!

A gong sounds. They all stop acting.

Cut to stock film of ladies applauding.

Pull out from this stock film to see that it is on a screen in a presentation studio. A glittery compère is also applauding sycophantically at his desk, above which is the glittery slogan 'Most Awful Family in Britain, 1974. Sponsored by "Heart Attacko Margarine"'.

Presenter (MICHAEL) A very good try there, by the Garibaldi family of Droitwich in Worcestershire. Professor...

Pull out further to pick up a panel of three distinguished, rather academic-looking people.

Professor K (ERIC) Well, I can't make up my mind about this family... I don't think there was the sustained awfulness that we really need. I mean, the father was appalling...

Two other members of the panel nod vigorous agreement.

Lady Organs (TERRY J) Appalling... yes...

Professor K He was dirty, smelly and distasteful... and I liked him very much... but..

Presenter Lady Organs?

Lady Organs Well... they were an unpleasant family certainly, but I don't think we had enough of the really gross awfulness that we're looking for...

Presenter Well, harsh words there for the Garibaldi family of Droitwich in Worcestershire, at present holders of the East Midlands Most Awful Family Award (Lower Middle-Class Section) but unable today to score more than fifteen on our disgustometer. Well with the scores all in from the judges, the Garibaldis are number three... and a surprise number two ... the Fanshaw-Chumleighs of Berkshire ... *(he turns to the screen)*

A very elegant breakfast table in beautifully tasteful surroundings. Four upper-class folk – two women (Michael and Graham), two men (Eric and Terry J) – are talking most incredibly loudly at each other, with quite appalling accents. An appalling din altogether. They talk just about at the same time as each other.

First Person What a super meal.

Second Person Absolutely super. Pat and Max are coming down from Eton to help Daddy count money.

Third Person How absolutely super.

Fourth Person My man at Poirer's says I could have my whole body lifted for £5,500.

Fourth Person How super ... *(etc.)*

Cut back to the panel nodding thoughtfully.

Presenter Well, some of the wonderful behaviour that made the Fanshaw-Chumleighs the second Most Awful Family in Britain 1974. But the winners, by a clear ten point margin, are once again the awful Jodrell family of Durham. Unfortunately, we're not allowed to show you some of the performance that won them an award, but I assure you it was of the very highest standard, was it not, Lady Organs?

Lady Organs Oh, yes, superb ... Mr Jodrell – you know, the old grandfather, who licks the ...

Presenter *(hurriedly)* Yes, yes ...

Lady Organs He's superb. His gobbing is consistent and accurate. His son is a dirty foul little creature, and those frightful scabs which Mrs Jodrell licks off the cat are ...

Presenter *(during this speech we cut to the same image on a TV screen)* Well, thank you very much, Lady Organs ... and from all of us all, well done to the Jodrells ... and to all of you, not forgetting those of you who may be halfway in between, without whom, of course, and not forgetting who made it all possible, when, and we'll be back, until then and so it's goodnight from me and here's wishing you a safe journey home, thank you for watching this show, don't forget it was all great fun, I've enjoyed it, and I hope you watching at home have enjoyed it too.

He is switched off, and fades into a dot. Pull back to reveal that the TV which has just been switched off is in a dirty old sitting room in which all the characters are really unpleasant Pepperpots. They are dressed more or less identically, except that son has a school cap and a blazer over his Pepperpot gear. He has a satchel and National Health glasses. The father has moustache and glasses and a Fair-Isle jersey.

Mother (ERIC) The Jodrells win every bloody year ... makes you vomit ... Dad?

Dad (TERRY J) Yes?

Mother Get your stinking feet off the bread.

Dad I'm only wiping the cat's do's off.

Son (TERRY G) Mum?

Mother Shut yer face, Douglas.

Son I wanted some corn-plasters.

Mother Shut up and eat what you got.

A cat set into the wall, i.e. a glove puppet, screeches as if someone had pulled its tail outside.

Dad Some fat bastard at the door! *(to the cat)* Shut up! *(she slaps it; it expires)* She takes a couple of milk bottles out. Standing on the doorstep is a man with a Nordic accent in female national costume. He has a tray labelled 'Icelandic Honey Week'

Man (GRAHAM) A strong hive of bees contains approximately 75,000 bees. Each honey bee must make 154 trips to collect one teaspoon of honey. Hello, sir.

Dad What do you want!

Man Would you like to buy some of our honey, sir?

Mother What you doing in here?

Man Which would you like, the Californian Orange Blossom, the Mexican, the New Zealand, or the Scottish Heather?

Mother He can't eat honey. It makes him go plop plops.

Man Come on, please try some.

Dad All right I'll have some Icelandic Honey.

Man No, there is no such thing.

Dad You mean you don't make any honey at all?

Man No, no, we must import it all. Every bally drop. We are a gloomy people. It's so crikey cold and dark up there, and only fish to eat. Fish and imported honey. Oh strewth!

Mother Well why do you have a week?

Man Listen Buster! In Reykyavik it is dark for eight months of the year, and it's cold enough to freeze your wrists off and there's only golly fish to eat. Administrative errors are bound to occur in enormous quantities. Look at this – it's all a mistake. It's a real pain in the sphincter! Icelandic Honey Week? My Life!

Mother Well why do you come in here trying to flog the stuff, then?

Man Listen Cowboy. I got a job to do. It's a stupid, pointless job but at least it keeps me away from Iceland, all right? The leg of the worker bee has...

They slam the door on him. Someone rather like Jeremy Thorpe looks round the door and waves as they do so.

Animated titles. then cut to a drawing of Indians attacking a fort.

Music: 'The Big Country' theme.

Voice Over (TERRY J) *and* SUPERIMPOSED ROLLER CAPTION:
'IN THE SPRING OF 1863 THE COMANCHES RALLIED UNDER THEIR WARRIOR LEADER CONCHITO IN A FINAL DESPERATE ATTEMPT TO DRIVE THE WHITE MAN FROM THE RICH HUNTING LANDS OF THEIR ANCESTORS. THE US CAVALRY WERE DRAWN UP AT FORT WORTH, AND THE SCENE WAS SET FOR A FINAL ALL-OUT ONSLAUGHT THAT COULD SET THE NEW TERRITORIES ABLAZE.'

Cut to a doctor's surgery. It has a wall shrine with a photo of Christiaan Barnard with flowers and candles in front of it. The doctor is talking to an embarrassed-looking man (Terry G).

Doctor (GRAHAM) Well, Mr Cotton, you have what we in the medical profession call a naughty complaint. My advice to you is to put this paper bag over your head – it has little holes there for your eyes, you see – and to ring this bell, and to take this card along to your hospital. *(he hands him card three feet long which reads 'For Special Treatment')* And I shall inform all your relatives and friends and anyone else I bump into. OK ... cash, wasn't it? *(the man hands over wad of fivers)* Thank you very much. Get out. *(the man gets up to go)* Dirty little man. *(he picks up big text book entitled 'Medical Practice' and flicks through the pages)* Hmm ... hmm ... Hippocratic Oath ... it's not in there ... jolly good. Very useful. Next!

An out-of-vision scream. A man staggers in clutching his bleeding stomach. Lots of blood pours out of him throughout the scene.

Doctor Ah, yes you must be Mr Williams.

Williams (TERRY J) *(obviously fatally wounded)* Y ... yes ...

Doctor Well, do take a seat. What seems to be the trouble?

Williams I've ... I've just been stabbed by your nurse ...

Doctor Oh dear ... well I'd probably better have a look at you then. Could you fill in this form first? *(he hands him a form)*

Williams She just stabbed me ...

Doctor Yes. She's an unpredictable sort. Look, you seem to be bleeding rather badly. I think you'd better hurry up and fill in that form.

Williams Ahhh ... couldn't ... I ... do ... it ... later, doctor!

Doctor No, no. You'd have bled to death by then. Can you hold a pen?

Williams I'll try.

With great effort he releases one of his hands from his bleeding stomach.

Doctor Yes, it's a hell of a nuisance all this damn paperwork, really it is ... *(he gets up and strolls around fairly unconcerned)* it's a real nightmare, this damned paperwork. It really is a hell of a nuisance. Something ought to be done about it.

Williams Do I have to answer all the questions, doctor?

Doctor No, no, no, just fill in as many as you can – no need to go into too much detail. I don't know why we bother with it all, really, it's such a nuisance. Well let's see how you've done, then . . . *(Williams half collapses)* Oh dear oh dear . . . that's not very good, is it. Look, surely you knew number four!

Williams No . . . I didn't . . .

Doctor It's from 'The Merchant of Venice' – even *I* know that!

Williams *(bleeding profusely)* It's going on the carpet, doctor.

Doctor Oh don't worry about that! Look at this – number six – the Treaty of Versailles! Didn't you know that? Oh, my God.

Williams Ahgg . . . aghhh.

Doctor And number nine – Emerson Fittipaldi! *(gives Williams a look)* Virginia *Wade*? You must be mad!

The nurse enters with a smoking revolver.

Nurse (CAROL) Oh doctor, I've just shot another patient. I don't think there's any point in your seeing him.

Doctor You didn't *kill* him, did you?

Nurse 'fraid so.

Doctor You mustn't *kill* them, nurse.

Nurse Oh, I'm sorry doctor. It was just on the spur of the moment. Rather silly really.

She exits, taking a sword from the wall. Through the next bit of the scene we hear screams off.

Williams I'm sorry about the carpet, doctor.

Doctor Mr Williams, I'm afraid I can't give you any marks, so I won't be able to recommend you for hospital. Tell you what – I'll stop the bleeding – but strictly speaking I shouldn't even do that on marks like these . . .

The nurse enters covered in blood.

Nurse There are no more patients now, doctor.

Doctor Oh well, let's go and have lunch, then.

Nurse What about . . . er . . . *(she points to Williams who is lying on the floor gurgling by this time)*

Doctor Ah yes – look, Mr Williams we're just popping out for a bite of lunch while we've got a spare moment, you know. Look, have another bash at the form . . . and if at least you can answer the question on history right, then we may be able to give you some morphine or something like that, OK?

Williams Thank you, doctor, thank you . . .

Cut to a large country house sitting room, dominated by large grinning portrait of Jeremy Thorpe. A bishop is sitting at a desk, typing. A brigadier in full military uniform just to below the chest, then a patch of bare midriff, with belly button showing, then a lavender tutu, incredibly hairy legs, thick army socks and high heels, is dictating.

Brigadier (ERIC) Dear Sir, I wish to protest in the strongest possible terms. Yours sincerely, Brigader N. F. Marwood-Git (retired). Read that back, will you, Brian.

Bishop (MICHAEL) And when he had built up Cedron, he sent Horsemen there, and an host of footmen to the end that issuing out they might make outroads upon the ways of Judea, as the King commanded them...

Brigadier Good! Pop it in an envelope and bung it off! It's no good bottling these things up, Brian. If you feel them you must say them or you'll just go mad...

Bishop Oh yes indeed... as the book of Maccabee said... as the flea is like unto an oxen, so is the privet hedge liken unto a botanist black in thy sight, O Lord!

Brigadier Quite... Look why don't you just nip out for lunch, Brian...

Bishop Yea... as Raymond Chandler said, it was one of those days when Los Angeles felt like a rock-hard fig.

Brigadier Brian, let's stop this pretending, shall we.

Bishop Oh... yea... as Dirk Bogarde said in his autobiography...

Brigadier Brian... let's stop all this futile pretence... I've... I've always been moderately fond of you...

Bishop Well to be quite frank, Brigadier... one can't walk so closely with a chap like you for... for so long without... feeling something deep down inside, even if it isn't anything... anything... very much.

Brigadier Well, splendid... Brian... er... well I don't suppose there's much we can do, really.

Bishop Not on television... no...

Brigadier No... they... they are a lot more permissive these days than they *used* to be...

Bishop Ah yes... but not with this sort of thing...

Brigadier No... I suppose they've... got to draw the line somewhere...

Bishop Yes...

Brigadier Well take a letter, Brian. Dear Sir, I wish to protest...

Cut to an animation sketch.

Voice Over (MICHAEL) CAPTION: 'THERE NOW FOLLOWS AN APPEAL ON BEHALF OF EXTREMELY RICH PEOPLE WHO HAVE ABSOLUTELY NOTHING WRONG WITH THEM'

Sir Pratt (GRAHAM) *(at a large leather-topped desk with an elaborate table lamp)* Hello. I'd like to talk to you tonight about a minority group of people who have no mental or physical handicaps and, who, through no fault of their own, have never been deprived, and consequently are forced to live in conditions of extreme luxury. This often ignored minority, is very rarely brought to the attention of the general public. The average man in the street scarcely gives a second thought to these extremely well-off people. He, quite simply, fails to appreciate the pressures vast quantities of money just do not bring. Have you at home, ever had to cope with this problem ... *(cut to a rich young yachting type surrounded by girls in bikinis)* or this ... *(cut to a rich woman loading her chauffeur with all kinds of expensive parcels)* or even this ... *(cut to a still of Centre Point)* I know it's only human to say, 'Oh this will never happen to me', and of course, it won't! I'm asking you, please, please, send *no* contributions, however large, to me.

We see the last bit on a TV in Mrs What-a-long-name-this-is-hardly-worth-typing-but-never-mind-it-doesn't-come-up-again's-living-room. Ding-dong of doorbell. A cupboard door opens, and the middle-aged man we saw in first scene comes out. He has no iguana on his shoulder.

Mrs Long Name (TERRY J) All right. I'll go.

TV Voice (MICHAEL) There now follows a Party Political Broadcast on behalf of the Liberal Par ...

She turns it off. The TV set just folds up as if empty and collapses on to the floor. Dust rises. She goes into the hallway to the front door (singing 'Anything Goes' by the other Cole Porter to herself) and opens it. A man with a briefcase stands there.

Mr Vernon (ERIC) Hello, madam ... *(comes in)*

Mrs Long Name Ah hello ... you must have come about ...

Mr Vernon Finishing the sentences, yes.

Mrs Long Name Oh ... well ... perhaps you'd like to ...

Mr Vernon Come through this way ... certainly ... *(they go through into the sitting room)* Oh, nice place you've got here.

Mrs Long Name Yes ... well ... er ... we ...

Mr Vernon Like it?

Mrs Long Name Yes ... yes we certainly ...

Mr Vernon Do ... Good! Now then ... when did you first start ...

Mrs Long Name ... finding it difficult to ...

Mr Vernon Finish sentences ... yes.

Mrs Long Name Well it's not me, it's my ...

Mr Vernon Husband?

Mrs Long Name Yes. He ...

Mr Vernon Never lets you finish what you've started.

Mrs Long Name Quite. I'm beginning to feel ...

Mr Vernon That you'll never finish a sentence again as long as you live.

Mrs Long Name Exact ...

Mr Vernon ly. It must be awful.

Mrs Long Name It's driving me ...

Mr Vernon To drink?

Mrs Long Name No, rou...
Mr Vernon nd the be...
Mrs Long Name en...
Mr Vernon d...
Mrs Long Name Yes...
Mr Vernon May I...
Mrs Long Name Take a seat...
Mr Vernon Thank you. *(he sits)* You see, our method is to reassure the patient by recreating normal... er...
Mrs Long Name Conditions?
Mr Vernon Yes. Then we try to get them in a position where they suddenly find that they're completing *other* people's sentences...
Mrs Long Name *(with self-wonder)* Themselves!
Mr Vernon Spot on Mrs...
Mrs Long Name *(hesitantly)* Smith?
Mr Vernon Good! Well, try not to overdo it to...
Mrs Long Name *(with growing confidence)* Begin with...?
Mr Vernon Good. Just keep it to one or two...
Mrs Long Name *(faster)* Words...
Mr Vernon To start off with, otherwise you may find that you're...
Mrs Long Name Taking on too long a sentence and getting completely... er...
Mr Vernon Stuck. Good. Yes. Well that's about it...
Mrs Long Name *(completely confident now)* for now, so...
Mr Vernon Thanks very much for calling.
Mrs Long Name Not at all.
Mr Vernon And, er...
Mrs Long Name Just like to say
Mr Vernon Thank you very much for coming along.
Mrs Long Name Not at all
Mr Vernon And good...
Mrs Long Name Bye, Mr...
Mr Vernon Vernon.

Mrs Long Name leaves. Mr Vernon shuts the door. A girl's voice comes from sitting room.

Girl's Voice Carl?
Mr Vernon Yes, dear?
Girl's Voice I've just had another baby.
Mr Vernon Oh, no! How many's that now?

Girl's Voice Twelve since lunch . . . Oh! There's another one!

Cut to exterior of Mrs Long Name's house. She comes out and sets off purposefully up the road, passing four Pepperpot nannies digging up the road. They are wearing the usual slippers, paisley dresses and knotted handkerchiefs. One wears a helmet. One works a pneumatic drill. She is stripped to the waist wearing a big pink bra. Behind, heroic shots of Mrs Long Name walking out of town, through suburbs, into neat country, then into wilder country. She finally stops in close-up, and looks up with inspiration in her eyes.

Cut to a linkman standing before Stonehenge.

Linkman (MICHAEL) This is Stonehenge . . . and it's from here we go to Africa.

Jeremy Thorpe appears at the edge of shot and waves.

Cut to as overgrown, jungleoid a location as Torquay can provide. A very big thick tree in the foreground. David Attenborough pushes through jungle towards camera. He has damp sweat patches under his arms which grow perceptibly during the scene. He has two African guides in the background both with saxophones round their necks.

Attenborough (MICHAEL) *(slapping the side of a tree)* Well here it is at last . . . the goal of our quest. After six months and three days we've caught up with the legendary walking tree of Dahomey, Quercus Nicholas Parsonus, resting here for a moment, on its long journey south. It's almost incredible isn't it, to think that this huge tree has walked over two thousand miles across this inhospitable terrain to stop here, maybe just to take in water before the two thousand miles on to Cape Town, where it lives. It's almost unimaginable, I find – the thought of this mighty tree strolling through Nigeria, perhaps swaggering a little as it crosses the border into Zaire, hopping through the tropical rain forests, trying to find a quiet grove where it could jump around on its own, sprinting up to Zambia for the afternoon, then nipping back . . . *(a native whispers in his ear)* Oh, super . . . well, I've just been told that this is *not* in fact the legendary walking tree of Dahomey, this is one of Africa's many stationary trees, Arborus Bamber Gascoignus. In fact we've just missed the walking tree . . . it left here at eight o'clock this morning . . . was heading off in that direction . . . so we'll see if we can go and catch it up. Come on boys.

They move off. At this point we notice that there are two other saxophone-wearing natives, a trumpeter, a trombonist, a double bassist, a guitarist, and finally a man with a drum kit tied to his back. Mix through to them on the move in another part of the jungle. Sweat is now spraying out from under Attenborough's armpits as if from a watering can.

Attenborough Well, we're still keeping up with it, but it's setting a furious pace. Early this morning we thought we'd spotted it, but it turned out to be an Angolan sauntering tree, Amazellus Robin Ray, out walking with a Gambian Sidling Bush... *(Jeremy Thorpe leans in the background and waves to camera)* So on we go... it's going to be difficult – the walking tree can achieve speeds of up to fifty miles an hour, especially when it's in a hurry. *(Rupert the bearer points excitedly)* Super! Well, Rupert has spotted something... this could be it... a walking tree on the move... *(they move off; by this time waterspray is gushing out from all over his chest)* But, what Rupert had in fact discovered was something very different...

He stops him, they kneel down. Cut to their eyeline. In the distance, amongst low bushes and thick undergrowth, six Africans dressed immaculately in cricket gear having a game of cricket. Cut to Attenborough, Rupert and one other bearer watching. Attenborough is looking down at something he is holding. The other two are gazing wide-eyed at the cricketers.

Attenborough The Turkish Little Rude Plant. *(he holds up, carefully and wondrously, a plant which has green outer leaves splayed back to reveal a small, accurately sculpted bum)* This remarkably smutty piece of flora was used by the Turks to ram up each other's... *(Rupert nudges him and points excitedly at the batsmen)* Ah no! In fact it was something even more interesting... *(Attenborough points, apparently at the batsmen, but he has clearly got it wrong again)* Yes, there it was, over the other side of the clearing, the legendary Puking Tree of Mozambique... *(Rupert nudges him again)*

Cut to an animated professor.

Voice (MICHAEL) No, what they had come across was a tribe lost to man since time immemorial... the legendary Batsmen of the Kalahari... *(cut to a shot of natives playing cricket)*

Voice Over (TERRY J) Primitive customs still survive here as if the march of time had passed them by. But for all the mumbo-jumbo and superstition, the Batsmen of the Kalahari are formidable fighters, as we can see on this rare footage of them in action against Warwickshire.

Cut to a big county ground pavilion in mid-shot. We zoom in on the commentator on a balcony.

Commentator (MICHAEL) Warwickshire had dismissed the Kalahari Batsmen for 140, and then it was their turn to face this extraordinary Kalahari attack. Pratt was the first to go, but Pratt and Pratt put on a second wicket stand of nought, which was broken by Odinga in his most hostile mood.

A compilation of the day's play. Natives in normal cricket gear. Pratt at crease as per usual cricket coverage. Cut to a low shot of the bowler thundering up towards the wicket. Cut away to the batsman preparing to take the shot. Cut back to the bowler. As he reaches the crease he produces a spear and raises it to shoulder height and hurls it. Cut to batsman who is hit full in the stomach. His bat dislodges the bails. There is a 'howzat' from all the native fielders. He makes an annoyed gesture as if he were Colin Cowdrey caught clean bowled, and sinks to the ground.

CAPTION: 'B. PRATT'

Voice Over (MICHAEL) That's B. Pratt, hit wicket – 0. But Pratt and Z. Pratt dug in and took the score to a half... *(cut to the new batting partnership; B. Pratt's body is still on the ground)* before Z. Pratt ran away. *(Z. Pratt reaching the pavilion, running with a hail of spears and arrows coming after him)* But out came M.J.K. Pratt... *(cut to M.J.K. Pratt coming out pulling on gloves etc.)* to play a real captain's innings. *(he reaches the crease and takes guard, the bowler bowls)* He'd taken his own score up to nought when he mistimed a shot of Bowanga and was lbw. *(a huge spear sticks right through the lower part of his leg; a big appeal and he turns and limps manfully off)*

CAPTION: 'M.J.K. PRATT'

Voice Over Typical of Umbonga's hostile opening spell was his dismissal of V.E. Pratt, who offered no resistance to this delivery... *(cut to native bowler bowling a machete; it hits the ground and does a leg spin up, slicing off the batsman's head as he waves his bat)* ... and he was caught behind.

The batsman's severed head lands in the wicket keeper's gloves. He throws it in the air with a flourish.

CAPTION: 'V.E. PRATT'

Jeremy Thorpe appears and waves.

Cut to the presenter from 'World's Most Awful Family 1974'.

Presenter (MICHAEL) But by lunch the situation had changed dramatically.

Voice Over (GRAHAM) *and* CAPTION: 'C.U. PRATT KILLED OUTRIGHT, BOWLED ODINGA – 0.

P.B.T.R. PRATT LEGS OFF BEFORE WICKET, BOWLED ODINGA – 0.

B.B.C.T.V. PRATT ASSEGAI UP JACKSEY, BOWLED UNBOKO – 0.

Z. PRATT MACHETE BEFORE WICKET, BOWLED UMBONGA – 0.

M.J.K. PRATT STUMP THROUGH HEAD, BOWLED UMBONGA – 0.

V.E. PRATT RAN AWAY – 0.

P.D.A. PRATT RETIRED HURT – 0.

W.G. PRATT RETIRED VERY HURT – 0.

PRATT DIED OF FRIGHT, BOWLED ODINGA – 0.

Y.E.T.A.N.O.T.H.E.R. PRATT NOT OUT BUT DREADFULLY HURT – 139.'

Cut back to the presenter. Behind him the 'World's Most Awful Family' sign is crossed out and replaced with 'Sport'.

Presenter And so with the tension colossal as we come up to the last ball... that's all from us.

Roll credits on black background. The first part of the signature tune is played very hesitantly on guitar.

PARTY POLITICAL BROADCAST ON BEHALF OF THE LIBERAL PARTY
WAS CONCEIVED, WRITTEN AND PERFORMED BY
J. THORPE (AGE 2)

C. SMITH (AGE 1½)

L. BYERS (AGE 0)

UNSUCCESSFUL CANDIDATES
GRAHAM CHAPMAN
LEICESTER NORTH (LOST DEPOSIT)

TERRY GILLIAM
MINNEAPOLIS NORTH (LOST DEPOSIT TWICE)

ERIC IDLE
SOUTH SHIELDS NORTH (LOST DEPOSIT BUT FOUND AN OLD ONE WHICH HE COULD USE)

TERRY JONES
COLWYN BAY NORTH (SMALL DEPOSIT ON HIS TROUSERS)
MICHAEL PALIN
SHEFFIELD NORTH (LOST HIS TROUSERS)

MORE UNSUCCESSFUL CANDIDATES
CAROL CLEVELAND (LIBERAL)

BOB E. RAYMOND (VERY LIBERAL)

PETER BRETT (EXTREMELY LIBERAL AND RATHER RUDE)

EVEN MORE UNSUCCESSFUL CANDIDATES
DOUGLAS ADAMS
SILLY WORD (NORTH)

NEIL INNES
SILLY WORDS AND MUSIC (NORTH)

(COPYRIGHT 1984 THORPE-O-HITS LTD)

MAKE-UP AND HAIRDRESSING
JO GRIMOND
MORE MAKE-UP
MAGGIE WESTON
EVEN MORE MAKE-UP
ANDREW ROSE (COSTUMES NORTH)

MUCH MORE MAKE-UP
STAN SPEEL (FILM CAMERAMAN NORTH)

MAKE-UP AND SOUND RECORDING
RON (NORTH) BLIGHT
ROSTRUM CAMERA WITH MAKE-UP
PETER WILLIS
FILM EDITOR AND NOT MAKE-UP
BOB DEARBERG
NOT FILM EDITOR NOT MAKE-UP BUT DUBBING MIXER

ROD GUEST
LIGHTING, MAKE-UP AND PRICES AND INCOMES POLICY
JIMMY PURDIE
VISUAL EFFECTS AND MR THORPE'S WIGS
JOHN HORTON
PRODUCTION ASSISTANT
BRIAN JONES (MAKE-UP NORTH)
DESIGNER (NORTH)
VALERIE WARRENDER (FAR TOO LIBERAL)
PRODUCED BY
MR LLOYD GEORGE (WHO KNEW IAN MACNAUGHTON'S FATHER)
A BBC-LIBERAL-TV-PARTY PRODUCTION (NORTH)

Nine O'Clock News intro in the newsroom behind. Behind the newsreader several men including Jeremy Thorpe are drinking and celebrating. A woman is dancing on the table.

Newsreader (ERIC) Good evening. Over 400,000 million pounds were wiped off the value of shares this afternoon, when someone in the Stock Exchange coughed. Sport: capital punishment is to be re-introduced in the first and second division. Any player found tackling from behind or controlling the ball with the lower part of the arm will be hanged. But the electric chair remains the standard punishment for threatening the goalie. Referee's chairman, Len Goebbels said 'at last the referee has been given teeth'. Finally, politics: the latest opinion poll published today shows Labour ahead with 40%, the AA second with 38% and not surprisingly Kentucky Fried Chicken running the Liberals a very close third. And now back to me. Hello. And now it's time to go over to Hugh Delaney in Paignton.

Cut to the linkman on the pier at Paignton. A smallish crowd is gathered behind him including Jeremy Thorpe who waves at the camera from the back.

Linkman (MICHAEL) Hello and welcome to Paignton, because it's *from* Paignton that we take you straight back to the studio.

Cut to a man in swimming trunks and a snorkel pushed back on his head, standing in the studio holding a stuffed polecat on a pole.

Man (GRAHAM) Hello. And it's from here we go over there.

Cut to the 'Most Awful Family' presenter.

Presenter Well we're already here so let's go over there.

Cut back to the newsreader.

Newsreader Welcome back. And now it's time for part eight of our series about the life and work of Ursula Hitler, the Surrey housewife who revolutionized British beekeeping in the nineteen-thirties.

Voice Over (MICHAEL) and CAPTION: 'THAT WAS A PARTY POLITICAL BROADCAST ON BEHALF OF THE LIBERAL PARTY'

His voice breaks up with giggles. Fade to blackout. The end.

Appendix

Transmission details

Episode number	Series/number	Transmission date	Number as recorded	Recording date
	First Series			
One	1/1	5-10-69	2	7-9-69
Two	1/2	12-10-69	1	30-8-69
Three	1/3	19-10-69	3	14-8-69
Four	1/4	26-10-69	4	21-9-69
Five	1/5	16-11-69	5	3-10-69
Six	1/6	23-11-69	7	5-11-69
Seven	1/7	30-11-69	6	10-10-69
Eight	1/8	7-12-69	8	25-11-69
Nine	1/9	14-12-69	10	7-12-69
Ten	1/10	21-12-69	9	30-11-69
Eleven	1/11	28-12-69	11	14-12-69
Twelve	1/12	4-1-70	12	21-12-69
Thirteen	1/13	11-1-70	13	4-1-70
	Second Series			
Fourteen	2/1	15-9-70	4	9-7-70
Fifteen	2/2	22-9-70	3	2-7-70
Sixteen	2/3	29-9-70	5	16-7-70
Seventeen	2/4	20-10-70	9	18-9-70
Eighteen	2/5	27-10-70	7	10-9-70
Nineteen	2/6	3-11-70	8	10-9-70
Twenty	2/7	10-11-70	11	2-10-70
Twenty-one	2/8	17-11-70	12	9-10-70
Twenty-two	2/9	24-11-70	10	25-9-70
Twenty-three	2/10	1-12-70	2	2-7-70
Twenty-four	2/11	8-12-70	6	23-7-70
Twenty-five	2/12	15-12-70	1	25-6-70
Twenty-six	2/13	22-12-70	3	16-10-70

Episode number	Series/ number	Transmission date	Number as recorded	Recording date
	Third Series			
Twenty-seven	3/1	19-10-72	5	14-1-72
Twenty-eight	3/2	26-10-72	7	28-1-72
Twenty-nine	3/3	2-11-72	1	4-12-71
Thirty	3/4	9-11-72	2	11-12-71
Thirty-one	3/5	16-11-72	9	24-4-72
Thirty-two	3/6	23-11-72	6	21-1-72
Thirty-three	3/7	30-11-72	4	7-1-72
Thirty-four	3/8	7-12-72	10	4-5-72
Thirty-five	3/9	14-12-72	11	11-5-72
Thirty-six	3/10	21-12-72	13	25-5-72
Thirty-seven	3/11	4-1-73	8	17-4-72
Thirty-eight	3/12	11-1-73	3	18-12-71
Thirty-nine	3/13	18-1-73	12	18-5-72
	Fourth Series			
Forty	4/1	31-10-74	1	12-10-74
Forty-one	4/2	7-11-74	2	19-10-74
Forty-two	4/3	14-11-74	3	26-10-74
Forty-three	4/4	21-11-74	4	2-11-74
Forty-four	4/5	28-11-74	5	9-11-74
Forty-five	4/6	5-12-74	6	16-11-74

Index

Agatha Christie sketch (railway timetables), 4
Anagram quiz, 92
Anne Elk, 118
Ant communication, 265
'Anything Goes In' (song), 280
Apology, 147
Apology for violence and nudity, 81
Apology (politicians), 128
Appeal on behalf of extremely rich people, 334
Argument clinic, 85
Army captain as clown, 99
Art gallery strike, 21
At home with the ant and other pets, 264
Attenborough, David, 337
Attenborough, Dickie, 227

Basingstoke in Westphalia, 280
Batsmen of the Kalahari, the, 338
BBC is short of money, the, 71
BBC News (handovers), 341
BBC programme planners, 220
Biggles dictates a letter, 134
Bingo-crazed Chinese, 157

Black Eagle, the, 15
'Blood, Devastation, Death, War and Horror', 91
Blood donor, 234
Bogus psychiatrists, 293
Bomb on plane, 165
'Book at Bedtime', a, 211
Boxing commentary, 302
Boxing match aftermath, 300
'Boxing Tonight'—Jack Bodell v. Sir Kenneth Clark, 194
Brigadier and Bishop, 333
British Well-Basically Club, the, 176
Bull-fighting, 176
Bus conductor sketch, 97
Buying an ant, 258

Cheap-Laughs, the, 175
Cheese shop, 141
City gents vox pops, 9
Climbing the north face of the Uxbridge Road, 136
Coal mine (historical argument), 30
Commercials 33
Communist quiz, 19
Conquistador coffee campaign, 1

Court martial, 279
Court (phrase-book), 17
Court scene - multiple murderer, 45
Court scene (Viking), 47
Crackpot Religions Ltd, 9
Credits of the year, 237
Cricket match (assegais), 338
Crossing the Atlantic on a tricycle, 13
Cycling tour, the, 148

'Dad's Doctors' (trail), 225
'Dad's Pooves' (trail), 225
David Niven's fridge, 229
Dentists, 305
Department store, 257
Different endings, 273
Dirty Hungarian phrase-book, 16
Dirty vicar sketch, 238
Doctor, 198
Doctor whose patients are stabbed by his nurse, a, 332
Documentary on ants, 266

Erizabeth L, 76
Elizabethan pornography smugglers, 181
Emigration from Surbiton to Hounslow, 60
Everest climbed by hairdressers, 107
Expedition to Lake Pahoe, 128
Exploding version of 'The Blue Danube', 38

Farming club, 66
Film director (teeth) 7

Film trailer 283
Fire brigade, 109
Fish-slapping dance, 69
Fraud film squad, 77
Free repetition of doubtful words sketch, by an underrated author, the, 187

George III, 246
Gestures to indicate pauses in a televised talk, 100
Girls' boarding school, 38
Gumby brain specialist 122
Gumby flower arranging, 26

Hamlet and Ophelia, 300
Hitting on the head lessons, 88
Hospital for over-actors, 25
Hospital run by RSM, 36
Housing project built by characters from nineteenth-century English literature, 166
'How not to be seen', 12
How to feed a goldfish, 34
How to rid the world of all known diseases, 63

Icelandic Honey Week, 272, 331
Icelandic saga, 47
Ideal Loon Exhibition, 204
Inspector Flying Fox of the Yard, 89
Insurance sketch, 35
International Wife-swapping, 235
Interview in filing cabinet, 13
'Is there?' ... life after death?, 188

'Jack in a Box', 153
Job hunter, 2
Jungle restaurant, 80

Kamikaze Scotsmen, 212
Ken Russell's 'Gardening Club', 81

Language laboratory, 113
Last five miles of the M2, the, 284
Lifeboat, 137
Lifeboat (cannibalism), 40
Life and death struggles, 95
'Life of Tchaikowsky', the, 66
'Light Entertainment Awards', 227
Live from Epsom, 305
Lost World of Roiurama, the, 82
Louis XIV, 243
Lupins, 195, 201, 203

M1 interchange built by characters from 'Paradise Lost', 167
Man who collects birdwatcher's eggs, the, 35
Man who finishes other people's sentences, the, 335
Man who is alternately rude and polite, the, 240
Man who makes people laugh uncontrollably, the, 98
Man who says words in the wrong order, the, 189
Man who says things in a very roundabout way, the, 32
Man who speaks in anagrams, the, 91
Man who speaks only the beginnings of words, the, 33
Man who speaks only the ends of words, the, 32
Man who speaks only the middles of words, the, 33
Mary recruitment office, 96
Merchant banker, 92
Minister for Not Listening to People, the, 126
Molluscs – 'live' TV documentary, 124
'Money Programme, The', 75
Mongolfier Brothers, the, 240
Monty Python's Flying Circus again in thirty seconds, 14
Moore, Dennis, 194, 196, 201, 206
'Mortuary Hour', 170
'Most Awful Family in Britain', 329
Mountaineer 38
Mrs Niggerbaiter explodes, 64
Mrs Premise and Mrs Conclusion visit Jean-Paul Sartre, 54
Mystico and Janet – flats built by hypnosis, 167

Naked man, a, 166
'Nationwide', 295
Neurotic announcers, 100
Neutron, Mr, 311
New brain from Curry's, 231
Newsflash (Germans) 291
News with Richard Baker, the, 147
News with Richard Baker (vision only), the, 101
No time to lose, 214

Off-licence, 205
Old lady snoopers, 138
One more minute of Monty Python's Flying Circus, 90
Oscar Wilde sketch, 228
Olympic hide-and-seek final, 172
Our Eamonn, 110

Pantomime horses, 94
'Pantomime Horse is a Secret Agent film', the, 102
'Party hints' with Veronica Smalls, 112
Party Political Broadcast (choreographed), 210
Pasolini's film 'The Third Test Match', 229
Penguins, 218
Philip Jenkinson on cheese westerns, 145
Piston engine (a bargain), 303
Pither, Mr, 148
Poetry reading (ants), 268
Police helmets, 296
Pornographic bookshop, 181
Post box ceremony, 310
'Prejudice' 208
Prices on the planet Algon, 177
Programme titles conference, 285
Public are idiots, the, 284
Puss in Boots, 72

Queen Victoria handicap, 306
Queen will be watching, the, 30

RAF banter, 277

Ramsay MacDonald striptease, 2
'Redgauntlet', 211
Repeating groove, 2
Rival documentaries, 223
Rogers, Clodagh, 153
Room in Polonius's house, a, 305

Salvation fuzz, 79
Sam Peckinpah's 'Salad Days', 146
Schoolboys Life Assurance Company, 62
Seashore interlude film, 147
Sherry-drinking vicar, 191
Show-jumping (musicals), 290
Show so far, the, 141
Shunt, Mr Neville, 6, 7
Silliest interview we've ever had, the, 132
Silliest sketch we've ever done, the, 133
Silly disturbances (the Reverend Arthur Belling), 186
Six more minutes of Monty Python's Flying Circus, 85
Smolensk, 156
Spam, 26
'Spot the Loony', 221
Stock Exchange report, 53
'Storage Jars', 140
Submarine, 39
'Summarize Proust Competition', 105

Teddy Salad (CIA agent), 313
Ten seconds of sex, 166
Thames TV introduction, 227

Theory on Brontosauruses by Anne Elk (Miss), 118
'There is nothing quite so wonderful as money' (song), 75
Thripshaw's disease, 189
Tory Housewives Clean-up Campaign, 121
Toupee, 270
Travel agent, 114
Trim-Jeans Theatre, 68
Trivialising the war 278
Trotsky, 155
Tudor jobs agency, 180
Tuesday documentary/children's story/party political broadcast, 127
'TV4 or not TV4' discussion, 199

Undertakers sketch, 42

Unexploded Scotsman, 221
'Up Your Pavement', 276

Vicar/salesman, 64

Walking tree of Dahomey, the, 337
Watney's Red Barrel, 116
What the stars foretell, 196
'When does a dream begin' (song), 291
Whicker Island, 57
Woody and tinny words, 287

'Ypres 1914', 23
'Ypres 1914' (abandoned), 20
'Yummy yummy', 14

Zeppelin, 251, 255